HISTORY OF PHOENICIA
George Rawlinson

PREFACE

Histories of Phoenicia or of the Phoenicians were written towards the middle of the present century by Movers and Kenrick. The elaborate work of the former writer01 collected into five moderate-sized volumes all the notices that classical antiquity had preserved of the Religion, History, Commerce, Art, &c., of this celebrated and interesting nation. Kenrick, making a free use of the stores of knowledge thus accumulated, added to them much information derived from modern research, and was content to give to the world in a single volume of small size,02 very scantily illustrated, the ascertained results of criticism and inquiry on the subject of the Phoenicians up to his own day. Forty-four years have since elapsed; and in the course of them large additions have been made to certain branches of the inquiry, while others have remained very much as they were before. Travellers, like Robinson, Walpole, Tristram, Renan, and Lortet, have thrown great additional light on the geography, geology, fauna, and flora of the country. Excavators, like Renan and the two Di Cesnolas, have caused the soil to yield up most valuable remains bearing upon the architecture, the art, the industrial pursuits, and the manners and customs of the people. Antiquaries, like M. Clermont-Ganneau and MM. Perrot and Chipiez, have subjected the remains to careful examination and criticism, and have definitively fixed the character of Phoenician Art, and its position in the history of artistic effort. Researches are still being carried on, both in Phoenicia Proper and in the Phoenician dependency of Cyprus, which are likely still further to enlarge our knowledge with respect to Phoenician Art and Archæology; but it is not probable that they will affect seriously the verdict already delivered by competent judges on those subjects. The time therefore appeared to the author to have come when, after nearly half a century of silence, the history of the people might appropriately be rewritten. The subject had long engaged his thoughts, closely connected as it is with the histories of Egypt, and of the "Great Oriental Monarchies," which for thirty years have been to him special objects of study; and a work embodying the chief results of the recent investigations seemed to him a not unsuitable termination to the historical efforts which his resignation of the Professorship of Ancient History at Oxford, and his entrance upon a new sphere of labour, bring naturally to an end.

The author wishes to express his vast obligations to MM. Perrot and Chipiez for the invaluable assistance which he has derived from their great work,03 and to their publishers, the MM. Hachette, for their liberality in allowing him the use of so large a number of MM. Perrot and Chipiez' Illustrations. He is also much beholden to the same gentlemen for the use of charts and drawings originally published in the "Géographie Universelle." Other works from which he has drawn either materials or illustrations, or both, are (besides Movers' and Kenrick's) M. Ernest Renan's "Mission de Phénicie," General Di Cesnola's "Cyprus," A. Di Cesnola's "Salaminia," M. Ceccaldi's "Monuments Antiques de Cypre," M. Daux's "Recherches sur les Emporia Phéniciens," the "Corpus Inscriptionum Semiticarum," M. Clermont-Ganneau's "Imagerie Phénicienne," Mr. Davis's "Carthage and her Remains," Gesenius's "Scripturæ Linguæque Phoeniciæ Monumenta," Lortet's "La Syrie d'aujourd'hui," Serra di Falco's "Antichità della Sicilia," Walpole's "Ansayrii," and Canon Tristram's "Land of Israel." The difficulty has been to select from these copious stores the most salient and noteworthy facts, and to marshal them in such a form as would make them readily intelligible to the ordinary English reader. How far he has succeeded in doing this he must leave the public to judge. In making his bow to them as a "Reader" and Writer "of Histories,"04 he has to thank them for a degree of favour which has given a ready sale to all his previous works, and has carried some of them through several editions.

CANTERBURY: August 1889.

CHAPTER I—THE LAND

Phoenicia—Origin of the name—Spread of the name
southwards—Real length of Phoenicia along the coast—
Breadth and area—General character of the region—The
Plains—Plain of Sharon—Plain of Acre—Plain of Tyre—Plain
of Sidon—Plain of Berytus—Plain of Marathus—Hilly
regions—Mountain ranges—Carmel—Casius—Bargylus—Lebanon—
Beauty of Lebanon—Rivers—The Litany—The Nahr-el-Berid—
The Kadisha—The Adonis—The Lycus—The Tamyras—The
Bostrenus—The Zaherany—The Headlands—Main
characteristics, inaccessibility, picturesqueness,
productiveness.

Phoenicé, or Phoenicia, was the name originally given by the Greeks—and afterwards adopted
from them by the Romans—to the coast region of the Mediterranean, where it faces the west
between the thirty-second and the thirty-sixth parallels. Here, it would seem, in their early
voyagings, the Pre-Homeric Greeks first came upon a land where the palm-tree was not only
indigenous, but formed a leading and striking characteristic, everywhere along the low sandy
shore lifting its tuft of feathery leaves into the bright blue sky, high above the undergrowth of
fig, and pomegranate, and alive. Hence they called the tract Phoenicia, or "the Land of Palms;"
and the people who inhabited it the Phoenicians, or "the Palm-tree people."

The term was from the first applied with a good deal of vagueness. It was probably originally
given to the region opposite Cyprus, from Gabala in the north—now Jebili—to Antaradus
(Tortosa) and Marathus (Amrith) towards the south, where the palm-tree was first seen
growing in rich abundance. The palm is the numismatic emblem of Aradus,11 and though not
now very frequent in the region which Strabo calls "the Aradian coast-tract,"12 must anciently
have been among its chief ornaments. As the Grecian knowledge of the coast extended
southward, and a richer and still richer growth of the palm was continually noticed, almost
every town and every village being embosomed in a circle of palm groves, the name extended
itself until it reached as far south at any rate as Gaza, or (according to some) as Rhinocolura
and the Torrens Ægypti. Northward the name seems never to have passed beyond Cape
Posideium (Possidi) at the foot of Mount Casius, the tract between this and the range of Taurus
being always known as Syria, never as Phoenecia or Phoenicé.

The entire length of the coast between the limits of Cape Possidi and Rhinocolura is, without
reckoning the lesser indentations, about 380 miles, or nearly the same as that of Portugal. The
indentations of the coast-line are slight. From Rhinocolura to Mount Carmel, a distance of 150
miles, not a single strong promontory asserts itself, nor is there a single bay of sufficient depth
to attract the attention of geographers. Carmel itself is a notable headland, and shelters a bay
of some size; but these once passed the old uniformity returns, the line being again almost
unbroken for a distance of seventy-five miles, from Haifa to Beyrout (Berytus). North of
Beyrout we find a little more variety. The coast projects in a tolerably bold sweep between the
thirty-fourth parallel and Tripolis (Tarabulus) and recedes almost correspondingly between
Tripolis and Tortosa (Antaradus), so that a deepish bay is formed between Lat. 34° 27′ and
Lat. 34° 45′, whence the line again runs northward unindented for fifty miles, to beyond
Gabala (Jebili). After this, between Gabala and Cape Posideium there is considerable
irregularity, the whole tract being mountainous, and spurs from Bargylus and Casius running

down into the sea and forming a succession of headlands, of which Cape Posideium is the most remarkable.

But while the name Phoenicia is applied geographically to this long extent—nearly 400 miles—of coast-line, historically and ethnically it has to be reduced within considerably narrower limits. A race, quite distinct from that of the Phoenicians, was settled from an early date on the southern portion of the west Asian coast, where it verges towards Africa. From Jabneh (Yebna) southwards was Palestine, the country of the Philistines, perhaps even from Joppa (Jaffa), which is made the boundary by Mela.13 Thus at least eighty miles of coast-line must be deducted from the 380, and the length of Phoenicia along the Mediterranean shore must be regarded as not exceeding three hundred miles.

The width varied from eight or ten miles to thirty. We must regard as the eastern boundary of Phoenicia the high ridge which forms the watershed between the streams that flow eastward toward the Orontes, Litany, and Jordan, and those that flow westward into the Mediterranean. It is difficult to say what was the average width, but perhaps it may be fairly estimated at about fifteen miles. In this case the entire area would have been about 4,500 square miles.

The tract was one of a remarkably diversified character. Lofty mountain, steep wooded hill, chalky slope, rich alluvial plain, and sandy shore succeeded each other, each having its own charm, which was enhanced by contrast. The sand is confined to a comparatively narrow strip along the seashore,14 and to the sites of ancient harbours now filled up. It is exceedingly fine and of excellent silicious quality, especially in the vicinity of Sidon and at the foot of Mount Carmel. The most remarkable plains are those of Sharon, Acre, Tyre, Sidon, Beyrout, and Marathus. Sharon, so dear to the Hebrew poets,15 is the maritime tract intervening between the highland of Samaria and the Mediterranean, extending from Joppa to the southern foot of Carmel—a distance of nearly sixty miles—and watered by the Chorseas, the Kaneh, and other rivers. It is a smooth, very slightly undulating tract, about ten miles in width from the sea to the foot of the mountains, which rise up abruptly from it without any intervening region of hills, and seem to bound it as a wall, above which tower the huge rounded masses of Ebal and Gerizim, with the wooded cone, on which stood Samaria, nestling at their feet.16 The sluggish streams, several of them containing water during the whole of the year, make their way across it between reedy banks,17 and generally spread out before reaching the shore into wide marshes, which might be easily utilised for purposes of irrigation. The soil is extremely rich, varying from bright red to deep black, and producing enormous crops of weeds or grain, according as it is cultivated or left in a state of nature. Towards the south the view over the region has been thus described: "From Ramleh there is a wide view on every side, presenting a prospect rarely surpassed in richness and beauty. I could liken it to nothing but the great plain of the Rhine by Heidelberg or, better still, to the vast plains of Lombardy, as seen from the cathedral of Milan and elsewhere. In the east the frowning mountains of Judah rose abruptly from the tract at their foot; while on the west, in fine contrast, the glittering waves of the Mediterranean Sea associated our thoughts with Europe. Towards the north and south, as far as the eye could reach, the beautiful plain was spread out like a carpet at our feet, variegated with tracts of brown from which the crops had just been taken, and with fields still rich with the yellow of the ripe corn, or green with the springing millet. Immediately below us the eye rested on the immense olive groves of Ramleh and Lydda, and the picturesque towers and minarets and domes of these large villages. In the plain itself were not many villages, but the tract of hills and the mountain-side beyond, especially in the north-east, were perfectly studded with them, and as now seen in the reflected beams of the setting sun they seemed like white villas and hamlets among the dark hills, presenting an appearance of thriftiness and beauty which certainly would not stand a closer examination."18 Towards its northern end Sharon is narrowed by the low hills which gather round the western flanks of Carmel, and gradually encroach upon the plain until it terminates against the shoulder of the mountain itself, leaving only a narrow beach at the foot of the promontory by which it is possible to communicate with the next plain towards the north.19

Compared with Sharon the plain of Acre is unimportant and of small extent. It reaches about eight miles along the shore, from the foot of Carmel to the headland on which the town of Acre stands, and has a width between the shore and the hills of about six miles. Like Sharon it is noted for its fertility. Watered by the two permanent streams of the Kishon and the Belus, it possesses a rich soil, which is said to be at present "perhaps the best cultivated and producing the most luxuriant crops, both of corn and weeds, of any in Palestine."110 The Kishon waters it on the south, where it approaches Carmel, and is a broad stream,111 though easily fordable towards its mouth. The Belus (Namâané) flows through it towards the north, washing Acre itself, and is a stream of even greater volume than the Kishon, though it has but a short course. The third of the Phoenician plains, as we proceed from south to north, is that of Tyre. This is a long but comparatively narrow strip, reaching from the Ras-el-Abiad towards the south to Sarepta on the north, a distance of about twenty miles, but in no part more than five miles across, and generally less than two miles. It is watered about midway by the copious stream of the Kasimiyeh or Litany, which, rising east of Lebanon in the Buka'a or Coelesyrian valley, forces its way through the mountain chain by a series of tremendous gorges, and debouches upon the Tyrian lowland about three miles to the south-east of the present city, near the modern Khan-el-Kasimiyeh, whence it flows peaceably to the sea with many windings through a broad low tract of meadow-land. Other rills and rivulets descending from the west flank of the great mountain increase the productiveness of the plain, while copious fountains of water gush forth with surprising force in places, more especially at Ras-el-Ain, three miles from Tyre, to the south.112 The plain is, even at the present day, to a large extent covered with orchards, gardens, and cultivated fields, in which are grown rich crops of tobacco, cotton, and cereals.

The plain of Sidon, which follows that of Tyre, and is sometimes regarded as a part of it,113 extends from a little north of Sarepta to the Ras-el-Jajunieh, a distance of about ten miles, and resembles that of Tyre in its principal features. It is long and narrow, never more than about two miles in width, but well-watered and very fertile. The principal streams are the Bostrenus (Nahr-el-Auly) in the north, just inside the promontory of Jajunieh, the Nahr-Sanîk, south of Sidon, a torrent dry in the summer-time,114 and the Nahr-ez-Zaherany, two and a half miles north of Sarepta, a river of moderate capacity. Fine fountains also burst from the earth in the plain itself, as the Ain-el-Kanterah and the Ain-el-Burâk,115 between Sarepta and the Zaherany river. Irrigation is easy and is largely used, with the result that the fruits and vegetables of Saïda and its environs have the name of being among the finest of the country.116

The plain of Berytus (Beyrout) is the most contracted of all the Phoenician plains that are at all noticeable. It lies south, south-east, and east of the city, intervening between the high dunes or sand-hills which form the western portion of the Beyrout peninsula, and the skirts of Lebanon, which here approach very near to the sea. The plain begins at Wady Shuweifat on the south, about four miles from the town of Beyrout, and extends northwards to the sea on the western side of the Nahr Beyrout. The northern part of the plain is known as Ard-el-Burâjineh. The plain is deficient in water,117 yet is cultivated in olives and mulberries, and contains the largest olive grove in all Syria. A little beyond its western edge is the famous pine forest118 from which (according to some) Berytus derived its name.119

The plain of Marathus is, next to Sharon, the most extensive in Phoenicia. It stretches from Jebili (Gabala) on the north to Arka towards the south, a distance of about sixty miles, and has a width varying from two to ten miles. The rock crops out from it in places and it is broken between Tortosa and Hammam by a line of low hills running parallel with the shore.120 The principal streams which water it are the Nahr-el-Melk, or Badas, six miles south of Jebili, the Nahr Amrith, a strong running brook which empties itself into the sea a few miles south of Tortosa (Antaradus), the Nahr Kublé, which joins the Nahr Amrith near its mouth, and the Eleutherus or Nahr-el-Kabir, which reaches the sea a little north of Arka. Of these the Eleutherus is the most important. "It is a considerable stream even in summer, and in the rainy season it is a barrier to intercourse, caravans sometimes remaining encamped on its banks for several weeks, unable to cross."121 The soil of the plain is shallow, the rock lying always near the surface; the streams are allowed to run to waste and form marshes, which breed malaria; a scanty population scarcely attempts more than the rudest and most inefficient cultivation; and the consequence is that the tract at present is almost a desert. Nature, however, shows its capabilities by covering it in the spring-time from end to end with a "carpet of flowers."122 From the edges of the plains, and sometimes from the very shore of the sea, rise up chalky slopes or steep rounded hills, partly left to nature and covered with trees and shrubs, partly at the present day cultivated and studded with villages. The hilly region forms generally an intermediate tract between the high mountains and the plains already described; but, not unfrequently, it commences at the water's edge, and fills with its undulations the entire space, leaving not even a strip of lowland. This is especially the case in the central region between Berytus and Arka, opposite the highest portion of the Lebanon; and again in the north between Cape Possidi and Jebili, opposite the more northern part of Bargylus. The hilly region in these places is a broad tract of alternate wooded heights and deep romantic valleys, with streams murmuring amid their shades. Sometimes the hills are cultivated in terraces, on which grow vines and olives, but more often they remain in their pristine condition, clothed with masses of tangled underwood.

The mountain ranges, which belong in some measure to the geography of Phoenicia, are four in number—Carmel, Casius, Bargylus, and Lebanon. Carmel is a long hog-backed ridge, running in almost a straight line from north-west to south-east, from the promontory which forms the western protection of the bay of Acre to El-Ledjun, on the southern verge of the great plain of Esdraelon, a distance of about twenty-two miles. It is a limestone formation, and rises up abruptly from the side of the bay of Acre, with flanks so steep and rugged that the traveller must dismount in order to ascend them,123 but slopes more gently towards the south, where it is comparatively easy of access. The greatest elevation which it attains is about Lat. 32° 4´, where it reaches the height of rather more than 1,200 feet; from this it falls gradually as it nears the shore, until at the convent, with which the western extremity is crowned, the height above the sea is no more than 582 feet. In ancient times the whole mountain was thickly wooded,124 but at present, though it contains "rocky dells" where there are "thick jungles of copse,"125 and is covered in places with olive groves and thickets of dwarf oak, yet its appearance is rather that of a park than of a forest, long stretches of grass alternating with patches of woodland and "shrubberies, thicker than any in Central Palestine," while the larger trees grow in clumps or singly, and there is nowhere, as in Lebanon, any dense growth, or even any considerable grove, of forest trees. But the beauty of the tract is conspicuous; and if Carmel means, as some interpret, a "garden" rather than a "forest," it may be held to well justify its appellation. "The whole mountain-side," says one traveller,126 "was dressed with blossoms and flowering shrubs and fragrant herbs." "There is not a flower," says another,127 "that I have seen in Galilee, or on the plains along the coast, that I do not find on Carmel, still the fragrant, lovely mountain that he was of old."

The geological structure of Carmel is, in the main, what is called "the Jura formation," or "the upper oolite"—a soft white limestone, with nodules and veins of flint. At the western extremity, where it overhangs the Mediterranean, are found chalk, and tertiary breccia formed of fragments of chalk and flint. On the north-east of the mountain, beyond the Nahr-el-Mukattah, plutonic rocks appear, breaking through the deposit strata, and forming the beginning of the basalt formation which runs through the plain of Esdraelon to Tabor and the Sea of Galilee.128 Like most limestone formations, Carmel abounds in caves, which are said to be more than 2,000 in number,129 and are often of great length and extremely tortuous. Carmel, the great southern headland of Phoenicia, is balanced in a certain sense by the extreme northern headland of Casius. Mount Casius is, strictly speaking, the termination of a spur from Bargylus; but it has so marked and peculiar a character that it seems entitled to separate description. Rising up abruptly from the Mediterranean to the height of 5,318 feet, it dominates the entire region in its vicinity, and from the sea forms a landmark that is extraordinarily conspicuous. Forests of fine trees clothe its flanks, but the lofty summit towers high above them, a bare mass of rock, known at the present day as Jebel-el-Akra, or "the Bald Mountain." It is formed mainly of the same cretaceous limestone as the other mountains of these parts, and like them has a rounded summit; but rocks of igneous origin enter into its geological structure; and in its vegetation it more resembles the mountain ranges of Taurus and Amanus than those of southern Syria and Palestine. On its north-eastern prolongation, which is washed by the Orontes, lay the enchanting pleasure-ground of Daphné, bubbling with fountains, and bright with flowering shrubs, where from a remote antiquity the Syrians held frequent festival to their favourite deity—the "Dea Syra"—the great nature goddess.

The elevated tract known to the ancients as Bargylus, and to modern geographers as the Ansayrieh or Nasariyeh mountain-region, runs at right angles to the spur terminating in the Mount Casius, and extends from the Orontes near Antioch to the valley of the Eleutherus. This is a distance of not less than a hundred miles. The range forms the western boundary of the lower Coelesyrian valley, which abuts upon it towards the east, while westward it looks down upon the region, partly hill, partly lowland, which may be regarded as constituting "Northern Phoenicia." The axis of the range is almost due north and south, but with a slight deflection towards the south-east. Bargylus is not a chain comparable to Lebanon, but still it is a romantic and picturesque region. The lower spurs towards the west are clothed with olive grounds and vineyards, or covered with myrtles and rhododendrons; between them are broad open valleys, productive of tobacco and corn. Higher up "the scenery becomes wild and bold; hill rises to mountain; soft springing green corn gives place to sterner crag, smooth plain to precipitous heights;"130 and if in the more elevated region the majesty of the cedar is wanting, yet forests of fir and pine abound, and creep up the mountain-side, in places almost to the summit, while here and there bare masses of rock protrude themselves, and crag and cliff rise into the clouds that hang about the highest summits. Water abounds throughout the region, which is the parent of numerous streams, as the northern Nahr-el-Kebir, which flows into the sea by Latakia, the Nahr-el-Melk, the Nahr Amrith, the Nahr Kublé, the Nahr-el-Abrath, and many others. From the conformation of the land they have of necessity short courses; but each and all of them spread along their banks a rich verdure and an uncommon fertility.

But the great range of Phoenicia, its glory and its boast is Lebanon. Lebanon, the "White Mountain"131—"the Mont Blanc of Palestine"132—now known as "the Old White-headed Man" (Jebel-esh-Sheikh), or "the Mountain of Ice" (Jebel-el-Tilj), was to Phoenicia at once its protection, the source of its greatness, and its crowning beauty. Extended in a continuous line for a distance of above a hundred miles, with an average elevation of from 6,000 to 8,000 feet, and steepest on its eastern side, it formed a wall against which the waves of eastern invasion naturally broke—a bulwark which seemed to say to them, "Thus far shall ye go, and no further." The flood of conquest swept along its eastern flank, down the broad vale of the Buka'a, and then over the hills of Galilee; but its frowning precipices and its lofty crest deterred or baffled the invader, and the smiling region between its summit and the Mediterranean was, in the early times at any rate, but rarely traversed by a hostile army. This western region it was which held those inexhaustible stores of forest trees that supplied Phoenicia with her war ships and her immense commercial navy; here were the most productive valleys, the vineyards, and the olive grounds, and here too were the streams and rills, the dashing cascades, the lovely dells, and the deep gorges which gave her the palm over all the surrounding countries for variety of picturesque scenery.

The geology of the Lebanon is exceedingly complicated. "While the bulk of the mountain, and all the higher ranges, are without exception limestone of the early cretaceous period, the valleys and gorges are filled with formations of every possible variety, sedimentary, metamorphic, and igneous. Down many of them run long streams of trap or basalt; occasionally there are dykes of porphyry and greenstone, and then patches of sandstone, before the limestone and flint recur."133 Some slopes are composed entirely of soft sandstone;

many patches are of a hard metallic-sounding trap or porphyry; but the predominant formation is a greasy or powdery limestone, bare often, but sometimes clothed with a soft herbage, or with a thick tangle of shrubs, or with lofty forest trees. The ridge of the mountain is everywhere naked limestone rock, except in the comparatively few places which attain the highest elevation, where it is coated or streaked with snow. Two summits are especially remarkable, that of Jebel Sunnin towards the south, which is a conspicuous object from Beyrout,134 and is estimated to exceed the height of 9,000 feet,135 and that of Jebel Mukhmel towards the north, which has been carefully measured and found to fall a very little short of 10,200 feet.136 The latter, which forms a sort of amphitheatre, circles round and impends over a deep hollow or basin, opening out towards the west, in which rise the chief sources that go to form the romantic stream of the Kadisha. The sides of the basin are bare and rocky, fringed here and there with the rough knolls which mark the deposits of ancient glaciers, the "moraines" of the Lebanon. In this basin stand "the Cedars." It is not indeed true, as was for a long time supposed, that the cedar grove of Jebel Mukhmel is the sole remnant of that primeval cedar-forest which was anciently the glory of the mountain. Cedars exist on Lebanon in six other places at least, if not in more. Near Tannurin, on one of the feeders of the Duweir, a wild gorge is clothed from top to bottom with a forest of trees, untouched by the axe, the haunt of the panther and the bear, which on examination have been found to be all cedars, some of a large size, from fifteen to eighteen feet in girth. They grow in clusters, or scattered singly, in every variety of situation, some clinging to the steep slopes, or gnarled and twisted on the bare hilltops, others sheltered in the recesses of the dell. There are also cedar-groves at B'sherrah; at El Hadith; near Dûma, five hours south-west of El Hadith; in one of the glens north of Deir-el-Kamar, at Etnub, and probably in other places.137 But still "the Cedars" of Jebel Mukhmel are entitled to pre-eminence over all the rest, both as out-numbering any other cluster, and still more as exceeding all the rest in size and apparent antiquity. Some of the patriarchs are of enormous girth; even the younger ones have a circumference of eighteen feet; and the height is such that the birds which dwell among the upper branches are beyond the range of an ordinary fowling-piece.

But it is through the contrasts which it presents that Lebanon has its extraordinary power of attracting and delighting the traveller. Below the upper line of bare and worn rock, streaked in places with snow, and seamed with torrent courses, a region is entered upon where the freshest and softest mountain herbage, the greenest foliage, and the most brilliant flowers alternate with deep dells, tremendous gorges, rocky ravines, and precipices a thousand feet high. Scarcely has the voyager descended from the upper region of naked and rounded rock, when he comes upon "a tremendous chasm—the bare amphitheatre of the upper basin contracts into a valley of about 2,000 feet deep, rent at its bottom into a cleft a thousand feet deeper still, down which dashes a river, buried between these stupendous walls of rock. All above the chasm is terraced as far as the eye can reach with indefatigable industry. Tiny streamlets bound and leap from terrace to terrace, fertilising them as they rush to join the torrent in the abyss. Some of the waterfalls are of great height and of considerable volume. From one spot may be counted no less than seven of these cascades, now dashing in white spray over a cliff, now lost under the shade of trees, soon to reappear over the next shelving rock."138 Or, to quote from another writer,139—"The descent from the summit is gradual, but is everywhere broken by precipices and towering rocks, which time and the elements have chiselled into strange fantastic shapes. Ravines of singular wildness and grandeur furrow the whole mountain-side, looking in many places like huge rents. Here and there, too, bold promontories shoot out, and dip perpendicularly into the bosom of the Mediterranean. The ragged limestone banks are scantily clothed with the evergreen oak, and the sandstone with pines; while every available spot is carefully cultivated. The cultivation is wonderful, and shows what all Syria might be of under a good government. Miniature fields of grain are often seen where one would suppose that the eagles alone, which hover round them, could have planted the seed.

Fig-trees cling to the naked rock; vines are trained along narrow ledges; long ranges of mulberries on terraces like steps of stairs cover the more gentle declivities; and dense groves of olives fill up the bottoms of the glens. Hundreds of villages are seen, here built amid labyrinths of rock, there clinging like swallows' nests to the sides of cliffs, while convents, no less numerous, are perched on the top of every peak. When viewed from the sea on a morning in early spring, Lebanon presents a picture which once seen is never forgotten; but deeper still is the impression left on the mind, when one looks down over its terraced slopes clothed in their gorgeous foliage, and through the vistas of its magnificent glens, on the broad and bright Mediterranean."

The eastern flank of the mountain falls very far short of the western both in area and in beauty. It is a comparatively narrow region, and presents none of the striking features of gorge, ravine, deep dell, and dashing stream which diversify the side that looks westward. The steep slopes are generally bare, the lower portion only being scantily clothed with deciduous oak, for the most part stunted, and with low scrub of juniper and barberry.140 Towards the north there is an outer barrier, parallel with the main chain, on which follows a tolerably flat and rather bare plain, well watered, and with soft turf in many parts, which gently slopes to the foot of the main ascent, a wall of rock generally half covered with snow, up which winds the rough track whereby travellers reach the summit. Rills of water are not wanting; flowers bloom to the very edge of the snow, and the walnut-tree flourishes in sheltered places to within two or three thousand feet of the summit; but the general character of the tract is bare and bleak; the villages are few; and the terraced cultivation, which adds so much to the beauty of the western side, is wanting. In the southern half of the range the descent is abrupt from the crest of the mountain into the Buka'a, or valley of the Litany, and the aspect of the mountain-side is one of "unrelieved bareness."141

There is, however, one beauty at one point on this side of the Lebanon range which is absent from the more favoured western region. On the ascent from Baalbek to the Cedars the traveller comes upon Lake Lemone, a beautiful mountain tarn, without any apparent exit, the only sheet of water in the Lebanon. Lake Lemone is of a long oval shape, about two miles from one end to the other, and is fed by a stream entering at either extremity, that from the north, which comes down from the village of Ainât, being the more important. As the water which comes into the lake cannot be discharged by evaporation, we must suppose some underground outlet,142 by which it is conveyed, through the limestone, into the Litany.

The eastern side of Lebanon drains entirely into this river, which is the only stream whereto it gives birth. The Litany is the principal of all the Phoenician rivers, for the Orontes must be counted not to Phoenicia but to Syria. It rises from a small pool or lake near Tel Hushben,143 about six miles to the south-west of the Baalbek ruins. Springing from this source, which belongs to Antilibanus rather than to Lebanon, the Litany shortly receives a large accession to its waters from the opposite side of the valley, and thus augmented flows along the lower Buka'a in a direction which is generally a little west of south, receiving on either side a number of streams and rills from both mountains, and giving out in its turn numerous canals for irrigation. As the river descends with numerous windings, but still with the same general course, the valley of the Buka'a contracts more and more, till finally it terminates in a gorge of a most extraordinary character. Nothing in the conformation of the strata, or in the lie of ground, indicates the coming marvel144—the roots of Lebanon and Hermon appear to intermix—and the further progress of the river seems to be barred by a rocky ridge stretching across the valley from east to west, when lo! suddenly the ridge is cut, as if by a knife, and a deep and narrow chasm opens in it, down which the stream plunges in a cleft 200 feet deep, and so narrow that in one place it is actually bridged over by masses of rock which have fallen from the cliffs above.145 In the gully below fig-trees and planes, besides many shrubs, find a footing, and the moist walls of rock on either side are hung with ferns of various kinds, among which is conspicuous the delicate and graceful maidenhair. Further down the chasm deepens, first to 1,000 and then to 1,500 feet, "the torrent roars in the gorge, milk-white and swollen often with the melting snow, overhung with semi-tropical oleanders, fig-trees, and oriental planes, while the upper cliffs are clad with northern vegetation, two zones of climate thus being visible at once."146 Where the gorge is the deepest, opposite the Castle of Belfort (the modern Kulat-esh-Shukif), the river suddenly makes a turn at right angles, altering its course from nearly due south to nearly due west, and cuts through the remaining roots of Lebanon, still at the bottom of a tremendous fissure, and still raging and chafing for a distance of fifteen miles, until at length it debouches on the coast plain, and meanders slowly through meadows to the sea,147 which it enters about five miles to the north of Tyre. The course of the Litany may be roughly estimated at from seventy to seventy-five miles.

The other streams to which Lebanon gives birth flow either from its northern or its western flank. From the northern flank flows one stream only, the Nahr-el-Kebir or Eleutherus. The course of this stream is short, not much exceeding thirty miles. It rises from several sources at the edge of the Coelesyrian valley, and, receiving affluents from either side, flows westward between Bargylus and Lebanon to the Mediterranean, which it enters between Orthosia (Artousi) and Marathus (Amrith) with a stream, the volume of which is even in the summer-time considerable. In the rainy season it constitutes an important impediment to intercourse, since it frequently sweeps away any bridge which may be thrown across it, and is itself unfordable. Caravans sometimes remain encamped upon its banks for weeks, waiting until the swell has subsided and crossing is no longer dangerous.148

From the western flank of Lebanon flow above a hundred streams of various dimensions, whereof the most important are the Nahr-el-Berid or river of Orthosia, the Kadisha or river of Tripolis, the Ibrahim or Adonis, the Nahr-el-Kelb or Lycus, the Damour or Tamyras, the Auly (Aouleh) or Bostrenus, and the Zaherany, of which the ancient name is unknown to us. The Nahr-el-Berid drains the north-western angle of the mountain chain, and is formed of two main branches, one coming down from the higher portion of the range, about Lat. 34° 20´, and flowing to the north-west, while the other descends from a region of much less elevation, about Lat. 34° 30´, and runs a little south of west to the point of junction. The united stream then forces its way down a gorge in a north-west direction, and enters the sea at Artousi, probably the ancient Orthosia.149 The length of the river from its remotest fountain to its mouth is about twenty miles.

The Kadisha or "Holy River" has its source in the deep basin already described, round which rise in a semicircle the loftiest peaks of the range, and on the edge of which stand "the Cedars." Fed by the perpetual snows, it shortly becomes a considerable stream, and flows nearly due west down a beautiful valley, where the terraced slopes are covered with vineyards and mulberry groves, and every little dell, every nook and corner among the jagged rocks, every ledge and cranny on precipice-side, which the foot of man can reach, or on which a basket of earth can be deposited, is occupied with patch of corn or fruit-tree.150 Lower down near Canobin the valley contracts into a sublime chasm, its rocky walls rising perpendicularly a thousand feet on either side, and in places not leaving room for even a footpath beside the stream that flows along the bottom.151 The water of the Kadisha is "pure, fresh, cool, and limpid,"152 and makes a paradise along its entire course. Below Canobin the stream sweeps round in a semicircle towards the north, and still running in a picturesque glen, draws near to Tripolis, where it bends towards the north-west, and enters the sea after passing through the town. Its course, including main windings, measures about twenty-five miles.

The Ibrahim, or Adonis, has its source near Afka (Apheca) in Lat. 34° 4´ nearly. It bursts from a cave at the foot of a tremendous cliff, and its foaming waters rush down into a wild chasm.153 Its flow is at first towards the north-west, but after receiving a small tributary from the north-east, it shapes its course nearly westward, and pursues this direction, with only slight bends to the north and south, for the distance of about fifteen miles to the sea. After heavy rain in Lebanon, its waters, which are generally clear and limpid, become tinged with the earth which the swollen torrent detaches from the mountain-side,154 and Adonis thus "runs purple to the sea"—not however once a year only, but many times. It enters the Mediterranean about four miles south of Byblus (Jebeil) and six north of Djouni.

The Lycus or Nahr-el-Kelb ("Dog River") flows from the northern and western flanks of Jebel Sunnin. It is formed by the confluence of three main streams. One of these rises near Afka, and runs to the south of west, past the castle and temples of Fakra, to its junction with the second stream, which is formed of several rivulets flowing from the northern flank of Sunnin. Near Bufkeiya the river constituted by the union of these two branches is joined by a third stream flowing from the western flank of Sunnin with a westerly course, and from this point the Lycus pursues its way in the same general direction down a magnificent gorge to the Mediterranean. Both banks are lofty, but especially that to the south, where one of Lebanon's great roots strikes out far, and dips, a rocky precipice, into the bosom of the deep.155 Low in the depths of the gorge the mad torrent dashes over its rocky bed in sheets of foam, its banks fringed with oleander, which it bathes with its spray. Above rise jagged precipices of white limestone, crowned far overhead by many a convent and village.156 The course of the Nahr-el-Kelbis about equal to that of the Adonis.

The Damour or Tamyras drains the western flank of Lebanon to the south of Jebel Sunnin (about Lat. 33° 45′), the districts known as Menassif and Jourd Arkoub, about Barouk and Deir-el-Kamar. It collects the waters from an area of about 110 square miles, and carries them to the sea in a course which is a little north of west, reaching it half-way between Khan Khulda (Heldua) and Nebbi Younas. The scenery along its banks is tame compared with that of the more northern rivers.

The Nahr-el-Auly or Bostrenus rises from a source to the north-east of Barouk, and flows in a nearly straight course to the south-west for a distance of nearly thirty-five miles, when it is joined by a stream from Jezzin, which flows into it from the south-east. On receiving this stream, the Auly turns almost at a right angle, and flows to the west down the fine alluvial track called Merj Bisry, passing from this point through comparatively low ground, and between swelling hills, until it reaches the sea two miles to the north of Sidon. Its entire course is not less than sixty miles.

The Zaherany repeats on a smaller scale the course of the Bostrenus. It rises near Jerjû'a from the western flank of Jebel Rihan, the southern extremity of the Lebanon range, and flows at first to the south-west. The source is "a fine large fountain bursting forth with violence, and with water enough for a mill race."157 From this the river flows in a deep valley, brawling and foaming along its course, through tracts of green grass shaded by black walnut-trees for a distance of about five miles, after which, just opposite Jerjû'a, it breaks through one of the spurs from Rihan by a magnificent chasm. The gorge is one "than which there are few deeper or more savage in Lebanon. The mountains on each side rise up almost precipitously to the height of two or three thousand feet above the stream, that on the northern bank being considerably the higher. The steep sides of the southern mountain are dotted with shrub, oak, and other dwarf trees."158 The river descends in its chasm still in a south-west direction until, just opposite Arab Salim, it "turns round the precipitous corner or bastion of the southern Rihan into a straight valley," and proceeds to run due south for a short distance. Meeting, however, a slight swell of ground, which blocks what would seem to have been its natural course, the river "suddenly turns west," and breaking through a low ridge by a narrow ravine, pursues its way by a course a little north of west to the Mediterranean, which it enters about midway between Sidon and Sarepta.159 The length of the stream, including main windings, is probably not more than thirty-five miles.

We have spoken of the numerous promontories, terminations of spurs from the mountains, which break the low coast-line into fragments, and go down precipitously into the sea. Of these there are two between Tyre and Acre, one known as the Ras-el-Abiad or "White Headland," and the other as the Ras-en-Nakura. The former is a cliff of snow-white chalk interspersed with black flints, and rises perpendicularly from the sea to the height of three hundred feet.160 The road, which in some places impends over the water, has been cut with great labour through the rock, and is said by tradition to have been the work of Alexander the

Great. Previously, both here and at the Ras-en-Nakura, the ascent was by steps, and the passes were known as the Climaces Tyriorum, or "Staircases of the Tyrians." Another similar precipice guards the mouth of the Lycus on its south side and has been engineered with considerable skill, first by the Egyptians and then by the Romans.161 North of this, at Djouni, the coast road "traverses another pass, where the mountain, descending to the water, has been cut to admit it."162 Still further north, between Byblus and Tripolis, the bold promontory known to the ancients as Theu-prosopon, and now called the Ras-esh-Shakkah, is still unconquered, and the road has to quit the shore and make its way over the spur by a "wearisome ascent"163 at some distance inland. Again, "beyond the Tamyras the hills press closely on the sea,"164 and there is "a rocky and difficult pass, along which the path is cut for some distance in the rock."165

The effect of this conformation of the country was, in early times, to render Phoenicia untraversable by a hostile army, and at the same time to interpose enormous difficulties in the way of land communication among the natives themselves, who must have soon turned their thoughts to the possibility of communicating by sea. The various "staircases" were painful and difficult to climb, they gave no passage to animals, and only light forms of merchandise could be conveyed by them. As soon as the first rude canoe put forth upon the placid waters of the Mediterranean, it must have become evident that the saving in time and labour would be great if the sea were made to supersede the land as the ordinary line of communication.

The main characteristics of the country were, besides its inaccessibility, its picturesqueness and its productiveness. The former of these two qualities seems to have possessed but little attraction for man in his primitive condition. Beauties of nature are rarely sung of by early poets; and it appears to require an educated eye to appreciate them. But productiveness is a quality the advantages of which can be perceived by all. The eyes which first looked down from the ridge of Bargylus or Lebanon upon the well-watered, well-wooded, and evidently fertile tract between the mountain summits and the sea, if they took no note of its marvellous and almost unequalled beauty, must at any rate have seen that here was one of earth's most productive gardens—emphatically a "good land," that might well content whosoever should be so fortunate as to possess it. There is nothing equal to it in Western Asia. The Damascene oasis, the lower valley of the Orontes, the Ghor or Jordan plain, the woods of Bashan, and the downs of Moab are fertile and attractive regions; but they are comparatively narrow tracts and present little variety; each is fitted mainly for one kind of growth, one class of products. Phoenicia, in its long extent from Mount Casius to Joppa, and in its combination of low alluvial plain, rich valley, sunny slopes and hills, virgin forests, and high mountain pasturage, has soils and situations suited for productions of all manner of kinds, and for every growth, from that of the lowliest herb to that of the most gigantic tree. In the next section an account of its probable products in ancient times will be given; for the present it is enough to note that Western Asia contained no region more favoured or more fitted by its general position, its formation, and the character of its soil, to become the home of an important nation.

CHAPTER II—CLIMATE AND PRODUCTIONS

Climate of Phoenicia—Varieties—Climate of the coast, in
the south, in the north—Climate of the more elevated
regions—Vegetable productions—Principal trees—Most
remarkable shrubs and fruit-trees—Herbs, flowers, and
garden vegetables—Zoology—Land animals—Birds—Marine and
fresh-water fish—Principal shell-fish—Minerals.

The long extent of the Phoenician coast, and the great difference in the elevation of its various parts, give it a great diversity of climate. Northern Phoenicia is many degrees colder than southern; and the difference is still more considerable between the coast tracts and the more elevated portions of the mountain regions. The greatest heat is experienced in the plain of Sharon,21 which is at once the most southern portion of the country, and the part most remote from any hills of sufficient elevation to exert an important influence on the temperature. Neither Carmel on the north, nor the hills of Samaria on the east, produce any sensible effect on the climate of the Sharon lowland. The heat in summer is intense, and except along the river courses the tract is burnt up, and becomes little more than an expanse of sand. As a compensation, the cold in winter is very moderate. Snow scarcely ever falls, and if there is frost it is short-lived, and does not penetrate into the ground.22

Above Carmel the coast tract is decidedly less hot than the region south of it, and becomes cooler and cooler as we proceed northwards. Northern Phoenicia enjoys a climate that is delightful, and in which it would be difficult to suggest much improvement. The summer heat is scarcely ever too great, the thermometer rarely exceeding 90° of Fahrenheit,23 and often sinking below 70°. Refreshing showers of rain frequently fall, and the breezes from the north, the east, and the south-east, coming from high mountain tracts which are in part snow-clad, temper the heat of the sun's rays and prevent it from being oppressive. The winter temperature seldom descends much below 50°; and thus the orange, the lemon and the date-palm flourish in the open air, and the gardens are bright with flowers even in December and January. Snow falls occasionally, but it rarely lies on the ground for more than a few days, and is scarcely ever so much as a foot deep. On the other hand, rain is expected during the winter-time, and the entire line of coast is visited for some months with severe storms and gales, accompanied often by thunder and violent rain,24 which strew the shore with wrecks and turn even insignificant mountain streams into raging torrents. The storms come chiefly from the west and north-west, quarters to which the harbours on the coast are unfortunately open.25 Navigation consequently suffers interruption; but when once the winter is past, a season of tranquillity sets in, and for many months of the year—at any rate from May to October26—the barometer scarcely varies, the sky is unclouded, and rain all but unknown.

As the traveller mounts from the coast tract into the more elevated regions, the climate sensibly changes. An hour's ride from the plains, when they are most sultry, will bring him into a comparatively cool region, where the dashing spray of the glacier streams is borne on the air, and from time to time a breeze that is actually cold comes down from the mountain-tops.27 Shade is abundant, for the rocks are often perpendicular, and overhand the road in places, while the dense foliage of cedars, or pines, or walnut-trees, forms an equally effectual screen against the sun's noonday rays. In winter the uplands are, of course, cold. Severe weather prevails in them from November to March;28 snow falls on all the high ground, while it rains on the coast and in the lowlands; the passes are blocked; and Lebanon and Bargylus replenish the icy stories which the summer's heat has diminished.

The vegetable productions of Phoenicia may be best considered under the several heads of trees, shrubs, herbs, flowers, fruit-trees, and garden vegetables. The chief trees were the palm-tree, the sycamore, the maritime pine, and the plane in the lowlands; in the highlands the cedar, Aleppo pine, oak, walnut, poplar, acacia, shumac, and carob. We have spoken of the former abundance of the palm. At present it is found in comparatively few places, and seldom in any considerable numbers. It grows singly, or in groups of two or three, at various points of the coast from Tripolis to Acre, but is only abundant in a few spots more towards the south, as at Haifa, under Carmel, where "fine date-palms" are numerous in the gardens,29 and at Jaffa, where travellers remark "a broad belt of two or three miles of date-palms and orange-groves laden with fruit."210 The wood was probably not much used as timber except in the earliest times, since Lebanon afforded so many kinds of trees much superior for building purposes. The date-palm was also valued for its fruit, though the produce of the Phoenician groves can never have been of a high quality.

The sycamore, or sycamine-fig, is a dark-foliaged tree, with a gnarled stem when it is old;211

it grows either singly or in clumps, and much more resembles in appearance the English oak than the terebinth does, which has been so often compared to it. The stem is short, and sends forth wide lateral branches forking out in all directions, which renders the tree very easy to climb. It bears a small fig in great abundance, and probably at all seasons, which, however, is "tasteless and woody,"212 though eaten by the inhabitants. The sycamore is common along the Phoenician lowland, but is a very tender tree and will not grow in the mountains.

The plane-tree, common in Asia Minor, is not very frequent either in Phoenicia or Palestine. It occurs, however, on the middle course of the Litany, where it breaks through the roots of Lebanon,213 and also in many of the valleys214 on the western flank of the mountain. The maritime pine (Pinus maritama) extends in forests here and there along the shore,215 and is found of service in checking the advance of the sand dunes, which have a tendency to encroach seriously on the cultivable soil.

Of the upland trees the most common is the oak. There are three species of oak in the country. The most prevalent is an evergreen oak (Quercus pseudococcifera), sometimes mistaken by travellers for a holly, sometimes for an ibex, which covers in a low dense bush many miles of the hilly country everywhere, and occasionally becomes a large tree in the Lebanon valleys,216 and on the flanks of Casius and Bargylus. Another common oak is Quercus Ægilops, a much smaller and deciduous tree, very stout-trunked, which grows in scattered groups on Carmel and elsewhere, "giving a park-like appearance to the landscape."217 The third kind is Quercus infectoria, a gall-oak, also deciduous, and very conspicuous from the large number of bright, chestnut-coloured, viscid galls which it bears, and which are now sometimes gathered for exportation.218

Next to the oak may be mentioned the walnut, which grows to a great size in sheltered positions in the Lebanon range, both upon the eastern and upon the western flank;219 the poplar, which is found both in the mountains220 and in the low country, as especially about Beyrout;221 the Aleppo pine (Pinus halepensis), of which there are large woods in Carmel, Lebanon, and Bargylus,222 while in Casius there is an enormous forest of them;223 and the carob (Ceratonia siliqua), or locust-tree, a dense-foliaged tree of a bright lucid green hue, which never grows in clumps or forms woods, but appears as an isolated tree, rounded or oblong, and affords the best possible shade.224 In the vicinity of Tyre are found also large tamarisks, maples, sumachs, and acacias.225

But the tree which is the glory of Phoenicia, and which was by far the most valuable of all its vegetable productions, is, of course, the cedar. Growing to an immense height, and attaining an enormous girth, it spreads abroad its huge flat branches hither and thither, covering a vast space of ground with its "shadowing shroud,"226 and presenting a most majestic and magnificent appearance. Its timber may not be of first-rate quality, and there is some question whether it was really used for the masts of their ships by the Phoenicians,227 but as building material it was beyond a doubt most highly prized, answering sufficiently for all the purposes required by architectural art, and at the same time delighting the sense of smell by its aromatic odour. Solomon employed it both for the Temple and for his own house;228 the Assyrian kings cut it and carried it to Nineveh;229 Herod the Great used it for the vast additions that he made to Zerubbabel's temple;230 it was exported to Egypt and Asia Minor; the Ephesian Greeks constructed of cedar, probably of cedar from Lebanon, the roof of their famous temple of Diana.231 At present the wealth of Lebanon in cedars is not great, but the four hundred which form the grove near the source of the Kadisha, and the many scattered cedar woods in other places, are to be viewed as remnants of one great primeval forest, which originally covered all the upper slopes on the western side, and was composed, if not exclusively, at any rate predominantly, of cedars.232 Cultivation, the need of fuel, and the wants of builders, have robbed the mountain of its primitive bright green vest, and left it either bare rock or terraced garden; but in the early times of Phoenicia, the true Lebanon cedar must undoubtedly have been its chief forest tree, and have stood to it as the pine to the Swiss Alps and the chestnut to the mountains of North Italy.

Of shrubs, below the rank of trees, the most important are the lentisk (Pistachia lentiscus), the bay, the arbutus (A. andrachne), the cypress, the oleander, the myrtle, the juniper, the barberry, the styrax (S. officinalis), the rhododendron, the bramble, the caper plant, the small-leaved holly, the prickly pear, the honeysuckle, and the jasmine. Myrtle and rhododendron grow luxuriantly on the flanks of Bargylus, and are more plentiful than any other shrubs in that region.233 Eastern Lebanon has abundant scrub of juniper and barberry;234 while on the western slopes their place is taken by the bramble, the myrtle, and the clematis.235 The lentisk, which rarely exceeds the size of a low bush, is conspicuous by its dark evergreen leaves and numerous small red berries;236 the arbutus—not our species, but a far lighter and more ornamental shrub, the Arbutus andrachne—bears also a bright red fruit, which colours the thickets;237 the styrax, famous for yielding the gum storax of commerce, grows towards the east end of Carmel, and is a very large bush branching from the ground, but never assuming the form of a tree; it has small downy leaves, white flowers like orange blossoms, and round yellow fruit, pendulous from slender stalks, like cherries.238 Travellers in Phoenicia do not often mention the caper plant, but it was seen by Canon Tristram hanging from the fissures of the rock, in the cleft of the Litany,239 amid myrtle and bay and clematis. The small-leaved holly was noticed by Mr. Walpole on the western flank of Bargylus.240 The prickly pear is not a native of Asia, but has been introduced from the New World. It has readily acclimatised itself, and is very generally employed, in Phoenicia, as in the neighbouring countries, for hedges.241

The fruit-trees of Phoenicia are numerous, and grow most luxuriantly, but the majority have no doubt been introduced from other countries, and the time of their introduction is uncertain. Five, however, may be reckoned as either indigenous or as cultivated at any rate from a remote antiquity—the vine, the olive, the date-palm, the walnut, and the fig. The vine is most widely spread. Vineyards cover large tracts in the vicinity of all the towns; they climb up the sides of Carmel, Lebanon, and Bargylus,242 hang upon the edge of precipices, and greet the traveller at every turn in almost every region. The size of individual vines is extraordinary. "Stephen Schultz states that in a village near Ptolemaïs (Acre) he supped under a large vine, the stem of which measured a foot and a half in diameter, its height being thirty feet; and that the whole plant, supported on trellis, covered an area of fifty feet either way. The bunches of grapes weighed from ten to twelve pounds and the berries were like small plums."243 The olive in Phoenicia is at least as old as the Exodus, for it was said of Asher, who was assigned the more southern part of that country—"Let him be acceptable to his brethren, and let him dip his foot in oil."244 Olives at the present day clothe the slopes of Lebanon and Bargylus above the vine region,245 and are carried upward almost to the very edge of the bare rock. They yield largely, and produce an oil of an excellent character. Fine olive-groves are also to be seen on Carmel,246 in the neighbourhood of Esfia. The date-palm has already been spoken of as a tree, ornamenting the landscape and furnishing timber of tolerable quality. As a fruit-tree it is not greatly to be prized, since it is only about Haifa and Jaffa that it produces dates,247 and those of no high repute. The walnut has all the appearance of being indigenous in Lebanon, where it grows to a great size,248 and bears abundance of fruit. The fig is also, almost certainly, a native; it grows plentifully, not only in the orchards about towns, but on the flanks of Lebanon, on Bargylus, and in the northern Phoenician plain.249

The other fruit-trees of the present day are the mulberry, the pomegranate, the orange, the lemon, the lime, the peach, the apricot, the plum, the cherry, the quince, the apple, the pear, the almond, the pistachio nut, and the banana. The mulberry is cultivated largely on the Lebanon250 in connection with the growth of silkworms, but is not valued as a fruit-tree. The pomegranate is far less often seen, but it is grown in the gardens about Saida,251 and the fruit has sometimes been an article of exportation.252 The orange and lemon are among the commonest fruits, but are generally regarded as comparatively late introductions. The lime is not often noticed, but obtains mention in the work of Mr. Walpole.253 The peach and apricot are for the most part standard trees, though sometimes trained on trellises.254 They were perhaps derived from Mesopotamia or Persia, but at what date it is quite impossible to conjecture. Apples, pears, plums, cherries, quinces, are not unlikely to have been indigenous, though of course the present species are the result of long and careful cultivation. The same may be said of the almond and the pistachio nut. The banana is a comparatively recent importation. It is grown along the coast from Jaffa as far north as Tripolis, and yields a fruit which is said to be of excellent quality.255

Altogether, Phoenicia may be pronounced a land of fruits. Hasselquist says,256 that in his time Sidon grew pomegranates, apricots, figs, almonds, oranges, lemons, and plums in such abundance as to furnish annually several shiploads for export, while D'Arvieux adds to this list pears, peaches, cherries, and bananas.257 Lebanon alone can furnish grapes, olives, mulberries, figs, apples, apricots, walnuts, cherries, peaches, lemons, and oranges. The coast tract adds pomegranates, limes, and bananas. It has been said that Carmel, a portion of Phoenicia, is "the garden of Eden run wild;"258 but the phrase might be fitly applied to the entire country.

Of herbs possessing some value for man, Phoenicia produces sage, rosemary, lavender, rue, and wormwood.259 Of flowers she has an extraordinary abundance. In early spring (March and April) not only the plains, but the very mountains, except where they consist of bare rock, are covered with a variegated carpet of the loveliest hues260 from the floral wealth scattered over them. Bulbous plants are especially numerous. Travellers mention hyacinths, tulips, ranunculuses, gladioli, anemones, orchises, crocuses of several kinds—blue and yellow and white, arums, amaryllises, cyclamens, &c., besides heaths, jasmine, honeysuckle, clematis, multiflora roses, rhododendrons, oleander, myrtle, astragalus, hollyhocks, convolvuli, valerian, red linum, pheasant's eye, guelder roses, antirrhinums, chrysanthemums, blue campanulas, and mandrakes. The orchises include "Ophrys atrata, with its bee-like lip, another like the spider orchis, and a third like the man orchis;"261 the cyclamens are especially beautiful, "nestling under every stone and lavish of their loveliness with graceful tufts of blossoms varying in hue from purest white to deepest purple pink."262 The multiflora rose is not common, but where it grows "covers the banks of streams with a sheet of blossom;"263 the oleanders fringe their waters with a line of ruby red; the mandrake (Mandragora officinalis) is "one of the most striking plants of the country, with its flat disk of very broad primrose-like leaves, and its central bunch of dark blue bell-shaped blossom."264 Ferns also abound, and among them is the delicate maidenhair.265

The principal garden vegetables grown at the present day are melons, cucumbers, gourds, pumpkins, turnips, carrots, and radishes.266 The kinds of grain most commonly cultivated are wheat, barley, millet, and maize. There is also an extensive cultivation of tobacco, indigo, and cotton, which have been introduced from abroad in comparatively modern times. Oil, silk, and fruits are, however, still among the chief articles of export; and the present wealth of the country is attributable mainly to its groves and orchards, its olives, mulberries, figs, lemons, and oranges.

The zoology of Phoenicia has not until recently attracted very much attention. At present the list of land animals known to inhabit it is short,267 including scarcely more than the bear, the leopard or panther, the wolf, the hyæna, the jackal, the fox, the hare, the wild boar, the ichneumon, the gazelle, the squirrel, the rat, and the mole. The present existence of the bear within the limits of the ancient Phoenicia has been questioned,268 but the animal has been seen in Lebanon by Mr. Porter,269 and in the mountains of Galilee by Canon Tristram.270 The species is the Syrian bear (Ursus syriacus), a large and fierce beast, which, though generally frugivorous, will under the presser of hunger attack both men and animals. Its main habitat is, no doubt, the less accessible parts of Lebanon; but in the winter it will descend to the villages and gardens, where it often does much damage.271 The panther or leopard has, like the bear, been seen by Mr. Porter in the Lebanon range;272 and Canon Tristram, when visiting Carmel, was offered the skin of an adult leopard273 which had probably been killed in that neighbourhood. Anciently it was much more frequent in Phoenicia and Palestine than it is at present, as appears by the numerous notices of it in Scripture.274 Wolves, hyænas, and jackals are comparatively common. They haunt not only Carmel and Lebanon, but many portions of the coast tract. Canon Tristram obtained from Carmel "the two largest hyænas that he had ever seen,"275 and fell in with jackals in the vicinity.276 Wolves seem to be more scarce, though anciently very plentiful.

The favourite haunts of the wild boar (Sus scrofa) in Phoenicia are Carmel277 and the deep valleys on the western slope of Lebanon. The valley of the Adonis (Ibrahim) is still noted for them,278 but, except on Carmel, they are not very abundant. Foxes and hares are also somewhat rare, and it is doubtful whether rabbits are to be found in any part of the country;279 ichneumons, which are tolerably common, seem sometimes to be mistaken for them. Gazelles are thought to inhabit Carmel,280 and squirrels, rats, and moles are common. Bats also, if they may be counted among land-animals, are frequent; they belong, it is probable, to several species, one of which is Xantharpyia ægyptiaca.281

If the fauna of Phoenicia is restricted so far as land-animals are concerned, it is extensive and varied in respect of birds. The list of known birds includes two sorts of eagle (Circaëtos gallicus and Aquila nævioïdes), the osprey, the vulture, the falcon, the kite, the honey-buzzard, the marsh-harrier, the sparrow-hawk, owls of two kinds (Ketupa ceylonensis and Athene meridionalis), the grey shrike (Lanius excubitor), the common cormorant, the pigmy cormorant (Græculus pygmæus), numerous seagulls, as the Adriatic gull (Larus melanocephalus), Andonieri's gull, the herring-gull, the Red-Sea-gull (Larus ichthyo-aëtos), and others; the gull-billed tern (Sterna anglica), the Egyptian goose, the wild duck, the woodcock, the Greek partridge (Caccabis saxatilis), the waterhen, the corncrake or landrail, the coot, the water-ouzel, the francolin; plovers of three kinds, green, golden, and Kentish; dotterels of two kinds, red-throated and Asiatic; the Manx shearwater, the flamingo, the heron, the common kingfisher, and the black and white kingfisher of Egypt, the jay, the wood-pigeon, the rock-dove, the blue thrush, the Egyptian fantail (Drymoeca gracilis), the redshank, the wheat-ear (Saxicola libanotica), the common lark, the Persian horned lark, the cisticole, the yellow-billed Alpine chough, the nightingale of the East (Ixos xanthopygius), the robin, the brown linnet, the chaffinch; swallows of two kinds (Hirundo cahirica and Hirundo rufula); the meadow bunting; the Lebanon redstart, the common and yellow water-wagtails, the chiffchaff, the coletit, the Russian tit, the siskin, the nuthatch, and the willow wren. Of these the most valuable for the table are the partridge, the francolin, and the woodcock. The Greek partridge is "a fine red-legged bird, much larger than our red-legged partridge, and very much better eating, with white flesh, and nearly as heavy as a pheasant."282 The francolin or black partridge is also a delicacy; and the woodcock, which is identical with our own, has the same delicate flavour.

The fish of Phoenicia, excepting certain shell-fish, are little known, and have seldom attracted the attention of travellers. The Mediterranean, however, where it washes the Phoenician coast, can furnish excellent mullet,283 while most of the rivers contain freshwater fish of several kinds, as the Blennius lupulus, the Scaphiodon capoëta, and the Anguilla microptera.284 All of these fish may be eaten, but the quality is inferior.

On the other hand, to certain of the shell-fish of Phoenicia a great celebrity attaches. The purple dye which gave to the textile fabrics of the Phoenicians a world-wide reputation was prepared from certain shell-fish which abounded upon their coast. Four existing species have been regarded as more or less employed in the manufacture, and it seems to be certain, at any rate, that the Phoenicians derived the dye from more shell-fish than one. The four are the Buccinum lapillus of Pliny,285 which is the Purpura lapillus of modern naturalists; the Murex trunculus; the Murex brandaris; and the Helix ianthina. The Buccinum derives its name from the form of the shell, which has a wide mouth, like that of a trumpet, and which after one or two twists terminates in a pointed head.286 The Murex trunculus has the same general form as the Buccinum; but the shell is more rough and spinous, being armed with a number of long thin projections which terminate in a sharp point.287 The Murex brandaris is a closely allied species, and "one of the most plentiful on the Phoenician coast."288 It is unlikely that the ancients regarded it as a different shell from Murex trunculus. The Helix ianthina has a wholly different character. It is a sort of sea-snail, as the name helix implies, is perfectly smooth, "very delicate and fragile, and not more than about three-quarters of an inch in diameter."289 All these shell-fish contain a sac or bag full of colouring matter, which is capable of being used as a dye. It is quite possible that they were all, more or less, made use of by the Phoenician dyers; but the evidence furnished by existing remains on the Tyrian coast is strongly in favour of the Murex brandaris as the species principally employed.290

The mineral treasures of Phoenicia have not, in modern times, been examined with any care. The Jura limestone, which forms the substratum of the entire region, cannot be expected to yield any important mineral products. But the sandstone, which overlies it in places, is "often largely impregnated with iron," and some strata towards the southern end of Lebanon are said to produce "as much as ninety per cent. of pure iron ore."291 An ochrous earth is also found in the hills above Beyrout, which gives from fifty to sixty per cent. of metal.292 Coal, too, has been found in the same locality, but it is of bad quality, and does not exist in sufficient quantity to form an important product. Limestone, both cretaceous and siliceous, is plentiful, as are sandstone, trap and basalt; while porphyry and greenstone are also obtainable.293 Carmel yields crystals of quarts and chalcedony,294 and the fine sand about Tyre and Sidon is still such as would make excellent glass. But the main productions of Phoenicia, in which its natural wealth consisted, must always have been vegetable, rather than animal or mineral, and have consisted in its timber, especially its cedars and pines; its fruits, as olives, figs, grapes, and, in early times, dates; and its garden vegetables, melons, gourds, pumpkins, cucumbers.

CHAPTER III—THE PEOPLE—ORIGIN AND CHARACTERISTICS

Semitic origin of the Phoenicians—Characteristics of the
Semites—Place of the Phoenicians within the Semitic group—
Connected linguistically with the Israelites and the Assyro-
Babylonians—Original seat of the nation, Lower Babylonia—
Special characteristics of the Phoenician people—Industry
and perseverance—Audacity in enterprise—Pliability and
adaptability—Acuteness of intellect—Business capacity—
Charge made against them of bad faith—Physical
characteristics.

The Phoenician people are generally admitted to have belonged to the group of nations known as Semitic. This group, somewhat irrelevantly named, since the descent of several of them from Shem is purely problematic, comprises the Assyrians, the later Babylonians, the Aramæans or Syrians, the Arabians, the Moabites, the Phoenicians, and the Hebrews. A single and very marked type of language belongs to the entire group, and a character of homogeneity may, with certain distinctions, be observed among all the various members composing it. The unity of language is threefold: it may be traced in the roots, in the inflections, and in the general features of the syntax. The roots are, as a rule, bilateral or trilateral, composed (that is) of two or three letters, all of which are consonants. The consonants determine the general sense of the words, and are alone expressed in the primitive writing; the vowel sounds do but modify more or less the general sense, and are unexpressed until the languages begin to fall into decay. The roots are, almost all of them, more or less physical and sensuous. They are derived in general from an imitation of nature. "If one looked only to the Semitic languages," says M. Renan,31 "one would say, that sensation alone presided over the first acts of the human intellect, and that language was primarily nothing but a mere reflex of the external world. If we run through the list of Semitic roots, we scarcely meet with a single one which does not present to us a sense primarily material, which is then transferred, by transitions more or less direct and immediate, to things which are intellectual." Derivative words are formed from the roots by a few simple and regular laws. The noun is scarcely inflected at all; but the verb has a marvellous wealth of conjugations, calculated to express excellently well the external relations of ideas, but altogether incapable of expressing their metaphysical relations, from the want of definitely marked tenses and moods. Inflections in general have a half-agglutinative character, the meaning and origin of the affixes and suffixes being palpable. Syntax scarcely exists, the construction of sentences having such a general character of simplicity, especially in narrative, that one might compare it with the naïve utterances of an infant. The utmost endeavour of the Semites is to join words together so as to form a sentence; to join sentences is an effort altogether beyond them. They employ the {lexis eiromene} of Aristotle,32 which proceeds by accumulating atom on atom, instead of attempting the rounded period of the Latins and Greeks.

The common traits of character among Semitic nations have been summed up by one writer under five heads:—1. Pliability combined with iron fixity of purpose; 2. Depth and force; 3. A yearning for dreamy ease; 4. Capacity for the hardest work; and 5. Love of abstract thought.33 Another has thought to find them in the following list:—1. An intuitive monotheism; 2. Intolerance; 3. Prophetism; 4. Want of the philisophic and scientific faculties; 5. Want of curiosity; 6. Want of appreciation of mimetic art; 7. Want of capacity for true political life.34 According to the latter writer, "the Semitic race is to be recognized almost entirely by negative characteristics; it has no mythology, no epic poetry, no science, no philosophy, no fiction, no plastic arts, no civil life; everywhere it shows absence of complexity; absence of combination; an exclusive sentiment of unity."35 It is not very easy to reconcile these two views, and not very satisfactory to regard a race as "characterised by negatives." Agreement should consist in positive features, and these may perhaps be found, first, in strength and depth of the religious feeling, combined with firm belief in the personality of the Deity; secondly, in dogged determination and "iron fixity of purpose;" thirdly, in inventiveness and skill in the mechanical arts and other industries; fourthly, in "capacity for hard work;" and, fifthly, in a certain adaptability and pliability, suiting the race for expansion and for commerce. All these qualities are perhaps not conspicuous in all the branches of the Semites, but the majority of them will be found united in all, and in some the combination would seem to be complete.

It is primarily on account of their language that the Phoenicians are regarded as Semites. When there are no historical grounds for believing that a nation has laid aside its own original form of speech, and adopted an alien dialect, language, if not a certain, is at least a very strong, evidence of ethnic character. Counter-evidence may no doubt rebut the prima facie presumption; but in the case of the Phoenicians no counter-evidence is producible. They belong to exactly that geographic zone in which Semitism has always had its chief seat; they cannot be shown to have been ever so circumstanced as to have had any inducement to change their speech; and their physical character and mental characteristics would, by themselves, be almost sufficient ground for assigning them to the type whereto their language points.

The place which the Phoenicians occupy within the Semitic group is a question considerably more difficult to determine. By local position they should belong to the western, or Aramaic branch, rather than to the eastern, or Assyro-Babylonian, or to the southern, or Arab. But the linguistic evidence scarcely lends itself to such a view, while the historic leads decidedly to an opposite conclusion. There is a far closer analogy between the Palestinian group of languages—Phoenician, Hebrew, Moabite, and the Assyro-Babylonian, than between either of these and the Aramaic. The Aramaic is scanty both in variety of grammatical forms and in vocabulary; the Phoenician and Assyro-Babylonian are comparatively copious.36 The Aramaic has the character of a degraded language; the Assyro-Babylonian and the Phoenician are modelled on a primitive type.37 In some respects Phoenician is even closer to Assyro-Babylonian than Hebrew is—e.g. in preferring at to ah for the feminine singular termination.38

The testimony of history to the origin of the Phoenicians is the following. Herodotus tells us that both the Phoenicians themselves, and the Persians best acquainted with history and antiquities, agreed in stating that the original settlements of the Phoenician people were upon the Erythræan Sea (Persian Gulf), and that they had migrated from that quarter at a remote period, and transferred their abode to the shores of the Mediterranean.39 Strabo adds that the inhabitants of certain islands in the Persian Gulf had a similar tradition, and showed temples in their cities which were Phoenician in character.310 Justin, or rather Trogus Pompeius, whom he abbreviated, writes as follows:—"The Syrian nation was founded by the Phoenicians, who, being disturbed by an earthquake, left their native land, and settled first of all in the neighbourhood of the Assyrian Lake, and subsequently on the shore of the Mediterranean, where they built a city which they called Sidon on account of the abundance of the fish; for the Phoenicians call a fish sidon."311 The "Assyrian lake" of this passage is probably the Bahr Nedjif, or "Sea of Nedjif," in the neighbourhood of the ancient Babylon, a permanent sheet of water, varying in its dimensions at different seasons, but generally about forty miles long, and from ten to twenty broad.312 Attempts have been made to discredit this entire story, but the highest living authority on the subject of Phoenicia and the Phoenicians adopts it as almost certainly true, and observes:—"The tradition relative to the sojourn of the Phoenicians on the borders of the Erythræan Sea, before their establishment on the coast of the Mediterranean, has thus a new light thrown upon it. It appears from the labours of M. Movers, and from the recent discoveries made at Nineveh and Babylon, that the civilisation and religion of Phoenicia and Assyria were very similar. Independently of this, the majority of modern critics admit it as demonstrated that the primitive abode of the Phoenicians ought to be placed upon the Lower Euphrates, in the midst of the great commercial and maritime establishments of the Persian Gulf, agreeable to the unanimous witness of all antiquity."313

If we pass from the probable origin of the Phoenician people, and their place in the Semitic group, to their own special characteristics, we shall find ourselves upon surer ground, though even here there are certain points which are debateable. The following is the account of their general character given by a very high authority, and by one who, on the whole, may be regarded as an admirer:—

"The Phoenicians form, in some respects, the most important fraction of the whole group of antique nations, notwithstanding that they sprang from the most obscure and insignificant families. This fraction, when settled, was constantly exposed to inroad by new tribes, was utterly conquered and subjected by utter strangers when it had taken a great place among the nations, and yet by industry, by perseverance, by acuteness of intellect, by unscrupulousness and wait of faith, by adaptability and pliability when necessary, and dogged defiance at other times, by total disregard of the rights of the weaker, they obtained the foremost place in the history of their times, and the highest reputation, not only for the things that they did, but for many that they did not. They were the first systematic traders, the first miners and metallurgists, the greatest inventors (if we apply such a term to those who kept an ever-watchful lookout for the inventions of others, and immediately applied them to themselves with some grand improvements on the original idea); they were the boldest mariners, the greatest colonisers, who at one time held not only the gorgeous East, but the whole of the then half-civilised West in fee—who could boast of a form of government approaching to constitutionalism, who of all nations of the time stood highest in practical arts and sciences, and into whose laps there flowed an unceasing stream of the world's entire riches, until the day came when they began to care for nothing else, and the enjoyment of material comforts and luxuries took the place of the thirst for and search after knowledge. Their piratical prowess and daring was undermined; their colonies, grown old enough to stand alone, fell away from them, some after a hard fight, others in mutual agreement or silently; and the nations in whose estimation and fear they had held the first place, and who had been tributary to them, disdained them, ignored them, and finally struck them utterly out of the list of nations, till they dwindled away miserably, a warning to all who should come after them."314

The prominent qualities in this description would seem to be industry and perseverance, audacity in enterprise, adaptability and pliability, acuteness of intellect, unscrupulousness, and want of good faith. The Phoenicians were certainly among the most industrious and persevering of mankind. The accounts which we have of them from various quarters, and the remains which cover the country that they once inhabited, sufficiently attest their unceasing and untiring activity through almost the whole period of their existence as a nation. Always labouring in their workshops at home in mechanical and æsthetic arts, they were at the same time constantly seeking employment abroad, ransacking the earth for useful or beautiful commodities, building cities, constructing harbours, founding colonies, introducing the arts of life among wild nations, mining and establishing fisheries, organising lines of land traffic, perpetually moving from place to place, and leaving wherever they went abundant proofs of their diligence and capacity for hard work. From Thasos in the East, where Herodotus saw "a large mountain turned topsy-turvy by the Phoenicians in their search for gold,"315 to the Scilly Islands in the West, where workings attributable to them are still to be seen, all the metalliferous islands and coast tracts bear traces of Phoenician industry in tunnels, adits, and air-shafts, while manufactured vessels of various kinds in silver, bronze, and terra-cotta, together with figures and gems of a Phoenician type, attest still more widely their manufacturing and commercial activity.

Audacity in enterprise can certainly not be denied to the adventurous race which, from the islands and coasts of the Eastern Mediterranean, launched forth upon the unknown sea in fragile ships, affronted the perils of waves and storms, and still more dreaded "monsters of the deep,"316 explored the recesses of the stormy Adriatic and inhospitable Pontus, steered their perilous course amid all the islets and rocks of the Ægean, along the iron-bound shores of Thrace, Euboea, and Laconia, first into the Western Mediterranean basin, and then through the Straits of Gibraltar into the wild and boundless Atlantic, with its mighty tides, its huge rollers, its blinding rains, and its frequent fogs. Without a chart, without a compass, guided only in their daring voyages by their knowledge of the stars, these bold mariners penetrated to the shores of Scythia in one direction; to Britain, if not even to the Baltic, in another; in a third to the Fortunate Islands; while, in a fourth, they traversed the entire length of the Red Sea, and entering upon the Southern Ocean, succeeded in doubling the Cape of Storms two thousand years before Vasco di Gama, and in effecting the circumnavigation of Africa.317 And, wild as the seas were with which they had to deal, they had to deal with yet wilder men. Except in Egypt, Asia Minor, Greece, and perhaps Italy, they came in contact everywhere with savage races; they had to enter into close relations with men treacherous, bloodthirsty, covetous— men who were almost always thieves, who were frequently cannibals, sometimes wreckers— who regarded foreigners as a cheap and very delicious kind of food. The pioneers of civilisation, always and everywhere, incur dangers from which ordinary mortals would shrink with dismay; but the earliest pioneers, the first introducers of the elements of culture among barbarians who had never heard of it, must have encountered far greater peril than others from their ignorance of the ways of savage man, and a want of those tremendous weapons of attack and defence with which modern explorers take care to provide themselves. Until the invention of gunpowder, the arms of civilised men—swords, and spears, and javelins, and the like— were scarcely a match for the cunningly devised weapons—boomerangs, and blow-pipes, and poisoned arrows, and lassoes318—of the savage.

The adaptability and pliability of the Phoenicians was especially shown in their power of obtaining the favourable regard of almost all the peoples and nations with which they came into contact, whether civilised or uncivilised. It is most remarkable that the Egyptians, intolerant as they usually were of strangers, should have allowed the Phoenicians to settle in their southern capital, Memphis, and to build a temple and inhabit a quarter there.319 It is also curious and interesting that the Phoenicians should have been able to ingratiate themselves with another most exclusive and self-sufficing people, viz. the Jews. Hiram's friendly dealings with David and Solomon are well known; but the continued alliance between the Phoenicians and the Israelites has attracted less attention. Solomon took wives from Phoenicia;320 Ahab married the daughter of Ithobalus, king of Sidon;321 Phoenicia furnished timber for the second Temple;322 Isaiah wound up his prophecy against Tyre with a consolation;323 our Lord found faith in the Syro-Phoenician woman;324 in the days of Herod Agrippa, Tyre and Sidon still desired peace with Judæa, "because their country was nourished by the king's country."325 And similarly Tyre had friendly relations with Syria and Greece, with Mesopotamia and Assyria, with Babylonia and Chaldæa. At the same time she could bend herself to meet the wants and gain the confidence of all the varieties of barbarians, the rude Armenians, the wild Arabs, the barbarous tribes of northern and western Africa, the rough Iberi, the passionate Gauls, the painted Britons, the coarse Sards, the fierce Thracians, the filthy Scyths, the savage races of the Caucasus. Tribes so timid and distrustful as those of Tropical Africa were lured into peaceful and friendly relations by the artifice of a "dumb commerce,"326 and on every side untamed man was softened and drawn towards civilisation by a spirit of accommodation, conciliation, and concession to prejudices.

If the Phoenicians are to be credited with acuteness of intellect, it must be limited to the field of practical enquiry and discovery. Whatever may be said with regard to the extent and variety of their literature—a subject which will be treated in another chapter—it cannot be pretended that humanity owes to them any important conquests of a scientific or philosophic character. Herodotus, who admires the learning of the Persians,327 the science of the Babylonians,328 and the combined learning and science of the Egyptians,329 limits his commendation of the Phoenicians to their skill in navigation, in mechanics, and in works of art.330 Had they made advances in the abstract, or even in the mixed, sciences, in mathematics, or astronomy, or geometry, in logic or metaphysics, either their writings would have been preserved, or at least the Greeks would have made acknowledgments of being indebted to them.331 But it is only in the field of practical matters that any such acknowledgments are made. The Greeks allow themselves to have been indebted to the Phoenicians for alphabetic writing, for advances in metallurgy, for improvements in shipbuilding, and navigation, for much geographic knowledge, for exquisite dyes, and for the manufacture of glass. There can be no doubt that the Phoenicians were a people of great practical ability, with an intellect quick to devise means to ends, to scheme, contrive, and execute, and with a happy knack of perceiving what was practically valuable in the inventions of other nations, and of appropriating them to their own use, often with improvements upon the original idea. But they were not possessed of any great genius or originality. They were, on the whole, adapters rather than inventors. They owed their idea of alphabetic writing to the Accadians,332 their weights and measures to Babylon,333 their shipbuilding probably to Egypt,334 their early architecture to the same country,335 their mimetic art to Assyria, to Egypt, and to Greece. They were not poets, or painters, or sculptors, or great architects, much less philosophers or scientists; but in the practical arts, and even in the practical sciences, they held a high place, in almost all of them equalling, and in some exceeding, all their neighbours.

We should be inclined also to assign to the Phoenicians, as a special characteristic, a peculiar capacity for business. This may be said, indeed, to be nothing more than acuteness of intellect applied in a particular way. To ourselves, however, it appears to be, in some sort, a special gift. As, beyond all question, there are many persons of extremely acute intellect who have not the slightest turn for business, or ability for dealing with it, so we think there are nations, to whom no one would deny high intellectual power, without the capacity in question. In its most perfect form it has belonged but to a small number of nations—to the Phoenicians, the Venetians, the Genoese, the English, and the Dutch. It implies, not so much high intellectual power, as a combination of valuable, yet not very admirable, qualities of a lower order. Industry, perseverance, shrewdness, quickness of perception, power of forecasting the future, power of organisation, boldness, promptness, are among the qualities needed, and there may be others discoverable by the skilful analyst. All these met in the Phoenicians, and met in the proportions that were needed for the combination to take full effect.

Whether unscrupulousness and want of good faith are rightly assigned to the Phoenicians as characteristic traits, is, at the least, open to doubt. The Latin writers, with whom the reproach contained in the expression "Punica fides" originated, are scarcely to be accepted as unprejudiced witnesses, since it is in most instances a necessity that they should either impute "bad faith" to the opposite side, or admit that there was "bad faith" on their own. The aspersions of an enemy are entitled to little weight. The cry of "perfide Albion" is often heard in the land of one of our near neighbours; but few Englishmen will admit the justice of it. It may be urged in favour of the Phoenicians that long-continued commercial success is impossible without fair-dealing and honesty; that where there is commercial fair-dealing and honesty, those qualities become part and parcel of the national character, and determine national policy; and, further, that in almost every one of the instances of bad faith alleged, there is at the least a doubt, of which the accused party ought to have the benefit. At any rate, let it be remembered that the charges made affect the Liby-Phoenicians alone, and not the Phoenicians of Asia, with whom we are here primarily concerned, and that we cannot safely, or equitably, transfer to a mother-country faults which are only even alleged against one of her colonies.

Physically, the Phoenicians appear to have resembled the Assyrians and the Jews. They had large frames strongly made, well-developed muscles, curled beards, and abundant hair. In their features they may have borne a resemblance, but probably not a very strong resemblance, to the Cypriots,336 who were a mixed people recruited from various quarters.337 In complexion they belonged to the white race, but were rather sallow than fair. Their hair was generally dark, though it may have been sometimes red. Some have regarded the name "Phoenician" as indicating that they were of a red or red-brown colour;338 but it is better to regard the appellation as having passed from the country to its people, and as applied to the country by the Greeks on account of the palm-trees which grew along its shores.

CHAPTER IV—THE CITIES

Importance of the cities in Phoenicia—Their names and
relative eminence—Cities of the first rank—Sidon—Tyre—
Arvad or Aradus—Marathus—Gebal or Byblus—Tripolis—Cities
of the second rank—Aphaca—Berytus—Arka—Ecdippa—Accho—
Dor—Japho or Joppa—Ramantha or Laodicea—Fivefold division
of Phoenicia.

Phoenicia, like Greece, was a country where the cities held a position of extreme importance. The nation was not a centralised one, with a single recognised capital, like Judæa, or Samaria, or Syria, or Assyria, or Babylonia. It was, like Greece, a congeries of homogeneous tribes, who had never been amalgamated into a single political entity, and who clung fondly to the idea of separate independence. Tyre and Sidon are often spoken of as if they were metropolitical cities; but it may be doubted whether there was ever a time when either of them could claim even a temporary authority over the whole country. Each, no doubt, from time to time, exercised a sort of hegemony over a certain number of the inferior cities; but there was no organised confederacy, no obligation of any one city to submit to another, and no period, as far as our knowledge extends, at which all the cities acknowledged a single one as their mistress.41 Between Tyre and Sidon there was especial jealousy, and the acceptance by either of the leadership of the other, even temporarily, was a rare fact in the history of the nation. According to the geographers, the cities of Phoenicia, from Laodicea in the extreme north to Joppa at the extreme south, numbered about twenty-five. These were Laodicea, Gabala,

Balanea, Paltos; Aradus, with its dependency Antaradus; Marathus; Simyra, Orthosia, and Arka; Tripolis, Calamus, Trieris, and Botrys; Byblus or Gebal; Aphaca; Berytus; Sidon, Sarepta, and Ornithonpolis; Tyre and Ecdippa; Accho and Porphyreon; Dor and Joppa. Of the twenty-five a certain number were, historically and politically, insignificant; for instance, Gabala, Balanea, Paltos, Orthosia, Calamus, Trieris, Botrys, Sarepta, Ornithonpolis, Porphyreon. Sarepta is immortalised by the memory of its pious widow,42 and Orthosia has a place in history from its connection with the adventures of Trypho;43 but the rest of the list are little more than "geographical expressions." There remain fifteen important cities, of which six may be placed in the first rank and nine in the second—the six being Tyre, Sidon, Aradus, Byblus or Gebal, Marathus, and Tripolis; the nine, Laodicea, Simyra, Arka, Aphaca, Berytus, Ecdippa, Accho, Dor, and Joppa. It will be sufficient in the present place to give some account of these fifteen.

There are some grounds for considering Sidon to have been the most ancient of the Phoenician towns. In the Book of Genesis Sidon is called "the eldest born of Canaan,"44 and in Joshua, where Tyre is simply a "fenced city" or fort,45 it is "Great Zidon."46 Homer frequently mentions it,47 whereas he takes no notice of Tyre. Justin makes it the first town which the Phoenicians built on arriving at the shores of the Mediterranean.48 The priority of Sidon in this respect was, however, not universally acknowledged, since Tyre claims on some of her coins to have been "the mother-city of the Sidonians,"49 and Marathus was also regarded as a city of the very highest antiquity.410 The city stood in Lat. 33° 34´ nearly, on the flat plain between the mountains and the shore, opposite a small promontory which projects into the sea towards the west, and is flanked towards the north-west and north by a number of rocky islands. The modern town of Saïda stands close upon the shore, occupying the greater part of the peninsula and a portion of the plain on which it abuts; but the ancient city is found to have been situated entirely in the plain, and its most western traces are almost half a mile from the nearest point of the present walls.411 The modern Saïda has clustered itself about what was the principal port of the ancient town, which lay north of the promontory, and was well protected from winds, on the west by the principal island, which has a length of 250 yards, and on the north by a long range of islets and reefs, extending in a north-easterly direction a distance of at least 600 yards. An excellent roadstead was thus formed by nature, which art early improved into a small but commodious harbour, a line of wall being carried out from the coast northwards to the most easterly of the islets, and the only unprotected side of the harbour being thus securely closed. There is reason to believe that this work was completed anterior to the time of Alexander,412 and was therefore due to the Phoenicians themselves, who were not blind to the advantages of closed harbours over open roadsteads. They seem also to have strengthened the natural barrier towards the north by a continuous wall of huge blocks along the reefs and the islets, portions of which are still in existence.

Besides this excellent harbour, 500 yards long by 200 broad, Sidon possessed on the southern side of the peninsula a second refuge for its ships, less safe, but still more spacious. This was an oval basin, 600 yards long from north to south, and nearly 400 broad from east to west, wholly surrounded by land on three sides, the north, the east, and the south, but open for the space of about 200 yards towards the west. In fine weather this harbour was probably quite as much used as the other; it was protected from all the winds that were commonly prevalent, and offered a long stretch of sandy shore free from buildings on which vessels could be drawn up. It is impossible to mark out the enceinte of the ancient town, or indeed to emplace it with any exactitude. Only scanty and scattered remains are left here and there between the modern city and the mountains. There is, however, towards the south an extensive necropolis,413 which marks perhaps the southern limits of the city, while towards the east the hills are penetrated by a number of sepulchural grottoes, and tombs of various kinds, which were also probably outside the walls. Were a northern necropolis to be discovered, some idea would be furnished of the extent of the city; but at present the plain has been very imperfectly examined in this direction. It is from the southern necropolis that the remarkable inscription was disinterred which first established beyond all possibility of doubt the fact that the modern Saïda is the representative of the ancient Sidon.414

Twenty miles to the south of Sidon was the still more important city—the double city—of Tzur or Tyre. Tzur signifies "a rock," and at this point of the Syrian coast (Lat. 33° 17´) there lay at a short distance from the shore a set of rocky islets, on the largest of which the original city seems to have been built. Indentations are so rare and so shallow along this coast, that a maritime people naturally looked out for littoral islands, as affording under the circumstances the best protection against boisterous winds; and, as in the north Aradus was early seized and occupied by Phoenician settlers, so in the south the rock, which became the heart of Tyre, was seized, fortified, covered with buildings, and converted from a bare stony eminence into a town. At the same time, or not much later, a second town grew up on the mainland opposite the isle; and the two together were long regarded as constituting a single city. After the time of Alexander the continental town went to decay; and the name of Palæ-Tyrus was given to it,415 to distinguish it from the still flourishing city on the island.

The islands of which we have spoken formed a chain running nearly in parallel to the coast. They were some eleven or twelve in number. The southern extremity of the chain was formed by three, the northern by seven, small islets.416 Intermediate between these lay two islands of superior size, which were ultimately converted into one by filling up the channel between them. A further enlargement was effected by means of substructions thrown out into the sea, probably on two sides, towards the east and towards the south. By these means an area was produced sufficient for the site of a considerable town. Pliny estimated the circumference of the island Tyre at twenty-two stades,417 or somewhat more than two miles and a half. Modern measurements make the actual present area one of above 600,000 square yards.418 The shape was an irregular trapezium, 1,400 yards along its western face, 800 yards along its southern one, 600 along the face towards the east, and rather more along the face towards the north-east.

The whole town was surrounded by a lofty wall, the height of which, on the side which faced the mainland, was, we are told, a hundred and fifty feet.419 Towards the south the foundations of the wall were laid in the sea, and may still be traced.420 They consist of huge blocks of stone strengthened inside by a conglomerate of very hard cement. The wall runs out from the south-eastern corner of what was the original island, in a direction a little to the south of west, till it reaches the line of the western coast, when it turns at a sharp angle, and rejoins the island at its south-western extremity. At present sea is found for some distance to the north of the wall, and this fact has been thought to show that originally it was intended for a pier or quay, and the space within it for a harbour;421 but the latest explorers are of opinion that the space was once filled up with masonry and rubbish, being an artificial addition to the island, over which, in the course of time, the sea has broken, and reasserted its rights.422

Like Sidon, Tyre had two harbours, a northern and a southern. The northern, which was called the "Sidonian," because it looked towards Sidon, was situated on the east of the main island, towards the northern end of it. On the west and south the land swept round it in a natural curve, effectually guarding two sides; while the remaining two were protected by art. On the north a double line of wall was carried out in a direction a little south of east for a distance of about three hundred yards, the space between the two lines being about a hundred feet. The northern line acted as a sort of breakwater, the southern as a pier. This last terminated towards the east on reaching a ridge of natural rock, and was there met by the eastern wall of the harbour, which ran out in a direction nearly due north for a distance of 250 yards, following the course of two reefs, which served as its foundation. Between the reefs was a space of about 140 feet, which was left open, but could be closed, if necessary, by a boom or chain, which was kept in readiness. The dimensions of this northern harbour are thought to have been about 370 yards from north to south, by about 230 from east to west,423 or a little short of those which have been assigned to the northern harbour of Sidon. Concerning the southern harbour there is considerable difference of opinion. Some, as Kenrick and M. Bertou, place it due south of the island, and regard its boundary as the line of submarine wall which we have already described and regarded as constituting the southern wall of the town. Others locate it towards the south-east, and think that it is now entirely filled up. A canal connected the two ports, so that vessels could pass from the one to the other.

The most remarkable of the Tyrian buildings were the royal palace, which abutted on the southern wall of the town, and the temples dedicated to Baal, Melkarth, Agenor, and Astarte or Ashtoreth.424 The probable character of the architecture of these buildings will be hereafter considered. With respect to their emplacement, it would seem by the most recent explorations that the temple of Baal, called by the Greeks that of the Olympian Zeus, stood by itself on what was originally a separate islet at the south-western corner of the city,425 while that of Melkarth occupied a position as nearly as possible central,426 and that of Agenor was placed near the point in which the island terminates toward the north.427 The houses of the inhabitants were closely crowded together, and rose to the height of several storeys.428 There was an open space for the transaction of business within the walls towards the east, called Eurychorus by those Phoenicians who wrote their histories in Greek.429 The town was full of dyeing establishments, which made it difficult to traverse.430 The docks and dockyards were towards the east.

The population of the island Tyre, when it was captured by Alexander, seems to have been about forty thousand souls.431 As St. Malo, a city less than one-third of the size, is known to have had at one time a population of twelve thousand,432 the number, though large for the area, would seem not to be incredible.

Of Palæ-Tyrus, or the continental Tyre, no satisfactory account can be given, since it has absolutely left no remains, and the classical notices on the subject are exceedingly scanty. At different periods of its history, its limits and extent probably varied greatly. Its position was nearly opposite the island, and in the early times it must have been, like the other coast towns, strongly fortified; but after its capture by Alexander the walls do not seem to have been restored, and it became an open straggling town, extending along the shore from the river Leontes (Litany) to Ras-el-Ain, a distance of seven miles or more. Pliny, who wrote when its boundary could still be traced, computed the circuit of Palæ-Tyrus and the island Tyre together at nineteen Roman miles,433 the circuit of the island by itself being less than three miles. Its situation, in a plain of great fertility, at the foot of the south-western spurs of Lebanon, and near the gorge of the Litany, was one of great beauty. Water was supplied to it in great abundance from the copious springs of Ras-el-Ain, which were received into a reservoir of an octagonal shape, sixty feet in diameter, and inclosed within walls eighteen feet in height,434 whence they were conveyed northwards to the heart of the city by an aqueduct, whereof a part is still remaining.

The most important city of Phoenicia towards the north was Arvad, or Aradus. Arvad was situated, like Tyre, on a small island off the Syrian coast, and lay in Lat. 34° 48′ nearly. It was distant from the shore about two miles and a half. The island was even smaller than that which formed the nucleus of Tyre, being only about 800 yards, or less than half a mile in length, by 500 yards, or rather more than a quarter of a mile in breadth.435 The axis of the island was from north-west to south-east. It was a bare rock, low and flat, without water, and without any natural soil. The iron coast was surrounded on three sides, the north, the west, and the south, by a number of rocks and small islets, which fringed it like the trimming of a shawl. Its Phoenician occupiers early converted this debatable territory, half sea half shore, into solid land, by filling up the interstices between the rocks with squared stones and a solid cement as hard as the rock itself, which remains to this day.436 The north-eastern portion, which has a length of 150 yards by a breadth of 125, is perfectly smooth and almost flat, but with a slight slope towards the east, which is thought to show that it was used as a sort of dry dock, on which to draw up the lighter vessels, for safety or for repairs.437 The western and southern increased the area for house-building. Anciently, as at Tyre, the houses were built very close together, and had several storeys,438 for the purpose of accommodating a numerous population. The island was wholly without natural harbour; but on the eastern side, which faced the mainland, and was turned away from the prevailing winds, the art and industry of the inhabitants constructed two ports of a fair size. This was effected by carrying out from the shore three piers at right angles into the sea, the central one to a distance of from seventy to a hundred yards, and the other two very nearly as far—and thus forming two rectangular basins, one on either side of the central pier, which were guarded from winds on three sides, and only open towards the east, a quarter from which the winds are seldom violent, and on which the mainland, less than three miles off, forms a protection. The construction of the central pier is remarkable. It is formed of massive blocks of sandstone, which are placed transversely, so that their length forms the thickness of the pier, and their ends the wall on either side. On both sides of the wall are quays of concrete.439

The line of the ancient enceinte may still be traced around the three outer sides of the island. It is a gigantic work, composed of stones from fifteen to eighteen feet long, placed transversely, like those of the centre pier, and in two places still rising to the height of five or six courses (from thirty to forty feet).440 The blocks are laid side by side without mortar; they are roughly squared, and arranged generally in regular courses; but sometimes two courses for a while take the place of one.441 There is a want of care in the arrangement of the blocks, joints in one course being occasionally directly over joints in the course below it. The stones are without any bevel or ornamentation of any kind. They have been quarried in the island itself, and the beds of rock from which they were taken may be seen at no great distance. At one point in the western side of the island, the native rock itself has been cut into the shape of the wall, and made to take the place of the squared stones for the distance of about ten feet.442 A moat has also been cut along the entire western side, which, with its glacis, served apparently to protect the wall from the fury of the waves.443

We know nothing of the internal arrangements of the ancient town beyond the fact of the closeness and loftiness of the houses. Externally Aradus depended on her possessions upon the mainland both for water and for food. The barren rock could grow nothing, and was moreover covered with houses. Such rainwater as fell on the island was carefully collected and stored in tanks and reservoirs,444 the remains of which are still to be seen. But the ordinary supply of water for daily consumption was derived in time of peace from the opposite coast. When this supply was cut off by an enemy Aradus had still one further resource. Midway in the channel between the island and the continent there burst out at the bottom of the sea a fresh-water spring of great strength; by confining this spring within a hemisphere of lead to which a leathern pipe was attached the much-needed fluid was raised to the surface and received into a vessel moored upon the spot, whence supplies were carried to the island.445 The phenomenon still continues, though the modern inhabitants are too ignorant and unskilful to profit by it.446 On the mainland Aradus possessed a considerable tract, and had a number of cities subject to her. Of these Strabo enumerates six, viz. Paltos, Balanea, Carnus—which he calls the naval station of Aradus—Enydra, Marathus, and Simyra.447 Marathus was the most important of these. Its name recalls the "Brathu" of Philo-Byblius448 and the "Martu" of the early Babylonian inscriptions,449 which was used as a general term by some of the primitive monarchs almost in the sense of "Syria." The word is still preserved in the modern "M'rith" or "Amrith," a name attached to some extensive ruins in the plain south-east of Aradus, which have been carefully examined by M. Renan.450 Marathus was an ancient Phoenician town, probably one of the most ancient, and was always looked upon with some jealousy by the Aradians, who ultimately destroyed it and partitioned out the territory among their own citizens.451 The same fate befell Simyra,452 a place of equal antiquity, the home probably of those Zemarites who are coupled with the Arvadites in Genesis.453 Simyra appears as "Zimirra" in the Assyrian inscriptions, where it is connected with Arka,454 which was not far distant. Its exact site, which was certainly south of Amrith, seems to be fixed by the name Sumrah, which attaches to some ruins in the plain about a mile and a half north of the Eleutherus (Nahr-el-Kebir) and within a mile of the sea.455 The other towns—Paltos,

Balanea, Carnus,456 and Enydra—were in the more northern portion of the plain, as was also Antaradus, now Tortosa, where there are considerable remains, but of a date long subsequent to the time of Phoenician ascendancy.

Of the remaining Phoenician cities the most important seems to have been Gebal, or Byblus. Mentioned under the name of Gubal in the Assyrian inscriptions as early as the time of Jehu457 (ab. B.C. 840), and glanced at even earlier in the Hebrew records, which tell of its inhabitants, the Giblites,458 Gebal is found as a town of note in the time of Alexander the Great,459 and again in that of Pompey.460 The traditions of the Phoenicians themselves made it one of the most ancient of the cities; and the historian Philo, who was a native of the place, ascribes its foundation to Kronos or Saturn.461 It was an especially holy city, devoted in the early times to the worship of Beltis,462 and in the later to that of Adonis.463 The position is marked beyond all reasonable doubt by the modern Jebeïl, which retains the original name very slightly modified, and answers completely to the ancient descriptions. The town lies upon the coast, in Lat. 34° 10′ nearly, about halfway between Tripolis and Berytus, four miles north of the point where the Adonis river (now the Ibrahim) empties itself into the sea. There is a "small but well-sheltered port,"464 formed mainly by two curved piers which are carried out from the shore towards the north and south, and which leave between them only a narrow entrance. The castle occupies a commanding position on a hill at a little distance from the shore, and has a keep built of bevelled stones of a large size. Several of them measure from fifteen to eighteen feet in length, and are from five to six feet thick.465 They were probably quarried by Giblite "stone-cutters," but placed in their present position during the middle ages.

Tripolis, situated halfway between Byblus and Aradus, was not one of the original Phoenician cities, but was a joint colony from the three principal settlements, Tyre, Sidon, and Aradus.466 The date of its foundation, and its native Phoenician name, are unknown to us: conjecture hovers between Hosah, Mahalliba, Uznu, and Siannu, maritime towns of Phoenicia known to the Assyrians,467 but unmentioned by any Greek author. The situation was a promontory, which runs out towards the north-west, in Lat. 34° 27′ nearly, for the distance of a mile, and is about half a mile wide. The site is "well adapted for a haven, as a chain of seven small islands, running out to the north-west, affords shelter in the direction from which the most violent winds blow."468 The remotest of these islands is ten miles distant from the shore.469 We are told that the colonists who founded Tripolis did not intermix, but had their separate quarters of the town assigned to them, each surrounded by its own wall, and lying at some little distance one from the other.470 There are no present traces of this arrangement, which seems indicative of distrust; but some remains have been found of a wall which was carried across the isthmus on the land side.471 Tripolis is now Tarabolus.

Aphaca, the only inland Phoenician town of any importance, is now Afka, and is visited by most travellers and tourists. It was situated in a beautiful spot at the head of the Adonis river,472 a sacred stream fabled to run with blood once a year, at the festival which commemorated the self-mutilation of the Nature-god Adonis. Aphaca was a sort of Delphi, a collection of temples rather than a town. It was dedicated especially to the worship of the Syrian goddess, Ashtoreth or Venus, sometimes called Beltis or Baaltis, whose orgies were of so disgracefully licentious a character that they were at last absolutely forbidden by Constantine. At present there are no remains on the ancient site except one or two ruins of edifices decidedly Roman in character.473 Nor is the gorge of the Adonis any richer in ancient buildings. There was a time when the whole valley formed a sort of "Holy Land,"474 and at intervals on its course were shown "Tombs of Adonis,"475 analogous to the artificial "Holy Sepulchres" of many European towns in the middle ages. All, however, have disappeared, and the traveller looks in vain for any traces of that curious cult which in ancient times made Aphaca and its river one of the most noted of the holy spots of Syria and a favourite resort of pilgrims.

Twenty-three miles south of Byblus was Berytus, which disputed with Byblus the palm of antiquity.476 Berytus was situated on a promontory in Lat. 33° 54′, and had a port of a fair size, protected towards the west by a pier, which followed the line of a ridge of rocks running out from the promontory towards the north. It was not of any importance during the flourishing Phoenician period, but grew to greatness under the Romans,477 when its harbour was much improved, and the town greatly extended.478 By the time of Justinian it had become the chief city of Phoenicia, and was celebrated as a school of law and science.479 The natural advantages of its situation have caused it to retain a certain importance, and in modern times it has drawn to itself almost the whole of the commerce which Europe maintains with Syria.

Arka, or Arqa, the home of the Arkites of Genesis,480 can never have been a place of much consequence. It lies at a distance of four miles from the shore, on one of the outlying hills which form the skirts of Lebanon, in Lat. 34° 33, Long. 33° 44′ nearly. The towns nearest to it were Orthosia, Simyra, and Tripolis. It was of sufficient consequence to be mentioned in the Assyrian Inscriptions,481 though not to attract the notice of Strabo.

Ecdippa, south of Tyre, in Lat. 33° 1′, is no doubt the scriptural Achzib,482 which was made the northern boundary of Asher at the division of the Holy Land among the twelve tribes. The Assyrian monarchs speak of it under the same name, but mention it rarely, and apparently as a dependency of Sidon.483 The old name, in the shortened form of "Zeb," still clings to the place.

Still further to the south, five miles from Ecdippa, and about twenty-two miles from Tyre, lay Akko or Accho, at the northern extremity of a wide bay, which terminates towards the south in the promontory of Carmel. Next to the Bay of St. George, near Beyrout, this is the best natural roadstead on the Syrian coast; and this advantage, combined with its vicinity to the plain of Esdraelon, has given to Accho at various periods of history a high importance, as in some sense "the key of Syria." The Assyrians, in their wars with Palestine and Egypt, took care to conquer and retain it.484 When the Ptolemies became masters of the tract between Egypt and Mount Taurus, they at once saw its value, occupied it, strengthened its defences, and gave it the name of Ptolemaïs. The old appellation has, however, reasserted itself; and, as Acre, the city played an important part in the Crusades, in the Napoleonic attempt on Egypt, and in the comparatively recent expedition of Ibrahim Pasha. It had a small port of its own to the south-east of the promontory on which it stood, which, like the other ports of the ancient Phoenicia, is at the present time almost wholly sanded up.485 But its roadstead was of more importance than its port, and was used by the Persians as a station for their fleet, from which they could keep watch on Egypt.486

South of Accho and south of Carmel, close upon the shore, which is here low and flat, was Dor, now Tantura, the seat of a kingdom in the time of Joshua,487 and allotted after its conquest to Manasseh.488 Here Solomon placed one of his purveyors,489 and here the great Assyrian monarch Tiglath-pileser II. likewise placed a "governor," about B.C. 732, when he reduced it.490 Dor was one of the places where the shell-fish which produced the purple dye were most abundant, and remained in the hands of the Phoenicians during all the political changes which swept over Syria and Palestine to a late period.491 It had fallen to ruin, however, by the time of Jerome,492 and the present remains are unimportant.

The extreme Phoenician city on the south was Japho or Joppa. It lay in Lat. 32° 2′, close to the territory of Dan,493 but continued to be held by the Phoenicians until the time of the Maccabees,494 when it became Jewish. The town was situated on the slope of a low hill near the sea, and possessed anciently a tolerable harbour, from which a trade was carried on with Tartessus.495 As the seaport nearest to Jerusalem, it was naturally the chief medium of the commerce which was carried on between the Phoenicians and the Jews. Thither, in the time of Solomon, were brought the floats of timber cut in Lebanon for the construction of the Temple and the royal palace; and thither, no doubt, were conveyed "the wheat, and the barley, and the oil, and the wine," which the Phoenicians received in return for their firs and cedars.496 A similar exchange of commodities was made nearly five centuries later at the same place, when the Jews returned from the captivity under Zerubbabel.497 In Roman times the foundation of

Cæsaræa reduced Joppa to insignificance; yet it still, as Jaffa or Yáfa, retains a certain amount of trade, and is famous for its palm-groves and gardens.

Joppa towards the south was balanced by Ramantha, or Laodicea, towards the north. Fifty miles north of Aradus and Antaradus (Tortosa), in Lat. 35° 30′ nearly, occupying the slope of a hill facing the sea, with chalky cliffs on either side, that, like those of Dover, whiten the sea, and with Mount Casius in the background, lay the most northern of all the Phoenician cities in a fertile and beautiful territory.498 The original appellation was, we are told, Ramantha,499 a name intended probably to mark the lofty situation of the place;4100 but this appellation was forced to give way to the Greek term, Laodicea, when Seleucus Nicator, having become king of Syria, partially rebuilt Ramantha and colonised it with Greeks.4101 The coins of the city under the Seleucidæ show its semi-Greek, semi-Phoenician character, having legends in both languages. One of these, in the Phoenician character, is read as l'Ladika am b'Canaan, i.e. "of Laodicea, a metropolis in Canaan," and seems to show that the city claimed not only to be independent, but to have founded, and to hold under its sway, a number of smaller towns.4102 It may have exercised a dominion over the entire tract from Mount Casius to Paltos, where the dominion of Aradus began. Laodicea is now Latakia, and is famous for the tobacco grown in the neighbourhood. It still makes use of its ancient port, which would be fairly commodious if it were cleared of the sand that at present chokes it.4103

It has been said that Phoenicia was composed of "three worlds" with distinct characteristics;4104 but perhaps the number of the "worlds" should be extended to five. First came that of Ramantha, reaching from the Mons Casius to the river Badas, a distance of about fifty miles, a remote and utterly sequestered region, into which neither Assyria nor Egypt ever thought of penetrating. Commerce with Cyprus and southern Asia Minor was especially open to the mariners of this region, who could see the shores of Cyprus without difficulty on a clear day. Next came the "world" of Aradus, reaching along the coast from the Badas to the Eleutherus, another stretch of fifty miles, and including the littoral islands, especially that of Ruad, on which Aradus was built. This tract was less sequestered than the more northern one, and contains traces of having been subjected to influences from Egypt at an early period. The gap between Lebanon and Bargylus made the Aradian territory accessible from the Coelesyrian valley; and there is reason to believe that one of the roads which Egyptian and Assyrian conquest followed in these parts was that which passed along the coast as far as the Eleutherus and then turned eastward and north-eastward to Emesa (Hems) and Hamath. It must have been conquerors marching by this line who set up their effigies at the mouth of the Nahr-el-Kelb, and those who pursued it would naturally make a point of reducing Aradus. Thus this second Phoenician "world" has not the isolated character of the first, but shows marks of Assyrian, and still more of early Egyptian, influence. The third Phoenician "world" is that of Gebal or Byblus. Its limits would seem to be the Eleutherus on the north, and on the south the Tamyras, which would allow it a length of a little above eighty miles. This district, it has been said, preserved to the last days of paganism a character which was original and well marked. Within its limits the religious sentiment had more intensity and played a more important part in life than elsewhere in Phoenicia. Byblus was a sort of Phoenician Jerusalem. By their turn of mind and by the language which they spoke, the Byblians or Giblites seem to have been, of all the Phoenicians, those who most resembled the Hebrews. King Jehavmelek, who probably reigned at Byblus about B.C. 400, calls himself "a just king," and prays that he may obtain favour in the sight of God. Later on it was at Byblus, and in the valleys of the Lebanon depending on it, that the inhabitants celebrated those mysteries of Astarte, together with that orgiastic worship of Adonis or Tammuz, which were so popular in Syria during the whole of the Greco-Roman period.4105 The fourth Phoenician "world" was that of Tyre and Sidon, beginning at the Tamyras and ending with the promontory of Carmel. Here it was that the Phoenician character developed especially those traits by which it is commonly known to the world at large—a genius for commerce and industry, a passion for the undertaking of long and perilous voyages, an adaptability to circumstances of all kinds, and an address in dealing with wild tribes of many different kinds which has rarely been equalled and never exceeded. "All that we are about to say of Phoenicia," declares the author recently quoted, "of its rapid expansion and the influence which it exercised over the nations of the West, must be understood especially of Tyre and Sidon. The other towns might furnish sailors to man the Tyrian fleet or merchandise for their cargo, but it was Sidon first and then (with even more determination and endurance) Tyre which took the initiative and the conduct of the movement; it was the mariners of these two towns who, with eyes fixed on the setting sun, pushed their explorations as far as the Pillars of Hercules, and eventually even further."4106 The last and least important of the Phoenician "worlds" was the southern one, extending sixty miles from Carmel to Joppa—a tract from which the Phoenician character was well nigh trampled out by the feet of strangers ever passing up and down the smooth and featureless region, along which lay the recognised line of route between Syria and Mesopotamia on the one hand, Philistia and Egypt on the other.4107

CHAPTER V—THE COLONIES

Circumstances which led the Phoenicians to colonise—Their colonies best grouped geographically—1. Colonies of the Eastern Mediterranean—in Cyprus, Citium, Amathus, Curium, Paphos, Salamis, Ammochosta, Tamisus, and Soli;—in Cilicia, Tarsus;—in Lycia, Phaselis;—in Rhodes, Lindus, Ialysus, Camirus;—in Crete, and the Cyclades;—in the Northern Egean; &c. 2. In the Central and Western Mediterranean—in Africa, Utica, Hippo-Zaritis, Hippo Regius, Carthage, Hadrumetum, Leptis Minor, Leptis Major, and Thapsus;—in Sicily, Motya, Eryx, Panormus, Solocis;—between Sicily and Africa, Cossura, Gaulos, and Melita;—in Sardinia, Caralis, Nora, Sulcis, and Tharros;—in the Balearic Isles;—in Spain, Malaca, Sex, Abdera. 3. Outside the Straits of Gibraltar;—in Africa, Tingis, and Lixus; in Spain, Tartessus, Gades, and Belon—Summary.

The narrowness of the territory which the Phoenicians occupied the military strength of their neighbours towards the north and towards the south, and their own preference of maritime over agricultural pursuits, combined to force them, as they began to increase and multiply, to find a vent for their superfluous population in colonies. The military strength of Philistia and Egypt barred them out from expansion upon the south; the wild savagery of the mountain races in Casius, northern Bargylus, and Amanus was an effectual barrier towards the north; but before them lay the open Mediterranean, placid during the greater portion of the year, and conducting to a hundred lands, thinly peopled, or even unoccupied, where there was ample room for any number of immigrants. The trade of the Phoenicians with the countries bordering the Eastern Mediterranean must be regarded as established long previously to the time when they began to feel cramped for space; and thus, when that time arrived, they had no difficulty in finding fresh localities to occupy, except such as might arise from a too abundant amplitude of choice. Right in front of them lay, at the distance of not more than seventy miles, visible from Casius in clear weather,51 the large and important island, once known as Chittim,52 and afterwards as Cyprus, which played so important a part in the history of the East from the time of Sargon and Sennacherib to that of Bragadino and Mustapha Pasha. To the right, well visible from Cyprus, was the fertile tract of Cilicia Campestris, which led on to the rich and picturesque regions of Pamphylia, Lycia, and Caria. From Caria stretched out, like a string of stepping-stones between Asia and Europe, the hundred islets of the Ægean, Cyclades, and Sporades, and others, inviting settlers, and conducting to the large islands of Crete and Euboea, and the shores of Attica and the Peloponnese. It is impossible to trace with any exactness the order in which the Phoenician colonies were founded. A thousand incidental circumstances—a thousand caprices—may have deranged what may be called the natural or geographical order, and have caused the historical order to diverge from it; but, on the whole, probably something like the geographical order was observed; and, at any rate, it will be most convenient, in default of sufficient data for an historical arrangement, to adopt in the present place a geographic one, and, beginning with those nearest to Phoenicia itself in the Eastern Mediterranean, to proceed westward to the Straits of Gibraltar, reserving for the last those outside the Straits on the shores of the Atlantic Ocean.

The nearest, and probably the first, region to attract Phoenician colonies was the island of Cyprus. Cyprus lies in the corner of the Eastern Mediterranean formed by the projection of Asia Minor from the Syrian shore. Its mountain chains run parallel with Taurus, and it is to Asia Minor that it presents its longer flank, while to Phoenicia it presents merely one of its extremities. Its length from east to west is 145 miles, its greatest width about sixty miles.53 Two strongly marked mountain ranges form its most salient features, the one running close along the north coast from Cape Kormaciti to Cape S. Andreas; the other nearly central, but nearer the south, beginning at Cape Renaouti in the west and terminating at Cape Greco. The mountain ranges are connected by a tract of high ground towards the centre, and separated by two broad plains,54 towards the east and west. The eastern plain is the more important of the two. It extends along the course of the Pediæus from Leucosia, or Nicosia, the present capital, to Salamis, a distance of thirty-five miles, and is from five to twelve miles wide. The fertility of the soil was reckoned in ancient times to equal that of Egypt.55 The western plain, that of Morfou, is much smaller, and is watered by a less important river. The whole island, when it first became known to the Phoenicians, was well wooded.56 Lovely glens opened upon them, as they sailed along its southern coast, watered by clear streams from the southern mountain-range, and shaded by thick woods of pine and cedar, the latter of which are said to have in some cases attained a greater size even than those of the Lebanon.57 The range was also prolific of valuable metals.58 Gold and silver were found in places, but only in small quantities; iron was yielded in considerable abundance; but the chief supply was that of copper, which derived its name from that of the island.59 Other products of the island were wheat of excellent quality; the rich Cyprian wine which retains its strength and flavour for well nigh a century, the henna dye obtained from the plant called copher or cyprus, the Lawsonia alba of modern botany; valuable pigments of various kinds, red, yellow, green, and amber; hemp and flax; tar, boxwood,510 and all the materials requisite for shipbuilding from the heavy timbers needed for the keel to the lightest spar and the flimsiest sail.511

The earliest of the Phoenician settlements in Cyprus seem to have lain upon its southern coast. Here were Citium, Amathus, Curium, and Paphus, the Palæ-paphus of the geographers, which have all yielded abundant traces of a Phoenician occupation at a very distant period. Citium, now Larnaka, was on the western side of a deep bay, which indents the more eastern portion of the southern coast, between the promontories of Citi and Pyla. It is sheltered from all winds except the south-east, and continues to the present day the chief port of the island. The Phoenician settlers improved on the natural position by the formation of an artificial basin, enclosed within piers, the lines of which may be traced, though the basin itself is sanded up.512 A plain extends for some distance inland, on which the palm-tree flourishes, and which is capable of producing excellent crops of wheat.513 Access to the interior is easy; for the mountain range sinks as it proceeds eastward, and between Citium and Dali (Idalium), on a tributary of the Pediæus, is of small elevation. There are indications that the Phoenicians did not confine themselves to the coast, but penetrated into the interior, and even settled there in large numbers. Idalium, sixteen miles north-west of Citium, and Golgi (Athiénau), ten miles nearly due north of the same, show traces of having supported for a considerable time a large

Phoenician population,514 and must be regarded as outposts advanced from Citium into the mountains for trading, and perhaps for mining purposes. Idalium (Dali) has a most extensive Phoenician necropolis; the interments have a most archaic character; and their Phoenician origin is indicated both by their close resemblance to interments in Phoenicia proper and by the discovery, in connection with them, of Phoenician inscriptions.515 At Golgi the remains scarcely claim so remote an antiquity. They belong to the time when Phoenician art was dominated by a strong Egyptian influence, and when it also begins to have a partially Hellenic character. Some critics assign them to the sixth, or even to the fifth century, B.C.516

West of Citium, also upon the south coast, and in a favourable situation for trade with the interior, was Amathus. The name Amathus has been connected with "Hamath;"517 but there is no reason to suppose that the Hamathites were Phoenicians. Amathus, which Stephen of Byzantium calls "a most ancient Cyprian city,"518 was probably among the earliest of the Phoenician settlements in the island. It lay in the bay formed by the projection of Cape Gatto from the coast, and, like Citium, looked to the south-east. Westward and south-westward stretched an extensive plain, fertile and well-watered, shaded by carob and olive-trees,519 whilst towards the north were the rich copper mines from which the Amathusians derived much of their prosperity. The site has yielded a considerable amount of Phoenician remains— tombs, sarcophagi, vases, bowls, pateræ and statuettes.520 Many of the tombs resemble those at Idalium; others are stone chambers deeply buried in the earth. The mimetic art shows Assyrian and Egyptian influence, but is essentially Phoenician, and of great interest. Further reference will be made to it in the Chapter on the Æsthetic Art of the Phoenicians.

Still further to the west, in the centre of the bay enclosed between the promontories of Zeugari and Boosoura, was the colony of Curium, on a branch of the river Kuras. Curium lay wholly open to the south-western-gales, but had a long stretch of sandy shore towards the south-east, on which vessels could be drawn up. The town was situated on a rocky elevation, 300 feet in height, and was further defended by a strong wall, a large portion of which may still be traced.521 The richest discovery of Phoenician ornaments and objects of art that has yet been made took place at Curium, where, in the year 1874, General Di Cesnola happened upon a set of "Treasure Chambers" containing several hundreds of rings, gems, necklaces, bracelets, armlets, ear-rings, bowls, basins, jugs, pateræ, &c., in the precious metals, which have formed the principal material for all recent disquisitions on the true character and excellency of Phoenician art. Commencing with works of which the probable date is the fifteenth or sixteenth century B.C., and descending at least as far as the best Greek period522 (B.C. 500-400), embracing, moreover, works which are purely Assyrian, purely Egyptian, and purely Greek, this collection has yet so predominant a Phoenician character as to mark Curium, notwithstanding the contrary assertions of the Greeks themselves,523 for a thoroughly Phoenician town. And the history of the place confirms this view, since Curium sided with Amathus and the Persians in the war of Onesilus.524 No doubt, like most of the other Phoenician cities in Cyprus, it was Hellenised gradually; but there must have been many centuries during which it was an emporium of Phoenician trade and a centre of Phoenician influence.

Where the southern coast of Cyprus begins to trend to the north-west, and a river of some size, the Bocarus or Diorizus, reaches the sea, stood the Phoenician settlement of Paphos, founded (as was said525) by Cinyras, king of Byblus. Here was one of the most celebrated of all the temples of Astarté or Ashtoreth,526 the Phoenician Nature-Goddess; and here ruled for many centuries the sacerdotal class of the Cinyridæ. The remains of the temple have been identified, and will be described in a future chapter. They have the massive character of all early Phoenician architecture.

Among other Phoenician settlements in Cyprus were, it is probable, Salamis, Ammochosta (now Famagosta), Tamasus, and Soli. Salamis must be regarded as originally Phoenician on account of the name, which cannot be viewed as anything but another form of the Hebrew "Salem," the alternative name of Jerusalem.527 Salamis lay on the eastern coast of the island at the mouth of the main river, the Pediæus. It occupied the centre of a large bay which looked towards Phoenicia, and would naturally be the place where the Phoenicians would first land. There is no natural harbour beyond that afforded by the mouth of the Pediæus, but a harbour was easily made by throwing out piers into the bay; and of this, which is now sanded up, the outline may be traced.528 There are, however, no remains, either at Salamis or in the immediate neighbourhood, which can claim to be regarded as Phoenician; and the glories of the city belong to the history of Greece.

Ammochosta was situated within a few miles of Salamis, towards the south.529 Its first appearance in history belongs to the reign of Esarhaddon (B.C. 680), when we find it in a list of ten Cyprian cities, each having its own king, who acknowledged for their suzerain the great monarch of Assyria.530 Soon afterwards it again occurs among the cities tributary to Asshur-bani-pal.531 Otherwise we have no mention of it in Phoenician times. As Famagosta it was famous in the wars between the Venetians and the Turks.

Tamasus, or Tamassus, was an inland city, and the chief seat of the mining operations which the Phoenicians carried on in the island in search of copper.532 It lay a few miles to the west of Idalium (Dali), on the northern flank of the southern mountain chain. The river Pediæus flowed at its feet. Like Ammochosta, it appears among the Cyprian towns which in the seventh century B.C. were tributary to the Assyrians.533 The site is still insufficiently explored.

Soli lay upon the coast, in the recess of the gulf of Morfou.534 The fiction of its foundation by Philocyprus at the suggestion of Solon535 is entirely disproved by the occurrence of the name in the Assyrian lists of Cyprian towns a century before Solon's time. Its sympathies were with the Phoenician, and not with the Hellenic, population of the island, as was markedly shown when it joined with Amathus and Citium in calling to Artaxerxes for help against Evagoras.536 The city stood on the left bank of the river Clarius, and covered the northern slope of a low hill detached from the main range, extending also over the low ground at the foot of the hill to within a short distance of the shore, where are to be seen the remains of the ancient harbour. The soil in the neighbourhood is very rich, and adapted for almost any kind of cultivation.537 In the mountains towards the south were prolific veins of copper.

The northern coast of the island between Capes Cormaciti and S. Andreas does not seem to have attracted the Phoenicians, though there are some who regard Lapethus and Cerynia as Phoenician settlements.538 It is a rock-bound shore of no very tempting aspect, behind which the mountain range rises up steeply. Such Phoenician emigrants as held their way along the Salaminian plain and, rounding Cape S. Andreas, passed into the channel that separates Cyprus from the mainland, found the coast upon their right attract them far more than that upon their left, and formed settlements in Cilicia which ultimately became of considerable importance. The chief of these was Tars or Tarsus, probably the Tarshish of Genesis,539 though not that of the later Books, a Phoenician city, which has Phoenician characters upon its coins, and worshipped the supreme Phoenician deity under the title of "Baal Tars," "the Lord of Tarsus."540 Tarsus commanded the rich Cilician plain up to the very roots of Taurus, was watered by the copious stream of the Cydnus, and had at its mouth a commodious harbour. Excellent timber for shipbuilding grew on the slopes of the hills bounding the plain, and the river afforded a ready means of floating such timber down to the sea. Cleopatra's ships are said to have been derived from the Cilician forests, which Antony made over to her for the purpose.541 Other Phoenician settlements upon the Cilician coast were, it is probable, Soli, Celenderis, and Nagidus.

Pursuing their way westward, in search of new abodes, the emigrants would pass along the coast, first of Pamphylia and then of Lycia. In Pamphylia there is no settlement that can be with confidence assigned to them; but in Lycia it would seem that they colonised Phaselis, and perhaps other places. The mountain which rises immediately behind Phaselis was called "Solyma;"542 and a very little to the south was another mountain known as "Phoenicus."543 Somewhat further to the west lies the cape still called Cape Phineka,544 in which the root Phoenix ({phoinix}) is again to be detected. A large district inland was named Cabalis or

Cabalia,545 or (compare Phoen. and Heb. gebal, mod. Arab. jebel) the "mountain" country. Phaselis was situated on a promontory projecting south-eastward into the Mediterranean,546 and was reckoned to have three harbours,547 which are marked in the accompanying chart. Of these the principal one was that on the western side of the isthmus, which was formed by a stone pier carried out for more than two hundred yards into the sea, and still to be traced under the water.548 The other two, which were of smaller size, lay towards the east. The Phoenicians were probably tempted to make a settlement at the place, partly by the three ports, partly by the abundance of excellent timber for shipbuilding which the neighbourhood furnishes. "Between Phaselis and Cape Avora, a little north of it," says a modern traveller, "a belt of large and handsome pines borders the shore for some miles."549

From Lycia the Asiatic coast westward and north-westward was known as Caria; and here Phoenician settlements appear to have been numerous. The entire country was at any rate called Phoenicé by some authors.550 But the circumstances do not admit of our pointing out any special Phoenician settlements in this quarter, which early fell under almost exclusive Greek influence. There are ample grounds, however, for believing that the Phoenicians colonised Rhodes at the south-western angle of Asia Minor, off the Carian coast. According to Conon,551 the earliest inhabitants of Rhodes were the Heliades, whom the Phoenicians expelled. The Phoenicians themselves were at a later date expelled by the Carians, and the Carians by the Greeks. Ergeias, however, the native historian, declared552 that the Phoenicians remained, at any rate in some parts of the island, until the Greeks drove them out. Ialysus was, he said, one of their cities. Dictys Cretensis placed Phoenicians, not only in Ialysus, but in Camirus also.553 It is the conclusion of Kenrick that "the Phoenician settlement in Rhodes was the first which introduced civilisation among the primeval inhabitants, and that they maintained their ascendancy till the rise of the naval power of the Carians. These new settlers reduced the Phoenicians to the occupancy of three principal towns"—i.e. Lindus, Ialysus, and Camirus; but "from these too they were expelled by the Dorians, or only allowed to remain at Ialysus as the hereditary priesthood of their native god."554 Rhodes is an island about one-fourth the size of Cyprus, with its axis from the north-east to the south-west. It possesses excellent harbours, accessible from all quarters,555 and furnishing a secure shelter in all weathers. The fertility of the soil is great; and the remarkable history of the island shows the importance which attaches to it in the hands of an enterprising people. Turkish apathy has, however, succeeded in reducing it to insignificance.

The acquisition of Rhodes led the stream of Phoenician colonisation onwards in two directions, south-westward and north-westward. South-westward, it passed by way of Carpathus and Casus to Crete, and then to Cythera; north-westward, by way of Chalcia, Telos, and Astypalæa, to the Cyclades and Sporades. The presence of the Phoenicians in Crete is indicated by the haven "Phoenix," where St. Paul's conductors hoped to have wintered their ship;556 by the town of Itanus, which was named after a Phoenician founder,557 and was a staple of the purple-trade,558 and by the existence near port Phoenix of a town called "Araden." Leben, on the south coast, near Cape Leo, seems also to have derived its name from the Semitic word for "lion."559 Crete, however, does not appear to have been occupied by the Phoenicians at more than a few points, or for colonising so much as for trading purposes. They used its southern ports for refitting and repairing their ships, but did not penetrate into the interior, must less attempt to take possession of the whole extensive territory. It was otherwise with the smaller islands. Cythera is said to have derived its name from the Phoenician who colonised it, and the same is also reported of Melos.560 Ios was, we are told, originally called Phoenicé;561 Anaphé had borne the name of Membliarus, after one of the companions of Cadmus;562 Oliarus, or Antiparos, was colonised from Sidon.563 Thera's earliest inhabitants were of the Phoenician race;564 either Phoenicians or Carians had, according to Thucydides,565 colonised in remote times "the greater part of the islands of the Ænean." There was a time when probably all the Ægean islands were Phoenician possessions, or at any rate acknowledged Phoenician influence, and Siphnus gave its gold, its silver,566 and its lead,567 Cythera its shell-fish,568 Paros its marble, Melos its sulphur and its alum,569 Nisyrus its millstones,570 and the islands generally their honey,571 to increase the wealth and advance the commercial interests of their Phoenician masters.

From the Sporades and Cyclades the advance was easy to the islands of the Northern Ægean, Lemnos, Imbrus, Thasos, and Samothrace. The settlement of the Phoenicians in Thasos is attested by Herodotus, who says that the Tyrian Hercules (Melkarth) was worshipped there,572 and ascribes to the Phoenicians extensive mining operations on the eastern shores of the island between Ænyra and Coenyra.573 A Phoenician occupation of Lemnos, Imbrus, and Samothrace is indicated by the worship in those islands of the Cabeiri,574 who were undoubtedly Phoenician deities. Whether the Phoenicians passed from these islands to the Thracian mainland, and worked the gold-mines of Mount Pangæus in the vicinity of Philippi, may perhaps be doubtful, but such seems to have been the belief of Strabo and Pliny.575 Strabo also believed that there had been a Semitic element in the population of Euboea which had been introduced by Cadmus;576 and a Phoenician settlement in Boeotia was the current tradition of the Greek writers upon primitive times, whether historians or geographers.577 The further progress of the Phoenician settlements northward into the Propontis and the Euxine is a point whereon different opinions may be entertained. Pronectus, on the Bithynian, and Amastris, on the Paphlagonian coast, have been numbered among the colonies of the Phoenicians by some;578 while others have gone so far as to ascribe to them the colonisation of the entire countries of Bithynia, Mariandynia, and Paphlagonia.579 The story of the Argonauts may fairly be held to show580 that Phoenician enterprise early penetrated into the stormy and inhospitable sea which washes Asia Minor upon the north, and even reached its deepest eastern recess; but it is one thing to sail into seas, and, landing where the natives seem friendly, to traffic with the dwellers on them—it is quite another thing to attempt a permanent occupation of portions of their coasts. To do so often provokes hostility, and puts a stop to trade instead of encouraging it. The Phoenicians may have been content to draw their native products from the barbarous tribes of Northern Asia Minor and Western Thrace—nay, even of Southern Scythia—without risking the collisions that might have followed the establishment of settlements.

As with the Black Sea, so with the Adriatic, the commercial advantages were not sufficient to tempt the Phoenicians to colonise. From Crete and Cythera they sent their gaze afar, and fixed it midway in the Mediterranean, at the western extremity of the eastern basin, on the shores of Sicily, and the vast projection from the coast of North Africa which goes forth to meet them. They knew the harbourless character of the African coast west of Egypt, and the dangers of the Lesser and Greater Syrtes. They knew the fertility of the Tunisian projection, the excellence of its harbours, and the prolificness of the large island that lay directly opposite. Here were the tracts where they might expand freely, and which would richly repay their occupation of them. It was before the beginning of the eleventh century B.C.—perhaps some centuries before— that the colonisation of North Africa by the Phoenicians was taken in hand:581 and about the same time, in all probability, the capes and isles about Sicily were occupied,582 and Phoenician influence in a little time extended over the entire island.

In North Africa the first colony planted is said to have been Utica. Utica was situated a little to the west of Carthage, at the mouth of the Mejerda or Bagradas river.583 It stood on a rocky promontory which ran out into the sea eastward, and partially protected its harbour. At the opposite extremity, towards the north, ran out another promontory, the modern Ras Sidi Ali-el-Mekki, while the mouth of the harbour, which faced to the south-east, was protected by some islands. At present the deposits of the Mejerda have blocked up almost the whole of this ancient port, and the rocky eminence upon which the city stood looks down on three sides upon a broad alluvial plain, through which the Mejerda pursues a tortuous course to the sea.584 The remains of the ancient town, which occupy the promontory and a peninsula projecting from it, include a necropolis, an amphitheatre, a theatre, a castle, the ruins of a temple, and some remains of baths; but they have nothing about them bearing any of the characteristics of Phoenician architecture, and belong wholly to the Roman or post-Roman period. The neighbourhood is productive of olives, which yield an excellent oil; and in the hills towards the south-west are veins of lead, containing a percentage of silver, which are thought to bear traces of having been worked at a very early date.585

Near Utica was founded, probably not many years later, the settlement of Hippo-Zaritis, of which the name still seems to linger in the modern Bizerta. Hippo-Zaritis stood on the west bank of a natural channel, which united with the sea a considerable lagoon or salt lake, lying south of the town. The channel was kept open by an irregular flux and reflux, the water of the lake after the rainy season flowing off into the sea, and that of the sea, correspondingly, in the dry season passing into the lake.586 At the present time the lake is extraordinarily productive of fish,587 and the sea outside yields coral;588 but otherwise the advantages of the situation are not great.

Two degrees further to the west, on a hill overlooking the sea, and commanding a lovely prospect over the verdant plain at its base, watered by numerous streams, was founded the colony of Hippo Regius, memorable as having been for five-and-thirty years the residence of St. Augustine. The Phoenicians were probably attracted to the site by the fertility of the soil, the unfailing supplies of water, and the abundant timber and rich iron ore of the neighbouring mountains.589 Hippo Regius is now Bona, or rather has been replaced by that town, which lies about a mile and a half north of the ancient Hippo, close upon the coast, in the fertile tract formed by the soil brought down by the river Seybouse. The old harbour of Hippo is filled up, and the remains of the ancient city are scanty; but the lovely gardens and orchards, which render Bona one of the most agreeable of Algerian towns, sufficiently explain and justify the Phoenician choice of the site.590

In the same bay with Utica, further to the south, and near its inner recess, was founded, nearly three centuries after Utica, the most important of all the Phoenician colonies, Carthage. The advantages of the locality are indicated by the fact that the chief town of Northern Africa, Tunis, has grown up within a short distance of the site. It combined the excellences of a sheltered situation, a good soil, defensible eminences, and harbours which a little art made all that was to be desired in ancient times and with ancient navies. These basins, partly natural, partly artificial, still exist;591 but their communication with the sea is blocked up, as also is the channel which connected the military harbour with the harbours of commerce. The remains of the ancient town are mostly beneath the surface of the soil, but modern research has uncovered a portion of them, and brought to light a certain number of ruins which belong probably to the very earliest period. Among these are walls in the style called "Cyclopian," built of a very hard material, and more than thirty-two feet thick, which seem to have surrounded the ancient Byrsa or citadel, and which are still in places sixteen feet high.592 The Roman walls found emplaced above these are of far inferior strength and solidity. An extensive necropolis lies north of the ancient town, on the coast near Cape Camart.

Another early and important Phoenician settlement in these parts was Hadrumetum or Adrymes,593 which seems to be represented by the modern Soûsa. Hadrumetum lay on the eastern side of the great Tunisian projection, near the southern extremity of a large bay which looks to the east, and is now known as the Gulf of Hammamet. Its position was upon the coast at the edge of the vast plain called at present the "Sahel of Soûsa," which is sandy, but immensely productive of olive oil. "Millions of olive-trees," it is said, "cover the tract,"594 and the present annual exportation amounts to 40,000 hectolitres.595 Ancient remains are few, but the Cothon, or circular harbour, may still be traced, and in the necropolis, which almost wholly encircles the town, many sepulchral chambers have been found, excavated in the chalk, closely resembling in their arrangements those of the Phoenician mainland.

South of Hadrumetum, at no great distance, was Leptis Minor, now Lemta. The gulf of Hammamet terminates southwards in the promontory of Monastir, between which and Ras Dimas is a shallow bay looking to the north-east. Here was the Lesser Leptis, so called to distinguish it from the larger city of the same name between the Lesser and the Greater Syrtis;

it was, however, a considerable town, as appears from its remains. These lie along the coast for two miles and a half in Lat. 35° 43′, and include the ruins of an aqueduct, of a theatre, of quays, and of jetties.596 The neighbourhood is suited for the cultivation of the olive.

The Greater Leptis (Leptis Major) lay at a considerable distance from the Lesser one. Midway in the low African coast which intervenes between the Tunisian projection and the Cyrenaic one, about Long. 14° 22′ E. of Greenwich, are ruins, near a village called Lebda, which, it is generally agreed, mark the site of this ancient city. Leptis Major was a colony from Sidon, and occupied originally a small promontory, which projects from the coast in a north-easterly direction, and attains a moderate elevation above the plain at its base. Towards the mainland it was defended by a triple line of wall still to be traced, and on the sea-side by blocks of enormous strength, which are said to resemble those on the western side of the island of Aradus 597 In Roman times the town, under the name of Neapolis,598 attained a vast size, and was adorned with magnificent edifices, of which there are still numerous remains. The neighbourhood is rich in palm-groves and olive-groves,599 and the Cinyps region, regarded by Herodotus as the most fertile in North Africa,5100 lies at no great distance to the east.

Ten miles east, and a little south of Leptis Minor,5101 was Thapsus, a small town, but one of great strength, famous as the scene of Julius Cæsar's great victory over Cato.5102 It occupied a position close to the promontory now known as Ras Dimas, in Lat. 35° 39′, Long. 11° 3′, and was defended by a triple enclosure, whereof considerable remains are still existing. The outermost of the three lines appears to have consisted of little more than a ditch and a palisaded rampart, such as the Romans were accustomed to throw up whenever they pitched a camp in their wars; but the second and third were more substantial. The second, which was about forty yards behind the first, was guarded by a deeper ditch, from which rose a perpendicular stone wall, battlemented at top. The third, forty yards further back, resembled the second, but was on an enlarged scale, and the wall was twenty feet thick.5103 Such triple enclosures are thought to be traceable in other Phoenician settlements also;5104 but in no case are the remains so perfect as at Thapsus. The harbour, which lay south of the town, was protected from the prevalent northern and north-eastern winds by a huge mole or jetty, carried out originally to a distance of 450 yards from the shore, and still measuring 325 yards. The foundation consists of piles driven into the sand, and placed very close together; but the superstructure is a stone wall thirty-five feet thick, and still rising to a height of ten feet above the surface of the water.5105

It is probable that there were many other early Phoenician settlements on the North African seaboard; but those already described were certainly the most important. The fertile coast tract between Hippo Regius and the straits is likely to have been occupied at various points from an early period. But none of these small trading settlements attained to any celebrity; and thus it is unnecessary to go into particulars respecting them.

In Sicily the permanent Phoenician settlements were chiefly towards the west and the north-west. They included Motya, Eryx, Panormus (Palermo), and Soloeis. That the Phoenicians founded Motya, Panormus, and Soloeis is distinctly stated by Thucydides;5106 while Eryx is proved to have been Phoenician by its remains. Motya, situated on a littoral island less than half a mile from the western shore, in Lat. 38° nearly, has the remains of a wall built of large stones, uncemented, in the Phoenician manner,5107 and carried, like the western wall of Aradus, so close to the coast as to be washed by the waves. It is said by Diodorus to have been at one time a most flourishing town.5108 The coins have Phoenician legends.5109

Eryx lay about seven miles to the north-east of Motya, in a very strong position. Mount Eryx (now Mount Giuliano), on which it was mainly built, rises to the height of two thousand feet above the plain,5110 and, being encircled by a strong wall, was rendered almost impregnable. The summit was levelled and turned into a platform, on which was raised the temple of Astarte or Venus.5111 An excellent harbour, formed by Cape Drepanum (now Trapani), lay at its base. There were springs of water within the walls which yielded an unfailing supply. The walls were of great strength, and a considerable portion of them is still standing, and attests the skill of the Phoenician architects. The blocks in the lower courses are mostly of a large size, some of them six feet long, or more, and bear in many cases the well-known Phoenician mason-marks.5112 They are laid without cement, like those of Aradus and Sidon, and recall the style of the Aradian builders, but are at once less massive and arranged with more skill. The breadth of the wall is about seven feet. At intervals it is flanked by square towers projecting from it, which are of even greater strength than the curtain between them, and which were carried up to a greater height. The doorways in the wall are numerous, and are of a very archaic character, being either covered in by a single long stone lintel or else terminating in a false arch.5113 The commercial advantages of Eryx were twofold, consisting in the produce of the sea as well as in that of the shore. The shore is well suited for the cultivation of the vine,5114 while the neighbouring sea yields tunny-fish, sponges, and coral.5115 Panormus (now Palermo) occupies a site almost unequalled by any other Mediterranean city, a site which has conferred upon it the title of "the happy," and has rendered it for above a thousand years the most important place in the island. "There is no town in Europe which enjoys a more delicious climate, none so charming to look on from a distance, none more delightfully situated in a nest of verdure and flowers. Its superb mountains, with their bare flanks pierced along their base with grottoes, enclose a marvellous garden, the famous 'Shell of Gold,' in the midst of which are seen the numerous towers and domes, the fan-like foliage of the palms, the spreading branches of the pines, and Mount Reale on the south towering over all with its vast mass of convents and churches."5116 The harbour lies open to the north; but the Phoenician settlers, here as elsewhere, no doubt made artificial ports by means of piers and moles, which have, however, disappeared on this much-frequented site, where generation after generation has been continually at work building and destroying. Panormus has left us no antique remains beyond its coins, which are abundant, and show that the native name of the settlement was Mahanath.5117 Mahanath was situated about forty miles east of Eryx, on the northern coast of the island.

Solus, or Soloeis, the Soluntum of the Romans (now Solanto), lay on the eastern side of the promontory (Cape Zafferana) which shuts in the bay of Palermo on the right. It stood on a slope at the foot of a lofty hill, overlooking a small round port, and was fortified by a wall of large squared blocks of stone,5118 which may be still distinctly traced. The site has yielded sarcophagi of an unmistakably Phoenician character,5119 and other objects of a high antiquity which recall the Phoenician manner;5120 but the chief remains belong to the Greco-Roman times.

The islands in the strait which separates the North African coast from Sicily were also colonised by the Phoenicians. These were three in number, Cossura (now Pantellaria), Gaulos (now Gozzo), and Melita (now Malta). Cossura, the most western of the three, lay about midway in the channel, but nearer to the African coast, from which it is distant not more than about thirty-five miles. It is a mass of igneous rock, which was once a volcano, and which still abounds in hot springs and in jets of steam.5121 There was no natural harbour of any size, but the importance of the position was such that the Phoenicians felt bound to occupy the island, if only to prevent its occupation by others. The soil was sterile; but the coins, which are very numerous,5122 give reason to suppose that the rocks were in early times rich in copper.

Gaulos (now Gozzo) forms, together with Malta and some islets, an insular group lying between the eastern part of Sicily and the Lesser Syrtis. It is situated in Lat. 36° 2′, Long. 12° 10′ nearly, and is distant from Sicily only about fifty miles. The colonisation of the island by the Phoenicians, asserted by Diodorus,5123 is entirely borne out by the remains, which include a Phoenician inscription of some length,5124 coins with Phoenician legends,5125 and buildings, believed to be temples, which have Phoenician characteristics.5126 Some of the blocks of stone employed in their construction have a length of nearly twenty feet,5127 with a width and height proportionate; and all are put together without cement or mortar of any kind. A conical stone of the kind known to have been used by the Phoenicians in their worship was found in one of the temples.5128 Gaulos had a port which was reckoned sufficiently commodious, and which lay probably towards the south-east end of the island.

Melita, or Malta, which lies at a short distance from Gozzo, to the south-east, is an island of more than double the size, and of far greater importance. It possesses in La Valetta one of the best harbours, or rather two of the best harbours, in the world. All the navies of Europe could anchor comfortably in the "great port" to the east of the town. The western port is smaller, but is equally well sheltered. Malta has no natural product of much importance, unless it be the honey, after which some think that it was named.5129 The island is almost treeless, and the light powdery soil gives small promise of fertility. Still, the actual produce, both in cereals and in green crops, is large; and the oranges, especially those known as mandarines, are of superior quality. Malta also produced, in ancient as in modern times, the remarkable breed of small dogs5130 which is still held in such high esteem. But the Phoenician colonisation must have taken place rather on account of the situation and the harbour than on account of the products. From Sicily and North Africa the tide of emigration naturally and easily flowed on into Sardinia, which is distant, from the former about 150 and from the latter about 115 miles. The points chosen by the Phoenician settlers lay in the more open and level region of the south and the south-west, and were all enclosed within a line which might be drawn from the coast a little east of Cagliari to the northern extremity of the Gulf of Oristano.5131 The tract includes some mountain groups, but consists mainly of the long and now marshy plain, called the "Campidano," which reaches across the island from Cagliari on the southern to Oristano on the western coast. This plain, if drained, would be by far the most fertile part of the island; and was in ancient times exceedingly productive in cereals, as we learn from Diodorus.5132 The mountains west of it, especially those about Iglesias, contain rich veins of copper and of lead, together with a certain quantity of silver.5133 Good harbours exist at Cagliari, at Oristano, and between the island of S. Antioco and the western shore. It was at these points especially that the Phoenicians made their settlements, the most important of which were Caralis (Cagliari), Nora, Sulcis, and Tharros. Caralis, or Cagliari, the present capital, lies at the bottom of a deep bay looking southwards, and has an excellent harbour, sheltered in all weathers. There are no remains of Phoenician buildings; but the neighbourhood yields abundant specimens of Phoenician art in the shape of tombs, statuettes, vases, bottles, and the like.5134 Caralis was probably the first of the settlements made by the Phoenicians in Sardinia; it would attract them by its harbour, its mines, and the fertility of its neighbourhood. From Caralis they probably passed to Nora, which lay on the same bay to the south-west; and from Nora they rounded the south-western promontory of Sardinia, and established themselves on the small island now known as the Isola di San Antioco, where they built a town which they called Sulchis or Sulcis.5135 Sulcis has yielded votive tablets of the Phoenician type, tombs, vases, &c.5136 The island was productive of lead, and had an excellent harbour towards the north, and another more open one towards the south. Finally, mid-way on the west coast, at the northern extremity of the Gulf of Oristano, the Phoenicians occupied a small promontory which projects into the sea southwards and there formed a settlement which became known as Tharras or Tharros.5137 Very extensive remains, quite unmistakably Phoenician, including tombs, cippi, statuettes in metal and clay, weapons, and the like, have been found on the site.5138

The passage would have been easy from Sardinia to Corsica, which is not more than seven miles distant from it; but Corsica seems to have possessed no attraction for the Phoenicians proper, who were perhaps deterred from colonising it by its unhealthiness, or by the savagery of its inhabitants. Or they may have feared to provoke the jealousy of the Tyrrhenians, off whose coast the island lay, and who, without having any colonising spirit themselves, disliked the too near approach of rivals.5139 At any rate, whatever the cause, it seems to have been left to the Carthaginians, to bring Corsica within the range of Phoenician influence; and even the Carthaginians did little more than hold a few points on its shores as stations for their ships.5140

If from Sardinia the Phoenicians ventured on an exploring voyage westward into the open

Mediterranean, a day's sail would bring them within sight of the eastern Balearic Islands, Minorca and Majorca. The sierra of Majorca rises to the height of between 3,000 and 4,000 feet,5141 and can be seen from a great distance. The occupation of the islands by "the Phoenicians" is asserted by Strabo,5142 but we cannot be sure that he does not mean Phoenicians of Africa, i.e. Carthaginians. Still, on the whole, modern criticism inclines to the belief that, even before the foundation of Carthage, Phoenician colonisation had made its way into the Balearic Islands, directly, from the Syrian coast.5143 Some resting-places between the middle Mediterranean and Southern Spain must have been a necessity; and as the North African coast west of Hippo offered no good harbours, it was necessary to seek them elsewhere. Now Minorca has in Port Mahon a harbour of almost unsurpassed excellence,5144 while in Majorca there are fairly good ports both at Palma and at Aleudia.5145 Ivica is less well provided, but there is one of some size, known as Pormany (i.e. "Porta magna"), on the western side of the island, and another, much frequented by fishing-boats,5146 on the south coast near Ibiza. The productions of the Balearides were not, perhaps, in the early times of much importance, since the islands are not, like Sardinia, rich in metals, nor were the inhabitants sufficiently civilised to furnish food supplies or native manufactures in any quantity. If, then, the Phoenicians held them, it must have been altogether for the sake of their harbours.

The colonies of the Mediterranean have now been, all of them, noticed, excepting those which lay upon the south coast of Spain. Of these the most important were Malaca (now Malaga), Sex or Sexti, and Abdera (now Adra). Malaca is said by Strabo to have been "Phoenician in its plan,"5147 Abdera is expressly declared by him to have been "a Phoenician settlement,"5148 while Sexti has coins which connect it with early Phoenician legends.5149 The mountain range above Malaca was anciently rich in gold-mines;5150 Sexti was famous for its salt-pans;5151 Abdera lay in the neighbourhood of productive silver-mines.5152 These were afterwards worked from Carthagena, which was a late Carthaginian colony, founded by Asdrubal, the uncle of Hannibal. Malaga and Carthagena (i.e. New-Town) had well-sheltered harbours; but the ports of Sexti and Abdera were indifferent.

Outside the Straits of Gibraltar, on the shores of the Atlantic, were two further sets of Phoenician colonies, situated respectively in Africa and in Spain. The most important of those in Africa were Tingis (now Tangiers) and Lixus (now Chemmish), but besides these there were a vast number of staples ({emporia}) without names,5153 spread along the coast as far as Cape Non, opposite the Canary Islands. Tingis, a second Gibraltar, lay nearly opposite that wonderful rock, but a little west of the narrowest part of the strait. It had a temple of the Tyrian Hercules, said to have been older than that at Gades;5154 and its coins have Phoenician legends.5155 The town was situated on a promontory running out to the north-east at the extremity of a semicircular bay about four miles in width, and thus possessed a harbour not to be despised, especially on such a coast. The country around was at once beautiful and fertile, dotted over with palms, and well calculated for the growth of fruit and vegetables. The Atlas mountains rose in the background, with their picturesque summits, while in front were seen the blue Mediterranean, with its crisp waves merging into the wilder Atlantic, and further off the shores of Spain, lying like a blue film on the northern horizon.5156

While Tingis lay at the junction of the two seas, on the northern African coast, about five miles east of Cape Spartel, Lixus was situated on the open Atlantic, forty miles to the south of that cape, on the West African coast, looking westward towards the ocean. The streams from Atlas here collect into a considerable river, known now as the Wady-el-Khous, and anciently as the Lixus.5157 The estuary of this river, before reaching the sea, meanders through the plain of Sidi Oueddar, from time to time returning upon itself, and forming peninsulas, which are literally almost islands.5158 From this plain, between two of the great bends made by the stream, rose in one place a rocky hill; and here the Phoenicians built their town, protecting it along the brow of the hill with a strong wall, portions of which still remain in place.5159 The blocks are squared, carefully dressed, and arranged in horizontal courses, without any cement.

Some of them are as much as eleven feet long by six feet or somewhat more in height. The wall was flanked at the corners by square towers, and formed a sort of irregular hexagon, above a mile in circumference.5160 A large building within the walls seems to have been a temple;5161 and in it was found one of those remarkable conical stones which are known to have been employed in the Phoenician worship. The estuary of the river formed a tolerably safe harbour for the Phoenician ships, and the valley down which the river flows gave a ready access into the interior.

In Spain, outside the Pillars of Hercules, the chief Phoenician settlements were Tartessus, Agadir or Gades, and Belon. Tartessus has been regarded by some as properly the name of a country rather than a town;5162 but the statements of the Greek and Roman geographers to the contrary are too positive to be disregarded. Tartessus was a town in the opinions of Scymnus Chius, Strabo, Mela, Pliny, Festus Avienus, and Pausanias,5163 who could not be, all of them, mistaken on such a point. It was a town named from, or at any rate bearing the same name with, an important river of southern Spain,5164 probably the Guadalquivir. It was not Gades, for Scymnus Chius mentions both cities as existing in his day;5165 it was not Carteia, for it lay west of Gades, while Carteia lay east. Probably it occupied, as Strabo thought, a small island between two arms of the Guadalquivir, and gradually decayed as Gades rose to importance. It certainly did not exist in Strabo's time, but five or six centuries earlier it was a most flourishing place.5166 If it is the Tarshish of Scripture, its prosperity and importance must have been even anterior to the time of Solomon, whose "navy of Tarshish" brought him once in every three years "gold, and silver, and ivory, and apes, and peacocks."5167 The south of Spain was rich in metallic treasures, and yielded gold, silver, copper, iron, lead, and tin;5168 trade along the west coast of Africa would bring in the ivory and apes abundant in that region; while the birds called in our translation of the Bible "peacocks" may have been guinea-fowl. The country on either side of the Guadalquivir to a considerable distance took its name from the city, being called Tartessis.5169 It was immensely productive. "The wide plains through which the Guadalquiver flows produced the finest wheat, yielding an increase of a hundredfold; the oil and the wine, the growth of the hills, were equally distinguished for their excellence. The wood was not less remarkable for its fineness than in modern times, and had a native colour beautiful without dye."5170 Nor were the neighbouring sea and stream less bountiful. The tunny was caught in large quantities off the coast, shell-fish were abundant and of unusual size,5171 while huge eels were sometimes taken by the fishermen, which, when salted, formed an article of commerce, and were reckoned a delicacy at Athenian tables.5172

Gades is said to have been founded by colonists from Tyre a few years anterior to the foundation of Utica by the same people.5173 Utica, as we have seen, dated from the twelfth century before Christ. The site of Gades combined all the advantages that the Phoenicians desired for their colonies. Near the mouth of the Guadalete there detaches itself from the coast of Spain an island eleven miles in length, known now as the "Isla de Leon," which is separated from the mainland for half its length by a narrow but navigable channel, while to this there succeeds on the north an ample bay, divided into two portions, a northern and a southern.5174 The southern, or interior recess, is completely sheltered from all winds; the northern lies open to the west, but is so full of creeks, coves, and estuaries as to offer a succession of fairly good ports, one or other of which would always be accessible. The southern half of the island is from one to four miles broad; but the northern consists of a long spit of land running out to the north-west, in places not more than a furlong in width, but expanding at its northern extremity to a breadth of nearly two miles. The long isthmus, and the peninsula in which it ends, have been compared to the stalk and blossom of a flower.5175 The flower was the ancient Gades, the modern Cadiz. The Phoenician occupation of the site is witnessed to by Strabo, Diodorus, Scymnus Chius, Mela, Pliny, Velleius Paterculus, Ælian and Arrian,5176 and is further evidenced by the numerous coins which bear the legend of "Agadir" in Phoenician characters.5177 But the place itself retains no traces of the Phoenician occupation. The famous temple of Melkarth, with its two bronze pillars in front bearing inscriptions, has wholly perished, as have all other vestiges of the ancient buildings. This is the result of the continuous occupation of the site, which has been built on successively by Phoenicians, Carthaginians, Romans, Vandals, Moors, and Spaniards. The space is somewhat confined, and the houses in ancient times were, we are told, closely crowded together,5178 as they were at Aradus and Tyre. But the advantages of the harbour and the productiveness of the vicinity more than made up for this inconvenience. Gades may have been, as Cadiz is now said to be, "a mere silver plate set down upon the edge of the sea,"5179 but it was the natural centre of an enormous traffic. It had easy access by the valley of a large stream to the interior with its rich mineral and vegetable products; it had the command of two seas, the Atlantic and the Mediterranean; it trained its sailors to affront greater perils than any which the Mediterranean offers; and it enjoyed naturally by its position an almost exclusive commerce with the Northern Atlantic, with the western coasts of Spain and Gaul, with Britain, North Germany, and the Baltic. Compared with Gades and Tartessus, Belon was an insignificant settlement. Its name5180 and coins5181 mark it as Phoenician, but it was not possessed of any special advantages of situation. The modern Bolonia, a little south of Cadiz, is thought to mark the site.5182 We have reached now the limits of Phoenician colonisation towards the West. While their trade was carried, especially from Gades, into Luisitania and Gallæcia on the one hand, and into North-western Africa on the other, reaching onward past these districts to Gaul and Britain, to the Senegal and Gambia, possibly to the Baltic and the Fortunate Islands, the range of their settlements was more circumscribed. As, towards the north-east, though their trade embraced the regions of Colchis and Thrace, of the Tauric Chersonese, and Southern Scythia, their settlements were limited to the Ægean and perhaps the Propontis, so westward they seem to have contented themselves with occupying a few points of vantage on the Spanish and West African coasts, at no great distance from the Straits, and from these stations to have sent out their commercial navies to sweep the seas and gather in the products of the lands which lay at a greater distance. The actual extent of their trade will be considered in a later chapter. We have been here concerned only with their permanent settlements or colonies. These, it has been seen, extended from the Syrian coast to Cyprus, Cilicia, Rhodes, Crete, the islands and shores of the Ægean and Propontis, the coasts of Sicily, Sardinia, and North Africa, the Balearic Islands, Southern Spain, and North-western Africa as far south as Cape Non. The colonisation was not so continuous as the Greek, nor was it so extensive in one direction,5183 but on the whole it was wider, and it was far bolder and more adventurous. The Greeks, as a general rule, made their advances by slow degrees, stealing on from point to point, and having always friendly cities near at hand, like an army that rests on its supports. The Phoenicians left long intervals of space between one settlement and another, boldly planted them on barbarous shores, where they had nothing to rely on but themselves, and carried them into regions where the natives were in a state of almost savagery. The commercial motive was predominant with them, and gave them the courage to plunge into wild seas and venture themselves among even wilder men. With the Greeks the motive was generally political, and a safe home was sought, where social and civil life might have free scope for quiet development.

CHAPTER VI—ARCHITECTURE

Origin of the architecture in rock dwellings—Second style,
a combination of the native rock with the ordinary wall—
Later on, the use of the native rock, discarded—Employment
of huge blocks of stone in the early walls—Absence of
cement—Bevelling—Occurrence of Cyclopian walls—Several

architectural members comprised in one block—Phoenician shrines—The Maabed and other shrines at Amrith—Phoenician temples—Temple of Paphos—Adjuncts to temples—Museum of Golgi—Treasure chambers of Curium—Walls of Phoenician towns—Phoenician tombs—Excavated chambers—Chambers built of masonry—Groups of chambers—Colonnaded tomb—Sepulchral monuments—The Burdj-el-Bezzâk—The Kabr Hiram—The two Méghâzil—Tomb with protected entrance—Phoenician ornamentation—Pillars and their capitals—Cornices and mouldings—Pavements in mosaic and alabaster—False arches—Summary.

The architecture of the Phoenicians began with the fashioning of the native rock—so abundant in all parts of the country where they had settled themselves—into dwellings, temples, and tombs. The calcareous limestone, which is the chief geological formation along the Syrian coast, is worked with great ease; and it contains numerous fissures and caverns,61 which a very moderate amount of labour and skill is capable of converting into fairly comfortable dwelling-places. It is probable that the first settlers found a refuge for a time in these natural grottos, which after a while they proceeded to improve and enlarge, thus obtaining a practical power of dealing with the material, and an experimental knowledge of its advantages and defects. But it was not long before these simple dwellings ceased to content them, and they were seized with an ambition to construct more elaborate edifices—edifices such as they must have seen in the lands through which they had passed on their way from the shores of the Persian Gulf to the seaboard of the Mediterranean. They could not at once, however, divest themselves of their acquired habits, and consequently, their earliest buildings continued to have, in part, the character of rock dwellings, while in part they were constructions of the more ordinary and regular type. The remains of a dwelling-house at Amrith,62 the ancient Marathus, offer a remarkable example of this intermixture of styles. The rock has been cut away so as to leave standing two parallel walls 33 yards long, 19 feet high, and 2 1/2 feet thick, which are united by transverse party-walls formed in the same way.63 Windows and doorways are cut in the walls, some square at top, some arched. At the two ends the main walls were united partly by the native rock, partly by masonry. The northern wall was built of masonry from the very foundation, the southern consisted for a portion of its height of the native rock, while above that were several courses of stones carrying it up further. At Aradus and at Sidon, similarly, the town walls are formed in many places of native rock, squared and smoothed, up to a certain height, after which courses of stone succeed each other in the ordinary fashion. It is as if the Phoenician builders could not break themselves of an inveterate habit, and rather than disuse it entirely submitted to an intermixture which was not without a certain amount of awkwardness.

Another striking example of the mixed system is found at a little distance from Amrith, in the case of a building which appears to have been a shrine, tabernacle, or sanctuary. The site is a rocky platform, about a mile from the shore. Here the rock has been cut away to a depth varying from three to six yards, and a rectangular court has been formed, 180 feet long by 156 feet wide, in the centre of which has been left a single block of the stone, still of one piece with the court, which rises to a height of ten feet, and forms the basis or pedestal of the shrine itself.64 The shrine is built of a certain number of large blocks, which have been quarried and brought to the spot; it has a stone roof with an entablature, and attains an elevation above the court of not less than twenty-seven feet. The dimensions of the shrine are small, not much exceeding seventeen feet each way.65

From constructions of this mixed character the transition was easy to buildings composed entirely of detached stones put together in the ordinary manner. Here, what is chiefly remarkable in the Phoenician architecture is the tendency to employ, especially for the foundations and lower courses of buildings, enormous blocks. When the immovable native rock is no longer available, the resource is to make use of vast masses of stone, as nearly immovable as possible. The most noted example is that of the substructions which supported the platform whereon stood the Temple of Jerusalem, which was the work of the Phoenician builders whom Hiram lent to Solomon.66 These substructions, laid bare at their base by the excavations of the Palestine Exploration Fund, are found to consist of blocks measuring from fifteen to twenty-five feet in length, and from ten to twelve feet in height. The width of the blocks at the angles of the wall, where alone it can be measured, is from twelve to eighteen feet. At the south-west angle no fewer than thirty-one courses of this massive character have been counted by the recent explorers, who estimate the weight of the largest block at something above a hundred tons!67

A similar method of construction is found to have prevailed at Tyre, at Sidon, at Aradus, at Byblus, at Leptis Major, at Eryx, at Motya, at Gaulos, and at Lixus on the West African coast. The blocks employed do not reach the size of the largest discovered at Jerusalem, but still are of dimensions greatly exceeding those of most builders, varying, as they do, from six feet to twenty feet in length, and being often as much as seven or eight feet in breadth and height. As the building rises, the stones diminish in size, and the upper courses are often in no way remarkable. Stones of various sizes are used, and often the courses are not regular, but one runs into another. A tower in the wall of Eryx is a good specimen of this kind of construction.68

Where the stones are small, mortar has been employed by the builders, but where they are of a large size, they are merely laid side by side in rows or courses, without mortar or cement of any kind, and remain in place through their own mass and weight. In the earliest style of building the blocks are simply squared,69 and the wall composed of them presents a flat and level surface, or one only broken by small and casual irregularities; but, when their ideas became more advanced, the Phoenicians preferred that style of masonry which is commonly regarded as peculiarly, if not exclusively, theirs610—the employment of large blocks with deeply bevelled edges. The bevel is a depression round the entire side of the stone, which faces outwards, and may be effected either by a sloping cut which removes the right-angle from the edge, or by two cuts, one perpendicular and the other horizontal, which take out from the edge a rectangular bar or plinth. The Phoenician bevelling is of this latter kind, and is generally accompanied by an artificial roughening of the surface inside the bevel, which offers a strong contrast to the smooth and even surface of the bevel itself.611 The style is highly ornamental and effective, particularly where a large space of wall has to be presented to the eye, unbroken by door or window.612

Occasionally, but very rarely, and only (so far as appears) in their remoter dependencies, the Phoenicians constructed their buildings in the rude and irregular way, which has been called Cyclopian, employing unhewn polygonal blocks of various sizes, and fitting them roughly together. The temples discovered in Malta and Gozzo have masonry of this description.613

A peculiarity in Phoenician architecture, connected with the preference for enormous blocks over stones of a moderate size, is the frequent combination in a single mass of distinct architectural members; for instance, of the shaft and capital of pillars, of entire pediments with a portion of the wall below them, and of the walls of monuments with the cornice and architrave. M. Renan has made some strong remarks on this idiosyncrasy. "In the Grecian style," he says, "the beauty of the wall is a main object with the architect, and the wall derives its beauty from the divisions between the stones, which observe symmetrical laws, and are in agreement with the general lines of the edifice. In a style of this kind the stones of a wall have, all of them, the same dimension, and this dimension is determined by the general plan of the building; or else, as in the kind of work which is called 'pseud-isodomic,' the very irregularity of the courses is governed by a law of symmetry. The stones of the architrave, the metopes, the triglyphs, are, all of them, separate blocks, even when it would have been perfectly easy to have included in a single block all these various members. Such facts, as one observes frequently in Syria, where three or four architectural members are brought out from a single block, would have appeared to the Greeks monstrous, since they are the negation of all logic."614

In cannot be denied that the habit of preferring large to small blocks, even in monuments of a very moderate size, involved the Phoenician architects in awkwardnesses and anomalies, which offend a cultivated taste; but it should be remembered, on the other hand, that massiveness in the material conduces greatly to stability, and that, in lands where earthquakes are frequent, as they are along all the Mediterranean shores, not many monuments would have survived the lapse of three thousand years had the material employed been of a less substantial and solid character.

Among the Phoenician constructions, of which it is possible to give some account at the present day, without drawing greatly on the imagination, are their shrines, their temples, the walls of their towns, and, above all, their tombs. Recent researches in Phoenicia Proper, in Cyprus, Sicily, Africa, and the smaller Mediterranean islands, have brought to light numerous remains previously unknown; the few previously known remains have been carefully examined, measured, and in some cases photographed; and the results have been made accessible to the student in numerous well-illustrated publications. When Movers and Kenrick published their valuable works on the history of Phoenicia, and the general characteristics of the Phoenician people, it was quite impossible to do more than form conjectures concerning their architecture from a few coins, and a few descriptions in ancient writers. It is now a matter of comparatively little difficulty to set before the public descriptions and representations which, if they still leave something to be desired in the way of completeness, are accurate, so far as they go, and will give a tolerably fair idea of the architectural genius of the people.

One very complete and two ruined shrines have been found in Phoenicia Proper, in positions and of a character which, in the judgment of the best antiquaries, mark them as the work of the ancient people. All these are situated on the mainland, near the site of Marathus, which lay nearly opposite the island of Ruad, the ancient Aradus. The shrine which is complete, or almost complete, bears the name of "the Maabed" or "Temple." Its central position, in the middle of an excavated court, and its mixed construction, partly of native rock and partly of quarried stone, have been already described. It remains to give an account of the shrine or tabernacle itself.615 This is emplaced upon the mass of rock left to receive it midway in the court, and is a sort of cell, closed in on three sides by walls, and open on one side, towards the north. The cell is formed of four quarried blocks, which are laid one over the other. These are nearly of the same size, and similarly shaped, each of them enclosing the cell on three sides, towards the east, the south, and the west. The fourth, which is larger than any of the others, constitutes the roof. It is a massive stone, carefully cut, which projects considerably in front of the rest of the building, and is ornamented towards the top with a cornice and string-course, extending along the four sides.616 Internally the roof is scooped into a sort of shallow vault. The height of the shrine proper is about seventeen feet, and the elevation of the entire structure above the court in which it stands appears to be about twenty-seven feet. M. Renan conjectures that the projecting portion of the roof had originally the support of two pillars, which may have been either of wood, of stone, or of metal, and notes that there are two holes in the basement stone, into which the bottoms of the pillars were probably inserted.617 He imagines that the court was once enclosed completely by the construction of a wall at its northern end, and that the water from a spring, which still rises within the enclosure, was allowed to overflow the entire space, so that the shrine looked down upon a basin or shallow lake and glassed itself in the waters.618 An image of a deity may have stood in the cell under the roof, dimly visible to the worshipper between the two porch pillars.

The two ruined tabernacles lie at no great distance from the complete one, which has just been described. One of them is so injured that its plan is irrecoverable; but M. Renan carefully collected and measured the fragments of the other, and thus obtained sufficient data for its restoration.619 It was, he believes, a monolithic chamber, with a roof slightly vaulted, like that of the Maabed, having a length of eight feet, a breadth of five, and a height of about ten feet, and ornamented externally with a very peculiar cornice. This consisted of a series of carvings, representing the fore part of an uræus or basilisk serpent, uprearing itself against the wall of the shrine, which were continued along the entire front of the chamber. There was also an internal ornamentation of the roof, consisting of a winged circle of an Egyptian character—a favourite subject with the Phoenician artists620—the circle having an uræus erect on either side of it, and also of another winged figure which appeared to represent an eagle.621 The monolithic chamber was emplaced upon a block of stone, ten feet in length and breadth, and six feet in height, which itself stood upon a much smaller stone, and overhung it on all sides. A flight of six steps, cut in the upper block at either side, gave access to the chamber, which, however, as it stood in a pool of water, must have been approached by a boat. The entire height of the shrine above the water must have been about eighteen feet.

Some other ruined shrines have been found in the more distant of the Phoenician settlements, and representations of them are common upon the stelæ, set up in temples as votive offerings. On these last the uræus cornice is frequently repeated, and the figure of a goddess sometimes appears, standing between the pillars which support the front of the shrine.622 There is a decided resemblance between the Phoenician shrines and the small Egyptian temples, which have been called mammeisi, the chief difference being that the latter are for the most part peristylar.623 M. Renan says of the Maabed, or main shrine at Amrith:—"L'aspect général de l'édifice est Egyptian, mais avec une certaine part d'originalité. Le bandeau et la corniche sur les quatre côtés de la stalle supériere en sont le seul ornement. Cette simplicité, cette sévérité de style, jointes à l'idée de force et de puissance qu'éveillent les dimensions énormes des matériaux employés, sont des caractères que nous avons déjà signalés dans les monumens funéraires d'Amrith."624

From the shrines of the Phoenicians we may now pass to their temples, of which, however, the remains are, unfortunately, exceedingly scanty. Of real temples, as distinct from shrines, Phoenicia Proper does not present to us so much as a single specimen. To obtain any idea of them, we must quit the mother country, and betake ourselves to the colonies, especially to those island colonies which have been less subjected than the mainland to the destructive ravages of barbarous conquerors, and the iconoclasm of fanatical populations. It is especially in Cyprus that we meet with extensive remains, which, if not so instructive as might have been wished, yet give us some important and interesting information.

The temple of Paphos, according to the measurements of General Di Cesnola,625 was a rectangular building, 221 feet long by 167 feet wide, built along its lower corners of large blocks of stone, but probably continued above in an inferior material, either wood or unbaked brick.626 The four corner-stones are still standing in their proper places, and give the dimensions without a possibility of mistake. Nothing is known of the internal arrangements, unless we attach credit to the views of the savant Gerhard, who, in the early years of the present century, constructed a plan from the reports of travellers, in which he divided the building into a nave and two aisles, with an ante-chapel in front, and a sacrarium at the further extremity.627 M. Gerhard also added, beyond the sacrarium, an apse, of which General Di Cesnola found no traces, but which may possibly have disappeared in the course of the sixty years which separated the observations of M. Gerhard's informants from the researches of the later traveller. The arrangement into a nave and two aisles is, to a certain extent, confirmed by some of the later Cyprian coins, which certainly represent Cyprian temples, and probably the temple of Paphos.628 The floor of the temple was, in part at any rate, covered with mosaic.629

This large building, which extended over an area of 36,800 square feet, was emplaced within a sacred court, surrounded by a peribolus, or wall of enclosure, built of even larger blocks than the temple itself, and entered by at least one huge doorway. The width of this entrance, situated near a corner of the western wall, was nearly eighteen feet.630 On one side of it were found still fixed in the wall the sockets for the bolts on which the door swung, in length six inches, and of proportionate width and depth. The peribolus was rectangular, like the temple, and was built in lines parallel to it. The longer sides measured 690 and the shorter 530 feet. One block, which was of blue granite and must have come either from Asia Minor or from Egypt, measured fifteen feet ten inches in length, with a width of seven feet eleven inches, and a depth of two feet five inches.631 It is thought that the court was probably surrounded by a colonnade or cloister,632 though no traces have been at present observed either of the pillars which must have supported such a cloister or of the rafters which must have formed its roof. Ponds,633 fountains, shrubberies, gardens, groves of trees, probably covered the open space between the cloister and the temple, while well-shaded walks led across it from the gates of the enclosure to those of the sanctuary.

If we allow ourselves to indulge our fancy for a brief space, and to complete the temple according to the idea which the coins above represented naturally suggest, we may suppose that it did, in fact, consist of a nave, two aisles, and a cell, or "holy of holies," the nave being of superior height to the aisles, and rising in front into a handsome façade, like the western end of a cathedral flanked by towers. Through the open doorway between the towers might be seen dimly the sacred cone or pillar which was emblematic of deity; on either side the eye caught the ends of the aisles, not more than half the height of the towers, and each crowned with a strongly projecting cornice, perhaps ornamented with a row of uræi. In front of the two aisles, standing by themselves, were twin columns, like Jachin and Boaz before the Temple of Solomon. The aisles were certainly roofed: whether the nave also was covered in, or whether, like the Greek hypæthral temples, it lay open to the blue vault of heaven, is perhaps doubtful. The walls of the buildings, after a few courses of hewn stone, were probably of wood, perhaps of cedar, enriched with the precious metals, and the pavement was adorned with a mosaic of many colours, "white, yellow, red, brown, and rose."634 Outside the temple was a mass of verdure. "In the sacred precinct, and in its dependencies, all breathed of voluptuousness, all spoke to the senses. The air of the place was full of perfumes, full of soft and caressing sounds. There was the murmur of rills which flowed over a carpet of flowers; there was, in the foliage above, the song of the nightingale, and the prolonged and tender cooing of the dove; there were, in the groves around, the tones of the flute, the instrument which sounds the call to pleasure, and summons to the banquet chamber the festive procession and the bridal train. Beneath the shelter of tents, or of light booths with walls formed by the skilful interlacing of a green mass of boughs, through which the myrtle and the laurel spread their odours, dwelt the fair slaves of the goddess, those whom Pindar called, in the drinking-song which he composed for Theoxenus of Corinth, 'the handmaids of persuasion.'"635 Here and there in the precincts, sacred processions took their prescribed way; ablutions were performed; victims led up to the temple; votive offerings hung on the trees; festal dances, it may be, performed; while in the cloister which skirted the peribolus, dealers in shrines and images chaffered with their customers, erotic poets sang their lays, lovers whispered, fortune-tellers plied their trade, and a throng of pilgrims walked lazily along, or sat on the ground, breathing in the soft, moist air, feasting their eyes upon the beauty of upspringing fountain and flowering shrub, and lofty tree, while their ears drank in the cadences of the falling waters, the song of the birds, and the gay music which floated lightly on the summer breeze.

Phoenician temples had sometimes adjuncts, as cathedrals have their chapter-houses and muniment rooms, which were at once interesting and important. There has been discovered at Athiénau in Cyprus—the supposed site of Golgi—a ruined edifice, which some have taken for a temple,636 but which appears to have been rather a repository for votive offerings, a sort of ecclesiastical museum. A picture of the edifice, as he conceives it to have stood in its original condition, has been drawn by one of its earliest visitants. "The building," he says,637 "was constructed of sun-dried bricks, forming four walls, the base of which rested upon a substruction of solid stone-work. The walls were covered, as are the houses of the Cypriot peasants of to-day, with a stucco which was either white or coloured, and which was impenetrable by rain. Wooden pillars with stone capitals supported internally a pointed roof, which sloped at a low angle. It formed thus a sort of terrace, like the roofs that we see in

Cyprus at the present day. This roof was composed of a number of wooden rafters placed very near each other, above which was spread a layer of rushes and coarse mats, covered with a thick bed of earth well pressed together, equally effective against the entrance of moisture and against the sun's rays. Externally the building must have presented a very simple appearance. In the interior, which received no light except from the wide doorways in the walls, an immovable and silent crowd of figures in stone, with features and garments made more striking by the employment of paint, surrounded, as with a perpetual worship, the mystic cone. Stone lamps, shaped like diminutive temples, illumined in the corners the grinning ex-votos which hung upon the walls, and the curious pictures with which they were accompanied. Grotesque bas-reliefs adorned the circuit of the edifice, where the slanting light was reflected from the white and polished pavement-stones."638 In length and breadth the chamber measured sixty feet by thirty; the thickness of the basement wall was three feet.639 Midway between the side walls stood three rows of large square pedestals—regularly spaced, and dividing the interior into four vistas or avenues, which some critics regard as bases for statues, and some as supports for the pillars which sustained the roof.640 Two stone capitals of pillars were found within the area of the chamber; and it is conjectured that the entire disappearance of the shafts may be accounted for by their having been of wood,641 the employment of wooden shafts with stone bases and capitals being common in Cyprus at the present time.642 Against each of the four walls was a row of pedestals touching each other, which had certainly been bases for statues, since the statues were found lying, mostly broken, in front of them. The figures varied greatly in size, some being colossal, others mere statuettes. Most probably all were votive offerings, presented by those who imagined that they had been helped by the god of the temple to which the chamber belonged, as an indication of their gratitude. The number of pedestals found along one of the walls was seventy-two,643 and the original number must have been at least three times as great.

Another Cyprian temple, situated at Curium, not far from Paphos, contained a very remarkable crypt, which appears to have been used as a treasure-house.644 It was entered by means of a flight of steps which conducted to a low and narrow passage cut in the rock, and giving access to a set of three similar semi-circular chambers, excavated side by side, and separated one from another by doors. Beyond the third of these, and at right angles to it, was a fourth somewhat smaller chamber, which gave upon a second passage that it was found impossible to explore.645 The three principal chambers were fourteen feet six inches in height, twenty-three feet long, and twenty-one feet broad. The fourth was a little smaller,646 and shaped somewhat irregularly. All contained plate and jewels of extraordinary richness, and often of rare workmanship. "The treasure found," says M. Perrot, "surpassed all expectation, and even all hope. Never had such a discovery been made of such a collection of precious articles, where the material was of the richest, and the specimens of different styles most curious. There were many bracelets of massive gold, and among them two which weighed a pound apiece, and several others of a weight not much short of this. Gold was met with in profusion under all manner of forms—finger-rings, ear-rings, amulets, flasks, small bottles, hair-pins, heavy necklaces. Silver was found in even greater abundance, both in ornaments and in vessels; besides which there were articles in electrum, which is an amalgam of silver with gold. Among the stones met with were rock-crystals, carnelians, onyxes, agates, and other hard stones of every variety; and further there were paste jewels, cylinders in soft stone, statuettes in burnt clay, earthen vases, and also many objects in bronze, as lamps, tripods, candelabra, chairs, vases, arms, &c. &c. A certain amount of order reigned in the repository. The precious objects in gold were collected together principally in the first chamber. The second contained the silver vessels, which were arranged along a sort of shelf cut in the rock, at the height of about eight inches above the floor. Unfortunately the oxydation of these vessels had proceeded to such lengths, that only a very small number could be extracted from the mass, which for the most part crumbled into dust at the touch of a finger. The third chamber held lamps and fibulæ in bronze, vases in alabaster, and, above all, the groups and vessels modelled in clay; while the fourth was the repository of the utensils in bronze, and of a certain number which were either in copper or in iron. In the further passage, which was not completely explored, there were nevertheless found seven kettles in bronze."647

In the construction of the walls of their towns, especially of those which were the most ancient, the feature which is most striking at first sight is that on which some remarks have already been made, the attachment of the lower portion of the wall to the soil from which the wall springs. At Sidon, at Aradus, and at Semar-Gebeil, the enceinte which protected the town consisted, up to the height of ten or twelve feet, of native rock, cut to a perpendicular face, upon which were emplaced several courses of hewn stone. The principle adopted was to utilise the rock as far as possible, and then to supplement what was wanting by a superstructure of masonry. Large blocks of stone, shaped to fit the upper surface of the rock, were laid upon it, generally endways, that is, with their smallest surface outwards, their length forming the thickness of the wall, which was sometimes as much as fifteen or twenty feet.648 The massive blocks, once placed, were almost immovable, and it was considered enough to lay them side by side, without clamps or mortar, since their own weight kept them in place. It was not thought of much consequence whether the joints of the courses coincided or not; though care was taken that, if a coincidence occurred in two courses, it should not be repeated in the third.649 The elevation of walls does not seem to have often exceeded from thirty to forty feet, though Diodorus makes the walls of Carthage sixty feet high,650 and Arrian gives to the wall of Tyre which faced the continent the extraordinary height of a hundred and fifty feet.651 If we may generalise from the most perfect specimens of Phoenician town-walls that are still fairly traceable, as those of Eryx and Lixus,652 we may lay it down, that such walls were usually flanked, at irregular intervals, by square or rectangular towers, which projected considerably beyond the line of the curtain. The towers were of a more massive construction than the wall itself, especially in the lower portion, where vast blocks were common. The wall was also broken at intervals by gates, some of which were posterns, either arched or covered in by flat stones,653 while others were of larger dimensions, and were protected, on one side or on both, by bastions. The sites of towns were commonly eminences, and the line of the walls followed the irregularities of the ground, crowning the slopes where they were steepest. Sometimes, as at Carthage and Thapsus, where the wall had to be carried across a flat space, the wall of defence was doubled, or even tripled. The restorations of Daux654 contain, no doubt, a good deal that is fanciful; but they give, probably, a fair idea of the general character of the so-called "triple wall" of certain Phoenician cities. The outer line, or {proteikhisma}, was little more than an earthwork, consisting of a ditch, with the earth from it thrown up inwards, crowned perhaps at top with a breastwork of masonry. The second line was far more elaborate. There was first a ditch deeper than the outer one, while behind this rose a perpendicular battlemented wall to the height, from the bottom of the ditch, of nearly forty feet. In the thickness of the wall, which was not much less than the height, were chambers for magazines and cisterns, while along the top, behind the parapet, ran a platform, from which the defenders discharged their arrows and other missiles against the enemy. Further back, at the distance of about thirty yards, came the main line of defence, which in general character resembled the second, but was loftier and stronger. There was, first, a third ditch (or moat, if water could be introduced), and behind it a wall thirty-five feet thick and sixty feet high, pierced by two rows of embrasures from which arrows could be discharged, and having a triple platform for the defenders. This wall was kept entirely clear of the houses of the town, and the different storeys could be reached by sloping ascents or internal staircases. It was flanked at intervals by square towers, somewhat higher than the walls, which projected sufficiently for the defenders to enfilade the assailants when they approached the base of the curtain.

The tombs of the Phoenicians were, most usually, underground constructions, either simple excavations in the rock, or subterranean chambers, built of hewn stone, at the bottom of sloping passages, or perpendicular shafts, which gave access to them. The simpler kinds bear a close resemblance to the sepulchres of the Jews. A chamber is opened in the rock, in the sides of which are hollowed out, horizontally, a number of caverns or loculi, each one intended to receive a corpse.655 If more space is needed, a passage is made from one of the sides of the chamber to a certain distance, and then a second chamber is excavated, and more loculi are formed; and the process is repeated as often as necessary. But chambers thus excavated were apt to collapse, especially if the rock was of the soft and friable nature so common in Phoenicia Proper and in Cyprus; on which account, in such soils, the second kind of tomb was preferred, sepulchural chambers being solidly built,656 either singly or in groups, each made to hold a certain number of sarcophagi. The most remarkable tombs of this class are those found at Amathus, on the south coast of Cyprus, by General Di Cesnola. They lie at the depth of from forty to fifty-five feet below the surface of the soil,657 and are square chambers, built of huge stones, carefully squared, some of them twenty feet in length, nine in breadth, and three in thickness, and even averaging a length of fourteen feet.658 Two shapes occur. Some of the tombs are almost perfect cubes, the upright walls rising to a height of twelve or fifteen feet, and being then covered in by three or four long slabs of stone. Others resemble huts, having a gable at either end, and a sloping roof formed of slabs which meet and support each other. A squared doorway, from five to six feet in height, gives entrance to the tombs at one end, and has for ornament a fourfold fillet, which surrounds it on three sides. Otherwise, ornamentation is absent, the stonework of both walls and roofs being absolutely plain and bare. Internally the chambers present the same naked appearance, walls and roofs being equally plain, and the floor paved with oblong slabs of stone, about a foot and a half in length. The grouped chambers are of several kinds. Sometimes there are two chambers only, one opening directly into the other, and not always similarly roofed. Occasionally, groups of three are found, and there are examples of groups of four. In these instances, the exact symmetry is remarkable. A single doorway of the usual character gives entrance to a nearly square chamber, the exact dimensions of which are thirteen feet four inches by twelve feet two inches. Midway in the side and opposite walls are three other doorways, each of them three foot six inches in width, which lead into exactly similar square chambers, having a length of twelve feet two inches, and a width of ten feet nine.659

Chambers of the character here described contain in almost every instance stone sarcophagi. These are ranged along the walls, at a little distance from them. The chambers commonly contain two or three; but sometimes one sarcophagus is superimposed upon another, and in this way the number occasionally reaches to six.660 Mostly, the sarcophagi are plain, or nearly so, but are covered over with a sloping lid. Sometimes, however, they are elaborately carved, and constitute works of art, which are of the highest value. An account will be given of the most remarkable of these objects in the chapter on Phoenician Æsthetic Art.

Another distinct type of Phoenician tomb is that which is peculiar to Nea-Paphos, and which is thought by some to have been employed exclusively by the High Priests of the great temple there.661 The peculiarity of these burial-places is, that the sepulchral chambers are adjuncts of a quadrangular court open to the sky, and surrounded by a colonnade supported on pillars.662 The court, the colonnade, the pillars, the entablature, and the chambers, with their niches for the dead, are all equally cut out of the rock, as well as the passage by which the court is entered, at one corner of the quadrangle. The columns are either square or rounded, the rounded ones having capitals resembling those of the Doric order; and the entablature is also a rough imitation of the Doric triglyphs, and guttæ. The entrances to the sepulchral chambers are under the colonnade, behind the pillars;663 and the chambers contain, beside niches, a certain number of bases for sarcophagi, but no sarcophagi have been found in them. The quadrangle is of a small size, not more than about eighteen feet each way.

Thus far we have described that portion of the sepulchral architecture of the Phoenicians which is most hidden from sight, lying, as it does, beneath the surface of the soil. With tombs of this quiet character the Phoenicians were ordinarily contented. They were not, however, wholly devoid of those feelings with respect to their dead which have caused the erection, in most parts of the world, of sepulchral monuments intended to attract the eye, and to hand on to later ages the memory of the departed. Well acquainted with Egypt, they could not but have been aware from the earliest times of those massive piles which the vanity of Egyptian monarchs had raised up for their own glorification on the western side of the valley of the Nile; nor in later days could such monuments have escaped their notice as the Mausoleum of Halicarnassus664 or the Tomb of the Maccabees.665 Accordingly, we find them, at a very remote period, not merely anxious to inter their dead decently and carefully in rock tombs or subterranean chambers of massive stone, but also wishful upon occasions to attract attention to the last resting-places of their great men, by constructions which showed themselves above the ground, and had some architectural pretensions. One of these, situated near Amrith, the ancient Marathus, is a very curious and peculiar structure. It is known at the present day as the Burdj-el-Bezzâk,666 and was evidently constructed to be, like the pyramids, at once a monument and a tomb. It is an edifice, built of large blocks of stone, and rising to a height of thirty-two feet above the plain at its base, so contrived as to contain two sepulchral chambers, the one over the other. Externally, the monument is plain almost to rudeness, being little more than a cubic mass, broken only by two doorways, and having for its sole ornament a projecting cornice in front. Internally, there is more art and contrivance. The chambers are very carefully constructed, and contain a number of niches intended to receive sarcophagi, the lower having accommodation for three and the upper for twelve bodies.667 It is thought that originally the cubic mass, which is all that now remains, was surmounted by a pyramidical roof, many stones from which were found by M. Renan among the débris that were scattered around. The height of the monument was thus increased by perhaps one-half, and did not fall much short of sixty-five feet.668 The cornice, which is now seen on one side only, and which is there imperfect, originally, no doubt, encircled the entire edifice.

The other constructions erected by the Phoenicians to mark the resting-places of their dead are simple monuments erected near, and generally over, the tombs in which the bodies are interred. The best known is probably that in the vicinity of Tyre, which the natives call the Kabr-Hiram, or "Tomb of Hiram."669 No great importance can be attached to this name, which appears to be a purely modern one;670 but the monument is undoubtedly ancient, perhaps as ancient as any other in Phoenicia.671 It is composed of eight courses of huge stones superimposed one upon another,672 the blocks having in some cases a length of eleven or twelve feet, with a breadth of seven or eight, and a depth of three feet. The courses retreat slightly, with the exception of the fifth, which projects considerably beyond the line of the fourth and still more beyond that of the sixth. The whole effect is less that of a pyramid than of a stelé or pillar, the width at top being not very much smaller than that at the base. The monument is a solid mass, and is not a square but a rectangular oblong, the broader sides measuring fourteen feet and the narrower about eight feet six inches. Two out of the eight courses are of the nature of substructions, being supplemental to the rock, which supplies their place in part; and it is only recently that they have been brought to light by means of excavation. Hence the earlier travellers speak of the monument as having no more than six courses. The present height above the soil is a little short of twenty-five feet. A flight of steps cut in the rock leads down from the monument to a sepulchral chamber, which, however, contains neither sepulchral niche nor sarcophagus.

But the most striking of the Phoenician sepulchral monuments are to be found in the north of Phoenicia, and not in the south, in the neighbourhood, not of Tyre and Sidon, but of Marathus and Aradus. Two of them, known as the Méghâzil,673 form a group which is very remarkable, and which, if we may trust the restoration of M. Thobois,674 must have had considerable architectural merit. Situated very near each other, on the culminating point of a great plateau of rock, they dominate the country far and wide, and attract the eye from a long distance. One seems to have been in much simpler and better taste than the other. M. Renan calls it "a real masterpiece, in respect of proportion, of elegance, and of majesty."675 It is built altogether in three stages. First, there is a circular basement story flanked by four figures of lions, attached to the wall behind them, and only showing in front of it their heads, their shoulders, and their fore paws. This basement, which has a height of between seven and eight feet, is surmounted by a cylindrical tower in two stages, the lower stage measuring fourteen and the upper, which is domed, ten feet. The basement is composed of four great stones, the entire tower above it is one huge monolith. An unusual and very effective ornamentation crowns both stages of the tower, consisting of a series of gradines at top with square machicolations below.

The other monument of the pair, distant about twenty feet from the one already described, is architecturally far less happy. It is composed of four members, viz. a low plinth for base, above this a rectangular pedestal, surmounted by a strong band or cornice; next, a monolithic cylinder, without ornaments, which contracts slightly as it ascends; and, lastly, a pentagonal pyramid at the top. The pedestal is exceedingly rough and unfinished; generally, the workmanship is rude, and the different members do not assort well one with another. Still it would seem that the two monuments belong to the same age and are parts of the same plan.676 Their lines are parallel, as are those of the subterranean apartments which they cover, and they stand within a single enclosure. Whether the same architect designed them both it is impossible to determine, but if so he must have been one of the class of artists who have sometimes happy and sometimes unhappy inspirations.

Both the Méghâzil are superimposed upon subterranean chambers, containing niches for bodies, and reached by a flight of steps cut in the rock, the entrance to which is at some little distance from the monuments.677 But there is nothing at all striking or peculiar in the chambers, which are without ornament of any kind.

Another tomb, in the vicinity of the Méghâzil, is remarkable chiefly for the care taken to shelter and protect the entrance to the set of chambers which it covers.678 The monument is a simple one. A square monolith, crowned by a strong cornice, stands upon a base consisting of two steps. Above the cornice is another monolith, the lower part squared and the upper shaped into a pyramid. The upper part of the pyramid has crumbled away, but enough remains to show the angle of the slope, and to indicate for the original erection a height of about twenty feet. At the distance of about ten yards from the base of the monument is a second erection, consisting of two tiers of large stones, which roof in the entrance to a flight of eighteen steps. These steps lead downwards to a sloping passage, in which are sepulchral niches, and thence into two chambers, the inner one of which is almost directly under the main monument. Probably, a block of stone, movable but removed with difficulty, originally closed the entrance at the point where the steps begin. This stone ordinarily prevented ingress, but when a fresh corpse was to be admitted, or funeral ceremonies were to be performed in one of the chambers, it could be "rolled"679 or dragged away.

Phoenician architects were, as a general rule, exceedingly sparing in the use of ornament. Neither the pillar, nor the arch, much less the vault, was a feature in their principal buildings, which affected straight lines, right-angles, and a massive construction, based upon the Egyptian. The pillar came ultimately to be adopted, to a certain extent, from the Greeks; but only the simplest forms, the Doric and Ionic, were in use, if we except certain barbarous types which the people invented for themselves. The true arch was scarcely known in Phoenicia, at any rate till Roman times, though false arches were not infrequent in the gateways of towns and the doors of houses.680 The external ornamentation of buildings was chiefly by cornices of various kinds, by basement mouldings, by carvings about doorways,681 by hemispherical or pyramidical roofs, and by the use of bevelled stones in the walls. The employment of animal forms in external decoration was exceedingly rare; and the half lions of the circular Méghâzil of Amrith are almost unique.

In internal ornamentation there was greater variety. Pavements were sometimes of mosaic, and glowed with various colours;682 sometimes they were of alabaster slabs elaborately patterned. Alabaster slabs also, it is probable, adorned the walls of temples and houses, excepting where woodwork was employed, as in the Temple of Solomon. There is much richness and beauty in many of the slabs now in the Phoenician collection of the Louvre,683 especially in those which exhibit the forms of sphinxes or griffins. Many of the patterns most affected are markedly Assyrian in character, as the rosette, the palm-head, the intertwined ribbons, and the rows of gradines which occur so frequently. Even the Sphinxes are rather Assyrian than Egyptian in character; and exhibit the recurved wings, which are never found in the valley of the Nile. In almost all the forms employed there is a modification of the original type, sufficient to show that the Phoenician artist did not care merely to reproduce.

On the whole the architecture must be pronounced wanting in originality and in a refined taste. What M. Renan says of Phoenician art in general684 is especially true of Phoenician architecture. "Phoenician art, which issued, as it would seem, originally from mere troglodytism, was, from the time when it arrived at the need of ornament, essentially an art of imitation. That art was, above all, industrial; that art never raised itself for its great public monuments to a style that was at once elegant and durable. The origin of Phoenician architecture was the excavated rock, not the column, as was the case with the Greeks. The wall replaced the excavated rock after a time, but without wholly losing its character. There is nothing that leads us to believe that the Phoenicians knew how to construct a keyed vault. The monolithic principle which dominated the Phoenician and Syrian art, even after it had taken Greek art for its model, is the exact contrary of the Hellenic style. Greek architecture starts from the principle of employing small stones, and proclaims the principal loudly. At no time did the Greeks extract from Pentelicus blocks at all comparable for size with those of Baalbek or of Egypt; they saw no use in doing so; on the contrary, with masses of such enormity, which it is desired to use in their entirety, the architect is himself dominated; the material, instead of being subordinate to the design of the edifice, runs counter to the design and contradicts it. The monuments on the Acropolis of Athens would be impossible with blocks of the size usual in Syria."685 Thus there is always something heavy, rude, and coarse in the Phoenician buildings, which betray their troglodyte origin by an over-massive and unfinished appearance.

There is also a want of originality, more especially in the ornamentation. Egypt, Assyria, and Greece have furnished the "motives" which lie at the root of almost all the decorative art that is to be met with, either in the mother country or in the colonies. Winged disks, uræi, scarabs, sphinxes, have been adopted from Egypt; Assyria has furnished gradines, lotus blossoms, rosettes, the palm-tree ornament, the ribbon ornament, and the form of the lion; Greece has supplied pillars, pediments, festoons, and chimæras. Native talent has contributed little or nothing to the ornamentation of buildings, if we except the modification of the types which have been derived from foreign sources.

Finally, there is a want of combination and general plan in the Phoenician constructions where they fall into groups. "This is sensibly felt," according to M. Renan, "at Amrith, at Kabr-Hiram, and at Um-el-Awamid. In the remains still visible in these localities there are many fine ideas, many beautiful details; but they do not fall under any general dominant plan, as do the buildings on the Acropolis of Athens. One seems to see a set of people who are fond of working in stone for its own sake, but who do not care to arrive at a mutual understanding in order to produce in common a single work, since they do not know that it is the conception of a grand whole which constitutes greatness in art. Hence the incompleteness of the monuments; there is not a tomb to which the relations of the deceased have deemed it fitting to give the finishing touches; there is everywhere a certain egotism, like that which in later times prevented the Mussulman monuments from enduring. A passing pleasure in art does not induce men to finish, since finishing requires a certain stiffness of will. In general, the ancient Phoenicians appear to have had the spirit of sculptors rather than of architects. They did not construct in great masses, but every one laboured on his own account. Hence there was no exact measurement, and no symmetry. Even the capitals of the columns at Um-el-Awamid are not alike; in the portions which most evidently correspond the details are different."686

CHAPTER VII—ÆSTHETIC ART

Recent discoveries of Phoenician artistic remains—
Phoenician sculpture—Statues and busts—Animal forms—Bas-
reliefs—Hercules and Geryon—Scenes on sarcophagi—
Phoenicians metal castings—Jachin and Boaz—Solomon's
"Molten Sea"—Solomon's lavers—Statuettes in bronze—
Embossed work upon cups and pateræ—Cup of Præneste—
Intaglios on cylinders and gems—Phoenician painting—Tinted
statues—Paintings on terra-cotta and clay.

Phoenician æsthetic art embraced sculpture, metal-casting, intaglio, and painting to a small extent. Situated as the Phoenicians were, in the immediate neighbourhood of nations which had practised from a remote antiquity the imitation of natural forms, and brought into contact by their commercial transactions with others, with whom art of every kind was in the highest esteem—adroit moreover with their hands, clever, active, and above all else practical—it was scarcely possible that they should not, at an early period in their existence as a nation, interest themselves in what they found so widely appreciated, and become themselves ambitious of producing such works as they saw everywhere produced, admired, and valued. The mere commercial instinct would lead them to supply a class of goods which commanded a high price in the world's markets; while it is not to be supposed that they were, any more than other nations, devoid of those æsthetic propensities which find a vent in what are commonly called the "fine arts," or less susceptible of that natural pleasure which successful imitation evokes from all who find themselves capable of it. Thus, we might have always safely concluded, even without any material evidence of it, that the Phoenicians had an art of their own, either original or borrowed; but we are now able to do more than this. Recent researches in Phoenicia Proper, in Cyprus, in Sardina, and elsewhere, have recovered such a mass of Phoenician artistic remains, that it is possible to form a tolerably complete idea of the character of their æsthetic art, of its methods, its aims, and its value.

Phoenician sculpture, even at its best, is somewhat rude. The country possesses no marble, and has not even any stone of a fine grain. The cretaceous limestone, which is the principal geological formation, is for the most part so pierced with small holes and so thickly sown with fossil shells as to be quite unsuited for the chisel; and even the better blocks, which the native sculptors were careful to choose, are not free from these defects, and in no case offer a grain that is satisfactory. To meet these difficulties, the Phoenician sculptor occasionally imported his blocks either from Egypt or from the volcanic regions of Taurus and Amanus;71 but it was not until he had transported himself to Cyprus, and found there an abundance of a soft, but fairly smooth, compact, and homogeneous limestone, that he worked freely, and produced either statues or bas-reliefs in any considerable number.72 The Cyprian limestone is very easy to work. "It is a whitish stone when it comes out of the quarry, but by continued exposure to the air the tone becomes a greyish yellow, which, though a little dull, is not disagreeable to the eye. The nail can make an impression on it, and it is worked by the chisel much more easily and more rapidly than marble. But it is in the plastic arts as in literature and poetry—what costs but little trouble has small chance of enduring. The Cyprian limestone is too soft to furnish the effects and the contrasts which marble offers, so to speak, spontaneously; it is incapable of receiving the charming polish which makes so strong an opposition to the dark shadows of the parts where the chisel has scooped deep. The chisel, whatever efforts it may make and however laboriously it may be applied, cannot impress on such material the strong and bold touches which indicate the osseous structure, and make the muscles and the veins show themselves under the epidermis in Greek statuary. The sculptor's work is apt to be at once finikin and lax; it wants breadth, and it wants decision. Moreover, the material, having little power of resistance, retains but ill what the chisel once impressed; the more delicate markings and the more lifelike touches that it once received, it loses easily through friction or exposure to rough weather. A certain number of the sculptured figures found by M. Di Cesnola at Athiénau were discovered under conditions that were quite peculiar, having passed from the shelter of a covered chamber to that of a protecting bed of dust, which had hardened and adhered to their surfaces; and these figures had preserved an unusual freshness, and seem as if just chiselled; but, saving these exceptions, the Cypriot figures have their angles rounded, and their projections softened down. It is like a page of writing, where the ink, before it had time to dry, preserving its sharpness of tone, has been absorbed by the blotting paper and has left only pale and feeble traces."73

Another striking defect in the Phoenician, or at any rate in the Cyprio-Phoenician, sculpture, and one that cannot be excused on account of any inherent weakness in the material, is the thinness and flatness of the greater part of the figures. The sculptor seems to have been furnished by the stonecutter, not so much with solid blocks of stone, as with tolerably thick slabs.74 These he fashioned carefully in front, and produced statues, which, viewed in front, are lifelike and fairly satisfactory. But to the sides and back of the slab he paid little attention, not intending that his work should be looked at from all quarters, but that the spectator should directly face it. The statues were made to stand against walls,75 or in niches, or back to back, the heels and backs touching;76 they were not, properly speaking, works in the round, but rather alti relievi a little exaggerated, not actually part of the wall, but laid closely against it. A striking example of this kind of work may be seen in a figure now at New York, which appears to represent a priest, whereof a front view is given by Di Cesnola in his "Cyprus," and a side view by Perrot and Chipiez in their "History of Ancient Art." The head and neck are in good proportion, but the rest of the figure is altogether unduly thin, while for some space above the feet it is almost literally a slab, scarcely fashioned at all.

This fault is less pronounced in some statues than in others, and from a certain number of the statuettes is wholly absent. This is notably the case in a figure found at Golgi, which represents a female arrayed in a long robe, the ample folds of which she holds back with one hand, while the other hand is advanced, and seems to have held a lotus flower. Three graceful tresses fall on either side of the neck, round which is a string of beads or pearls, with an amulet as pendant; while a long veil, surmounted by a diadem, hangs from the back of the head. This statue is in no respect narrow or flat, as may be seen especially from the side view given by Di Cesnola;77 but it is short and inelegant, though not wanting in dignity; and it is disfigured by sandalled feet of a very disproportionate size, which stand out offensively in front. The figure has been viewed as a representation of the goddess Astarte or Ashtoreth;78 but the identification can scarcely be regarded as more than a reasonable conjecture.

The general defects of Phoenician statuary, besides want of finish and flatness, are a stiff and conventional treatment, recalling the art of Egypt and Assyria, a want of variety, and a want of life. Most of the figures stand evenly on the two feet, and have the arms pendant at the two sides, with the head set evenly, neither looking to the right nor to the left, while even the arrangement of the drapery is one of great uniformity. In the points where there is any variety, the variety is confined within very narrow limits. One foot may be a little advanced;79 one arm may be placed across the breast, either as confined by the robe,710 or as holding something, e.g. a bird or a flower.711 In female figures both arms may be laid along the thighs,712 or both be bent across the bosom, with the hands clasping the breasts,713 or one hand may be so placed, and the other depend in front.714 The hair and beard are mostly arranged with the utmost regularity in crisp curls, resembling the Assyrian; where tresses are worn, they are made to hang, whatever their number, with exact uniformity on either side.715 Armlets and bracelets appear always in pairs, and are exactly similar; the two sides of a costume correspond perfectly; and in the groups the figures have, as nearly as possible, the same attitude.

Repose is no doubt the condition of human existence which statuary most easily and most naturally expresses; and few things are more obnoxious to a refined taste than that sculpture which, like that of Roubiliac, affects movement, fidget, flutter, and unquiet. But in the Phoenician sculpture the repose is overdone; except in the expression of faces, there is scarcely any life at all. The figures do nothing; they simply stand to be looked at. And they stand stiffly, sometimes even awkwardly, rarely with anything like elegance or grace. The heads, indeed, have life and vigour, especially after the artists have become acquainted with Greek models;716 but they are frequently too large for the bodies whereto they are attached, and the face is apt to wear a smirk that is exceedingly disagreeable. This is most noticeable in the Cypriot series, as will appear by the accompanying representations; but it is not confined to them, since it reappears in the bronzes found in Phoenicia Proper.

Phoenician statues are almost always more or less draped. Sometimes nothing is worn besides the short tunic, or shenti, of the Egyptians, which begins below the navel and terminates at the knee.717 Sometimes there is added to this a close-fitting shirt, like a modern "jersey," which has short sleeves and clings to the figure, so that it requires careful observation to distinguish between a statue thus draped and one which has the shenti only.718 But there are also a number of examples where the entire figure is clothed from the head to the ankles, and nothing is left bare but the face, the hands, and the feet. A cap, something like a Phrygian bonnet, covers the head; a long-sleeved robe reaches from the neck to the ankles, or sometimes rests upon the feet; and above this is a mantle or scarf thrown over the left shoulder, and hanging down nearly to the knees. Ultimately a drapery greatly resembling that of the Greeks seems to have been introduced; a long cloak, or chlamys, is worn, which falls into numerous folds, and is disposed about the person according to the taste and fancy of the wearer, but so as to leave the right arm free.719 Statues of this class are scarcely distinguishable from Greek statues of a moderately good type.

Phoenician sculptors in the round did not very often indulge in the representation of animal forms. The lion, however, was sometimes chiselled in stone, either partially, as in a block of stone found by M. Renan at Um-el-Awamid, or completely, as in a statuette brought by General Di Cesnola from Cyprus. The representations hitherto discovered have not very much merit. We may gather from them that the sculptors were unacquainted with the animal itself, had never seen the king of beasts sleeping in the shade or stretching himself and yawning as he awoke, or walking along with a haughty and majestic slowness, or springing with one bound upon his prey, but had simply studied without much attention or interest the types furnished them by Egyptian or Assyrian artists, who were familiar with the beast himself. The representations are consequently in every case feeble and conventional; in some they verge on the ridiculous. What, for instance, can be weaker than the figure above given from the great work of Perrot and Chipiez, with its good-humoured face, its tongue hanging out of its mouth, its tottering forelegs, and its general air of imbecility? The lioness' head represented in the same work is better, but still leaves much to be desired, falling, as it does, very far behind the best Assyrian models. Nor were the sculptors much more successful in their mode of expressing animals with whose forms they were perfectly well acquainted. The sheep carried on the back of a shepherd, brought from Cyprus and now in the museum of New York, is a very ill-shaped sheep, and the doves so often represented are very poor doves.720 They are just recognisable, and that is the most that can be said for them. A dog in stone,721 found at Athiénau, is somewhat better, equally the dogs of the Egyptians and Assyrians. On the other hand, the only fully modelled horses that have been found are utterly childish and absurd.722 The reliefs of the Phoenicians are very superior to their statues. They vary in their character from almost the lowest kind of relief to the highest. On dresses, on shields, on slabs, and on some sarcophagi it is much higher than is usual even in Greece. A bas-relief of peculiar interest was discovered at Athiénau by General Di Cesnola, and has been represented both by him and by the Italian traveller Ceccaldi.723 It represents Hercules capturing the cattle of Geryon from the herdsman Eurytion, and gives us reason to believe that that myth was a native Phoenician legend adopted by the Greeks, and not a Hellenic one imported into Phoenicia. The general character of the sculpture is archaic and Assyrian; nor is there a trace of Greek influence about it. Hercules, standing on an elevated block of stone at the extreme left, threatens the herdsman, who responds by turning towards him, and making a menacing gesture with his right hand, while in his left, instead of a club, he carries an entire tree. His hair and beard are curled in the Assyrian fashion, while his figure, though short, is strong and muscular. In front of him are his cattle, mixed up in a confused and tangled mass, some young, but most of them full grown, and amounting to the number of seventeen. They are in various attitudes, and are drawn with much spirit, recalling groups of cattle in the sculptures of Assyria and Egypt, but surpassing any such group in the vigour of their life and movement. Above, in an upper field or plain, divided from the under one by a horizontal line, is the triple-headed dog, Orthros, running full speed towards Hercules, and scarcely checked by the arrow which has met him in mid career, and entered his neck at the point of junction between the second and the third head.724 The bas-relief is three feet two inches in length, and just a little short of two feet in height. It served to ornament a huge block of stone which formed the pedestal of a colossal statue of Hercules, eight feet nine inches high.725

A sarcophagus, on which the relief is low, has been described and figured by Di Cesnola,726 who discovered it in the same locality as the sculpture which has just engaged our attention. The sarcophagus, which had a lid guarded by lions at the four corners, was ornamented at both ends and along both sides by reliefs. The four scenes depicted appear to be distinct and separate. At one end Perseus, having cut off Medusa's head and placed it in his wallet, which he carries behind him by means of a stick passed over his shoulder, departs homewards followed by his dog. Medusa's body, though sunk upon one knee, is still upright, and from the bleeding neck there spring the forms of Chrysaor and Pegasus. At the opposite end of the tomb is a biga drawn by two horses, and containing two persons, the charioteer and the owner, who is represented as bearded, and rests his hand upon the chariot-rim. The horse on the right hand, which can alone be distinctly seen, is well proportioned and spirited. He is impatient and is held in by the driver, and prevented from proceeding at more than a foot's pace. On the longer sides are a hunting scene, and a banqueting scene. In a wooded country, indicated by three tall trees, a party, consisting of five individuals, engages in the pleasures of the chase. Four of the five are accoutred like Greek soldiers; they wear crested helmets, cuirasses, belts, and a short tunic ending in a fringe: the arms which they carry are a spear and a round buckler or shield. The fifth person is an archer, and has a lighter equipment; he wears a cloth about his loins, a short tunic, and a round cap on his head. The design forms itself into two groups. On the right two of the spearmen are engaged with a wild boar, which they are wounding with their lances; on the left the two other spearmen and the archer are attacking a wild bull. In the middle a cock separates the two groups, while at the two extremities two animal forms, a horse grazing and a dog trying to make out a scent, balance each other. The fourth side of the sarcophagus presents us with a banqueting scene. On four couches, much like the Assyrian,727 are arranged the banqueters. At the extreme right the couch is occupied by a single person, who has a long beard and extends a wine-cup towards an attendant, a naked youth, who is advancing towards him with a wine-jug in one hand, and a ladle or strainer in the other. The three other couches are occupied respectively by three couples, each comprising a male and a female. The male figure reclines in the usual attitude, half sitting and half lying, with the left arm supported on two pillows;728 the female sits on the edge of the couch, with her feet upon a footstool. The males hold wine-cups; of the females, one plays upon the lyre, while the two others fondle with one hand their lover or husband. A fourth female figure, erect in the middle between the second and third couches, plays the double flute for the delectation of the entire party. All the figures, except the boy attendant, are decently draped, in robes with many folds, resembling the Greek. At the side of each couch is a table, on which are spread refreshments, while at the extreme left is a large bowl or amphora, from which the wine-cups may be replenished. This is placed under the shade of a tree, which tells us that the festivity takes place in a garden.729

No one can fail to see, in this entire series of sculptures, the dominant influence of Greece. While the form of the tomb, and the lions that ornament the covering, are unmistakably Cyprio-Phoenician, the reliefs contain scarcely a feature which is even Oriental; all has markedly the colouring and the physiognomy of Hellenism. Yet Cyprian artists probably executed the work. There are little departures from Greek models, which indicate the "barbarian" workman, as the introduction of trees in the backgrounds, the shape of the furniture, the recurved wings of the Gorgon, and the idea of hunting the wild bull. But the figures, the proportions, the draperies, the attitudes, the chariot, the horse, are almost pure Greek. There is a grace and ease in the modelling, an elegance, a variety, to which Asiatic art, left to itself, never attained. The style, however, is not that of Greece at its best, but of archaic Greece. There is something too much of exact symmetry, both in the disposition of the groups and in the arrangement of the accessories; nay, even the very folds of the garments are over-stiff and regular. All is drawn in exact profile; and in the composition there is too much of balance and correspondence. Still, a new life shows itself through the scenes. There is variety in the movements; there is grace and suppleness in the forms; there is lightness in the outline, vigour in the attitudes, and beauty spread over the whole work. It cannot be assigned an earlier date than the fifth century B.C., and is most probably later,730 since it took time for improved style to travel from the head-centres of Greek art to the remoter provinces, and still more time for it to percolate through the different layers of Greek society until it reached the stratum of native Cyprian artistic culture.

We may contrast with the refined work of the Athiénau sarcophagus the far ruder, but more genuinely native, designs of a tomb of the same kind found on the site of Amathus.731 On this sarcophagus, the edges of which are most richly adorned with patterning, there are, as upon the other, four reliefs, two of them occupying the sides and two the ends. Those at the ends are curious, but have little artistic merit. They consist, in each case, of a caryatid figure four times repeated, representations, respectively, of Astarté and of a pygmy god, who, according to some, is Bes, and, according to others, Melkarth or Esmun.732 The figures of Astarté are rude, as are generally her statues.733 They have the hair arranged in three rows of crisp curls, the arms bent, and the hands supporting the breasts. The only ornament worn by them is a double necklace of pearls or round beads. The representations of the pygmy god have more interest. They remind us of what Herodotus affirms concerning the Phoenician pataikoi, which were used for the figure-heads of ships,734 and which he compares to the Egyptian images of Phthah, or Ptah, the god of creation. They are ugly dwarf figures, with a large misshapen head, a bushy beard, short arms, fat bodies, a short striped tunic, and thick clumsy legs. Only one of the four figures is at present complete, the sarcophagus having been entered by breaking a hole into it at this end.

The work at the sides is much superior to that at the ends. The two panels represent, apparently, a single scene. The scene is a procession, but whether funeral or military it is hard to decide.735 First come two riders on horseback, wearing conical caps and close-fitting jerkins; they are seated on a species of saddle, which is kept in place by a board girth passing round the horse's belly, and by straps attached in front. The two cavaliers are followed by four bigæ. The first contains the principal personages of the composition, who sits back in his car, and shades himself with a parasol, the mark of high rank in the East, while his charioteer sits in front of him and holds the reins. The second car has three occupants; the third two; and the fourth also two, one of whom leans back and converses with the footmen, who close the procession. These form a group of three, and seem to be soldiers, since they bear shield and spear; but their costume, a loose robe wrapped round the form, is rather that of civilians. The horses are lightly caparisoned, with little more than a head-stall and a collar; but they carry on their heads a conspicuous fan-like crest.736 MM. Perrot and Chipiez thus sum up their description of this monument:—"Both in the ornamentation and in the sculpture properly so-called there is a mixture of two traditions and two inspirations, diverse one from the other. The persons who chiselled the figures in the procession which fills the two principal sides of the sarcophagus were the pupils of Grecian statuaries; they understood how to introduce variety into the attitudes of those whom they represented, and even into the movements of the horses. Note, in this connection, the steeds of the two cavaliers in front; one of them holds up his head, the other bends it towards the ground. The draperies are also cleverly treated, especially those of the foot soldiers who bring up the rear, and resemble in many respects the costume of the Greeks. On the other hand, the types of divinity, repeated four times at the two ends of the monument, have nothing that is Hellenic about them, but are borrowed from the Pantheon of Phoenicia. Even in the procession itself—the train of horsemen, footmen, and chariots, which is certainly the sculptor's true subject—there are features which recall the local customs and usages of the East. The conical caps of the two cavaliers closely resemble those which we see on the heads of many of the Cyprian statues; the parasol which shades the head of the great person in the first biga is the symbol of Asiatic royalty; lastly, the fan-shaped plume which rises above the heads of all the chariot horses is an ornament that one sees in the same position in Assyria and in Lycia, whensoever the sculptor desires to represent horses magnificently caparisoned."737

Sarcophagi recently exhumed in the vicinity of Sidon are said to be adorned with reliefs superior to any previously known specimens of Phoenician art. As, however, no drawings or photographs of these sculptures have as yet reached Western Europe, it will perhaps be sufficient in this place to direct attention to the descriptions of them which an eye-witness has published in the "Journal de Beyrout."738 No trustworthy critical estimate can be formed from mere descriptions, and it will therefore be necessary to reserve our judgment until the sculptures themselves, or correct representations of them, are accessible.

The metal castings of the Phoenicians, according to the accounts which historians give of them, were of a very magnificent and extraordinary character. The Hiram employed by Solomon in the ornamentation of the Temple at Jerusalem, who was a native of Tyre,739 designed and executed by his master's orders a number of works in metal, which seem to have been veritable masterpieces. The strangest of all were the two pillars of bronze, which bore the names of "Jachin" and "Boaz,"740 and stood in front of the Temple porch, or possibly under it.741 These pillars, with their capitals, were between thirty-four and thirty-five feet high, and had a diameter of six feet.742 They were cast hollow, the bronze whereof they were composed having a uniform thickness of three inches,743 or thereabouts. Their ornamentation was elaborate. A sort of chain-work covered the "belly" or lower part of the capitals,744 while above and below were representations of pomegranates in two rows, probably at the top and bottom of the "belly," the number of the pomegranates upon each pillar being two hundred.745 At the summit of the whole was a sort of "lily-work"746 or imitation of the lotus blossom, a "motive" adopted from Egypt. Various representations of the pillars have been attempted in works upon Phoenician art, the most remarkable being those designed by M. Chipiez, and published in the "Histoire de l'Art dans l'Antiquité."747 Perhaps, however, there is more to be said in favour of M. de Vogüé's view, as enunciated in his work on the Jewish Temple.

The third great work of metallurgy which Hiram constructed for Solomon was "the molten sea."748 This was an enormous bronze basin, fifteen feet in diameter, supported on the backs of twelve oxen, grouped in sets of three.749 The basin stood fourteen or fifteen feet above the level of the Temple Court,750 and was a vast reservoir, always kept full of water, for the ablutions of the priests. There was an ornamentation of "knops" or "gourds," in two rows, about the "brim" of the reservoir; and it must have been supplied in its lower part with a set of stopcocks, by means of which the water could be drawn off when needed. Representations of the "molten sea" have been given by Mangeant, De Vogüé, Thenius, and others; but all of them are, necessarily, conjectural. The design of Mangeant is reproduced in the preceding representation. It is concluded that the oxen must have been of colossal size in order to bear a proper proportion to the basin, and not present the appearance of being crushed under an enormous weight.751

Next in importance to these three great works were ten minor ones, made for the Jewish

Temple by the same artist. These were lavers mounted on wheels,752 which could be drawn or pushed to any part of the Temple Court where water might be required. The lavers were of comparatively small size, capable of containing only one-fiftieth part753 of the contents of the "molten sea," but they were remarkable for their ornamentation. Each was supported upon a "base;" and the bases, which seem to have been panelled, contained, in the different compartments, figures of lions, oxen, and cherubim,754 either single or in groups. On the top of the base, which seems to have been square, was a circular stand or socket, a foot and a half in height, into which the laver or basin fitted.755 This, too, was panelled, and ornamented with embossed work, representing lions, cherubim, and palm-trees.756 Each base was emplaced upon four wheels, which are said to have resembled chariot wheels, but which were molten in one piece, naves, spokes, and felloes together.757 A restoration by M. Mangeant, given by Perrot and Chipiez in the fourth volume of their "History of Ancient Art," is striking, and leaves little to be desired.

Hiram is also said to have made for Solomon a number of pots, shovels, basins, flesh-hooks, and other instruments,758 which were all used in the Temple service; but as no description is given of any of these works, even their general character can only be conjectured. We may, however, reasonably suppose them not to have differed greatly from the objects of a similar description found in Cyprus by General Di Cesnola.759

From the conjectural, which may amuse, but can scarcely satisfy, the earnest student, it is fitting that we should now pass to the known and actual. Phoenician metal-work of various descriptions has been found recently in Phoenicia Proper, in Cyprus, and in Sardinia; and, though much of it consists of works of utility or of mere personal adornment, which belong to another branch of the present enquiry, there is a considerable portion which is more or less artistic and which rightly finds its place in the present chapter. The Phoenicians, though they did not, so far as we know, attempt with any frequency the production, in bronze or other metal, of the full-sized human form,760 were fond of fabricating, especially in bronze, the smaller kinds of figures which are known as "figurines" or "statuettes." They also had a special talent for producing embossed metal-work of a highly artistic character in the shape of cups, bowls, and dishes or pateræ, whereon scenes of various kinds were represented with a vigour and precision that are quite admirable. Some account of these two classes of works must here be given.

The statuettes commence with work of the rudest kind. The Phoenician sites in Sardinia have yielded in abundance grotesque figures of gods and men,761 from three or four to six or eight inches high, which must be viewed as Phoenician productions, though perhaps they were not the best works which Phoenician artists could produce, but such as were best suited to the demands of the Sardinian market. The savage Sards would not have appreciated beauty or grace; but to the savage mind there is something congenial in grotesqueness. Hence gods with four arms and four eyes,762 warriors with huge horns projecting from their helmets,763 tall forms of extraordinary leanness,764 figures with abnormally large heads and hands,765 huge noses, projecting eyes, and various other deformities. For the home consumption statuettes of a similar character were made; but they were neither so rude nor so devoid of artistic merit. There is one in the Louvre, which was found at Tortosa, in Northern Phoenicia, approaching nearly to the Sardinian type, while others have less exaggeration, and seem intended seriously. In Cyprus bronzes of a higher order have been discovered.766 One is a figure of a youth, perhaps Æsculapius, embracing a serpent; another is a female form of much elegance, which may have been the handle of a vase or jug; it springs from a grotesque bracket, and terminates in a bar ornamented at either end with heads of animals. The complete bronze figure found near Curium, which is supposed to represent Apollo and is figured by Di Cesnola,767 is probably not the production of a Phoenician artists, but a sculpture imported from Greece.

The embossed work upon cups and pateræ is sometimes of great simplicity, sometimes exceedingly elaborate. A patera of the simplest kind was found by General Di Cesnola in the treasury of Curium and is figured in his work.768 At the bottom of the dish, in the middle, is a rosette with twenty-two petals springing from a central disk; this is surrounded by a ring whereon are two wavy lines of ribbon intertwined. Four deer, with strongly recurved horns, spaced at equal intervals, stand on the outer edge of the ring in a walking attitude. Behind them and between them are a continuous row of tall stiff reeds terminating in blossoms, which are supposed to represent the papyrus plant. The reeds are thirty-two in number. We may compare with this the medallion at the bottom of a cup found at Cære in Italy, which has been published by Grifi.769 Here, on a chequered ground, stands a cow with two calves, one engaged in providing itself with its natural sustenance, the other disporting itself in front of its dam. In the background are a row of alternate papyrus blossoms and papyrus buds bending gracefully to the right and to the left, so as to form a sort of framework to the main design. Above the cow and in front of the papyrus plants two birds wing their flight from left to right across the scene.

A bronze bowl, discovered at Idalium (Dali) in Cyprus,770 is, like these specimens, Egyptian in its motive, but is more ambitious in that it introduces the human form. On a throne of state sits a goddess, draped in a long striped robe which reaches to the feet, and holding a lotus flower in her right hand and a ball or apple in her left. Bracelets adorn her wrists and anklets her feet. Behind her stands a band of three instrumental performers, all of them women, and somewhat variously costumed: the first plays the double pipe, the second performs on a lyre or harp, the third beats the tambourine. In front of the goddess is a table or altar, to which a votary approaches bringing offerings. Then follows another table whereon two vases are set; finally comes a procession of six females, holding hands, who are perhaps performing a solemn dance. Behind them are a row of lotus pillars, the supports probably of a temple, wherein the scene takes place. The human forms in this design are ill-proportioned, and very rudely traced. The heads and hands are too large, the faces are grotesque, and the figures wholly devoid of grace. Mimetic art is seen clearly in its first stage, and the Phoenician artist who has designed the bowl has probably fallen short of his Egyptian models.

Animal and human forms intermixed occur on a silver patera found at Athiénau, which is more complicated and elaborate than the objects hitherto described, but which is, like them, strikingly Egyptian.771 A small rosette occupies the centre; round it is, apparently, a pond or lake, in which fish are disporting themselves; but the fish are intermixed with animal and human forms—a naked female stretches out her arms after a cow; a man clothed in a shenti endeavours to seize a horse. The pond is edged by papyrus plants, which are alternately in blossom and in bud. A zigzag barrier separates this central ornamentation from that of the outer part of the dish. Here a marsh is represented in which are growing papyrus and other water-plants. Aquatic birds swim on the surface or fly through the tall reeds. Four boats form the chief objects in this part of the field. In one, which is fashioned like a bird, there sits under a canopy a grandee, with an attendant in front and a rower or steersman at the stern. Behind him, in a second boat, is a band consisting of three undraped females, one of whom plays a harp and another a tambourine, while the third keeps time with her hands. A man with a punt-pole directs the vessel from the stern. In the third boat, which has a freight of wine-jars, a cook is preparing a bird for the grandee's supper. The fourth boat contains three rowers, who possibly have the vessel of the grandee in tow. The first and second boats are separated by two prancing steeds, the second and third by two cows, the third and fourth by a chariot and pair. It is difficult to explain the mixture of the aquatic with the terrestrial in this piece; but perhaps the grandee is intended to be enjoying himself in a marshy part of his domain, where he might ride, drive, or boat, according to his pleasure. The whole scene is rather Egyptian than Phoenician or Cypriot, and one cannot help suspecting that the patera was made for an Egyptian customer.

There is a patera at Athens,772 almost certainly Phoenician, which may well be selected to introduce the more elaborate and complicated of the Phoenician works of art in this class. It has been figured,773 and carefully described by MM. Perrot and Chipiez in these terms:—

"The medallion in the centre is occupied by a rosette with eight points. The zone outside this, in which are distributed the personages represented, is divided into four compartments by four figures, which correspond to each other in pairs. They lift themselves out of a trellis-work, bounded on either side by a light pillar without a base. The capitals which crown the pillars recall those of the Ionic order, but the abacus is much more developed. A winged globe, stretching from pillar to pillar, roofs in this sort of little chapel; each is the shrine of a divinity. One of the divinities is that nude goddess, clasping her breasts with her hands, whom we have already met with in the Phoenician world more than once; the other is a bearded personage, whose face is framed in by his abundant hair; he appears to be dressed in a close-fitting garment, made of a material folded in narrow plaits. We do not know what name to give the personage. Each of the figures is repeated twice. The rest of the field is occupied by four distinct subjects, two of them being scenes of adoration. In one may be recognised the figure of Isis-Athor, seated on a sort of camp-stool, and giving suck to the young Horus;774 on an altar in front of the goddess is placed the disk of the moon, enveloped (as we have seen it elsewhere) by a crescent which recalls the moon's phases. Behind the altar stands a personage whose sex is not defined; the right hand, which is raised, holds a patera, while the left, which falls along the hip, has the ankh or crux ansata. Another of the scenes corresponds to this, and offers many striking analogies. The altar indeed is of a different form, but it supports exactly the same symbols. The goddess sits upon a throne with her feet on a footstool; she has no child; in one hand she holds out a cup, in the other a lotus blossom. The personage who confronts her wears a conical cap, and is clothed, like the worshipper of the corresponding representation, in a long robe pressed close to the body by a girdle à cordelière; he has also the crux ansata, and holds in the right hand an object the character and use of which I am unable to conjecture. We may associate with these two scenes of homage and worship another representation in which there figure three musicians. The instruments are the same as usual— the lyre, the tambourine, and the double pipe; two of the performers march at a steady pace; the third, the one who beats the metal(?) disk, dances, as he plays, with much vigour and spirit. In the last compartment we come again upon a group that we have already met with in one of the cups from Idalium.775 . . . A beardless individual, clothed in the shenti, has put his foot upon the body of a griffin, which, in struggling against the pressure, flings its hind quarters into the air in a sort of wild caper; the conqueror, however, holds it fast by the plume of feathers which rises from its head, and plunges his sword into its half-open beak. It is this group, drawn in relief, and on a larger scale, that we meet with for a second time on the Athenian patera; but in this case the group is augmented by a second personage, who takes part in the struggle. This is an old man with a beard who is armed with a formidable pike. Both the combatants wear conical caps upon their heads, similar to those which we have noticed as worn by a number of the statues from Cyprus; but the cap of the right-hand personage terminates in a button, whereto is attached a long appendage, which looks like the tail of an ox." The Egyptian character of much of this design is incontestable. The ankh, the lotus blossom in the hand, the winged disk, are purely Egyptian forms; the Isis Athor with Horus in her lap speaks for itself; and the worshipper in front of Isis has an unmistakably Egyptian head dress. But the contest with the winged griffin is more Assyrian than Egyptian; the seat whereon Isis sits recalls a well-known Assyrian type;776 one of the altars has a distinctly Assyrian character, while the band of musicians, the Astarté figures standing in their shrines, and the pillars which support, and frame in, the shrines are genuine Phoenician contributions. Artistically this patera is much upon a par with those from Dali and Athiénau, which have been already described.

Our space will not admit of our pursuing this subject much further. We cannot give descriptions of all the twenty pateræ,777 pronounced by the best critics to be Phoenician, which are contained in the museums of Europe and America. Excellent representations of most of these works of art will be found in Longpérier's "Musée Napoléon III.," in M. Clermont-Ganneau's "Imagerie Phénicienne," and in the "Histoire de l'Art dans l'Antiquité" of MM. Perrot et Chipiez. The bowls brought from Larnaca, from Curium, and from Amathus are especially interesting.778 We must, however, conclude our survey with a single specimen of the most elaborate kind of patera; and, this being the case, we cannot hesitate to give the preference to the famous "Cup of Præneste," which has been carefully figured and described in two of the three works above cited.779

The cup in question consists of a thin plate of silver covered over with a layer of gold; its greatest diameter is seven inches and three-fifths. The under or outside is without ornament; the interior is engraved with a number of small objects in low relief. In the centre, and surrounded by a circle of heads, there is a subject to which we shall presently have to return. The zone immediately outside this medallion, which is not quite an inch in width, is filled with a string of eight horses, all of them proceeding at a trot, and following each other to the right. Over each horse two birds fly in the same direction. The horses' tails are extraordinarily conventional, consisting of a stem with branches, and resembling a conventional palm branch. Outside this zone there is an exterior and a wider one, which is bounded on its outer edge by a huge snake, whose scaly length describes an almost exact circle, excepting towards the tail, where there are some slight sinuosities. This serpent, whose head reaches and a little passes the thin extremity of the tail, is "drawn," says M. Clermont-Ganneau, "with the hand of a master."780 It has been compared781 with the well-known Egyptian and Phoenician symbol for the {kosmos} or universe, which was a serpent with its tail in its mouth. "Naturally," he continues,782 "the outer zone by its very position offers the greatest room for development. The artist is here at his ease, and having before him a field relatively so vast, has represented on it a series of scenes, remarkably alike for the style of their execution, the diversity of their subject-matter, the number of the persons introduced, and the nature of the acts which they accomplish. . . . The scenes, however, are not, as some have imagined, a series of detached fantastic subjects, arbitrarily chosen and capriciously grouped, a mere confused mêlée of men, animals, chariots, and other objects; on the contrary, they form a little history, a plastic idyll, a story with a beginning, a middle, and an end. It is a narrative divided into nine scenes." (1) An armed hero, mounted in a car driven by a charioteer, quits in the morning a castle or fortified town. He is going to hunt, and carries his bow in his left hand. Over his head is an umbrella, the badge of his high rank, and his defence against the mid-day sun. A quiver hangs at the side of his chariot. He wears a conical cap, while the driver has his head bare, and leans forwards over the front of the car, seeming to shake the reins, and encourage the horses to mend their pace. (2) After the car has proceeded a certain distance, the hunter espies a stag upon a rocky hill. He stops his chariot, gets down, and leaving the driver in charge of the vehicle, ensconces himself behind a tree, and thus screened lets fly an arrow against the quarry, which strikes it midway in the chest. (3) Weak and bleeding copiously, the stag attempts to escape; but the hunter pursues and takes possession of him without having to shoot a second time. (4) The hour is come now for a rest. The sportsman has reached a wood, in which date-bearing palms are intermingled with trees of a different kind. He fastens his game to one of them, and proceeds to the skinning and the disembowelling. Meanwhile, his attendant detaches the horses from the car, relieves them of their harness, and proceeds to feed them from a portable manger. The car, left to itself, is tilted back, and stands with its pole in the air. (5) Food and drink having been prepared and placed on two tables, or altars, the hunter, seated on a throne under the shadow of his umbrella, pours a libation to the gods. They, on their part, scent the feast and draw near, represented by the sun and moon—a winged disk, and a crescent embracing a full orb. The feast is also witnessed by a spirit of evil, in the shape of a huge baboon or cynocephalous ape, who from a cavern at the foot of a wooded mountain, whereon a stag and a hare are feeding, furtively surveys the ceremony. (6) Remounting his chariot the hunter sets out on his return home, when the baboon quits his concealment, and rushes after him, threatening him with a huge stone. Hereupon a winged deity descends from heaven, and lifting into the air chariot, horses, charioteer, and hunter, enfolds them in an embrace and saves them. (7) The ape, baffled, pursues his way; the chariot is replaced on the earth. The hunter prepares his bow, places an arrow on the string, and hastily pursues his enemy, who is speedily overtaken and thrown to the ground by the horses. (8) The hunter dismounts, puts his foot upon the prostrate ape, and gives him the coup de grâce with a heavy axe or mace. A bird of prey hovers near, ready to descend upon the carcase. (9) The hero remounts his chariot, and returns to the castle or city which he left in the morning.783

We have now to return to the medallion which forms the centre of the cup. Within a circle of pearls or beads, similar to that separating the two zones, is a round space about two inches in diameter, divided into two compartments by a horizontal line. In the upper part are contained three human figures, and the figure of a dog. At the extreme left is a prisoner with a beard and long hair that falls upon his shoulders. His entire body is naked. Behind him his two arms are brought together, tied by a cord, and then firmly attached to a post. His knees are bent, but do not reach the ground, and his feet are placed with their soles uppermost against the post at its base. The attitude is one which implies extreme suffering.784 In front of the prisoner, occupying the centre of the medallion, is the main figure of the upper compartment, a warrior, armed with a spear, who pursues the third figure, a fugitive, and seems to be thrusting his spear into the man's back. Both have long hair, but are beardless; and wear the shenti for their sole garment. Between the legs of the main figure is a dog of the jackal kind, which has his teeth fixed in the heels of the fugitive, and arrests his flight. Below, in the second compartment, are two figures only, a man and a dog. The man is prostrate, and seems to be crawling along the ground, the dog stands partly on him, and appears to be biting his left heel. The interpretation which M. Clermont-Ganneau gives to this entire scene lacks the probability which attaches to his explanation of the outer scene. He suggests that the prisoner is the hunter of the other scene, plundered and bound by his charioteer, who is hastening away, when he is seized by his master's dog and arrested in his flight. The dog gnaws off his right foot and then attacks the left, while the fugitive, in order to escape his tormentor, has to crawl along the ground. But M. Clermont-Ganneau himself distrusts his interpretation,785 while he has convinced no other scholar of its soundness. Judicious critics will be content to wait the further researches which he promises, whereby additional light may perhaps be thrown on this obscure matter.

In its artistic character the "cup of Præneste" claims a high place among the works of art probably or certainly assignable to the Phoenicians. The relief is high; the forms, especially the animal ones, are spirited and well-proportioned. The horses are especially good. As M. Clermont-Ganneau says, "their forms and their movements are indicated with a great deal of precision and truth."786 They show also a fair amount of variety; they stand, they walk, they trot, they gallop at full speed, always truthfully and naturally. The stag, the hare, and the dog are likewise well portrayed; the ape has less merit; he is too human, too like a mere unkempt savage. The human forms are about upon a par with those of the Assyrians and Egyptians, which have evidently served for their models, the Assyrian for the outer zone, the Egyptian for the medallion. The encircling snake, as already observed, is a masterpiece. There is no better drawing in any of the other pateræ. At best they equal, they certainly do not surpass, the Prænestine specimen.

The intaglios of the Phoenicians are either on cylinders or on gems, and can rarely be distinguished, unless they are accompanied by an inscription, from the similar objects obtained in such abundance from Babylonia and Assyria. They reproduce, with scarcely any variation, the mythological figures and emblems native to those countries—the forms of gods and priests, of spirits of good and evil, of kings contending with lions, of sacred trees, winged circles, and the like—scarcely ever introducing any novelty. The greater number of the cylinders are very rudely cut. They have been worked simply by means of a splinter of obsidian,787 and are barbarous in execution, though interesting to the student of archaic art. The subjoined are specimens. No. 1 represents a four-winged genius of the Assyrian type, bearded, and clad in a short tunic and a long robe, seizing with either hand a winged griffin, or spirit of evil, and reducing them to subjection. In the field, towards the two upper corners, are the same four Phoenician characters, twice repeated; they designate, no doubt, the owner of the cylinder, which he probably used as a seal, and are read as Harkhu.788 No. 2, which is better cut than No. 1, represents a king of the Persian (Achæmenian) type,789 who stands between two rampant lions, and seizes each by the forelock. Behind the second lion is a sacred tree of a type that is not uncommon; and behind the tree is an inscription, which has been read as l'Baletân—i.e. "(the seal) of Baletan."790 This cylinder was found recently in the Lebanon.791 Nos. 3 and 4 come from Salamis in Cyprus, where they were found by M. Alexandre Di Cesnola,792 the brother of the General. No. 3 represents a robed figure holding two nondescript animals by the hind legs; the creatures writhe in his grasp, and turn their heads towards him, as though wishing to bite. The remainder of the field is filed with detached objects, scattered at random—two human forms, a griffin, two heads of oxen, a bird, two balls, three crosses, a sceptre, &c. The forms are, all of them, very rudely traced. No. 4 resembles in general character No. 3, but is even ruder. Three similar robed figures hold each other's hands and perhaps execute a dance around some religious object. Two heads of oxen or cows, with a disk between their horns, occupy the spaces intervening between the upper parts of the figures. In the lower portion of the field, the sun and moon fill the middle space, the sun, moon, and five planets the spaces to the right and to the left. Another cylinder from the same place (No. 5)793 is tolerably well designed and engraved. It shows us two persons, a man and a woman, in the act of presenting a dove to a female, who is probably the goddess Astarté, and who willingly receives it at their hands. Behind Astarté a seated lion echoes the approval of the goddess by raising one of his fore paws, while a griffin, who wholly disapproves of the offering, turns his back in disgust.

On another cylinder, which is certainly Phoenician, a rude representation of a sacred tree occupies the central position. To the left stands a worshipper with the right hand upraised, clad in a very common Assyrian dress. Over the sacred tree is a coarse specimen of the winged circle or disk, with head and tail, and fluttering ends of ribbon.794 On either side stand two winged genii, dressed in long robes, and tall stiff caps, such as are often seen on the heads of Persians in the Persepolitan sculptures, and on the darics.795 In the field is a Phoenician inscription, which is read as {...} or Irphael ben Hor'adad, "Irphael, the son of Horadad."796 Phoenician cylinders are in glass, green serpentine, cornaline, black hæmatite, steatite, and green jasper.797 They are scratched rather than deeply cut, and cannot be said ever to attain to any considerable artistic beauty. Those which have been here given are among the best; and they certainly fall short, both in design and workmanship, of many Assyrian, Babylonian, and even Persian specimens.

The gems, on the other hand, are in many cases quite equal to the Assyrian. There is one of special merit, which has been pronounced "an exquisite specimen of Phoenician lapidary art,"798 figured by General Di Cesnola in his "Cyprus."799 Two men in regular Assyrian costume, standing on either side of a "Sacred Tree," grasp, each of them, a branch of it. Above is a winged circle, with the wings curved so as to suit the shape of the gem. Below is an ornament, which is six times repeated, like the blossom of a flower; and below this is a trelliswork. The whole is cut deeply and sharply. Its Phoenician authorship is assured by its being an almost exact repetition of a group upon the silver patera found at Amathus.7100 Of other gems equally well engraved the following are specimens. No. 1 is a scarab of cornaline found by M. de Vogüé in Phoenicia Proper.7101 Two male figures in Assyrian costume face each other, their advanced feet crossing. Both hold in one hand the ankh or symbol of life. One has in the left hand what is thought to be a lotus blossom. The other has the right hand raised in the usual attitude of adoration. Between the figures, wherever there was space for them, are Phoenician characters, which are read as {...}, or l'Beka—i.e. "(the seal) of Beka."7102 No. 2, which has been set in a ring, is one of the many scarabs brought by General Di Cesnola from Cyprus.7103 It contains the figure of a hind, suckling her fawn, and is very delicately carved. The hind, however, is in an impossible attitude, the forelegs being thrown forwards, probably in order to prevent them from interfering with the figure of the fawn. Above the hind is an inscription, which appears to be in the Cyprian character, and which gives (probably) the name of the owner. No. 3 introduces us to domestic life. A grand lady, of Tyre perhaps or Sidon,7104 by name Akhot-melek, seated upon an elegant throne, with her feet upon a footstool, and dressed in a long robe which envelops the whole of her figure, receives at the hands of a female attendant a bowl or wine-cup, which the latter has just filled from an oenochoë of elegant shape, still held in her left hand. The attendant wears a striped robe reaching to the feet, and over it a tunic fastened round the waist with a belt. Her hair flows down on her shoulders, while that of her mistress is confined by a band, from which depends an ample veil, enveloping the cheeks, the back of the head, and the chin. We are told that such veils are still worn in the Phoenician country.7105 An inscription, in a late form of the Phoenician character, surrounds the two figures, and is read as {...} or l'Akhot-melek ishat Joshua(?)—i.e. "(the seal) of Akhot-melek, wife of Joshua."7106 No. 4 contains the figure of a lion, cut with much spirit. MM. Perrot et Chipiez say of it—"Among the numerous representations of lions that have been discovered in Phoenicia, there is none which can be placed on a par with that on the scarab bearing the name of 'Ashenel: small as it is, this lion has something of the physiognomy of those magnificent ones which we have borrowed from the bas-reliefs of the Assyrians. Still, the intaglio is in other respects decidedly Phoenician and not Assyrian. Observe, for instance, the beetle with the wings expanded, which fills up the lower part of the field; this is a motive borrowed from Egypt, which a Ninevite lapidary would certainly not have put in such a place."7107 The Phoenician inscription takes away all doubt as to the nationality. It reads as {...}, or 'Ashenêl, and no doubt designates the owner. No. 5 is beautifully engraved on a chalcedony. It represents a stag attacked by a griffin, which has jumped suddenly on its back. The drawing is excellent, both of the real and of the imaginary animal, and leaves nothing to be desired. The inscription, which occupies the upper part of the field to the right, is in Cyprian characters, and shows that the gem was the signet of a certain Akestodaros.7108

There are some Phoenician gems which are interesting from their subject matter without being especially good as works of art. One of these contains a representation of two men fighting.7109 Both are armed with two spears, and both carry round shields or bucklers. The warrior to the right wears a conical helmet, and is thought to be a native Cyprian;7110 he carries a shield without an umbo or boss. His adversary on the left wears a loose cap, or hood, the {pilos apages} of Herodotus,7111 and has a prominent umbo in the middle of his shield. He probably represents a Persian, and appears to have received a wound from his antagonist, which is causing him to sink to the ground. This gem was found at Curium in Cyprus by General Di Cesnola.

Another, found at the same place, exhibits a warrior, or a hunter, going forth to battle or to the chase in his chariot.7112 A large quiver full of arrows is slung at each side of his car. The warrior and his horse (one only is seen) are rudely drawn, but the chariot is very distinctly made out, and has a wheel of an Assyrian type. The Salaminians of Cyprus were famous for their war chariots,7113 of which this may be a representation.

The island of Sardinia has furnished a prodigious number of Phoenician seals. A single private collection contains as many as six hundred.7114 They are mostly scarabs, and the type of them is mostly Egyptian. Sometimes they bear the forms of Egyptian gods, as Horus, or Thoth, or Anubis;7115 sometimes cartouches with the names of kings as Menkara, Thothmes III., Amenophis III., Seti I., &c.;7116 sometimes mere sacred emblems, as the winged uræus, the disk between two uræi,7117 and the like. Occasionally there is the representation of a scene with which the Egyptian bas-reliefs have made us familiar:7118 a warrior has caught hold of his vanquished and kneeling enemy by a lock of his hair, and threatens him with an axe or mace, which he brandishes above his head. Or a lion takes the place of the captive man, and is menaced in the same way. Human figures struggling with lions, and lions killing wild bulls, are also common;7119 but the type in these cases is less Egyptian than Oriental.

Phoenician painting was not, like Egyptian, displayed upon the walls of temples, nor was it, like Greek, the production of actual pictures for the decoration of houses. It was employed to a certain extent on statues, not so as to cover the entire figure, but with delicacy and discretion, for the marking out of certain details, and the emphasising of certain parts of the design.7120 The hair and beard were often painted a brownish red; the pupil of the eye was marked by means of colour; and robes had often a border of red or blue. Statuettes were tinted more generally, whole vestments being sometimes coloured red or green,7121 and a gay effect being produced, which is said to be agreeable and harmonious.7122 But the nearest approach to painting proper which was made by the Phoenicians was upon their vessels in clay, in terra-cotta, and in alabaster. Here, though, the ornamentation was sometimes merely by patterns or bands,7123 there were occasionally real attempts to depict animal and human forms, which, if not very successful, still possess considerable interest. The noble amphora from Curium, figured by Di Cesnola,7124 contains above forty representations of horses, and nearly as many of birds. The shape of the horse is exceedingly conventional, the whole form being attenuated in the highest degree; but the animal is drawn with spirit, and the departure from nature is clearly intentional. In the animals that are pasturing, the general attitude is well seized; the movement is exactly that of the horse when he stretches his neck to reach and crop the grass.7125 In the birds there is equal spirit and greater truth to nature: they are in various attitudes, preening their feathers, pecking the ground, standing with head erect in the usual way. Other vases contain figures of cows, goats, stags, fish and birds of various kinds, while one has an attempt at a hippopotamus. The attempts to represent the human form are certainly not happy; they remind us of the more ambitious efforts of Chinese and Japanese art.

CHAPTER VIII—INDUSTRIAL ART AND MANUFACTURES

Phoenician textile fabrics, embroidered or dyed—Account of the chief Phoenician dye—Mollusks from which the purple was obtained—Mode of obtaining them—Mode of procuring the dye from them—Process of dyeing—Variety of the tints—Manufacture of glass—Story of its invention—Three kinds of Phoenician glass—1. Transparent colourless glass—2. Semi-transparent coloured glass—3. Opaque glass, much like porcelain—Description of objects in glass—Methods pursued in the manufacture—Phoenician ceramic art—Earliest specimens—Vases with geometrical designs—Incised patterning—Later efforts—Use of enamel—Great amphora of Curium—Phoenician ceramic art disappointing—Ordinary metallurgy—Implements—Weapons—Toilet articles—Lamp-stands and tripods—Works in iron and lead.

Phoenicia was celebrated from a remote antiquity for the manufacture of textile fabrics. The materials which she employed for them were wool, linen yarn, perhaps cotton, and, in the later period of her commercial prosperity, silk. The "white wool" of Syria was supplied to her in abundance by the merchants of Damascus,81 and wool of lambs, rams, and goats seems also to have been furnished by the more distant parts of Arabia.82 Linen yarn may have been imported from Egypt, where it was largely manufactured, and was of excellent quality;83 while raw silk is said to have been "brought to Tyre and Berytus by the Persian merchants, and there both dyed and woven into cloaks."84 The price of silk was very high, and it was customary in Phoenicia to intermix the precious material either with linen or with cotton;85 as is still done to a certain extent in modern times. It is perhaps doubtful whether, so far as the mere fabric of stuffs was concerned, the products of the Phoenician looms were at all superior to those which Egypt and Babylonia furnished, much less to those which came from India, and passed under the name of Sindones. Two things gave to the Phoenician stuffs that high reputation which caused them to be more sought for than any others; and these were, first, the brilliancy and beauty of their colours, and, secondly, the delicacy with which they were in many instances embroidered. We have not much trace of Phoenician embroidery on the representations of dresses that have come down to us; but the testimony of the ancients is unimpeachable,86 and we may regard it as certain that the art of embroidery, known at a very early date to the Hebrews,87 was cultivated with great success by their Phoenician neighbours, and under their auspices reached a high point of perfection. The character of the decoration is to be gathered from the extant statues and bas-reliefs, from the representations on pateræ, on cups, dishes, and gems. There was a tendency to divide the surface to be ornamented into parallel stripes or bands, and to repeat along the line a single object, or two alternately. Rosettes, monsters of various kinds, winged globes with uræi, scarabs, sacred trees, and garlands or blossoms of the lotus were the ordinary "motives."88 Occasionally human figures might be introduced, and animal forms even more frequently; but a stiff conventionalism prevailed, the same figures were constantly repeated, and the figures themselves had in few cases much beauty.

The brilliancy and beauty of the Phoenician coloured stuffs resulted from the excellency of their dyes. Here we touch a second branch of their industrial skill, for the principal dyes used were originally invented and continuously fabricated by the Phoenicians themselves, not imported from any foreign country. Nature had placed along the Phoenician coast, or at any rate along a great portion of it, an inexhaustible supply of certain shell-fish, or molluscs, which contained as a part of their internal economy a colouring fluid possessing remarkable, and indeed unique, qualities. Some account has been already given of the species which are thought to have been anciently most esteemed. They belong, mainly, to the two allied families of the Murex and the Buccinum or Purpura. Eight species of the former, and six of the latter, having their habitat in the Mediterranean, have been distinguished by some naturalists;89 but two of the former only, and one of the latter, appear to have attracted the attention of the Phoenicians. The Murex brandaris is now thought to have borne away the palm from all the others; it is extremely common upon the coast; and enormous heaps of the shells are found, especially in the vicinity of Tyre, crushed and broken—the débris, as it would seem, cast away by the manufacturers of old.810 The Murex trunculus, according to some, is just as abundant, in a crushed state, in the vicinity of Sidon, great banks of it existing, which are a hundred yards long and several yards thick.811 It is a more spinous shell than the M. brandaris, having numerous projecting points, and a generally rough and rugged appearance. The Purpura employed seems to have been the P. lapillus, a mollusc not confined to the Mediterranean, but one which frequents also our own shores, and was once turned to some account in Ireland.812 The varieties of the P. lapillus differ considerably. Some are nearly white, some greyish, others buff striped with brown. Some, again, are smooth, others nearly as rough as the Murex trunculus. The Helix ianthina, which is included by certain writers among the molluscs employed for dyeing purposes by the Phoenicians,813 is a shell of a completely different character, smooth and delicate, much resembling that of an ordinary land snail, and small compared to the others. It is not certain, however, that the helix, though abounding in the Eastern Mediterranean,814 ever attracted the notice of the Phoenicians.

The molluscs needed by the Phoenician dyers were not obtained without some difficulty. As the Mediterranean has no tides, it does not uncover its shores at low water like the ocean, or invite man to rifle them. The coveted shell-fish, in most instances, preferred tolerably deep water; and to procure them in any quantity it was necessary that they should be fished up from a depth of some fathoms. The mode in which they were captured was the following. A long rope was let down into the sea, with baskets of reeds or rushes attached to it at intervals, constructed like our lobster-traps or eel-baskets, with an opening that yielded easily to pressure from the outside, but resisted pressure from the inside, and made escape, when once the trap was entered, impossible. The baskets were baited with mussels or frogs, both of which had great attractions for the Purpuræ, and were seized and devoured with avidity. At the upper end of the rope was attached to a large piece of cork, which, even when the baskets were full, could not be drawn under water. It was usual to set the traps in the evening, and after waiting a night, or sometimes a night and a day, to draw them up to the surface, when they were generally found to be full of the coveted shell-fish.815

There were two ways in which the dye was obtained from the molluscs. Sometimes a hole was broken in the side of the shell, and the fish taken out entire.816 The sac containing the colouring matter, which is a sort of vein, beginning at the head of the animal, and following the tortuous line of the body as it twists through the spiral shell,817 was then carefully extracted, either while the mollusc was still alive, or as soon as possible after death, as otherwise the quality of the dye was impaired. This plan was pursued more especially with the larger species of Purpuræ, where the sac attained a certain size; while with a smaller kinds a different method was followed. In their case no attempt was made to extract the sac, but the entire fish was crushed, together with its shell, and after salt had been added in the proportion of twenty ounces to a hundred pounds of the pulp, three days were allowed for maceration; heat was then applied, and when, by repeated skimming, the coarse particles had been removed, the dye was left in a liquid state at the bottom. It was necessary that the vessel in which this final process took place should be of lead, and not of bronze or iron, since those metals gave the dye a disagreeable tinge.818

The colouring matter contained in the sac of the Purpuræ is a liquid of a creamy consistency, and of a yellowish-white hue. On extraction, it is at first decidedly yellow; then after a little time it becomes green; and, finally, it settles into some shade of violet or purple. Chemical analysis has shown that in the case of the Murex trunculus the liquid is composed of two elementary substances, one being cyanic acid, which is of a blue or azure colour, and the other being purpuric oxide, which is a bright red.819 In the case of the Murex brandaris one element only has been found: it is an oxide, which has received the name of oxyde tyrien.820 No naturalist has as yet discovered what purpose the liquid serves in the economy, or in the preservation, of the animal; it is certainly not exuded, as sepia is by the cuttle-fish, to cloud the water in the neighbourhood, and enable the creature to conceal itself.

Concerning the Phoenician process of dyeing, the accounts which have come down to us are at once confused and incomplete. Nothing is said with respect to their employment of mordants, either acid or alkali, and yet it is almost certain that they must have used one or the other, or both, to fix the colours, and render them permanent. The gamins of Tyre employ to this day mordants of each sort;821 and an alkali derived from seaweed is mentioned by Pliny as made use of for fixing some dyes,822 though he does not distinctly tell us that it was known to the Phoenicians or employed in fixing the purple. What we chiefly learn from this writer as to the dyeing process is823—first, that sometimes the liquid derived from the murex only, sometimes that of the purpura or buccinum only, was applied to the material which it was wished to colour, while the most approved hue was produced by an application of both dyes separately. Secondly, we are told that the material, whatever it might be, was steeped in the dye for a certain number of hours, then withdrawn for a while, and afterwards returned to the vat and steeped a second time. The best Tyrian cloths were called Dibapha, i.e. "twice dipped;" and for the production of the true "Tyrian purple" it was necessary that the dye obtained from the Buccinum should be used after that from the Murex had been applied. The Murex alone gave a dye that was firm, and reckoned moderately good; but the Buccinum alone was weak, and easily washed out.

The actual tints produced from the shell-fish appear to have ranged from blue, through violet and purple, to crimson and rose.824 Scarlet could not be obtained, but was yielded by the cochineal insect. Even for the brighter sorts of crimson some admixture of the cochineal dye was necessary.825 The violet tint was not generally greatly prized, though there was a period in the reign of Augustus when it was the fashion;826 redder hues were commonly preferred; and the choicest of all is described as "a rich, dark purple, the colour of coagulated blood."827

A deep crimson was also in request, and seems frequently to be intended when the term purple ({porphureos}, purpureus) is used.

A third industry greatly affected by the Phoenicians was the manufacture of glass. According to Pliny,828 the first discovery of the substance was made upon the Phoenician coast by a body of sailors whom he no doubt regarded as Phoenicians. These persons had brought a cargo of natrum, which is the subcarbonate of soda, to the Syrian coast in the vicinity of Acre, and had gone ashore at the mouth of the river Belus to cook their dinner. Having lighted a fire upon the sand, they looked about for some stones to prop up their cooking utensils, but finding none, or none convenient for the purpose, they bethought themselves of utilising for the occasion some of the blocks of natrum with which their ship was laden. These were placed close to the fire, and the heat was sufficient to melt a portion of one of them, which, mixing with the siliceous sand at its base, produced a stream of glass. There is nothing impossible or even very improbable in this story; but we may question whether the scene of it is rightly placed. Glass was manufactured in Egypt many centuries before the probable date of the Phoenician occupation of the Mediterranean coast; and, if the honour of the invention is to be assigned to a particular people, the Egyptians would seem to have the best claim to it. The process of glass-blowing is represented in tombs at Beni Hassan of very great antiquity,829 and a specimen of Egyptian glass is in existence bearing the name of a Usurtasen, a king of the twelfth dynasty.830 Natrum, moreover, was an Egyptian product, well known from a remote date, being the chief ingredient used in the various processes of embalming.831 Phoenicia has no natrum, and not even any vegetable alkali readily procurable in considerable quantity. There may have been an accidental discovery of glass in Phoenicia, but priority of discovery belonged almost certainly to Egypt; and it is, upon the whole, most probable that Phoenicia derived from Egypt her knowledge both of the substance itself and of the method of making it. Still, there can be no doubt that the manufacture was one on which the Phoenicians eagerly seized, and which they carried out on a large scale and very successfully. Sidon, according to the ancients,832 was the chief seat of the industry; but the best sand is found near Tyre, and both Tyre and Sarepta also seem to have been among the places where glassworks were early established. At Sarepta extensive banks of débris have been found, consisting of broken glass of many colours, the waste beyond all doubt of a great glass manufactory;833 at Tyre, the traces of the industry are less extensive,834 but on the other hand we have historical evidence that it continued to be practised there into the middle ages.835

The glass produced by the Phoenicians was of three kinds: first, transparent colourless glass, which the eye could see through; secondly, translucent coloured glass, through which light could pass, though the eye could not penetrate it so as to distinguish objects; and, thirdly, opaque glass, scarcely distinguishable from porcelain. Transparent glass was employed for mirrors, round plates being cast, which made very tolerable looking-glasses,836 when covered at the back by thin sheets of metal, and also for common objects, such as vases, urns, bottles, and jugs, which have been yielded in abundance by tombs of a somewhat late date in Cyprus.837 No great store, however, seems to have been set upon transparency, in which the Oriental eye saw no beauty; and the objects which modern research has recovered under this head at Tyre, in Cyprus, and elsewhere, seem the work of comparatively rude artists, and have little æsthetic merit. The shapes, however, are not inelegant.

The most beautiful of the objects in glass produced by the Phoenicians are the translucent or semi-transparent vessels of different kinds, most of them variously coloured, which have been found in Cyprus, at Camirus in Rhodes, and on the Syrian coast, near Beyrout and elsewhere.838 These comprise small flasks or bottles, from three to six inches long, probably intended to contain perfumes; small jugs (oenochoæ) from three inches in height to five inches; vases of about the same size; amphoræ pointed at the lower extremity; and other varieties. They are coloured, generally, either in longitudinal or in horizontal stripes and bands; but the bands often deviate from the straight line into zig-zags, which are always more or less irregular, like the zig-zags of the Norman builders, while sometimes they are deflected into crescents, or other curves, as particularly one resembling a willow-leaf. The colours are not very vivid, but are pleasing and well-contrasted; they are chiefly five—white, blue, yellow, green, and a purplish brown. Red scarcely appears, except in a very pale, pinkish form; and even in this form it is uncommon. Blue, on the other hand, is greatly affected, being sometimes used in the patterns, often taken for the ground, and occasionally, in two tints, forming both groundwork and ornamentation.839 It is not often that more than three hues are found on the same vessel, and sometimes the hues employed are only two. There are instances, however, and very admirable instances, of the employment, on a single vessel, of four hues.840

The colours were obtained, commonly, at any rate, from metallic oxides. The ordinary blue employed is cobalt, though it is suspected that there was an occasional use of copper. Copper certainly furnished the greens, while manganese gave the brown, which shades off into purple and into black. The beautiful milky white which forms the ground tint of some vases is believed to have been derived from the oxide of tin, or else from phosphate of chalk. It is said that the colouring matter of the patterns does not extend through the entire thickness of the glass, but lies only on the outer surface, being a later addition to the vessels as first made. Translucent coloured glass was also largely produced by the Phoenicians for beads and other ornaments, and also for the imitation of gems. The huge emerald of which Herodotus speaks,841 as "shining with great brilliancy at night" in the temple of Melkarth at Tyre, was probably a glass cylinder, into which a lamb was introduced by the priests. In Phoenician times the pretended stone is quite as often a glass paste as a real gem, and the case is the same with the scarabs so largely used as seals. In Phoenician necklaces, glass beads alternate frequently with real agates, onyxes, and crystals; while sometimes glass in various shapes is the only material employed. A necklace found at Tharros in Sardinia, and now in the collection of the Louvre, which is believed to be of Phoenician manufacture, is composed of above forty beads, two cylinders, four pendants representing heads of bulls, and one representing the face of a man, all of glass.842 Another, found by M. Renan in Phoenicia itself, is made up of glass beads imitating pearls, intermixed with beads of cornaline and agate.843

Another class of glass ornaments consists of small flat plaques or plates, pierced with a number of fine holes, which appear to have been sewn upon garments. These are usually patterned, sometimes with spirals, sometimes with rosettes, occasionally, though rarely, with figures. Messrs. Perrot and Chipiez represent one in their great work upon ancient art,844 where almost the entire field is occupied by a winged griffin, standing upright on its two hind legs, and crowned with a striped cap, or turban.

Phoenician opaque glass is comparatively rare, and possesses but little beauty. It was rendered opaque in various ways. Messrs. Perrot and Chipiez found that in a statue of Serapis, which they analysed, the glass was mixed with bronze in the proportions of ten to three. An opaque material of a handsome red colour was thus produced, which was heavy and exceedingly hard.845

The methods pursued by the Phoenician glass-manufacturers were probably much the same as those which are still employed for the production of similar objects, and involved the use of similar implements, as the blowpipe, the lathe, and the graver. The materials having been procured, they were fused together in a crucible or melting-pot by the heat of a powerful furnace. A blowpipe was then introduced into the viscous mass, a portion of which readily attached itself to the implement, and so much glass was withdrawn as was deemed sufficient for the object which it was designed to manufacture. The blower then set to work, and blew hard into the pipe until the glass at its lower extremity began to expand and gradually took a pear-shaped form, the material partially coolling and hardening, but still retaining a good deal of softness and pliability. While in this condition, it was detached from the pipe, and modelled with pincers or with the hand into the shape required, after which it was polished, and perhaps sometimes cut by means of the turning-lathe. Sand and emery were the chief polishers, and by their help a surface was produced, with which little fault could be found, being smooth, uniform, and brilliant. Thus the vessel was formed, and if no further ornament was required, the manufacture was complete—a jug, vase, alabastron, amphora, was produced, either transparent or of a single uniform tint, which might be white, blue, brown, green, &c., according to the particular oxide which had been thrown, with the silica and alkali, into the crucible. Generally, however, the manufacturer was not content with so simple a product: he aimed not merely at utility, but at beauty, and proceeded to adorn the work of his hands— whatever it was—with patterns which were for the most part in good taste and highly pleasing. These patterns he first scratched on the outer surface of the vessel with a graving tool; then, when he had made his depressions deep enough, he took threads of coloured glass, and having filled up with the threads the depressions which he had made, he subjected the vessel once more to such a heat that the threads were fused, and attached themselves to the ground on which they had been laid. In melting they would generally more than fill the cavities, overflowing them, and protruding from them, whence it was for the most part necessary to repeat the polishing process, and to bring by means of abrasion the entire surface once more into uniformity. There are cases where this has been incompletely done and where the patterns project; there are others where the threads have never thoroughly melted into the ground, and where in the course of time they have partially detached themselves from it; but in general the fusion and subsequent polishing have been all that could be wished, and the patterns are perfectly level with the ground and seem one with it.846

The running of liquid glass into moulds, so common nowadays, does not seem to have been practised by the Phoenicians, perhaps because their furnaces were not sufficiently hot to produce complete liquefaction. But—if this was so—the pressure of the viscous material into moulds cannot have been unknown, since we have evidence of the existence of moulds,847 and there are cases where several specimens of an object have evidently issued from a single matrix.848 Beads, cylinders, pendants, scarabs, amulets, were probably, all of them, made in this way, sometimes in translucent, sometimes in semi-opaque glass, as perhaps were also the plaques which have been already described.

The ceramic art of the Phoenicians is not very remarkable. Phoenicia Proper is deficient in clay of a superior character, and it was probably a very ordinary and coarse kind of pottery that the Phoenician merchants of early times exported regularly in their trading voyages, both inside and outside the Mediterranean. We hear of their carrying this cheap earthenware northwards to the Cassiterides or Scilly Islands,849 and southwards to the isle of Cerné, which is probably Arguin, on the West African coast;850 nor can we doubt that they supplied it also to the uncivilised races of the Mediterranean—the Illyrians, Ligurians, Sicels, Sards, Corsicans, Spaniards, Libyans. But the fragile nature of the material, and its slight value, have caused its entire disappearance in the course of centuries, unless in the shape of small fragments; nor are these fragments readily distinguishable from those whose origin is different. Phoenicia Proper has furnished no earthen vessels, either whole or in pieces, that can be assigned to a time earlier than the Greco-Roman period,851 nor have any such vessels been found hitherto on Phoenician sites either in Sardinia, or in Corsica, or in Spain, or Africa, or Sicily, or Malta, or Gozzo. The only places that have hitherto furnished earthen vases or other vessels presumably Phoenician are Jerusalem, Camirus in Rhodes, and Cyprus; and it is from the specimens found at these sites that we must form our estimate of the Phoenician pottery. The earliest specimens are of a moderately good clay, unglazed. They are regular in shape, being made by the help of a wheel, and for the most part not inelegant, though they cannot be said to possess any remarkable beauty. Many are without ornament of any kind, being apparently mere jars, used for the storing away of oil or wine; they have sometimes painted or scratched upon them, in Phoenician characters, the name of the maker or owner. A few rise somewhat above the ordinary level, having handles of some elegance, and being painted with designs and patterns, generally of a geometrical character. A vase about six inches high, found at Jerusalem, has, between horizontal bands, a series of geometric patterns, squares, octagons, lozenges, triangles, pleasingly arranged, and painted in brown upon a ground which is of a dull grey. At the top are two rude handles, between which runs a line of zig-zag, while at the bottom is a sort of stand or base. The shape is heavy and inelegant.852

Another vase of a similar character to this, but superior in many respects, was found by General Di Cesnola at Dali (Idalium), and is figured in his "Cyprus."853 This vase has the shape of an urn, and is ornamented with horizontal bands, except towards the middle, where it has its greatest diameter, and exhibits a series of geometric designs. In the centre is a lozenge, divided into four smaller lozenges by a St. Andrew's cross; other compartments are triangular, and are filled with a chequer of black and white, resembling the squares of a chessboard. Beyond, on either side, are vertical bands, diversified with a lozenge ornament. Two hands succeed, of a shape that is thought to have "a certain elegance."854 There is a rim, which might receive a cover, at top, and at bottom a short pedestal. The height of the vase is about thirteen inches.

In many of the Cyprian vases having a geometric decoration, the figures are not painted on the surface but impressed or incised. Messrs. Perrot and Chipiez regard this form of ornamentation as the earliest; but the beauty and finish of several vases on which it occurs is against the supposition. There is scarcely to be found, even in the range of Greek art, a more elegant form than that of the jug in black clay brought by General Di Cesnola from Alambra and figured both in his "Cyprus"855 and in the "Histoire de l'Art."856 Yet its ornamentation is incised. If, then, incised patterning preceded painted in Phoenicia, at any rate it held its ground after painting was introduced, and continued in vogue even to the time when Greek taste had largely influenced Phoenician art of every description.

The finest Phoenician efforts in ceramic art resemble either the best Egyptian or the best Greek. As the art advanced, the advantage of a rich glaze was appreciated, and specimens which seem to be Phoenician have all the delicacy and beauty of the best Egyptian faïence. A cup found at Idalium, plain on the outside, is covered internally with a green enamel, on which are patterns and designs in black.857 In a medallion at the bottom of the cup is the representation of a marshy tract overgrown with the papyrus plant, whereof we see both the leaves and blossoms, while among them, rushing at full speed, is the form of a wild boar. The rest of the ornamentation consists chiefly of concentric circles; but between two of the circles is left a tolerably broad ring, which has a pattern consisting of a series of broadish leaves pointing towards the cup's centre. Nothing can be more delicate, or in better taste, than the entire design.

The most splendid of all the Cyprian vases was found at Curium, and has been already represented in this volume. It is an amphora of large dimensions, ornamented in part with geometrical designs, in part with compartments, in which are represented horses and birds. The form, the designs, and the general physiognomy of the amphora are considered to be in close accordance with Athenian vases of the most antique school. The resemblance is so great that some have supposed the vase to have been an importation from Attica into Cyprus;858 but such conjectures are always hazardous; and the principal motives of the design are so frequent on the Cyprian vases, that the native origin of the vessel is at least possible, and the judgment of some of the best critics seems to incline in this direction.

Still, on the whole, the Cyprian ceramic art is somewhat disappointing. What is original in it is either grotesque, as the vases in the shape of animals,859 or those crowned by human heads,860 or those again which have for spout a female figure pouring liquid out of a jug.861 What is superior has the appearance of having been borrowed. Egyptian, Assyrian, and Greek art, each in turn, furnished shapes, designs, and patterns to the Phoenician potters, who readily adopted from any and every quarter the forms and decorations which hit their fancy. Their fancy was, predominantly, for the bizarre and the extravagant. Vases in the shape of helmets, in the shape of barrels, in the shape of human heads,862 have little fitness, and in the Cyprian specimens have little beauty; the mixture of Assyrian with Egyptian forms is incongruous; the birds and beasts represented are drawn with studied quaintness, a quaintness recalling the art of China and Japan. If there is elegance in some of the forms, it is seldom a very pronounced elegance; and, where the taste is best, the suspicion continually arises that a foreign model has been imitated. Moreover, from first to last the art makes little progress. There seems to have been an arrest of development.863 The early steps are taken, but at a certain point stagnation sets in; there is no further attempt to improve or advance; the artists are content to repeat themselves, and reproduce the patterns of the past. Perhaps there was no demand for ceramic art of a higher order. At any rate, progress ceases, and while Greece was rising to her grandest efforts, Cyprus, and Phoenicia generally, were content to remain stationary.

Besides their ornamental metallurgy, which has been treated of in a former chapter, the Phoenicians largely employed several metals, especially bronze and copper, in the fabrication of vessels for ordinary use, of implements, arms, toilet articles, furniture, &c. The vessels include pateræ, bowls, jugs, amphoræ, and cups;864 the implements, hatchets, adzes, knives, and sickles;865 the arms, spearheads, arrowheads, daggers, battle-axes, helmets, and shields;866 the toilet articles, mirrors, hand-bells, buckles, candlesticks, &c.;867 the furniture, tall candelabra, tripods, and thrones.868 The bronze is of an excellent quality, having generally about nine parts of copper to one of tin; and there is reason to believe that by the skilful tempering of the Phoenician metallurgists, it attained a hardness which was not often given it by others. The Cyprian shields were remarkable. They were of a round shape, slightly convex, and instead of the ordinary boss, had a long projecting cone in the centre. An actual shield, with the cone perfect, was found by General Di Cesnola at Amathus,869 and a projection of the same kind is seen in several of the Sardinian bronze and terra-cotta statuettes.870 Shields were sometimes elaborately embossed, in part with patterning, in part with animal and vegetable forms.871 Helmets were also embossed with care, and sometimes inscribed with the name of the maker or the owner.872

Some remains of swords, probably Phoenician, have been found in Sardinia. They vary from two feet seven inches to four feet two inches in length.873 The blade is commonly straight, and very thick in the centre, but tapers off on both sides to a sharp edge. The point is blunt, so that the intention cannot have been to use the weapon both for cutting and thrusting, but only for the former. It would scarcely make such a clean cut as a modern broadsword, but would no doubt be equally effectual for killing or disabling. Another weapon, found in Sardinia, and sometimes called a sword, is more properly a knife or dagger. In length it does not exceed seven or eight inches, and of this length more than a third is occupied by the handle.874 Below the handle the blade broadens for about an inch or an inch and a half; after this it contracts, and tapers gently to a sharp point. Such a weapon appears sometimes in the hand of a statuette.875

The bronze articles of the toilet recovered by recent researches in Cyprus and elsewhere are remarkable. The handle of a mirror found in Cyprus, and now in the Museum of New York, possesses considerable merit. It consists mainly of a female figure, naked, and standing upon a frog.876 In her hands she holds a pair of cymbals, which she is in the act of striking together. A ribbon, passed over her left shoulder, is carried through a ring, from which hangs a seal. On her arms and shoulders appear to have stood two lions, which formed side supports to the mirror that was attached to the figure's head. If the face of the cymbal-player cannot boast of much beauty, and her figure is thought to "lack distinction," still it is granted that the tout ensemble of the work was not without originality, and may have possessed a certain amount of elegance.877 The frog is particularly well modelled.

Some candlesticks found in the Treasury of Curium,878 and a tripod from the same place, seem to deserve a short notice. The candlesticks stand upon a sort of short pillar as a base, above which is the blossom of a flower inverted, a favourite Phoenician ornament.879 From this rises the lamp-stand, composed of three leaves, which curl outwards, and support between them a ring into which the bottom of the lamp fitted. The tripod880 is more elaborate. The legs, which are fluted, bulge considerably at the top, after which they bend inwards, and form a curve like one half of a Cupid's bow. To retain them in place, they are joined together by a sort of cross-bar, about half-way in their length; while, to keep them steady, they are made to rest on large flat feet. The circular hoop which they support is of some width, and is ornamented along its entire course with a zig-zag. From the hoop depend, half-way in the spaces between the legs, three rings, from each of which there hangs a curious pendant. Besides copper and bronze, the Phoenicians seem to have worked in lead and iron, but only to a small extent. Iron ore might have been obtained in some parts of their own country, but appears to have been principally derived from abroad, especially from Spain.881 It was worked up chiefly, so far as we know, into arms offensive and defensive. The sword of Alexander, which he received as a gift from the king of Citium,882 was doubtless in this metal, which is the material of a sword found at Amathus, and of numerous arrowheads.883 We are also told that Cyprus furnished the iron breast-plates worn by Demetrius Poliorcetes;884 and in pre-Homeric times it was a Phoenician—Cinyras—who gave to Agamemnon his breast-plate of steel, gold, and tin.885 That more remains of iron arms and implements have not been found on Phoenician sites is probably owing to the rapid oxydisation of the metal, which consequently decays and disappears. The Hiram who was sent to assist Solomon in building and furnishing the Temple of Jerusalem was, we must remember, "skilful to work," not only "in gold, and silver, and bronze," but also "in iron."886 Lead was largely furnished to the Phoenicians by the Scilly Islands,887 and by Spain.888 It has not been found in any great quantity on Phoenician sites, but still appears occasionally. Sometimes it is a solder uniting stone with bronze;889 sometimes it exists in thin sheets, which may have been worn as ornaments.890 In Phoenicia Proper it has been chiefly met with in the shape of coffins,891 which are apparently of a somewhat late date. They are formed of several sheets placed one over the other and then soldered together. There is generally on the lid and sides of the coffin an external ornamentation in a low relief, wherein the myth of Psyché is said commonly to play a part; but the execution is mediocre, and the designs themselves have little merit.

CHAPTER IX—SHIPS, NAVIGATION, AND COMMERCE

Earliest navigation by means of rafts and canoes—Model of a
very primitive boat—Phoenician vessel of the time of
Sargon—Phoenician biremes in the time of Sennacherib—
Phoenician pleasure vessels and merchant ships—Superiority
of the Phoenician war-galleys—Excellence of the
arrangements—Patæci—Early navigation cautious—Increasing
boldness—Furthest ventures—Extent of the Phoenician land
commerce—Witness of Ezekiel—Wares imported—Caravans—
Description of the land trade—Sea trade of Phoenicia—1.
With her own colonies—2. With foreigners—Mediterranean and
Black Sea trade—North Atlantic trade—Trade with the West
Coast of Africa and the Canaries—Trade in the Red Sea and
Indian Ocean.

The first attempts of the Phoenicians to navigate the sea which washed their coast were probably as clumsy and rude as those of other primitive nations. They are said to have voyaged from island to island, in their original abodes within the Persian Gulf, by means of rafts.91 When they reached the shores of the Mediterranean, it can scarcely have been long ere they constructed boats for fishing and coasting purposes, though no doubt such boats were of a very rude construction. Probably, like other races, they began with canoes, roughly hewn out of the trunk of a tree. The torrents which descended from Lebanon would from time to time bring down the stems of fallen trees in their flood-time; and these, floating on the Mediterranean waters, would suggest the idea of navigation. They would, at first, be hollowed out with hatchets and adzes, or else with fire; and, later on, the canoes thus produced would form the models for the earliest efforts in shipbuilding. The great length, however, would soon be found unnecessary, and the canoe would give place to the boat, in the ordinary acceptation of the term. There are models of boats among the Phoenician remains which have a very archaic character,92 and may give us some idea of the vessels in which the Phoenicians of the remoter times braved the perils of the deep. They have a keel, not ill shaped, a rounded hull, bulwarks, a beak, and a high seat for the steersman. The oars, apparently, must have been passed through interstices in the bulwark.

From this rude shape the transition was not very difficult to the bark represented in the sculptures of Sargon,93 which is probably a Phoenician one. Here four rowers, standing to their oars, impel a vessel having for prow the head of a horse and for stern the tail of a fish, both of them rising high above the water. The oars are curved, like golf or hockey-sticks, and are worked from the gunwale of the bark, though there is no indication of rowlocks. The vessel is without a rudder; but it has a mast, supported by two ropes which are fastened to the head and stern. The mast has neither sail nor yard attached to it, but is crowned by what is called a "crow's nest"—a bell-shaped receptacle, from which a slinger or archer might discharge missiles against an enemy.94

A vessel of considerably greater size than this, but of the same class—impelled, that is, by one bank of oars only—is indicated by certain coins, which have been regarded by some critics as Phoenician, by others as belonging to Cilicia.95 These have a low bow, but an elevated stern; the prow exhibits a beak, while the stern shows signs of a steering apparatus; the number of the oars on each side is fifteen or twenty. The Greeks called these vessels triaconters or penteconters. They are represented without any mast on the coins, and thus seem to have been merely row-boats of a superior character.

About the time of Sennacherib (B.C. 700), or a little earlier, some great advances seem to have been made by the Phoenician shipbuilders. In the first place, they introduced the practice of placing the rowers on two different levels, one above the other; and thus, for a vessel of the same length, doubling the number of the rowers. Ships of this kind, which the Greeks called "biremes," are represented in Sennacherib's sculptures as employed by the inhabitants of a Phoenician city, who fly in them at the moment when their town is captured, and so escape their enemy.96 The ships are of two kinds. Both kinds have a double tier of rowers, and both are guided by two steering oars thrust out from the stern; but while the one is still without mast or sail, and is rounded off in exactly the same way both at stem and stern, the other has a mast, placed about midship, a yard hung across it, and a sail close reefed to the yard, while the bow is armed with a long projecting beak, like a ploughshare, which must have been capable of doing terrible damage to a hostile vessel. The rowers, in both classes of ships, are represented as only eight or ten upon a side; but this may have arisen from artistic necessity, since a greater number of figures could not have been introduced without confusion. It is thought that in the beaked vessel we have a representation of the Phoenician war-galley; in the vessel without a beak, one of the Phoenician transport.97

A painting on a vase found in Cyprus exhibits what would seem to have been a pleasure-vessel.98 It is unbeaked, and without any sign of oars, except two paddles for steering with. About midship is a short mast, crossed by a long spar or yard, which carries a sail, closely reefed along its entire length. The yard and sail are managed by means of four ropes, which are, however, somewhat conventionally depicted. Both the head and stern of the vessel rise to a considerable height above the water, and the stern is curved, very much as in the war-galleys. It perhaps terminated in the head of a bird.

According to the Greek writers, Phoenician vessels were mainly of two kinds, merchant ships and war-vessels.99 The merchant ships were of a broad, round make, what our sailors would call "tubs," resembling probably the Dutch fishing-boats of a century ago. They were impelled both by oars and sails, but depended mainly on the latter. Each of them had a single mast of moderate height, to which a single sail was attached;910 this was what in modern times is called a "square sail," a form which is only well suited for sailing with when the wind is directly astern. It was apparently attached to the yard, and had to be hoisted together with the yard, along which it could be closely reefed, or from which it could be loosely shaken out. It was managed, no doubt, by ropes attached to the two lower corners, which must have been held in the hands of sailors, as it would have been most dangerous to belay them. As long as the wind served, the merchant captain used his sail: when it died away, or became adverse, he dropped yard and sail on to his deck, and made use of his oars.

Merchant ships had, commonly, small boats attached to them, which afforded a chance of safety if the ship foundered, and were useful when cargoes had to be landed on a shelving shore.911 We have no means of knowing whether these boats were hoisted up on deck until they were wanted, or attached to the ships by ropes and towed after them; but the latter arrangement is the more probable.

The war-galleys of the Phoenicians in the early times were probably of the class which the Greeks called triaconters or penteconters, and which are represented upon the coins. They were long open rowboats, in which the rowers sat, all of them, upon a level, the number of rowers on either side being generally either fifteen or twenty-five. Each galley was armed at its head with a sharp metal spike, or beak, which was its chief weapon of offence, vessels of this class seeking commonly to run down their enemy. After a time these vessels were superseded by biremes, which were decked, had masts and sails, and were impelled by rowers sitting at two different elevations, as already explained. Biremes were ere long superseded by triremes, or vessels with three banks of oars, which are said to have been invented at Corinth,912 but which came into use among the Phoenicians before the end of the sixth century B.C.913 In the third century B.C. the Carthaginians employed in war quadriremes, and even quinqueremes; but there is no evidence of the employment of either class of vessel by the Phoenicians of Phoenicia Proper.

The superiority of the Phoenician ships to others is generally allowed, and was clearly shown when Xerxes collected his fleet of twelve hundred and seven triremes against Greece. The fleet included contingents from Phoenicia, Cyprus, Egypt, Cilicia, Pamphylia, Lycia, Caria, Ionia, Æolis, and the Greek settlements about the Propontis.914 When it reached the Hellespont, the great king, anxious to test the quality of his ships and sailors, made proclamation for a grand sailing match, in which all who liked might contend. Each contingent probably—at any rate, all that prided themselves on their nautical skill—selected its best vessel, and entered it for the coming race; the king himself, and his grandees and officers, and all the army, stood or sat along the shore to see: the race took place, and was won by the Phoenicians of Sidon.915 Having thus tested the nautical skill of the various nations under his sway, the great king, when he ventured his person upon the dangerous element, was careful to embark in a Sidonian galley.916

A remarkable testimony to the excellence of the Phoenician ships with respect to internal arrangements is borne by Xenophon, who puts the following words into the mouth of Ischomachus, a Greek:917 "I think that the best and most perfect arrangement of things that I ever saw was when I went to look at the great Phoenician sailing-vessel; for I saw the largest amount of naval tackling separately disposed in the smallest stowage possible. For a ship, as you well know, is brought to anchor, and again got under way, by a vast number of wooden implements and of ropes and sails the sea by means of a quantity of rigging, and is armed with a number of contrivances against hostile vessels, and carries about with it a large supply of weapons for the crew, and, besides, has all the utensils that a man keeps in his dwelling-house, for each of the messes. In addition, it is laden with a quantity of merchandise which the owner carries with him for his own profit. Now all the things which I have mentioned lay in a space not much bigger than a room which would conveniently hold ten beds. And I remarked that they severally lay in a way that they did not obstruct one another, and did not require anyone to search for them; and yet they were neither placed at random, nor entangled one with another, so as to consume time when they were suddenly wanted for use. Also, I found the captain's assistant, who is called 'the look-out man,' so well acquainted with the position of all the articles, and with the number of them, that even when at a distance he could tell where everything lay, and how many there were of each sort, just as anyone who has learnt to read can tell the number of letters in the name of Socrates and the proper place for each of them. Moreover, I saw this man, in his leisure moments, examining and testing everything that a vessel needs when at sea; so, as I was surprised, I asked him what he was about, whereupon he replied—'Stranger, I am looking to see, in case anything should happen, how everything is arranged in the ship, and whether anything is wanting, or is inconveniently situated; for when a storm arises at sea, it is not possible either to look for what is wanting, or to put to right what is arranged awkwardly.'"

Phoenician ships seem to have been placed under the protection of the Cabeiri, and to have had images of them at their stem or stern or both.918 These images were not exactly "figure-heads," as they are sometimes called. They were small, apparently, and inconspicuous, being little dwarf figures, regarded as amulets that would preserve the vessel in safety. We do not see them on any representations of Phoenician ships, and it is possible that they may have been no larger than the bronze or glazed earthenware images of Phthah that are so common in Egypt. The Phoenicians called them pittuchim, "sculptures,"919 whence the Greek {pataikoi} and the French fétiche.

The navigation of the Phoenicians, in early times, was no doubt cautious and timid. So far from venturing out of sight of land, they usually hugged the coast, ready at any moment, if the sea or sky threatened, to change their course and steer directly for the shore. On a shelving coast they were not at all afraid to run their ships aground, since, like the Greek vessels, they could be easily pulled up out of reach of the waves, and again pulled down and launched, when the storm was over and the sea calm once more. At first they sailed, we may be sure, only in the daytime, casting anchor at nightfall, or else dragging their ships up upon the beach, and so awaiting the dawn. But after a time they grew more bold. The sea became familiar to them, the positions of coasts and islands relatively one to another better known, the character of the seasons, the signs of unsettled or settled weather, the conduct to pursue in an emergency, better apprehended. They soon began to shape the course of their vessels from headland to headland, instead of always creeping along the shore, and it was not perhaps very long before they would venture out of sight of land, if their knowledge of the weather satisfied them that the wind might be trusted to continue steady, and if they were well assured of the direction of the land that they wished to make. They took courage, moreover, to sail in the night, no less than in the daytime, when the weather was clear, guiding themselves by the stars, and particularly by the Polar star,920 which they discovered to be the star most nearly marking the true north. A passage of Strabo921 seems to show that—in the later times at any rate—they had a method of calculating the rate of a ship's sailing, though what the method was is wholly unknown to us. It is probable that they early constructed charts and maps, which however they would keep secret through jealousy of their commercial rivals.

The Phoenicians for some centuries confined their navigation within the limits of the Mediterranean, the Propontis, and the Euxine, land-locked seas, which are tideless and far less rough than the open ocean. But before the time of Solomon they had passed the Pillars of Hercules, and affronted the dangers of the Atlantic.922 Their frail and small vessels, scarcely bigger than modern fishing-smacks, proceeded southwards along the West African coast, as far as the tract watered by the Gambia and Senegal, while northwards they coasted along Spain, braved the heavy seas of the Bay of Biscay, and passing Cape Finisterre, ventured across the mouth of the English Channel to the Cassiterides. Similarly, from the West African shore, they boldly steered for the Fortunate Islands (the Canaries), visible from certain elevated points of the coast, though at 170 miles distance. Whether they proceeded further, in the south to the Azores, Madeira, and the Cape de Verde Islands, in the north to the coast of

Holland, and across the German Ocean to the Baltic, we regard as uncertain. It is possible that from time to time some of the more adventurous of their traders may have reached thus far; but their regular, settled, and established navigation did not, we believe, extend beyond the Scilly Islands and coast of Cornwall to the north-west, and to the south-west Cape Non and the Canaries.

The commerce of the Phoenicians was carried on, to a large extent, by land, though principally by sea. It appears from the famous chapter of Ezekiel923 which describes the riches and greatness of Tyre in the sixth century B.C. that almost the whole of Western Asia was penetrated by the Phoenician caravans, and laid under contribution to increase the wealth of the Phoenician traders.

"Thou, son of man, (we read) take up a lamentation for Tyre,
    and say
unto her,
O thou that dwellest at the entry of the sea,
Which art the merchant of the peoples unto many isles,
Thus saith the Lord God, Thou, O Tyre, hast said, I am perfect in
beauty.
Thy borders are in the heart of the sea;
Thy builders have perfected thy beauty.
They have made all thy planks of fir-trees from Senir;
They have taken cedars from Lebanon to make a mast for thee
Of the oaks of Bashan have they made thine oars;
They have made thy benches of ivory,
Inlaid in box-wood, from the isles of Kittim.
Of fine linen with broidered work from Egypt was thy sail,
That it might be to thee for an ensign;
Blue and purple from the isles of Elishah was thy awning.
The inhabitants of Zidon and of Arvad were thy rowers;
Thy wise men, O Tyre, were in thee—they were thy pilots.
The ancients of Gebal, and their wise men, were thy calkers;
All the ships of the sea, with their mariners, were in thee,
That they might occupy thy merchandise.
Persia, and Lud, and Phut were in thine army, thy men of war;
They hanged the shield and helmet in thee;
They set forth thy comeliness.
The men of Arvad, with thine army, were upon thy walls round about;
And the Gammadim were in thy towers;
They hanged their shields upon thy walls round about;
They have brought to perfection thy beauty.
Tarshish was thy merchant by reason of the multitude of all
    kinds of
riches;
With silver, iron, tin, and lead, they traded for thy wares.
Javan, Tubal, and Meshech, they were thy traffickers;
They traded the persons of men, and vessels of brass, for thy
merchandise.
They of the house of Togarmah traded for thy wares,
With horses, and with chargers, and with mules.
The men of Dedan were thy traffickers; many isles were the mart of
thy hands;
They brought thee in exchange horns of ivory, and ebony.
Syria was thy merchant by reason of the multitude of thy

handiworks;
They traded for thy wares with emeralds, purple, and broidered
    work,
And with fine linen, and coral, and rubies.
Judah, and the land of Israel, they were thy traffickers;
They traded for thy merchandise wheat of Minnith,
And Pannag, and honey, and oil, and balm.
Damascus was thy merchant for the multitude of thy handiworks;
By reason of the multitude of all kinds of riches;
With the wine of Helbon, and white wool.
Dedan and Javan traded with yarn for thy wares;
Bright iron, and cassia, and calamus were among thy merchandise.
Dedan was thy trafficker in precious cloths for riding;
Arabia, and all the princes of Kedar, they were the merchants
    of thy
hand,
In lambs, and rams, and goats, in these were they thy merchants.
The traffickers of Sheba and Raamah, they were thy traffickers;
They traded for thy wares with chief of all spices,
And with all manner of precious stones, and gold.
Haran, and Canneh, and Eden, the traffickers of Sheba,
Asshur and Chilmad, were thy traffickers:
They were thy traffickers in choice wares,
In wrappings of blue and broidered work, and in chests of rich
apparel,
Bound with cords, and made of cedar, among thy merchandise.
The ships of Tarshish were thy caravans for they merchandise;
And thou wast replenished, and made very glorious, in the heart of
the sea.
Thy rowers have brought thee into great waters;
The east wind hath broken thee in the heart of the sea.
Thy reaches, and thy wares, thy merchandise, thy mariners, and thy
pilots,
Thy calkers, and the occupiers of thy merchandise,
With all the men of war, that are in thee,
Shall fall into the heart of the seas in the day of thy ruin.
At the sound of thy pilot's cry the suburb's shall shake;
And all that handle the oar, the mariners, and all the pilots
    of the
sea,
They shall come down from their ships, they shall stand upon the
land,
And shall cause their voice to be heard over thee, and shall cry
bitterly,
And shall cast up dust upon their heads, and wallow in the ashes;
And they shall make themselves bald for thee, and gird them with
sackcloth,
And they shall weep for thee in bitterness of soul with bitter
mourning.
And in their wailing they shall take up a lamentation for thee,
And lament over thee saying, Who is there like Tyre,
Like her that is brought to silence in the midst of the sea?

When thy wares went forth out of the seas, thou filledst many
peoples;
Thou didst enrich the kings of the earth with thy merchandise and
thy riches.
In the time that thou was broken by the seas in the depths of the
waters,
Thy merchandise, and all thy company, did fall in the midst of
thee,
And the inhabitants of the isles are astonished at thee,
And their kings are sore afraid, they are troubled in their
countenance,
The merchants that are among the peoples, hiss at thee;
Thou art become a terror; and thou shalt never be any more."

Translating this glorious burst of poetry into prose, we find the following countries mentioned
as carrying on an active trade with the Phoenician metropolis:—Northern Syria, Syria of
Damascus, Judah and the land of Israel, Egypt, Arabia, Babylonia, Assyria, Upper
Mesopotamia,924 Armenia,925 Central Asia Minor, Ionia, Cyprus, Hellas or Greece,926 and
Spain.927 Northern Syria furnishes the Phoenician merchants with butz, which is translated
"fine linen," but is perhaps rather cotton,928 the "tree-wool" of Herodotus; it also supplies
embroidery, and certain precious stones, which our translators have considered to be coral,
emeralds, and rubies. Syria of Damascus gives the "wine of Helbon"—that exquisite liquor
which was the only sort that the Persian kings would condescend to drink929—and "white
wool," the dainty fleeces of the sheep and lambs that fed on the upland pastures of Hermon
and Antilibanus. Judah and the land of Israel supply corn of superior quality, called "corn of
Minnith"—corn, i.e. produced in the rich Ammonite country930—together with pannag, an
unknown substance, and honey, and balm, and oil. Egypt sends fine linen, one of her best
known products931—sometimes, no doubt, plain, but often embroidered with bright patterns,
and employed as such embroidered fabrics were also in Egypt,932 for the sails of pleasure-
boats. Arabia provides her spices, cassia, and calamus (or aromatic reed), and, beyond all
doubt, frankincense,933 and perhaps cinnamon and ladanum.934 She also supplies wool and
goat's hair, and cloths for chariots, and gold, and wrought iron, and precious stones, and ivory,
and ebony, of which the last two cannot have been productions of her own, but must have been
imported from India or Abyssinia.935 Babylonia and Assyria furnish "wrappings of blue,
embroidered work, and chests of rich apparel."936 Upper Mesopotamia partakes in this
traffic.937 Armenia gives horses and mules. Central Asia Minor (Tubal and Meshech)
supplies slaves and vessels of brass, and the Greeks of Ionia do the like. Cyprus furnishes
ivory, which she must first have imported from abroad.938 Greece Proper sends her shell-fish,
to enable the Phoenician cities to increase their manufacture of the purple dye.939 Finally,
Spain yields silver, iron, tin, and lead—the most useful of the metals—all of which she is
known to have produced in abundance.940

With the exception of Egypt, Ionia, Cyprus, Hellas, and Spain, the Phoenician intercourse with
these places must have been carried on wholly by land. Even with Egypt, wherewith the
communication by sea was so facile, there seems to have been also from a very early date a
land commerce. The land commerce was in every case carried on by caravans. Western Asia
has never yet been in so peaceful and orderly condition as to dispense prudent traders from the
necessity of joining together in large bodies, well provisioned and well armed, when they are
about to move valuable goods any considerable distance. There have always been robber-
tribes in the mountain tracts, and thievish Arabs upon the plains, ready to pounce on the
insufficiently protected traveller, and to despoil him of all his belongings. Hence the necessity
of the caravan traffic. As early as the time of Joseph—probably about B.C. 1600—we find a
company of the Midianites on their way from Gilead, with their camels bearing spicery, and
balm, and myrrh, going to carry it down to Egypt.941 Elsewhere we hear of the "travelling

companies of the Dedanim,"942 of the men of Sheba bringing their gold and frankincense;943 of a multitude of camels coming up to Palestine with wood from Kedar and Nebaioth.944 Heeren is entirely justified in his conclusion that the land trade of the Phoenicians was conducted by "large companies or caravans, since it could only have been carried on in this way."945

The nearest neighbours of the Phoenicians on the land side were the Jews and Israelites, the Syrians of Damascus, and the people of Northern Syria, or the Orontes valley and the tract east of it. From the Jews and Israelites the Phoenicians seem to have derived at all times almost the whole of the grain which they were forced to import for their sustenance. In the time of David and Solomon it was chiefly for wheat and barley that they exchanged the commodities which they exported,946 in that of Ezekiel it was primarily for "wheat of Minnith;"947 and a similar trade is noted on the return of the Jews from the captivity,948 and in the first century of our era.949 But besides grain they also imported from Palestine at some periods wine, oil, honey, balm, and oak timber.950 Western Palestine was notoriously a land not only of corn, but also of wine, of olive oil, and of honey, and could readily impart of its superfluity to its neighbour in time of need. The oaks of Bashan are very abundant, and seem to have been preferred by the Phoenicians to their own oaks as the material of oars.951 Balm, or basalm, was a product of the land of Gilead,952 and also of the lower Jordan valley, where it was of superior quality.953

From the Damascene Syrians we are told that Phoenicia imported "wine of Helbon" and "white wool."954 The "wine of Helbon" is reasonably identified with that {oinos Khalubonios} which is said to have been the favourite beverage of the Persian kings.955 It was perhaps grown in the neighbourhood of Aleppo.956 The "white wool" may have been furnished by the sheep that cropped the slopes of the Antilibanus, or by those fed on the fine grass which clothes most of the plain at its base. The fleece of these last is, according to Heeren,957 "the finest known, being improved by the heat of the climate, the continual exposure to the open air, and the care commonly bestowed upon the flocks." From the Syrian wool, mixed perhaps with some other material, seems to have been woven the fabric known, from the city where it was commonly made,958 as "damask."

According to the existing text of Ezekiel,959 Syria Proper "occupied in the fairs" of Phoenicia with cotton, with embroidered robes, with purple, and with precious stones. The valley of the Orontes is suitable for the cultivation of cotton; and embroidered robes would naturally be produced in the seat of an old civilisation, which Syria certainly was. Purple seems somewhat out of place in the enumeration; but the Syrians may have gathered the murex on their seaboard between Mt. Casius and the Gulf of Issus, and have sold what they collected in the Phoenician market. The precious stones which Ezekiel assigns to them are difficult of identification, but may have been furnished by Casius, Bargylus, or Amanus. These mountains, or at any rate Casius and Amanus, are of igneous origin, and, if carefully explored, would certainly yield gems to the investigator. At the same time it must be acknowledged that Syria had not, in antiquity, the name of a gem-producing country; and, so far, the reading of "Edom" for "Aram," which is preferred by many,960 may seem to be the more probable.

The commerce of the Phoenicians with Egypt was ancient, and very extensive. "The wares of Egypt" are mentioned by Herodotus as a portion of the merchandise which they brought to Greece before the time of the Trojan War.961 The Tyrians had a quarter in the city of Memphis assigned to them,962 probably from an early date. According to Ezekiel, the principal commodity which Egypt furnished to Phoenicia was "fine linen"963—especially the linen sails embroidered with gay patterns, which the Egyptian nobles affected for their pleasure-boats. They probably also imported from Egypt natron for their glass-works, papyrus for their documents, earthenware of various kinds for exportation, scarabs and other seals, statuettes and figures of gods, amulets, and in the later times sarcophagi.964 Their exports to Egypt consisted of wine on a large scale,965 tin almost certainly, and probably their peculiar purple fabrics, and other manufactured articles.

The Phoenician trade with Arabia was of especial importance, since not only did the great peninsula itself produce many of the most valuable articles of commerce, but it was also mainly, if not solely, through Arabia that the Indian market was thrown open to the Phoenician traders, and the precious commodities obtained for which Hindustan has always been famous. Arabia is par excellence the land of spices, and was the main source from which the ancient world in general, and Phoenicia in particular, obtained frankincense, cinnamon, cassia, myrrh, calamus or sweet-cane, and ladanum.966 It has been doubted whether these commodities were, all of them, the actual produce of the country in ancient times, and Herodotus has been in some degree discredited, but perhaps without sufficient reason. He is supported to a considerable extent by Theophrastus, the disciple of Aristotle, who says:967 "Frankincense, myrrh, and cassia grow in the Arabian districts of Saba and Hadramaut; frankincense and myrrh on the sides or at the foot of mountains, and in the neighbouring islands. The trees which produce them grow sometimes wild, though occasionally they are cultivated; and the frankincense-tree grows sometimes taller than the tree producing the myrrh." Modern authorities declare the frankincense-tree (Boswellia thurifera) to be still a native of Hadramaut;968 and there is no doubt that the myrrh-tree (Balsamodendron myrrha) also grows there. If cinnamon and cassia, as the terms are now understood, do not at present grow in Arabia, or nearer to Phoenicia than Hindustan, it may be that they have died out in the former country, or our modern use of the terms may differ from the ancient one. On the other hand, it is no doubt possible that the Phoenicians imagined all the spices which they obtained from Arabia to be the indigenous growth of the country, when in fact some of them were importations.

Next to her spices, Arabia was famous for the production of a superior quality of wool. The Phoenicians imported this wool largely. The flocks of Kedar are especially noted,969 and are said to have included both sheep and goats.970 It was perhaps a native woollen manufacture, in which Dedan traded with Tyre, and which Ezekiel notices as a trade in "cloths for chariots."971 Goat's hair was largely employed in the production of coverings for tents.972 Arabia also furnished Phoenicia with gold, with precious stones, with ivory, ebony, and wrought iron.973 The wrought iron was probably from Yemen, which was celebrated for its manufacture of sword blades. The gold may have been native, for there is much reason to believe that anciently the Arabian mountain ranges yielded gold as freely as the Ethiopian,974 with which they form one system; or it may have been imported from Hindustan, with which Arabia had certainly, in ancient times, constant communication. Ivory and ebony must, beyond a doubt, have been Arabian importations. There are two countries from which they may have been derived, India and Abyssinia. It is likely that the commercial Arabs of the south-east coast had dealings with both.975

Of Phoenician imports into Arabia we have no account; but we may conjecture that they consisted principally of manufactured goods, cotton and linen fabrics, pottery, implements and utensils in metal, beads, and other ornaments for the person, and the like. The nomadic Arabs, leading a simple life, required but little beyond what their own country produced; there was, however, a town population976 in the more southern parts of the peninsula, to which the elegancies and luxuries of life, commonly exported by Phoenicia, would have been welcome. The Phoenician trade with Babylonia and Assyria was carried on probably by caravans, which traversed the Syrian desert by way of Tadmor or Palmyra, and struck the Euphrates about Circesium. Here the route divided, passing to Babylon southwards along the course of the great river, and to Nineveh eastwards by way of the Khabour and the Sinjar mountain-range. Both countries seem to have supplied the Phoenicians with fabrics of extraordinary value, rich in a peculiar embroidery, and deemed so precious that they were packed in chests of cedar-wood, which the Phoenician merchants must have brought with them from Lebanon.977 The wares furnished by Assyria were in some cases exported to Greece,978 while no doubt in others they were intended for home consumption. They included cylinders in rock crystal, jasper, hematite, steatite, and other materials, which may sometimes have found purchasers in

Phoenicia Proper, but appear to have been specially affected by the Phoenician colonists in Cyprus.979 On her part Phoenicia must have imported into Assyria and Babylonia the tin which was a necessary element in their bronze; and they seem also to have found a market in Assyria for their own most valuable and artistic bronzes, the exquisite embossed pateræ which are among the most precious of the treasures brought by Sir Austen Layard from Nineveh.980 The nature of the Phoenician trade with Upper Mesopotamia is unknown to us; and it is not impossible that their merchants visited Haran,981 rather because it lay on the route which they had to follow in order to reach Armenia than because it possessed in itself any special attraction for them. Gall-nuts and manna are almost the only products for which the region is celebrated; and of these Phoenicia herself produced the one, while she probably did not need the other. But the natural route to Armenia was by way of the Coelesyrian valley, Aleppo and Carchemish, to Haran, and thence by Amida or Diarbekr to Van, which was the capital of Armenia in the early times.

Armenia supplied the Phoenicians with "horses of common and of noble breeds,"982 and also with mules.983 Strabo says that it was a country exceedingly well adapted for the breeding of the horse,984 and even notes the two qualities of the animal that it produced, one of which he calls "Nisæan," though the true "Nisæan plain" was in Media. So large was the number of colts bred each year, and so highly were they valued, that, under the Persian monarchy the Great King exacted from the province, as a regular item of its tribute, no fewer than twenty thousand of them annually.985 Armenian mules seem not to be mentioned by any writer besides Ezekiel; but mules were esteemed throughout the East in antiquity,986 and no country would have been more likely to breed them than the mountain tract of Armenia, the Switzerland of Western Asia, where such surefooted animals would be especially needed.

Armenia adjoined the country of the Moschi and Tibareni—the Meshech and Tubal of the Bible. These tribes, between the ninth and the seventh centuries B.C., inhabited the central regions of Asia Minor and the country known later as Cappadocia. They traded with Tyre in the "persons of men" and in "vessels of brass" or copper.987 Copper is found abundantly in the mountain ranges of these parts, and Xenophon remarks on the prevalence of metal vessels in the portion of the region which he passed through—the country of the Carduchians.988 The traffic in slaves was one in which the Phoenicians engaged from very early times. They were not above kidnapping men, women, and children in one country and selling them into another;989 besides which they seem to have frequented regularly the principal slave marts of the time. They bought such Jews as were taken captive and sold into slavery by the neighbouring nations,990 and they looked to the Moschi and Tibareni for a constant supply of the commodity from the Black Sea region.991 The Caucasian tribes have always been in the habit of furnishing slave-girls to the harems of the East, and the Thracians, who were not confined to Europe, but occupied a great part of Asia Minor, regularly trafficked in their children.992

Such was the extent of the Phoenician land trade, as indicated by the prophet Ezekiel, and such were, so far as is at present known, the commodities interchanged in the course of it. It is quite possible—nay, probable—that the trade extended much further, and certain that it must have included many other articles of commerce besides those which we have mentioned. The sources of our information on the subject are so few and scanty, and the notices from which we derive our knowledge for the most part so casual, that we may be sure what is preserved is but a most imperfect record of what was—fragments of wreck recovered from the sea of oblivion. It may have been a Phoenician caravan route which Herodotus describes as traversed on one occasion by the Nasamonians,993 which began in North Africa and terminated with the Niger and the city of Timbuctoo; and another, at which he hints as lying between the coast of the Lotus-eaters and Fezzan.994 Phoenician traders may have accompanied and stimulated the slave hunts of the Garamantians,995 as Arab traders do those of the Central African nations at the present day. Again, it is quite possible that the Phoenicians of Memphis designed and organised the caravans which, proceeding from Egyptian Thebes, traversed Africa from east to west along the line of the "Salt Hills," by way of Ammon, Augila, Fezzan, and the Tuarik country to Mount Atlas.996 We can scarcely imagine the Egyptians showing so much enterprise. But these lines of traffic can be ascribed to the Phoenicians only by conjecture, history being silent on the subject.

The sea trade of the Phoenicians was still more extensive than their land traffic. It is divisible into two branches, their trade with their own colonists, and that with the natives of the various countries to which they penetrated in their voyages. The colonies sent out from Phoenicia were, except in the single instance of Carthage, trading settlements, planted where some commodity or commodities desired by the mother-country abounded, and were intended to secure to the mother-country the monopoly of such commodity or commodities. For instance, Cyprus was colonised for the sake of its copper mines and its timber; Cilicia and Lycia for their timber only; Thasos for its gold mines; Salamis and Cythera for the purple trade; Sardinia and Spain for their numerous metals; North Africa for its fertility and for the trade with the interior. Phoenicia expected to derive, primarily, from each colony the commodity or commodities which had caused the selection of the site. In return she supplied the colonists with her own manufactured articles; with fabrics in linen, wool, cotton, and perhaps to some extent in silk; with every variety of pottery, from dishes and jugs of the plainest and most simple kind to the most costly and elaborate vases and amphoræ; with metal utensils and arms, with gold and silver ornaments, with embossed shields and pateræ, with faïnce and glass, and also with any foreign products or manufactures that they desired and that the countries within the range of her influence could furnish. Phoenicia must have imported into Cyprus, to suit a peculiar Cyprian taste, the Egyptian statuettes, scarabs, and rings,997 and the Assyrian and Babylonian cylinders, which have been found there. The tin which she brought from the Cassiterides she distributed generally, for she did not discourage her colonists from manufacturing for themselves to some extent. There was probably no colony which did not make its own bronze vessels of the commoner sort and its own coarser pottery.

In her trade with the nations who peopled the coasts of the Mediterranean, the Propontis, and the Black Sea, Phoenicia aimed primarily at disposing to advantage of her own commodities, secondarily at making a profit in commodities which she had obtained from other countries, and thirdly on obtaining commodities which she might dispose of to advantage elsewhere. Where the nations were uncivilised, or in a low condition of civilisation, she looked to making a large profit by furnishing them at a cheap rate with all the simplest conveniences of life, with their pottery, their implements and utensils, their clothes, their arms, the ornaments of their persons and of their houses. Underselling the native producers, she soon obtained a monopoly of this kind of trade, drove the native products out of the market, and imposed her own instead, much as the manufacturers of Manchester, Birmingham, and the Potteries impose their calicoes, their cutlery, and their earthenware on the savages of Africa and Polynesia. Where culture was more advanced, as in Greece and parts of Italy,998 she looked to introduce, and no doubt succeeded in introducing, the best of her own productions, fabrics of crimson, violet, and purple, painted vases, embossed pateræ, necklaces, bracelets, rings—"cunning work" of all manner of kinds999—mirrors, glass vessels, and smelling-bottles. At the same time she also disposed at a profit of many of the wares that she had imported from foreign countries, which were advanced in certain branches of art, as Egypt, Babylonia, Assyria, possibly India. The muslins and ivory of Hindustan, the shawls of Kashmir, the carpets of Babylon, the spices of Araby the Blest, the pearls of the Persian Gulf, the faïence and the papyrus of Egypt, would be readily taken by the more civilised of the Western nations, who would be prepared to pay a high price for them. They would pay for them partly, no doubt, in silver and gold, but to some extent also in their own manufactured commodities, Attica in her ceramic products, Corinth in her "brass," Etruria in her candelabra and engraved mirrors,9100 Argos in her highly elaborated ornaments.9101 Or, in some cases, they might make return out of the store wherewith nature had provided them, Euboea rendering her copper, the Peloponnese her "purple," Crete her timber, the Cyrenaica its silphium.

Outside the Pillars of Hercules the Phoenicians had only savage nations to deal with, and with these they seem to have traded mainly for the purpose of obtaining certain natural products, either peculiarly valuable or scarcely procurable elsewhere. Their trade with the Scilly Islands and the coast of Cornwall was especially for the procuring of tin. Of all the metals, tin is found in the fewest places, and though Spain seems to have yielded some anciently,9102 yet it can only have been in small quantities, while there was an enormous demand for tin in all parts of the old world, since bronze was the material almost universally employed for arms, tools, implements, and utensils of all kinds, while tin is the most important, though not the largest, element in bronze. From the time that the Phoenicians discovered the Scilly Islands—the "Tin Islands" (Cassiterides), as they called them—it is probable that the tin of the civilised world was almost wholly derived from this quarter. Eastern Asia, no doubt, had always its own mines, and may have exported tin to some extent, in the remoter times, supplying perhaps the needs of Egypt, Assyria, and Babylon. But, after the rich stores of the metal which our own islands possess were laid open, and the Phoenicians with their extensive commercial dealings, both in the West and in the East, became interested in diffusing it, British tin probably drove all other out of use, and obtained the monopoly of the markets wherever Phoenician influence prevailed. Hence the trade with the Cassiterides was constant, and so highly prized that a Phoenician captain, finding his ship followed by a Roman vessel, preferred running it upon the rocks to letting a rival nation learn the secret of how the tin-producing coast might be approached in safety.9103 With the tin it was usual for the merchants to combine a certain amount of lead and a certain quantity of skins or hides; while they gave in exchange pottery, salt, and articles in bronze, such as arms, implements, and utensils for cooking and for the table.9104

If the Phoenicians visited, as some maintain that they did,9105 the coasts of the Baltic, it must have been for the purpose of obtaining amber. Amber is thrown up largely by the waters of that land-locked sea, and at present especially abounds on the shore in the vicinity of Dantzic. It is very scarce elsewhere. The Phoenicians seem to have made use of amber in their necklaces from a very early date;9106 and, though they might no doubt have obtained it by land-carriage across Europe to the head of the Adriatic, yet their enterprise and their commercial spirit were such as would not improbably have led them to seek to open a direct communication with the amber-producing region, so soon as they knew where it was situated. The dangers of the German Ocean are certainly not greater than those of the Atlantic; and if the Phoenicians had sufficient skill in navigation to reach Britain and the Fortunate Islands, they could have found no very serious difficulty in penetrating to the Baltic. On the other hand, there is no direct evidence of their having penetrated so far, and perhaps the Adriatic trade may have supplied them with as much amber as they needed.

The trade of the Phoenicians with the west coast of Africa had for its principal objects the procuring of ivory, of elephant, lion, leopard, and deer-skins, and probably of gold. Scylax relates that there was an established trade in his day (about B.C. 350) between Phoenicia and an island which he calls Cerne, probably Arguin, off the West African coast. "The merchants," he says,9107 "who are Phoenicians, when they have arrived at Cerne, anchor their vessels there, and after having pitched their tents upon the shore, proceed to unload their cargo, and to convey it in smaller boats to the mainland. The dealers with whom they trade are Ethiopians; and these dealers sell to the Phoenicians skins of deer, lions, panthers, and domestic animals—elephants' skins also, and their teeth. The Ethiopians wear embroidered garments, and use ivory cups as drinking vessels; their women adorn themselves with ivory bracelets; and their horses also are adorned with ivory. The Phoenicians convey to them ointment, elaborate vessels from Egypt, castrated swine(?), and Attic pottery and cups. These last they commonly purchase [in Athens] at the Feast of Cups. These Ethiopians are eaters of flesh and drinkers of milk; they make also much wine from the vine; and the Phoenicians, too, supply some wine to them. They have a considerable city, to which the Phoenicians sail up." The river on which the city stood was probably the Senegal.

It will be observed that Scylax says nothing in this passage of any traffic for gold. We can scarcely suppose, however, that the Phoenicians, if they penetrated so far south as this, could remain ignorant of the fact that West Africa was a gold-producing country, much less that, being aware of the fact, they would fail to utilise it. Probably they were the first to establish that "dumb commerce" which was afterwards carried on with so much advantage to themselves by the Carthaginians, and whereof Herodotus gives so graphic an account. "There is a country," he says,9108 "in Libya, and a nation, beyond the Pillars of Hercules, which the Carthaginians are wont to visit, where they no sooner arrive than forthwith they unlade their wares, and having disposed them after an orderly fashion along the beach, there leave them, and returning aboard their ships, raise a great smoke. The natives, when they see the sample, come down to the shore, and laying out to view so much gold as they think the wares are worth, withdraw to a distance. The Carthaginians upon this come ashore again and look. If they think the gold to be enough, they take it and go their way; but if it does not seem to them sufficient, they go aboard ship once more, and wait patiently. Then the others approach and add to their gold, till the Carthaginians are satisfied. Neither party deals unfairly by the other: for they themselves never touch the gold till it comes up to the worth of their goods, nor do the natives ever carry off the goods until the gold has been taken away."

The nature of the Phoenician trade with the Canaries, or Fortunate Islands, is not stated by any ancient author, and can only be conjectured. It would scarcely have been worth the Phoenicians' while to convey timber to Syria from such a distance, or we might imagine the virgin forests of the islands attracting them.9109 The large breed of dogs from which the Canaries derived their later name9110 may perhaps have constituted an article of export even in Phoenician times, as we know they did later, when we hear of their being conveyed to King Juba;9111 but there is an entire lack of evidence on the subject. Perhaps the Phoenicians frequented the islands less for the sake of commerce than for that of watering and refitting the ships engaged in the African trade, since the natives were less formidable than those who inhabited the mainland.9112

There was one further direction in which the Phoenicians pushed their maritime trade, not perhaps continuously, but at intervals, when their political relations were such as to give them access to the sea which washed Asia on the south and on the southeast. The nearest points at which they could embark for the purpose of exploring or utilising the great tract of ocean in this quarter were the inner recesses of the two deep gulfs known as the Persian and the Arabian. It has been thought by some9113 that there were times in their history when the Phoenicians had the free use of both these gulfs, and could make the starting-point of their eastern explorations and trading voyages either a port on one of the two arms into which the Red Sea divides towards the north, or a harbour on the Persian Gulf near its north-western extremity. But the latter supposition rests upon grounds which are exceedingly unsafe and uncertain. That the Phoenicians migrated at some remote period from the shores of the Persian Gulf to the Mediterranean may be allowed to be highly probable; but that, after quitting their primitive abodes and moving off nearly a thousand miles to the westward, they still maintained a connection with their early settlements and made them centres for a trade with the Far East, is as improbable a hypothesis as any that has ever received the sanction of men of learning and repute. The Babylonians, through whose country the connection must have been kept up, were themselves traders, and would naturally keep the Arabian and Indian traffic in their own hands; nor can we imagine them as brooking the establishment of a rival upon their shores. The Arabians were more friendly; but they, too, would have disliked to share their carrying trade with a foreign nation. And the evidence entirely fails to show that the Phoenicians, from the time of their removal to the Mediterranean, ever launched a vessel in the Persian Gulf, or had any connection with the nations inhabiting its shores, beyond that maintained by the caravans which trafficked by land between the Phoenician cities and the men of Dedan and Babylon.9114

It was otherwise with the more western gulf. There, certainly, from time to time, the

Phoenicians launched their fleets, and carried on a commerce which was scarcely less lucrative because they had to allow the nations whose ports they used a participation in its profits. It is not impossible that, occasionally, the Egyptians allowed them to build ships in some one or more of their Red Sea ports, and to make such port or ports the head-quarters of a trade which may have proceeded beyond the Straits of Babelmandeb and possibly have reached Zanzibar and Ceylon. At any rate, we know that, in the time of Solomon, two harbours upon the Red Sea were open to them—viz. Eloth and Ezion-Geber—both places situated in the inner recess of the Elanitic Gulf, or Gulf of Akaba, the more eastern of the two arms into which the Red Sea divides. David's conquest of Edom had put these ports into the possession of the Israelites, and the friendship between Hiram and Solomon had given the Phoenicians free access to them. It was the ambition of Solomon to make the Israelites a nautical people, and to participate in the advantages which he perceived to have accrued to Phoenicia from her commercial enterprise. Besides sharing with the Phoenicians in the trade of the Mediterranean,9115 he constructed with their help a fleet at Ezion-Geber upon the Red Sea,9116 and the two allies conjointly made voyages to the region, or country, called Ophir, for the purpose of procuring precious stones, gold, and almug-wood.9117 Ophir is, properly speaking, a portion of Arabia,9118 and Arabia was famous for its production of gold,9119 and also for its precious stones.9120 Whether it likewise produced almug-trees is doubtful;9121 and it is quite possible that the joint fleet went further than Ophir proper, and obtained the "almug-wood" from the east coast of Africa, or from India. The Somauli country might have been as easily reached as South-eastern Arabia, and if India is considerably more remote, yet there was nothing to prevent the Phoenicians from finding their way to it.9122 We have, however, no direct evidence that their commerce in the Indian Ocean ever took them further than the Arabian coast, about E. Long. 55°.

CHAPTER X—MINING

Surface gathering of metals, anterior to mining—Earliest
known mining operations—Earliest Phoenician mining in
Phoenicia Proper—Mines of Cyprus—Phoenician mining in
Thasos and Thrace—in Sardinia—in Spain—Extent of the
metallic treasures there—Phoenician methods not unlike
those of the present day—Use of shafts, adits, and
galleries—Roof of mines propped or arched—Ores crushed,
pounded, and washed—Use of quicksilver unknown—Mines
worked by slave labour.

The most precious and useful of the metals lie, in many places, so near the earth's surface that, in the earliest times, mining is unneeded and therefore unpractised. We are told that in Spain silver was first discovered in consequence of a great fire, which consumed all the forests wherewith the mountains were clothed, and lasted many days; at the end of which time the surface of the soil was found to be intersected by streams of silver from the melting of the superficial silver ore through the intense heat of the conflagration. The natives did not know what to do with the metal, so they bartered it away to the Phoenician traders, who already frequented their country, in return for some wares of very moderate value.101 Whether this tale be true or no, it is certain that even at the present day, in what are called "new countries," valuable metals often show themselves on the surface of the soil, either in the form of metalliferous earths, or of rocks which shine with spangles of a metallic character, or occasionally, though rarely, of actual masses of pure ore, sometimes encrusted with an oxide, sometimes bare, bright, and unmistakable. In modern times, whenever there is a rush into any gold region—whether California, or Australia, or South Africa—the early yield is from the surface. The first comers scratch the ground with a knife or with a pick-axe, and are rewarded by discovering "nuggets" of greater or less dimensions; the next flight of gold-finders search the beds of the streams; and it is not until the supply from these two sources begins to fail that mining, in the proper sense of the term, is attempted.

The earliest mining operations, whereof we have any record, are those conducted by the Egyptian kings of the fourth, fifth and twelfth dynasties, in the Sinaitic region. At two places in the mountains between Suez and Mount Sinai, now known as the Wady Magharah and Sarabit-el-Khadim, copper was extracted from the bosom of the earth by means of shafts laboriously excavated in the rocks, under the auspices of these early Pharaohs.102 Hence at the time of the Exodus the process of mining was familiar to the Hebrews, who could thus fully appreciate the promise,103 that they were about to be given "a good land"—"a land whose stones were iron, and out of whose hills they might dig brass." The Phoenicians, probably, derived their first knowledge of mining from their communications with the Egyptians, and no doubt first practised the art within the limits of their own territory—in Lebanon, Casius, and Bargylus. The mineral stores of these regions were, however, but scanty, and included none of the more important metals, excepting iron. The Phoenicians were thus very early in their history driven afield for the supply of their needs, and among the principal causes of their first voyages of discovery must be placed the desire of finding and occupying regions which contained the metallic treasures wherein their own proper country was deficient. It is probable that they first commenced mining operations on a large scale in Cyprus. Here, according to Pliny,104 copper was first discovered; and though this may be a fable, yet here certainly it was found in great abundance at a very early time, and was worked to such an extent, that the Greeks knew copper, as distinct from bronze, by no other name than that of {khalkos Kuprios}, whence the Roman Æs Cyprium, and our own name for the metal. The principal mines were in the southern mountain range, near Tamasus,105 but there were others also at Amathus, Soli, and Curium.106 Some of the old workings have been noticed by modern travellers, particularly near Soli and Tamasus,107 but they have neither been described anciently nor examined scientifically in modern times. The ore from which the metal was extracted is called chalcitis by Pliny,108 and may have been the "chalcocite" of our present metallurgical science, which is a sulphide containing very nearly eighty per cent. of copper. The brief account which Strabo gives of the mines of Tamasus shows that the ore was smelted in furnaces which were heated by wood fires. We gather also from Strabo that Tamasus had silver mines.

That the Phoenicians conducted mining operations in Thasos we know from Herodotus,109 and from other writers of repute1010 we learn that they extended these operations to the mainland opposite. Herodotus had himself visited Thasos, and tells us that the mines were on the eastern coast of the island, between two places which he calls respectively Ænyra and Coenyra. The metal sought was gold, and in their quest of it the Phoenicians had, he says, turned an entire mountain topsy-turvy. Here again no modern researches seem to have been made, and nothing more is known than that at present the natives obtain no gold from their soil, do not seek for it, and are even ignorant that their island was ever a gold-producing region.1011 The case is almost the same on the opposite coast, where in ancient times very rich mines both of gold and silver abounded,1012 which the Phoenicians are said to have worked, but where at the present day mining enterprise is almost at a standstill, and only a very small quantity of silver is produced.1013

Sardinia can scarcely have been occupied by the Phoenicians for anything but its metals. The southern and south-western parts of the island, where they made their settlements, were rich in copper and lead; and the position of the cities seems to indicate the intention to appropriate these metals. In the vicinity of the lead mines are enormous heaps of scoriæ, mounting up apparently to a very remote era.1014 The scoriæ are not so numerous in the vicinity of the copper mines, but "pigs" of copper have been found in the island, unlike any of the Roman period, which are perhaps Phoenician, and furnish specimens of the castings into which the metal was run, after it had been fused and to some extent refined. The weight of the pigs is from twenty-eight to thirty-seven kilogrammes.1015 Pigs of lead have also been found, but they are less frequent.

But all the other mining operations of the Phoenicians were insignificant compared with those of which the theatre was Spain. Spain was the Peru of the ancient world, and surpassed its modern rival, in that it produced not only gold and silver, but also copper, iron, tin, and lead. Of these metals gold was the least abundant. It was found, however, as gold dust in the bed of the Tagus;1016 and there were mines of it in Gallicia,1017 in the Asturias, and elsewhere. There was always some silver mixed with it, but in one of the Gallician mines the proportion was less than three per cent. Elsewhere the proportion reached to ten or even twelve and a half per cent.; and, as there was no known mode of clearing the gold from it, the produce of the Gallician mine was in high esteem and greatly preferred to that of any other. Silver was yielded in very large quantities. "Spain," says Diodorus Siculus,1018 "has the best and most plentiful silver from mines of all the world." "The Spanish silver," says Pliny,1019 "is the best." When the Phoenicians first visited Spain, they found the metal held in no esteem at all by the natives. It was the common material of the cheapest drinking vessels, and was readily parted with for almost anything that the merchants chose to offer. Much of it was superficial, but the veins were found to run to a great depth; and the discovery of one vein was a sure index of the near vicinity of more.1020 The out-put of the Spanish silver mines during the Phoenician, Carthaginian, and Roman periods was enormous, and cannot be calculated; nor has the supply even yet failed altogether. The iron and copper of Spain are also said to have been exceedingly abundant in ancient times,1021 though, owing to the inferior value of the metals, and to their wider distribution, but little is recorded with regard to them. Its tin and lead, on the other hand, as being metals found in comparatively few localities, receive not infrequent mention. The Spanish tin, according to Posidonius, did not crop out upon the surface,1022 but had to be obtained by mining. It was produced in some considerable quantity in the country of the Artabri, to the north of Lusitania,1023 as well as in Lusitania itself, and in Gallicia;1024 but was found chiefly in small particles intermixed with a dark sandy earth. Lead was yielded in greater abundance; it was found in Cantabria, in Bætica, and many other places.1025 Much of it was mixed with silver, and was obtained in the course of the operations by means of which silver was smelted and refined.1026 The mixed metal was called galena.1027 Lead, however, was also found, either absolutely pure,1028 or so nearly so that the alloy was inappreciable, and was exported in large quantities, both by the Phoenicians and the Carthaginians, and also by the Romans. It was believed that the metal had a power of growth and reproduction, so that if a mine was deserted for a while and then re-opened, it was sure to be found more productive than it was previously.1029 The fact seems to be simply that the supply is inexhaustible, since even now Spain furnishes more than half the lead that is consumed by the rest of Europe. Besides the ordinary metals, Spain was capable of yielding an abundance of quicksilver;1030 but this metal seems not to have attracted the attention of the Phoenicians, who had no use for it.

The methods employed by the Phoenicians to obtain the metals which they coveted were not, on the whole, unlike those which continue in use at the present day. Where surface gold was brought down by the streams, the ground in their vicinity, and such portions of their beds as could be laid bare, were searched by the spade; any earth or sand that was seen to be auriferous was carefully dug out and washed, till the earthy particles were cleared away, and only the gold remained. Where the metal lay deeper, perpendicular shafts were sunk into the ground to a greater or less depth—sometimes, if we may believe Diodorus,1031 to the depth of half a mile or more; from these shafts horizontal adits were carried out at various levels, and from the adits there branched lateral galleries, sometimes at right angles, sometimes obliquely, which pursued either a straight or a tortuous course.1032 The veins of metal were perseveringly followed up, and where faults occurred in them, filled with trap,1033 or other hard rock, the obstacle was either tunnelled through or its flank turned, and the vein still pursued on the other side. As the danger of a fall of material from the roofs of the adits and galleries was well understood, it was customary to support them by means of wooden posts, or, where the material was sufficiently firm, to arch them.1034 Still, from time to time, falls would occur, with great injury and loss of life to the miners. Nor was there much less danger where a mountain was quarried for the sake of its metallic treasures. Here, too, galleries were driven into the mountain-side, and portions of it so loosened that after a time they detached themselves and fell with a loud crash into a mass of débris 1035 It sometimes happened that, as the workings proceeded, subterranean springs were tapped, which threatened to flood the mine, and put an end to its further utilisation. In such cases, wherever it was possible, tunnels were constructed, and the water drained off to a lower level.1036 In the deeper mines this, of course, could not be done, and such workings had to be abandoned, until the invention of the Archimedes' screw (ab. B.C. 220-190), when the water was pumped up to the surface, and so got rid of.1037 But before this date Phoenicia had ceased to exist as an independent country, and the mines that had once been hers were either no longer worked, or had passed into the hands of the Romans or the Carthaginians.

When the various ores were obtained, they were first of all crushed, then pounded to a paste; after which, by frequent washings, the non-metallic elements were to a large extent eliminated, and the metallic ones alone left. These, being collected, were placed in crucibles of white clay,1038 which were then submitted to the action of a furnace heated to the melting point. This point could only be reached by the use of the bellows. When it was reached, the impurities which floated on the top of the molten metal were skimmed off, or the metal itself allowed, by the turning of a cock, to flow from an upper crucible into a lower one. For greater purity the melting and skimming process was sometimes repeated; and, in the case of gold, the skimmings were themselves broken up, pounded, and again submitted to the melting pot.1039 The use of quicksilver, however, being unknown, the gold was never wholly freed from the alloy of silver always found in it, nor was the silver ever wholly freed from an alloy of lead.1040

The Romans and Carthaginians worked their mines almost wholly by slave labour; and very painful pictures are drawn of the sufferings undergone by the unhappy victims of a barbarous and wasteful system.1041 The gangs of slaves, we are told, remained in the mines night and day, never seeing the sun, but living and dying in the murky and foetid atmosphere of the deep excavations. It can scarcely be hoped that the Phoenicians were wiser or more merciful. They had a large command of slave labour, and would naturally employ it where the work to be done was exceptionally hard and disagreeable. Moreover, the Carthaginians, their colonists, are likely to have kept up the system, whatever it was, which they found established on succeeding to the inheritance of the Phoenician mines, and the fact that they worked them by means of slaves makes it more than probable that the Phoenicians had done so before them.1042

When the metals were regarded as sufficiently cleansed from impurities, they were run into moulds, which took the form of bars, pigs, or ingots. Pigs of copper and lead have, as already observed, been found in Sardinia which may well belong to Phoenician times. There is also in the museum of Truro a pig of tin, which, as it differs from those made by the Romans, Normans, and later workers, has been supposed to be Phoenician.1043 Ingots of gold and silver have not at present been found on Phoenician localities; but the Persian practice, witnessed to by Herodotus,1044 was probably adopted from the subject nation, which confessedly surpassed all the others in the useful arts, in commerce, and in practical sagacity.

CHAPTER XI—RELIGION

Strength of the religious sentiment among the Phoenicians—
Proofs—First stage of the religion, monotheistic—Second
stage, a polytheism within narrow limits—Worship of Baal—
of Ashtoreth—of El or Kronos—of Melkarth—of Dagon—of
Hadad—of Adonis—of Sydyk—of Esmun—of the Cabeiri—of
Onca—of Tanith—of Beltis—Third stage marked by
introduction of foreign deities—Character of the Phoenician
worship—Altars and sacrifice—Hymns of praise, temples, and
votive offerings—Wide prevalence of human sacrifice and of
licentious orgies—Institution of the Galli—Extreme
corruption of the later religion—Views held on the subject
of a future life—Piety of the great mass of the people
earnest, though mistaken.

There can be no doubt that the Phoenicians were a people in whose minds religion and religious ideas occupied a very prominent place. Religiousness has been said to be one of the leading characteristics of the Semitic race;0111 and it is certainly remarkable that with that race originated the three principal religions, two of which are the only progressive religions, of the modern world. Judaism, Christianity, and Mohammedanism all arose in Western Asia within a restricted area, and from nations whose Semitic origin is unmistakable. The subject of ethnic affinities and differences, of the transmission of qualities and characteristics, is exceedingly obscure; but, if the theory of heredity be allowed any weight at all, there should be no difficulty in accepting the view that particular races of mankind have special leanings and aptitudes.

Still, the religiousness of the Phoenicians does not rest on any à priori arguments, or considerations of what is likely to have been. Here was a nation among whom, in every city, the temple was the centre of attraction, and where the piety of the citizens adorned every temple with abundant and costly offerings. The monarchs who were at the head of the various states showed the greatest zeal in continually maintaining the honour of the gods, repaired and beautified the sacred buildings, and occasionally added to their kingly dignity the highly esteemed office of High Priest.0112 The coinage of the country bore religious emblems,0113 and proclaimed the fact that the cities regarded themselves as under the protection of this or that deity. Both the kings and their subjects bore commonly religious names—names which designated them as the worshippers or placed them under the tutelage of some god or goddess. Abd-alonim, Abdastartus, Abd-osiris, Abdemon (which is properly Abd-Esmun), Abdi-milkut, were names of the former kind, Abi-baal (= "Baal is my father"), Itho-bal (= "with him is Baal"), Baleazar or Baal-azur (= "Baal protects"), names of the latter. The Phoenician ships carried images of the gods0114 in the place of figure-heads. Wherever the Phoenicians went, they bore with them their religion and their worship; in each colony they planted a temple or temples, and everywhere throughout their wide dominion the same gods were worshipped with the same rites and with the same observances.

In considering the nature of the Phoenician religion, we must distinguish between its different stages. There is sufficient reason to believe that originally, either when they first occupied their settlements upon the Mediterranean or before they moved from their primitive seats upon the shores of the Persian Gulf, the Phoenicians were Monotheists. We must not look for information on this subject to the pretentious work which Philo of Byblus, in the first or second century of our era, put forth with respect to the "Origines" of his countrymen, and attributed to Sanchoniatho;0115 we must rather look to the evidence of language and fact, records which may indeed be misread, but which cannot well be forged or falsified. These will show us that in the earliest times the religious sentiment of the Phoenicians acknowledged only a single deity—a single mighty power, which was supreme over the whole universe. The names by which they designated him were El, "great;" Ram or Rimmon, "high;" Baal, "Lord;"

Melek or Molech, "King;" Eliun, "Supreme;" Adonai, "My Lord;" Bel-samin, "Lord of Heaven," and the like.0116 Distinct deities could no more be intended by such names as these than by those under which God is spoken of in the Hebrew Scriptures, several of them identical with the Phoenician names—El or Elohim, "great;" Jehovah, "existing;" Adonai, "my Lord;" Shaddai, "strong;" El Eliun,0117 "the supreme Great One." How far the Phoenicians actually realised all that their names properly imply, whether they went so far as to divest God wholly of a material nature, whether they viewed Him as the Creator, as well as the Lord, of the world, are problems which it is impossible, with the means at present at our disposal, to solve. But they certainly viewed Him as "the Lord of Heaven,"0118 and, if so, no doubt also as the Lord of earth; they believed Him to be "supreme" or "the Most High;" and they realised his personal relation to each one of his worshippers, who were privileged severally to address Him as Adonai—"my Lord." It may be presumed that at this early stage of the religion there was no idolatry; when One God alone is acknowledged and recognised, the feeling is naturally that expressed in the Egyptian hymn of praise—"He is not graven in marble; He is not beheld; His abode is unknown; there is no building that can contain Him; unknown is his name in heaven; He doth not manifest his forms; vain are all representations."0119

But this happy state of things did not—perhaps we may say, could not—in the early condition of the human intelligence, last long. Fallen man, left to himself, very soon corrupts his way upon the earth; his hands deal with wickedness; and, in a little while, "every imagination of the thoughts of his heart is only evil continually."1110 When he becomes conscious to himself of sin, he ceases to be able to endure the thought of One Perfect Infinite Being, omnipotent, ever-present, who reads his heart, who is "about his path, and about his bed, and spies out all his ways."1111 He instinctively catches at anything whereby he may be relieved from the intolerable burden of such a thought; and here the imperfection of language comes to his aid. As he has found it impossible to express in any one word all that is contained in his idea of the Divine Being, he has been forced to give Him many names, each of them originally expressive of some one of that Being's attributes. But in course of time these words have lost their force—their meaning has been forgotten—and they have come to be mere proper names, designative but not significative. Here is material for the perverted imagination to work upon. A separate being is imagined answering to each of the names; and so the nomina become numina.1112 Many gods are substituted for one; and the idea of God is instantly lowered. The gods have different spheres. No god is infinite; none is omnipotent, none omnipresent; therefore none omniscient. The aweful, terrible nature of God is got rid of, and a company of angelic beings takes its place, none of them very alarming to the conscience.

In its second stage the religion of Phoenicia was a polytheism, less multitudinous than most others, and one in which the several divinities were not distinguished from one another by very marked or striking features. At the head of the Pantheon stood a god and a goddess—Baal and Ashtoreth. Baal, "the Lord," or Baal-samin,1113 "the Lord of Heaven," was compared by the Greeks to their Zeus, and by the Romans to their Jupiter. Mythologically, he was only one among many gods, but practically he stood alone; he was the chief of the gods, the main object of worship, and the great ruler and protector of the Phoenician people. Sometimes, but not always, he had a solar character, and was represented with his head encircled by rays.1114 Baalbek, which was dedicated to him, was properly "the city of the Sun," and was called by the Greeks Heliopolis. The solar character of Baal is, however, far from predominant, and as early as the time of Josiah we find the Sun worshipped separately from him,1115 no doubt under a different name. Baal is, to a considerable extent, a city god. Tyre especially was dedicated to him; and we hear of the "Baal of Tyre"1116 and again of the "Baal of Tarsus."1117 Essentially, he was the embodiment of the generative principle in nature—"the god of the creative power, bringing all things to life everywhere."1118 Hence, "his statue rode upon bulls, for the bull was the symbol of generative power; and he was also represented with bunches of grapes and pomegranates in his hand,"1119 emblems of productivity. The sacred conical stones and pillars dedicated in his temples1120 may have had their origin in a similar symbolism. As polytheistic systems had always a tendency to enlarge themselves, Baal had no sooner become a separate god, distinct from El, and Rimmon, and Molech, and Adonai, than he proceeded to multiply himself, and from Baal became Baalim,1121 either because the local Baals—Baal-Tzur, Baal-Sidon, Baal-Tars, Baal-Libnan, Baal-Hermon—were conceived of as separate deities, or because the aspects of Baal—Baal as Sun-God, Baal as Lord of Heaven, Baal as lord of flies,1122, &c.—were so viewed, and grew to be distinct objects of worship. In later times he was identified with the Egyptian Ammon, and worshipped as Baal-Hammon. Baal is known to have had temples at Baalbek, at Tyre, at Tarsus, at Agadir1123 (Gades), in Sardinia,1124 at Carthage, and at Ekron. Though not at first worshipped under a visible form, he came to have statues dedicated to him,1125 which received the usual honours. Sometimes, as already observed, his head was encircled with a representation of the solar rays; sometimes his form was assimilated to that under which the Egyptians of later times worshipped their Ammon. Seated upon a throne and wrapped in a long robe, he presented the appearance of a man in the flower of his age, bearded, and of solemn aspect, with the carved horn of a ram on either side of his forehead. Figures of rams also supported the arms of his throne on either side, and on the heads of these two supports his hands rested.1126

The female deity whose place corresponded to that of Baal in the Phoenician Pantheon, and who was in a certain sense his companion and counterpart, was Ashtoreth or Astarte. As Baal was the embodiment of the generative principle in nature, so was Ashtoreth of the receptive and productive principle. She was the great nature-goddess, the Magna Mater, regent of the stars, queen of heaven, giver of life, and source of woman's fecundity.1127 Just as Baal had a solar, so she had a lunar aspect, being pictured with horns upon her head representative of the lunar crescent.1128 Hence, as early as the time of Moses, there was a city on the eastern side of Jordan, named after her, Ashtoreth-Karnaim,1129 or "Astarte of the two horns." Her images are of many forms. Most commonly she appears as a naked female, with long hair, sometimes gathered into tresses, and with her two hands supporting her two breasts.1130 Occasionally she is a mother, seated in a comfortable chair, and nursing her babe.1131 Now and then she is draped, and holds a dove to her breast, or else she takes an attitude of command, with the right hand raised, as if to bespeak attention. Sometimes, on the contrary, her figure has that modest and retiring attitude which has caused it to be described by a distinguished archæologist1132 as "the Phoenician prototype of the Venus de Medici." The Greeks and Romans, who identified Baal determinately with their Zeus or Jupiter, found it very much more difficult to fix on any single goddess in their Pantheon as the correspondent of Astarte. Now they made her Hera or Juno, now Aphrodite or Venus, now Athene, now Artemis, now Selene, now Rhea or Cybele. But her aphrodisiac character was certainly the one in which she most frequently appeared. She was the goddess of the sexual passion, rarely, however, represented with the chaste and modest attributes of the Grecian Aphrodite-Urania, far more commonly with those coarser and more repulsive ones which characterise Aphrodite Pandemos.1133 Her temples were numerous, though perhaps not quite so numerous as those of Baal. The most famous were those at Sidon, Aphaca, Ashtoreth-Karnaim, Paphos, Pessinus, and Carthage. At Sidon the kings were sometimes her high-priests;1134 and her name is found as a frequent element in Phoenician personal names, royal and other: e.g.—Astartus, Abdastartus, Delæastartus, Am-ashtoreth, Bodoster, Bostor, &c.

The other principal Phoenician deities were El, Melkarth, Dagon, Hadad, Adonis, Sydyk, Eshmun, the Cabeiri, Onca, Tanith, Tanata, or Anaitis, and Baalith, Baaltis, or Beltis. El, or Il, originally a name of the Supreme God, became in the later Phoenician mythology a separate and subordinate divinity, whom the Greeks compared to their Kronos1135 and the Romans to their Saturn. El was the special god of Gebal or Byblus,1136 and was worshipped also with peculiar rites at Carthage.1137 He was reckoned the son of Uranus and the father of Beltis, to whom he delivered over as her especial charge the city of Byblus.1138 Numerous tales were told of him. While reigning on earth as king of Byblus, or king of Phoenicia, he had fallen in love with a nymph of the country, called Anobret, by whom he had a son named Ieoud. This son, much as he loved him, when great dangers from war threatened the land, he first invested with the emblems of royalty, and then sacrificed.1139 Uranus (Heaven) married his sister Ge (Earth), and Il or Kronos was the issue of this marriage, as also were Dagon, Bætylus, and Atlas. Ge, being dissatisfied with the conduct of her husband, induced her son Kronos to make war upon him, and Kronos, with the assistance of Hermes, overcame Uranus, and having driven him from his kingdom succeeded to the imperial power. Besides sacrificing Ieoud, Kronos murdered another of his sons called Sadid, and also a daughter whose name is not given. Among his wives were Astarte, Rhea, Dioné, Eimarmené, and Hora, of whom the first three were his sisters.1140 There is no need to pursue this mythological tangle. If it meant anything to the initiated, the meaning is wholly lost; and the stories, gravely as they are related by the ancient historian, to the modern, who has no key to them, are almost wholly valueless. Originally, Melkarth would seem to have been a mere epithet, representing one aspect of Baal. The word is formed from the two roots melek and kartha1141 (= Heb. kiriath, "city"), and means "King of the City," or "City King," which Baal was considered to be. But the two names in course of time drifted apart, and Melicertes, in Philo Byblius, has no connection at all with Baal-samin.1142 The Greeks, who identified Baal with their Zeus, viewed Melkarth as corresponding to their Heracles, or Hercules; and the later Phoenicians, catching at this identification, represented Melkarth under the form of a huge muscular man, with a lion's skin and sometimes with a club.1143 Melkarth was especially worshipped at Tyre, of which city he was the tutelary deity, at Thasos, and at Gades. Herodotus describes the temple of Hercules at Tyre, and attributes to it an antiquity of 2,300 years before his own time.1144 He also visited a temple dedicated to the same god at Thasos.1145 With Gades were connected the myths of Hercules' expedition to the west, of his erection of the pillars, his defeat of Chrysaor of the golden sword, and his successful foray upon the flocks and herds of the triple Geryon.1146 Whether these legends were Greek or Phoenician in origin is uncertain; but the Phoenicians, at any rate, adopted them, and here have been lately found on Phoenician sites representations both of Geryon himself,1147 and the carrying off by Hercules of his cattle.1148 The temple of Heracles at Gades is mentioned by Strabo1149 and others. It was on the eastern side of the island, where the strait between the island and the continent was narrowest. Founded about B.C. 1100, it continued to stand to the time of Silius Italicus, and, according to the tradition, had never needed repair.1150 An unextinguished fire had burnt upon its altar for thirteen hundred years; and the worship had remained unchanged—no image profaned the Holy of Holies, where the god dwelt, waited on by bare-footed priests with heads shaved, clothed in white linen robes, and vowed to celibacy.1151 The name of the god occurs as an element in a certain small number of Phoenician names of men—e.g. Bomilcar, Himilcar, Abd-Melkarth, and the like.

Dagon appears in scripture only as a Philistine god,1152 which would not prove him to have been acknowledged by the Phoenicians; but as Philo of Byblus admits him among the primary Phoenician deities, making him a son of Uranus, and a brother of Il or Kronis,1153 it is perhaps right that he should be allowed a place in the Phoenician list. According to Philo, he was the god of agriculture, the discoverer of wheat, and the inventor of the plough.1154 Whether he was really represented, as is commonly supposed,1155 in the form of a fish, or as half man and half fish, is extremely doubtful. In the Hebrew account of the fall of Dagon's image before the Ark of the Covenant at Ashdod there is no mention made of any "fishy part;" nor is there anything in the Assyrian remains to connect the name Dagon, which occurs in them, with the remarkable figure of a fish-god so frequent in the bas-reliefs. That figure would seem rather to represent, or symbolise, either Hea or Nin. The notion of Dagon's fishy form seems to rest entirely on an etymological basis—on the fact, i.e. that dag means "fish," in Hebrew. In Assyrian, however, kha is "fish," and not dag; while in Hebrew, though dag is "fish," dagan is "corn." It may be noted also that the Phoenician remains contain no representation of a fish deity. On the whole, it is perhaps best to be content with the account of Philo, and to regard the Phoenician Dagon as a "Zeus Arotrios"—a god presiding over agriculture and especially worshipped by husbandmen. The name, however, does not occur in the Phoenician remains which have come down to us.

Hadad, like Dagon, obtains his right to be included in the list of Phoenician deities solely from the place assigned to him by Philo. Otherwise he would naturally be viewed as an Aramean god, worshipped especially in Aram-Zobah, and in Syria of Damascus.1156 In Syria, he was identified with the sun;1157 and it is possible that in the Phoenician religion he was the Sun-God, worshipped (as we have seen) sometimes independently of Baal. His image was represented with the solar rays streaming down from it towards the earth, so as to indicate that the earth received from him all that made it fruitful and abundant.1158 Macrobius connects his name with the Hebrew chad, "one;" but this derivation is improbable.1159 Philo gives him the title of "King of Gods," and says that he reigned conjointly with Astarte and Demaroüs,1160 but this does not throw much light on the real Phoenician conception of him. The local name, Hadad-rimmon,1161 may seem to connect him with the god Rimmon, likewise a Syrian deity,1162 and it is quite conceivable that the two words may have been alternative names of the same god, just as Phoebus and Apollo were with the Greeks. We may conjecture that the Sun was worshipped under both names in Syria, while in Phoenicia Hadad was alone made use of. The worship of Baal as the Sun, which tended to prevail ever more and more, ousted Hadad from his place, and caused him to pass into oblivion.

Adonis was probably, like Hadad, originally a sun-god; but the myths connected with him gave him, at any rate in the late Phoenician times, a very distinct and definite personality. He was made the son of Cinryas, a mythic king of Byblus,1163 and the husband of Astarte or Ashtoreth. One day, as he chased the wild boar in Lebanon, near the sources of the river of Byblus, the animal which he was hunting turned upon him, and so gored his thigh that he died of the wound. Henceforth he was mourned annually. At the turn of the summer solstice, the anniversary of his death, all the women of Byblus went in a wild procession to Aphaca, in the Lebanon, where his temple stood, and wept and wailed on account of his death. The river, which his blood had once actually stained, turned red to show its sympathy with the mourners, and was thought to flow with his blood afresh. After the "weeping for Tammuz"1164 had continued for a definite time, the mourning terminated with the burial of an image of the god in the sacred precinct. Next day Adonis was supposed to return to life; his image was disinterred and carried back to the temple with music and dances, and every circumstance of rejoicing.1165 Wild orgies followed, and Aphaca became notorious for scenes to which it will be necessary to recur hereafter. The Adonis myth is generally explained as representing either the perpetually recurrent decay and recovery of nature, or the declension of the Sun as he moves from the summer to the winter constellations, and his subsequent return and reappearance in all his strength. But myths obtained a powerful hold on ancient imaginations, and the worshippers of Adonis probably in most cases forgot the symbolical character of his cult, and looked on him as a divine or heroic personage, who had actually gone through all the adventures ascribed to him in the legend. Hence the peculiarly local character of his worship, of which we find traces only at Byblus and at Jerusalem.

Sydyk, "Justice," or, the "Just One,"1166 whose name corresponds to the Hebrew Zadok or Zedek, appears in the Phoenician mythology especially as the father of Esmun and the Cabeiri. Otherwise he is only known as the son of Magus (!) and the discoverer of salt.1167 It is perhaps his name which forms the final element in Melchizedek, Adoni-zedek,1168 and the like. We have no evidence that he was really worshipped by the Phoenicians.

Esmun, on the other hand, the son of Sydyk, would seem to have been an object of worship almost as much as any other deity. He was the special god of Berytus,1169 but was honoured also in Cyprus, at Sidon, at Carthage, in Sardinia, and elsewhere.1170 His name forms a frequent element in Phoenician names, royal and other:—e.g. Esmun-azar, Esmun-nathan, Han-Esmun, Netsib-Esmun, Abd-Esmun, &c. According to Damascius,1171 he was the eighth son of Sydyk, whence his name, and the chief of the Cabeiri. Whereas they were dwarfish and misshapen, he was a youth of most beautiful appearance, truly worthy of admiration. Like

Adonis, he was fond of hunting in the woods that clothe the flanks of Lebanon, and there he was seen by Astronoë, the Phoenician goddess, the mother of the gods (in whom we cannot fail to recognise Astarte), who persecuted him with her attentions to such an extent that to escape her he was driven to the desperate resource of self-emasculation. Upon this the goddess, greatly grieved, called him Pæan, and by means of quickening warmth brought him back to life, and changed him from a man into a god, which he thenceforth remained. The Phoenicians called him Esmun, "the eighth," but the Greeks worshipped him as Asclepius, the god of healing, who gave life and health to mankind. Some of the later Phoenicians regarded him as identical with the atmosphere, which, they said, was the chief source of health to man.1172 But it is not altogether clear that the earlier Phoenicians attached to him any healing character.1173

The seven other Cabeiri, or "Great Ones," equally with Esmun the sons of Sydyk, were dwarfish gods who presided over navigation,1174 and were the patrons of sailors and ships. The special seat of their worship in Phoenicia Proper was Berytus, but they were recognised also in several of the Phoenician settlements, as especially in Lemnos, Imbrus, and Samothrace.1175 Ships were regarded as their invention,1176 and a sculptured image of some one or other of them was always placed on every Phoenician war-galley, either at the stern or stem of the vessel.1177 They were also viewed as presiding over metals and metallurgy,1178 having thus some points of resemblance to the Greek Hephæstus and the Latin Vulcan. Pigmy and misshapen gods belong to that fetishism which has always had charms for the Hamitic nations; and it may be suspected that the Phoenicians adopted the Cabeiri from their Canaanite predecessors, who were of the race of Ham.1179 The connection between these pigmy deities and the Egyptian Phthah, or rather Phthah-Sokari, is unmistakable, and was perceived by Herodotus.1180 Clay pigmy figurines found on Phoenician sites1181 very closely resemble the Egyptian images of that god; and the coins attributed to Cossura exhibit a similar dwarfish form, generally carrying a hammer in the right hand.1182 An astral character has been attached by some writers to the Cabeiri,1183 but chiefly on account of their number, which is scarcely a sufficient proof.

Several Greek writers speak of a Phoenician goddess corresponding to the Grecian Athene,1184 and some of them say that she was named Onga or Onca.1185 The Phoenician remains give us no such name; but as Philo Byblius has an "Athene" among his Phoenician deities, whom he makes the daughter of Il, or Kronos, and the queen of Attica,1186 it is perhaps best to allow Onca to retain her place in the Phoenician Pantheon. Philo says that Kronos by her advice shaped for himself out of iron a sword and a spear; we may therefore presume that she was a war-goddess (as was Pallas-Athene among the Greeks), whence she naturally presided over the gates of towns,1187 which were built and fortified for warlike purposes.

The worship of a goddess, called Tanath or Tanith, by the later Phoenicians, is certain, since, besides the evidence furnished by the name Abd-Tanith, i.e. "Servant of Tanith,"1188 the name Tanith itself is distinctly read on a number of votive tablets brought from Carthage, in a connection which clearly implies her recognition, not only as a goddess, but as a great goddess, the principal object of Carthaginian worship. The form of inscription on the tablets is, ordinarily, as follows:—1189

"To the great [goddess], Tanith, and
To our lord and master Baal-Hammon.
The offerer is ....,
Son of ...., son of ...."

Tanith is invariable placed before Baal, as though superior to him, and can be no other than the celestial goddess (Dea coelestis), whose temple in the Roman Carthage was so celebrated.1190 The Greeks regarded her as equivalent to their Artemis;1191 the Romans made her Diana, or Juno, or Venus.1192 Practically she must at Carthage have taken the place of Ashtoreth. Apuleius describes her as having a lunar character, like Ashtoreth, and calls her "the parent of all things, the mistress of the elements, the initial offspring of the ages, the highest of the deities, the queen of the Manes, the first of the celestials, the single representative of all the gods and goddesses, the one divinity whom all the world worships in many shapes, with varied rites, and under a multitude of names."1193 He says that she was represented as riding upon a lion, and it is probably her form which appears upon some of the later coins of Carthage, as well as upon a certain number of gems.1194 The origin of the name is uncertain. Gesenius would connect it at once with the Egyptian Neith (Nit), and with the Syrian Anaïtis or Tanaïtis;1195 but the double identification is scarcely tenable, since Anaïtis was, in Egypt, not Neith, but Anta.1196 The subject is very obscure, and requires further investigation.

Baaltis, or Beltis, was, according to Philo Byblius, the daughter of Uranus and the sister of Asthoreth or Astarte.1197 Il made her one of his many wives, and put the city of Byblus, which he had founded, under her special protection.1198 It is doubtful, however, whether she was really viewed by the Phoenicians as a separate goddess, and not rather as Ashtoreth under another name. The word is the equivalent of {...}, "my lady," a very suitable title for the supreme goddess. Beltis, indeed, in Babylonia, was distinct from Ishtar;1199 but this fact must not be regarded as any sufficient proof that the case was the same in Phoenicia. The Phoenician polytheism was decidedly more restricted than the Babylonian, and did not greatly affect the needless multiplication of divinities. Baaltis in Phoenicia may be the Beltis of Babylon imported at a comparatively late date into the country, but is more probably an alternative name, or rather, perhaps, a mere honorary title of Ashtoreth.11100

The chief characteristic of the third period of the Phoenician religion was the syncretistic tendency,11101 whereby foreign gods were called in, and either identified with the old national divinities, or joined with them, and set by their side. Ammon, Osiris, Phthah, Pasht, and Athor, were introduced from Egypt, Tanith from either Egypt or Syria, Nergal from Assyria, Beltis (Baaltis) perhaps from Babylon. The worship of Osiris in the later times appears from such names as Abd-Osir, Osir-shamar, Melek-Osir, and the like,11102 and is represented on coins with Phoenician legends, which are attributed either to Malta or Gaulos.11103 Osiris was, it would seem, identified with Adonis,11104 and was said to have been buried at Byblus;11105 which was near the mouth of the Adonis river. His worship was not perhaps very widely spread; but there are traces of it at Byblus, in Cyprus, and in Malta.11106 Ammon was identified with Baal in his solar character,11107 and was generally worshipped in conjunction with Tanith, more especially at Carthage.11108 He was represented with his head encircled by rays, and with a perfectly round face.11109 His common title was "Lord" {...}, but in Numidia he was worshipped as "the Eternal King" {...}.11110 As the giver of all good things, he held trees or fruits in his hands.11111

The Phoenicians worshipped their gods, like most other ancient nations, with prayer, with hymns of praise, with sacrifices, with processions, and with votive offerings. We do not know whether they had any regularly recurrent day, like the Jewish Sabbath, or Christian Sunday, on which worship took place in the temples generally; but at any rate each temple had its festival times, when multitudes flocked to it, and its gods were honoured with prolonged services and sacrifices on a larger scale than ordinary. Most festivals were annual, but some recurred at shorter intervals; and, besides the festivals, there was an every day cult, which was a duty incumbent upon the priests, but at which the private worshipper also might assist to offer prayer or sacrifice. The ordinary sacrificial animals were oxen, cows, goats, sheep, and lambs; swine were not offered, being regarded as unclean;11112 but the stag was an acceptable victim, at any rate on certain occasions.11113 At all functions the priests attended in large numbers, habited in white garments of linen or cotton, and wearing a stiff cap or mitre upon their heads:11114 on one occasion of a sacrifice Lucian counted above three hundred engaged in the ceremony.11115 It was the duty of some to slay the victims; of others to pour libations; of a third class to bear about pans of coal on which incense could be offered; of a fourth to attend upon the altars.11116 The priests of each temple had at their head a Chief or High

Priest, who was robed in purple and wore a golden tiara. His office, however, continued only for a year, when another was chosen to succeed him.11117

Ordinarily, sacrifices were offered, in Phoenicia as elsewhere, singly, and upon altars; but sometimes it was customary to have a great holocaust. Large trees were dug up by the roots, and planted in the court of the temple; the victims, whether goats, or sheep, or cattle of any other kind, were suspended by ropes from the branches; birds were similarly attached, and garments, and vessels in gold and silver. Then the images of the gods belonging to the temple were brought out, and carried in a solemn procession round the trees; after which the trees were set on fire, and the whole was consumed in a mighty conflagration.11118 The season for this great holocaust was the commencement of the spring-time, when the goodness of Heaven in once more causing life to spring up on every side seemed to require man's special acknowledgment.

Hymns of praise are spoken of especially in connection with this same Spring-Festival.11119 Votive offerings were continually being offered in every temple by such as believed that they had received any benefit from any god, either in consequence of their vows, or prayers, or even by the god's spontaneous action. The sites of temples yield numerous traces of such offerings. Sometimes they are in the shape of stone stelæ or pillars, inscribed and more or less ornamented,11120 sometimes of tablets placed within an ornamental border, and generally accompanied by some rude sculptures;11121 more often of figures, either in bronze or clay, which are mostly of a somewhat rude character. M. Renan observes with respect to these figures, which are extremely numerous:—"Ought we to see in these images, as has been supposed, long series of portraits of priests and priestesses continued through several centuries? We do not think so. The person represented in these statues appears to us to be the author of a vow or of a sacrifice made to the divinity of the temple . . . Vows and sacrifices were very fleeting things; it might be feared that the divinity would soon forget them. An inscription was already recognised as a means of rendering the memory of a vow more lasting; but a statue was a momento still more—nay, much more efficacious. By having himself represented under the eyes of the divinity in the very act of accomplishing his vow, a man called to mind, as one may say, incessantly the offering which he had made to the god, and the homage which he had rendered him. An idea of this sort is altogether in conformity with the materialistic and self-interested character of the Phoenician worship, where the vow is a kind of business affair, a matter of debtor and creditor account, in which a man stipulates very clearly what he is to give, and holds firmly that he is to be paid in return . . . We have then, in these statues, representations of pious men, who came one after another to acquit themselves of their debt in the presence of the divinity; in order that the latter should not forget that the debt was discharged, they set up their images in front of the god. The image was larger or smaller, more or less carefully elaborated, in a more or less valuable material, according to the means of the individual who consecrated it."11122

Thus far there was no very remarkable difference between the Phoenician religious system and other ancient Oriental worships, which have a general family likeness, and differ chiefly in the names and number of the deities, the simplicity or complication of the rites, and the greater or less power and dignity attached to the priestly office. In these several respects the Phoenician religion seems to have leant towards the side of simplicity, the divinities recognised being, comparatively speaking, few, priestly influence not great, and the ceremonial not very elaborate. But there were two respects in which the religion was, if not singular, at any rate markedly different from ordinary polytheisms, though less in the principles involved than in the extent to which they were carried out in practice. These were the prevalence of licentious orgies and of human sacrifice. The worship of Astarte was characterised by the one, the worship of Baal by the other. Phoenician mythology taught that the great god, Il or El, when reigning upon earth as king of Byblus, had, under circumstances of extreme danger to his native land, sacrificed his dearly loved son, Ieoud, as an expiatory offering. Divine sanction had thus been given to the horrid rite; and thenceforth, whenever in Phoenicia either public or private calamity threatened, it became customary that human victims should be selected, the nobler and more honourable the better, and that the wrath of the gods should be appeased by taking their lives. The mode of death was horrible. The sacrifices were to be consumed by fire; the life given by the Fire God he should also take back again by the flames which destroy being. The rabbis describe the image of Moloch as a human figure with a bull's head and outstretched arms;11123 and the account which they give is confirmed by what Diodorus relates of the Carthaginian Kronos. His image, Diodorus says,11124 was of metal, and was made hot by a fire kindled within it; the victims were placed in its arms and thence rolled into the fiery lap below. The most usual form of the rite was the sacrifice of their children— especially of their eldest sons11125—by parents. "This custom was grounded in part on the notion that children were the dearest possession of their parents, and, in part, that as pure and innocent beings they were the offerings of atonement most certain to pacify the anger of the deity; and further, that the god of whose essence the generative power of nature was had a just title of that which was begotten of man, and to the surrender of their children's lives . . . Voluntary offering on the part of the parents was essential to the success of the sacrifice; even the first-born, nay, the only child of the family, was given up. The parents stopped the cries of their children by fondling and kissing them, for the victim ought not to weep; and the sound of complaint was drowned in the din of flutes and kettledrums. Mothers, according to Plutarch,11126 stood by without tears or sobs; if they wept or sobbed they lost the honour of the act, and their children were sacrificed notwithstanding. Such sacrifices took place either annually or on an appointed day, or before great enterprises, or on the occasion of public calamities, to appease the wrath of the god."11127

In the worship of Astarte the prostitution of women, and of effeminate men, played the same part that child murder did in the worship of Baal. "This practice," says Dr. Döllinger,11128 "so widely spread in the world of old, the delusion that no service more acceptable could be rendered a deity than that of unchastity, was deeply rooted in the Asiatic mind. Where the deity was in idea sexual, or where two deities in chief, one a male and the other a female, stood in juxtaposition, there the sexual relation appeared as founded upon the essence of the deity itself, and the instinct and its satisfaction as that in men which most corresponded with the deity. Thus lust itself became a service of the gods; and, as the fundamental idea of sacrifice is that of the immediate or substitutive surrender of a man's self to the deity, so the woman could do the goddess no better service than by prostitution. Hence it was the custom [in some places] that a maiden before her marriage should prostitute herself once in the temple of the goddess;11129 and this was regarded as the same in kind with the offering of the first-fruits of the field." Lucian, a heathen and an eye-witness, tells us11130—"I saw at Byblus the grand temple of the Byblian Venus, in which are accomplished the orgies relating to Adonis; and I learnt the nature of the orgies. For the Byblians say that the wounding of Adonis by the boar took place in their country; and, in memory of the accident, they year by year beat their breasts, and utter lamentations, and go through the orgies, and hold a great mourning throughout the land. When the weeping is ended, first of all, they make to Adonis the offerings usually made to a corpse; after which, on the next day, they feign that he has come to life again, and hold a procession [of his image] in the open air. But previously they shave their heads, like the Egyptians when an Apis dies; and if any woman refuse to do so, she must sell her beauty during one day to all who like. Only strangers, however, are permitted to make the purchase, and the money paid is expended on a sacrifice which is offered to the goddess." "In this way," as Dr. Döllinger goes on to say, "they went so far at last as to contemplate the abominations of unnatural lust as a homage rendered to the deity, and to exalt it into a regular cultus. The worship of the goddess [Ashtoreth] at Aphaca in the Lebanon was specially notorious in this respect."11131 Here, according to Eusebius, was, so late as the time of Constantine the Great, a temple in which the old Phoenician rites were still retained. "This," he says, "was a grove and a sacred enclosure, not situated, as most temples are, in the midst of a city, and of market-places, and of broad streets, but far away from either road or path, on the rocky slopes of Libanus. It was dedicated to a shameful goddess, the goddess Aphrodite. A school of wickedness was this place for all such profligate persons as had ruined their bodies by excessive luxury. The men there were soft and womanish—men no longer; the dignity of their sex they rejected; with impure lust they thought to honour the deity. Criminal intercourse with women, secret pollutions, disgraceful and nameless deeds, were practised in the temple, where there was no restraining law, and no guardian to preserve decency."11132

One fruit of this system was the extraordinary institution of the Galli. The Galli were men, who made themselves as much like women as they could, and offered themselves for purposes of unnatural lust to either sex. Their existence may be traced in Israel and Judah,11133 as well as in Syria and Phoenicia.11134 At great festivals, under the influence of a strong excitement, amid the din of flutes and drums and wild songs, a number of the male devotees would snatch up swords or knives, which lay ready for the purpose, throw off their garments, and coming forward with a loud shout, proceed to castrate themselves openly. They would then run through the streets of the city, with the mutilated parts in their hands, and throw them into the houses of the inhabitants, who were bound in such case to provide the thrower with all the apparel and other gear needful for a woman.11135 This apparel they thenceforth wore, and were recognised as attached to the worship of Astarte, entitled to reside in her temples, and authorised to take part in her ceremonies. They joined with the priests and the sacred women at festival times in frenzied dances and other wild orgies, shouting, and cutting themselves on the arms, and submitting to be flogged one by another.11136 At other seasons they "wandered from place to place, taking with them a veiled image or symbol of their goddess, and clad in women's apparel of many colours, and with their faces and eyes painted in female fashion, armed with swords and scourges, they threw themselves by a wild dance into bacchanalian ecstasy, in which their long hair was draggled through the mud. They bit their own arms, and then hacked themselves with their swords, or scourged themselves in penance for a sin supposed to have been committed against the goddess. In these scenes, got up to aid the collection of money, by long practice they contrived to cut themselves so adroitly as not to inflict on themselves any very serious wounds."11137

It is difficult to estimate the corrupting effect upon practice and morals of a religious system which embraced within it so many sensual and degrading elements. Where impurity is made an essential part of religion, there the very fountain of life is poisoned, and that which should have been "a savour of life unto life"—a cleansing and regenerating influence—becomes "a savour of death unto death"—an influence leading on to the worst forms of moral degradation. Phoenician religion worked itself out, and showed its true character, in the first three centuries after our era, at Aphaca, at Hierapolis, and at Antioch, where, in the time of Julian, even a Libanius confessed that the great festival of the year consisted only in the perpetration of all that was impure and shameless, and the renunciation of every lingering spark of decency.11138

A vivid conception of another world, and of the reality of a life after death, especially if connected with a belief in future rewards and punishments, might have done much, or at any rate something, to counteract the effect upon morals and conduct of the degrading tenets and practices connected with the Astarte worship; but, so far as appears, the Phoenicians had a very faint and dim conception of the life to come, and neither hoped for happiness, nor feared misery in it. Their care for the preservation of their bodies after death, and the provision which in some cases they are seen to have made for them,11139 imply a belief that death was not the end of everything, and a few vague expressions in inscriptions upon tombs point to a similar conviction;11140 but the life of the other world seems to have been regarded as something imperfect and precarious11141—a sort of shadowy existence in a gloomy Sheôl, where was neither pleasure nor pain, neither suffering nor enjoyment, but only quietness and rest. The thought of it did not occupy men's minds, or exercise any perceptible influence over their conduct. It was a last home, whereto all must go, acquiesced in, but neither hoped for nor dreaded. A Phoenician's feelings on the subject were probably very much those expressed by

Job in his lament:—11142

"Why died I not from the womb? Why gave I not up the ghost at my
  birth?
Why did the knees prevent me? or why the breasts that I should
  suck?
For now should I have lain still and been quiet;
I should have slept, and then should I have been at rest;
I should have been with the kings and councillors of the earth,
Who rebuilt for themselves the cities that were desolate.
I should have been with the princes that had much gold,
And that filled their houses with silver . . .
There they that are wicked cease from troubling,
There they that are weary sink to rest;
There the prisoners are in quiet together,
And hear no longer the voice of the oppressor:
There are both the great and small, and the servant is freed from
  his master."

Still their religion, such as it was, had a great hold upon the Phoenicians. Parents gave to their children, almost always, religious names, recognising each son and daughter as a gift from heaven, or placing them under the special protection of the gods generally, or of some single divinity. It was piety, an earnest but mistaken piety, which so often caused the parent to sacrifice his child—the very apple of his eye and delight of his heart—that so he might make satisfaction for the sins which he felt in his inmost soul that he had committed. It was piety that filled the temples with such throngs, that brought for sacrifice so many victims, that made the worshipper in every difficulty put up a vow to heaven, and caused the payment of the vows in such extraordinary profusion. At Carthage alone there have been found many hundreds of stones, each one of which records the payment of a vow;11143 while other sites have furnished hundreds or even thousands of ex votos—statues, busts, statuettes, figures of animals, cylinders, seals, rings, bracelets, anklets, ear-rings, necklaces, ornaments for the hair, vases, amphoræ, oenochoæ, pateræ, jugs, cups, goblets, bowls, dishes, models of boats and chariots—indicative of an almost unexampled devotion. A single chamber in the treasury of Curium produced more than three hundred articles in silver and silver-gilt;11144 the temple of Golgi yielded 228 votive statues;11145 sites in Sardinia scarcely mentioned in antiquity have sufficed to fill whole museums with statuettes, rings, and scarabs. If the Phoenicians did not give evidence of the depth of their religious feeling by erecting, like most nations, temples of vast size and magnificence, still they left in numerous places unmistakable proof of the reality of their devotion to the unseen powers by the multiplicity, and in many cases the splendour,11146 of their votive offerings.

CHAPTER XII—DRESS, ORNAMENTS, AND SOCIAL HABITS

Dress of common men—Dress of men of the upper classes—
Treatment of the hair and beard—Male ornaments—Supposed
priestly costume—Ordinary dress of women—Arrangement of
their hair—Female ornaments—Necklaces—Bracelets—Ear-
rings—Ornaments for the hair—Toilet pins—Buckles—A
Phoenician lady's toilet table—Freedom enjoyed by
Phoenician women—Active habits of the men—Curious agate
ornament—Use in furniture of bronze and ivory.

The dress of the Phoenician men, especially of those belonging to the lower orders, consisted, for the most part, of a single close-fitting tunic, which reached from the waist to a little above the knee.0121 The material was probably either linen or cotton, and the simple garment was perfectly plain and unornamented, like the common shenti of the Egyptians. On the head was generally worn a cap of one kind or another, sometimes round, more often conical, occasionally shaped like a helmet. The conical head-dresses seem to have often ended in a sort of top-knot or button, which recalls the head-dress of a Chinese Mandarin.

Where the men were of higher rank, the shenti was ornamented, It was patterned, and parted towards the two sides, while a richly adorned lappet, terminating in uræi, fell down in front.0122 The girdle, from which it depended, was also patterned, and the shenti thus arranged was sometimes a not inelegant garment. In addition to the shenti, it was common among the upper classes to wear over the bust and shoulders a close-fitting tunic with short sleeves,0123 like a modern "jersey;" and sometimes two garments were worn, an inner robe descending to the feet, and an outer blouse or shirt, with sleeves reaching to the elbow.0124 Occasionally, instead of this outer blouse, the man of rank has a mantle thrown over the left shoulder, which falls about him in folds that are sufficiently graceful.0125 The conical cap with a top-knot is, with persons of this class, the almost universal head-dress.

Great attention seems to have been paid to the hair and beard. Where no cap is worn, the hair clings closely to the head in a wavy compact mass, escaping however from below the wreath or diadem, which supplies the place of a cap, in one or two rows of crisp, rounded curls.0126 The beard has mostly a strong resemblance to that affected by the Assyrians, and familiar to us from their sculptures. It is arranged in three, four, or five rows of small tight curls,0127 and extends from ear to ear around the cheeks and chin. Sometimes, however, in lieu of the many rows, we find one row only, the beard falling in tresses, which are curled at the extremity.0128 There is no indication of the Phoenicians having cultivated mustachios.

For ornaments the male Phoenicians wore collars, which were sometimes very elaborate, armlets, bracelets, and probably finger-rings. The collars resembled those of the Egyptians, being arranged in three rows, and falling far over the breast.0129 The armlets seem to have been plain, consisting of a mere twist of metal, once, twice, or thrice around the limb.1210 The royal armlets of Etyander, king of Paphos, are single twists of gold, the ends of which only just overlap: they are plain, except for the inscription, which reads Eteadoro to Papo basileos, or "The property of Etyander, king of Paphos."1211 Men's bracelets were similar in character. The finger-rings were either of gold or silver, and generally set with a stone, which bore a device, and which the wearer used as a seal.1212

The most elaborate male costume which has come down to us is that of a figure found at Golgi, and believed to represent a high priest of Ashtoreth. The conical head-dress is divided into partitions by narrow stripes, which, beginning at its lower edge, converge to a point at top. This point is crowned by the representation of a calf's or bull's head. The main garment is a long robe reaching from the neck to the feet, "worn in much the same manner as the peplos on early Greek female figures." Round the neck of the robe are two rows of stars painted in red, probably meant to represent embroidery. A little below the knee is another band of embroidery, from which the robe falls in folds or pleats, which gather closely around the legs. Above the long robe is worn a mantle, which covers the right arm and shoulder, and thence hangs down below the right knee, passing also in many folds from the shoulder across the breast, and thence, after a twist around the left arm, falling down below the left knee. The treatment of the hair is remarkable. Below the rim of the cap is the usual row of crisp curls; but besides these, there depend from behind the ears on either side of the neck three long tresses. The feet of the figure are naked. The right hand holds a cup by its foot between the middle and fore-fingers, while the left holds a dove with wings outspread.1213

Women were, for the most part, draped very carefully from head to foot. The nude figures which are found abundantly in the Phoenician remains1214 are figures of goddesses, especially of Astarte, who were considered not to need the ornament, or the concealment of dress. Human female figures are in almost every case covered from the neck to the feet, generally in garments with many folds, which, however, are arranged very variously. Sometimes a single robe of the amplest dimensions seems to envelop the whole form, which it completely conceals with heavy folds of drapery.1215 The long petticoat is sleeved, and gathered into a sinus below the breasts, about which it hangs loosely. Sometimes, on the contrary, the petticoat is perfectly plain, and has no folds.1216 Occasionally a second garment is worn over the gown or robe, which covers the left shoulder and the lap, descending to the knees, or somewhat lower.1217 The waist is generally confined by a girdle, which is knotted in front.1218 There are a few instances in which the feet are enclosed in sandals.1219

The hair of women is sometimes concealed under a cap, but generally it escapes from such confinement, and shows itself below the cap in great rolls, or in wavy masses, which flow off right and left from a parting over the middle of the forehead.1220 Tresses are worn occasionally: these depend behind either ear in long loose curls, which fall upon the shoulders.1221 Female heads are mostly covered with a loose hood, or cap; but sometimes the hair is merely encircled by a band or bands, above and below which it ripples freely.1222 Phoenician women were greatly devoted to the use of personal ornaments. It was probably from them that the Hebrew women of Isaiah's time derived the "tinkling ornaments of the feet, the cauls, the round tires like the moon, the chains, the bracelets, and the mufflers, the bonnets and the ornaments of the legs, and the head-bands, and the tablets, and the ear-rings, the rings and nose-jewels, the changeable suits of apparel, and the mantles, and the wimples, and the crisping pins, the glasses, and the fine linen, and the hoods, and the vails,"1223 which the prophet denounces so fiercely. The excavations made on Phoenician sites have yielded in abundance necklaces, armlets, bracelets, pendants to be worn as lockets, ear-rings, finger-rings, ornaments for the hair, buckles or brooches, seals, buttons, and various articles of the toilet such as women delight in.

Women wore, it appears, three or four necklaces at the same time, one above the other.1224 A string of small beads or pearls would closely encircle the neck just under the chin. Below, where the chest begins, would lie a second string of larger beads, perhaps of gold, perhaps only of glass, while further down, as the chest expands, would be rows of still larger ornaments, pendants in glass, or crystal, or gold, or agate modelled into the shape of acorns, or pomegranates, or lotus flowers, or cones, or vases, and lying side by side to the number of fifty or sixty. Several of the necklaces worn by the Cypriote ladies have come down to us. One is composed of a row of one hundred and three gold beads, alternately round and oval, to the oval ones of which are attached pendants, also in gold, representing alternately the blossom and bud of the lotus plant, except in one instance. The central bead of all has as its pendant a human head and bust, modelled in the Egyptian style, with the hair falling in lappets on either side of the face, and with a broad collar upon the shoulders and the breast.1225 Another consists of sixty-four gold beads, twenty-two of which are of superior size to the rest, and of eighteen pendants, shaped like the bud of a flower, and delicately chased.1226 There are others where gold beads are intermixed with small carnelian and onyx bugles, while the pendants are of gold, like the beads; or where gold and rock-crystal beads alternate, and a single crystal vase hangs as pendant in the middle; or where alternate carnelian and gold beads have as pendant a carnelian cone, a symbol of Astarte.1227 Occasionally the sole material used is glass. Necklaces have been found composed entirely of long oval beads of blue or greenish-blue glass; others where the colour of the beads is a dark olive;1228 others again, where all the component parts are of glass, but the colours and forms are greatly varied. In a glass necklace found at Tharros in Sardinia, besides beads of various sizes and hues, there are two long rough cylinders, four heads of animals, and a human head as central ornament. "Taken separately, the various elements of which this necklace is composed have little value; neither the heads of the animals, nor the bearded human face, perhaps representing Bacchus, are in good style; the cylinders and rounded beads which fill up the intermediate spaces between the principal objects are of very poor execution; but the mixture of whites, and greys, and yellows, and greens, and blues produces a whole which is harmonious and gay."1229 Perhaps the most elegant and tasteful necklace of all that have been discovered is the one made of a thick solid gold cord, very soft and elastic, which is figured on the page opposite.1230 At either extremity is a cylinder of very fine granulated work, terminating in one case in a lion's head of good execution, in the other surmounted by a simple cap. The lion's mouth holds a ring, while the cap supports a long hook, which seems to issue from a somewhat complicated knot, entangled wherein is a single light rosette. "In this arrangement, in the curves of the thin wire, which folds back upon itself again and again, there is an air of ease, an apparent negligence, which is the very perfection of technical skill."1231

The bracelets worn by the Phoenician ladies were of many kinds, and frequently of great beauty. Some were bands of plain solid gold, without ornament of any kind, very heavy, weighing from 200 to 300 grammes each.1232 Others were open, and terminated at either extremity in the head of an animal. One, found by General Di Cesnola at Curium in Cyprus,1233 exhibited at the two ends heads of lions, which seemed to threaten each other. The execution of the heads left nothing to be desired. Some others, found in Phoenicia Proper, in a state of extraordinary preservation, were of similar design, but, in the place of lions' heads, exhibited the heads of bull, with very short horns.1234 A third type aimed at greater variety, and showed the head of a wild goat at one end, and that of a ram at the other.1235 In a few instances, the animal representation appears at one extremity of the bracelet only, as in a specimen from Camirus, whereof the workmanship is unmistakably Phoenician, which has a lion's head at one end, and at the other tapers off, like the tail of a serpent.1236

A pair of bracelets in the British Museum, said to have come from Tharros, consist of plain thin circlets of gold, with a ball of gold in the middle. The ball is ornamented with spirals and projecting knobs, which must have been uncomfortable to the wearer, but are said not to be wanting in elegance.1237

There are other Phoenician bracelets of an entirely different character. These consist of broad flat bands, which fitted closely to the wrist, and were fastened round it by means of a clasp. Two, now in the Museum of New York, are bands of gold about an inch in width, ornamented externally with rosettes, flowers, and other designs in high relief, on which are visible in places the remains of a blue enamel.1238 Another is composed of fifty-four large-ribbed gold beads, soldered together by threes, and having for centre a gold medallion, with a large onyx set in it, and with four gold pendants.1239 A third bracelet of the kind, said to have been found at Tharros, consists of six plates, united by hinges, and very delicately engraved with patterns of a thoroughly Phoenician character, representing palms, volutes, and flowers.1240

But it is in their earrings that the Phoenician ladies were most curious and most fanciful. They present to us, as MM. Perrot and Chipiez note, "an astonishing variety."1241 Some, which must have been very expensive, are composed of many distinct parts, connected with each other by chains of an elegant pattern. One of the most beautiful specimens was found by General Di Cesnola in Cyprus.1242 There is a hook at top, by which it was suspended. Then follows a medallion, where the workmanship is of singular delicacy. A rosette occupies the centre; around it are a set of spirals, negligently arranged, and enclosed within a chain-like band, outside of which is a double beading. From the medallion depend by finely wrought chains five objects. The central chain supports a human head, to which is attached a conical vase, covered at top: on either side are two short chains, terminating in rings, from which hang small nondescript pendants: beyond are two longer chains, with small vases or bottles attached. Another, found in Sardinia, is scarcely less complicated. The ring which pierced the ear forms the handle of a kind of basket, which is covered with lines of bead-work: below, attached by means of two rings, is the model of a hawk with wings folded; below the hawk, again attached by a couple of rings, is a vase of elegant shape, decorated with small bosses, lozenges, and chevrons.1243 Other ear-rings have been found similar in type to this, but simplified by the omission of the bird, or of the basket.1244

An entirely different type is that furnished by an ear-ring in the Museum of New York brought from Cyprus, where the loop of the ornament rises from a sort of horse-shoe, patterned with bosses and spirals, and surrounded by a rough edging of knobs, standing at a little distance one from another.1245 Other forms found also in Cyprus are the ear-ring with the long pendant, which has been called "an elongated pear,"1246 ornamented towards the lower end with small blossoms of flowers, and terminating in a minute ball, which recalls the "drops" that are still used by the jewellers of our day; the loop which supports a crux ansata;1247 that which has attached to it a small square box, or measure containing a heap of grain, thought to represent wheat;1248 and those which support fruit of various kinds.1249 An ear-ring of much delicacy consists of a twisted ring, curved into a hook at one extremity, and at the other ending in the head of a goat, with a ring attached to it, through which the hook passes.1250 Another, rather curious than elegant, consists of a double twist, ornamented with lozenges, and terminating in triangular points finely granulated.1251

Ornaments more or less resembling this last type of ear-ring, but larger and coarser, have given rise to some controversy, having been regarded by some as ear-rings, by others as fastenings for the dress, and by a third set of critics as ornaments for the hair. They consist of a double twist, sometimes ornamented at one end only, sometimes at both. A lion's or a griffin's head crowns usually the principal end; round the neck is a double or triple collar, and below this a rosette, very carefully elaborated. In one instance two griffins show themselves side by side, exhibiting their heads, their chests, their wings, and their fore-paws or hands; between them is an ornament like that which commonly surmounts Phoenician stelæ; and below this a most beautiful rosette.1252 The fashioning shows that the back of the ornament was not intended to be seen, and favours the view that it was to be placed where a mass of hair would afford the necessary concealment.

The Phoenician ladies seem also to have understood the use of hair-pins, which were from two to three inches long, and had large heads, ribbed longitudinally, and crowned with two smaller balls, one above the other.1253 The material used was either gold or silver.

To fasten their dresses, the Phoenician ladies used fibulæ or buckles of a simple character. Brooches set with stones have not at present been found on Phoenician sites; but in certain cases the fibulæ show a moderate amount of ornament. Some have glass beads strung on the pin that is inserted into the catch; others have the rounded portion surmounted by the figure of a horse or of a bird.1254 Most fibulæ are in bronze; but one, found in the treasury of Curium, and now in the Museum of New York, was of gold.1255 This, however, was most probably a votive offering.

It is impossible at present to reproduce the toilet table of a Phoenician lady. We may be tolerably sure, however, that certain indispensable articles would not be lacking. Circular mirrors, either of polished metal, or of glass backed by a plate of tin or silver, would undoubtedly have found their place on them, together with various vessels for holding perfumes and ointments. A vase in rock crystal, discovered at Curium, with a funnel and cover in gold, the latter attached by a fine gold chain to one of its handles,1256 was doubtless a fine lady's favourite smelling bottle. Various other vessels in silver, of a small size,1257 as basins and bowls beautifully chased, tiny jugs, alabasti, ladles, &c., had also the appearance of belonging rather to the toilet table than to the plate-basket. Some of the alabasti would contain kohl or stibium, some salves and ointments, others perhaps perfumed washes for the complexion. Among the bronze objects found,1258 some may have been merely ornaments, others stands for rings, bracelets, and the like. One terra-cotta vase from Dali seems made for holding pigments,1259 and raises the suspicion that Phoenician, or at any rate Cyprian, beauties were not above heightening their charms by the application of paint.

Women in Phoenicia seem to have enjoyed considerable freedom. They are represented as banqueting in the company of men, sometimes sitting with them on the same couch, sometimes reclining with them at the same table.1260 Occasionally they delight their male companion by playing upon the lyre or the double pipe,1261 while in certain instances they are associated in bands of three, who perform on the lyre, the double pipe, and the tambourine.1262 They take part in religious processions, and present offerings to the deities.1263 The positions occupied in history by Jezebel and Dido fall in with these indications, and imply a greater approach to equality between the sexes in Phoenicia than in Oriental communities generally.

The men were, for Orientals, unusually hardy and active. In only one instance is there any appearance of the use of the parasol by a Phoenician.1264 Sandals are infrequently worn; neck, chest, arms, and legs are commonly naked. The rough life of seamen hardened the greater number: others hunted the wild ox and the wild boar1265 in the marshy plains of the coast tract, and in the umbrageous dells of Lebanon. Even the lion may have been affronted in the great mountain, and if we are unable to describe the method of its chase in Phoenicia, the reason is that the Phoenician artists have, in their representations of lion hunts, adopted almost exclusively Assyrian models.1266 The Phoenician gift of facile imitation was a questionable advantage, since it led the native artists continually to substitute for sketches at first hand of scenes with which they were familiar, conventional renderings of similar scenes as depicted by foreigners.

An ornament found in Cyprus, the intention of which is uncertain, finds its proper place in the present chapter, though we cannot attach it to any particular class of objects. It consists of a massive knob of solid agate, with a cylinder of the same both above and below, through which a rod, or bar, must have been intended to pass. Some archæologists see in it the top of a sceptre;1267 others, the head of a mace;1268 but there is nothing really to prove its use. We might imagine it the adornment of a throne or chair of state, or the end of a chariot pole, or a portion of the stem of a candelabrum. Antiquity has furnished nothing similar with which to compare it; and we only say of it, that, whatever was its purpose, so large and so beautiful a mass of agate has scarcely been met with elsewhere.1269 The cutting is such as to show very exquisitely the veining of the material.

Bronze objects in almost infinite variety have been found on Phoenician sites,1270 but only a few of them can have been personal ornaments. They comprise lamps, bowls, vases, jugs, cups, armlets, anklets, daggers, dishes, a horse's bit, heads and feet of animals, statuettes, mirrors, fibulæ, buttons, &c. Furniture would seem to have been largely composed of bronze, which sometimes formed its entire fabric, though generally confined to the ornamentation. Ivory was likewise employed in considerable quantities in the manufacture of furniture,1271 to which it was applied as an outer covering, or veneer, either plain, or more generally carved with a pattern or with figures. The "ivory house" of Ahab1272 was perhaps so called, not so much from the application of the precious material to the doors and walls, as from its employment in the furniture. There is every probability that it was the construction of Phoenician artists.

CHAPTER XIII—PHOENICIAN WRITING, LANGUAGE, AND LITERATURE

The Phoenician alphabet—Its wide use—Its merits—Question of its origin—Its defects—Phoenician writing and language— Resemblance of the language to Hebrew—In the vocabulary— In the grammar—Points of difference between Phoenician and Hebrew—Scantiness of the literature—Phoenician history of Philo Byblius—Extracts—Periplus of Hanno—Phoenician epigraphic literature—Inscription of Esmunazar—Inscription of Tabnit—Inscription of Jehav-melek—Marseilles inscription—Short inscriptions on votive offerings and tombs—Range of Phoenician book-literature.

The Phoenician alphabet, like the Hebrew, consisted of twenty-two characters, which had, it is probable, the same names with the Hebrew letters,0131 and were nearly identical in form with the letters used anciently by the entire Hebrew race. The most ancient inscription in the character which has come down to us is probably that of Mesha,0132 the Moabite king, which belongs to the ninth century before our era. The next in antiquity, which is of any considerable length, is that discovered recently in the aqueduct which brings the water into the pool of Siloam,0133 which dates probably from the time of Hezekiah, ab. B.C. 727-699. Some short epigraphs on Assyrian gems, tablets, and cylinders belong apparently to about the same period. The series of Phoenician and Cilician coins begins soon after this, and continues to the time of the Roman supremacy in Western Asia. The soil of Phoenicia Proper, and of the various countries where the Phoenicians established settlements or factories, as Cyprus, Malta, Sicily, Sardinia, Southern Gaul, Spain, and North Africa, has also yielded a large crop of somewhat brief legends, the "inscription of Marseilles"0134 being the most important of them. Finally there have been found within the last few years, in Phoenicia itself, near Byblus and Sidon, the three most valuable inscriptions of the entire series—those of Jehavmelek, Esmunazar and Tabnit—which have enabled scholars to place the whole subject on a scientific basis.

It is now clear that the same, or nearly the same, alphabet was in use from a very early date over the greater part of Western Asia—in Phoenicia, Moab, Judæa, Samaria, Lycia, Caria, Phrygia, &c.—that it was adopted, with slight alterations only, by the Etruscans and the Greeks, and that from them it was passed on to the nations of modern Europe, and acquired a quasi-universality. The invention of this alphabet was, by the general consent of antiquity, ascribed to the Phoenicians;0135 and though, if their claim to priority of discovery be disputed, it is impossible to prove it, their practical genius and their position among the nations of the earth are strong subsidiary arguments in support of the traditions.

The Phoenician alphabet, or the Syrian script, as some call it,0136 did not obtain its general prevalence without possessing some peculiar merits. Its primary merit was that of simplicity. The pictorial systems of the Egyptians and the Hittites required a hand skilled in drawing to express them; the cuneiform syllabaries of Babylonia, Assyria, and Elam needed an extraordinary memory to grasp the almost infinite variety in the arrangement of the wedges, and to distinguish each group from all the rest; even the Cypriote syllabary was of awkward and unnecessary extent, and was expressed by characters needlessly complicated. The Phoenician inventor, whoever he was, reduced letters to the smallest possible number, and expressed them by the simplest possible forms. Casting aside the idea of a syllabary, he reduced speech to its ultimate elements, and set apart a single sign to represent each possible variety of articulation, or rather each variety of which he was individually cognisant. How he fixed upon his signs, it is difficult to say. According to some, he had recourse to one or other of previously existing modes of expressing speech, and merely simplified the characters which he found in use. But there are two objections to this view. First, there is no known set of characters from which the early Phoenician can be derived with any plausability. Resemblances no doubt may be pointed out here and there, but taking the alphabet as a whole, and comparing it with any other, the differences will always be quite as numerous and quite as striking as the similarities. For instance, the writer of the article on the "Alphabet" in the "Encyclopædia Britannica" (1876) derives the Phoenician letters from letters used in the Egyptian hieratic writing,0137 but his own table shows a marked diversity in at least eleven instances, a slight resemblance in seven or eight, a strong resemblance in no more than two or three. Derivation from the Cypriote forms has been suggested by some; but here again eight letters are very different, if six or seven are similar. Recently, derivation from the Hittite hieroglyphs has been advocated,0138 but the alleged instances of resemblance touch nine characters only out of the twenty-two. And real resemblance is confined to three or four. Secondly, no theory of derivation accounts for the Phoenician names of their letters, which designate objects quite different from those represented by the Egyptian hieroglyphs, and equally different from those represented by the Hittite letters. For instance, the Egyptian a is the ill-drawn figure of an eagle, the Phoenician alef has the signification of "ox;" the b of the Egyptians is a hastily drawn figure of a crane, the Phoenician beth means "a house."

On the whole, it seems most probable that the Phoenicians began with their own hieroglyphical system, selecting an object to represent the initial sound of its name, and at first drawing that object, but that they very soon followed the Egyptian idea of representing the original drawing in a conventional way, by a few lines, straight or curved. Their hieroglyphic alphabet which is extant is an alphabet in the second stage, corresponding to the Egyptian hieratic, but not derived from it. Having originally represented their alef by an ox's head, they found a way of sufficiently indicating the head by three lines {...}, which marked the horns, the ears, and the face. Their beth was a house in the tent form; their gimel a camel, represented by its head and neck; their daleth a door, and so on. The object intended is not always positively known; but, where it is known, there is no difficulty in tracing the original picture in the later conventional sign.

The Phoenician alphabet was not without its defects. The most remarkable of these was the absence of any characters expressive of vowel sounds. The Phoenician letters are, all of them, consonants; and the reader is expected to supply the vowel sounds for himself. There was not even any system of pointing, so far as we know, whereby, as in Hebrew and Arabic, the proper sounds were supplied. Again, several letters were made to serve for two sounds, as beth for both b and v, pe for both p and f, shin for both s and sh, and tau for both t and th. There were no forms corresponding to the sounds j or w. On the other hand, there was in the alphabet a certain amount of redundancy. Tsade is superfluous, since it represents, not a simple elemental sound, but a combination of two sounds, t and s. Hence the Greeks omitted it, as did also the Oscans and the Romans. There is redundancy in the two forms for k, namely kaph and koph; in the two for t, namely teth and tau; and in the two for s, namely samech and shin. But no alphabet is without some imperfections, either in the way of excess or defect; and perhaps we ought to be more surprised that the Phoenician alphabet has not more faults than that it falls so far short of perfection as it does.

The writing of the Phoenicians was, like that of the majority of the Semitic nations, from right to left. The reverse order was entirely unknown to them, whether employed freely as an alternative, as in Egypt, or confined, as in Greece, to the alternate lines. The words were, as a general rule, undivided, and even in some instances were carried over the end of one line into the beginning of another. Still, there are examples where a sign of separation occurs between each word and the next;0139 and the general rule is, that the words do not run over the line. In the later inscriptions they are divided, according to the modern fashion, by a blank space;1310 but there seems to have been an earlier practice of dividing them by small triangles or by dots.

The language of the Phoenicians was very close indeed to the Hebrew, both as regards roots and as regards grammatical forms. The number of known words is small, since not only are the inscriptions few and scanty, but they treat so much of the same matters, and run so nearly in the same form, that, for the most part, the later ones contain nothing new but the proper names. Still they make known to us a certain number of words in common use, and these are almost always either identical with the Hebrew forms, or very slightly different from them, as the following table will demonstrate:—

Phoenician	Hebrew	English
Ab {...}	{...}	father
Aben {...}	{...}	stone
Adon {...}	{...}	lord
Adam {...}	{...}	man
Aleph {...}	{...}	an ox
Akh {...}	{...}	brother
Akhar {...}	{...}	after
Am {...}	{...}	mother

Anak {...}	{...}	I
Arets {...}	{...}	earth, land
Ash {...}	{...}	who, which
Barak {...}	{...}	to bless
Bath {...}	{...}	daughter
Ben {...}	{...}	son
Benben {...}	{...}	grandson
Beth {...}	{...}	house, temple
Ba'al {...}	{...}	lord, citizen
Ba'alat {...}	{...}	lady, mistress
Barzil {...}	{...}	iron
Dagan {...}	{...}	corn
Deber {...}	{...}	to speak, say
Daleth {...}	{...}	door
Zan {...}	{...}	this
Za {...}	{...}	this
Zereng {...}	{...}	seed, race
Har {...}	{...}	mountain
Han {...}	{...}	grace, favour
Haresh {...}	{...}	carpenter
Yom {...}	{...}	day, also sea
Yitten {...}	{...}	to give
Ish {...}	{...}	man
Ishath {...}	{...}	woman, wife
Kadesh {...}	{...}	holy
Kol {...}	{...}	every, all
Kol {...}	{...}	voice
Kohen {...}	{...}	priest
Kohenath {...}	{...}	priestess
Kara {...}	{...}	to call
Lechem {...}	{...}	bread
Makom {...}	{...}	a place
Makar {...}	{...}	a seller
Malakath {...}	{...}	work
Melek {...}	{...}	king
Mizbach {...}	{...}	altar
Na'ar {...}	{...}	boy, servant
Nehusht {...}	{...}	brass
Nephesh {...}	{...}	soul
Nadar {...}	{...}	to vow
'Abd {...}	{...}	slave, servant
'Am {...}	{...}	people
'Ain {...}	{...}	eye, fountain
'Ath {...}	{...}	time
'Olam {...}	{...}	eternity
Pen {...}	{...}	face
Per {...}	{...}	fruit
Pathach {...}	{...}	door
Rab {...}	{...}	lord, chief
Rabbath {...}	{...}	lady
Rav {...}	{...}	rain, irrigation
Rach {...}	{...}	spirit

Rapha {...}	{...}	physician
Shamam {...}	{...}	the heavens
Shemesh {...}	{...}	the sun
Shamang {...}	{...}	to hear
Shenath {...}	{...}	a year
Shad {...}	{...}	a field
Sha'ar {...}	{...}	a gate
Shalom {...}	{...}	peace
Shem {...}	{...}	a name
Shaphat {...}	{...}	a judge
Sopher {...}	{...}	a scribe
Sakar {...}	{...}	memory
Sar {...}	{...}	a prince
Tsedek {...}	{...}	just

The Phoenician numerals, so far as they are known to us, are identical, or nearly identical, with the Hebrew. 'Ahad {...} is "one;" shen {...}, "two;" shalish {...}, "three;" arba {...}, "four;" hamesh {...}, "five;" eshman {...}, "eight;" 'eser {...}, "ten;" and so on. Numbers were, however, by the Phoenicians ordinarily expressed by signs, not words—the units by perpendicular lines: | for "one," || for "two," ||| for "three," and the like; the tens by horizontal ones, either simple, {...}, or hooked at the right end, {...}; twenty by a sign resembling a written capital n, {...}; one hundred by a sign still more complicated, {...}.

The grammatical inflexions, the particles, the pronouns, and the prepositions are also mostly identical. The definite article is expressed, as in Hebrew, by h prefixed. Plurals are formed by the addition of m or th. The prefix eth {...} marks the accusative. There is a niphal conjugation, formed by prefixing n. The full personal pronouns are anak {...} = "I" (compare Heb. {...}); hu {...}, "he" (compare Heb. {...}); hi {...}, "she" (compare Heb. {...}); anachnu, "we" (compare Heb. {...}); and the suffixed pronouns are -i, "me, my;" -ka, "thee, thy;" -h (pronounced as -oh or -o), "him, his" (compare Heb. {...}); -n "our," perhaps pronounced nu; and -m, "their, them," pronounced om or um (compare Heb. {...}). Vau prefixed means "and;" beth prefixed "in;" kaph prefixed "as;" lamed prefixed "of" or "to;" 'al {...} is "over;" ki {...} "because;" im {...}, "if;" hazah, zath, or za {...}, "this" (compare Heb. {...}); and ash {...}, "who, which" (compare Heb. {...}). Al {...} and lo {...} are the negatives (compare Heb. {...}). The redundant use of the personal pronoun with the relative is common.

Still, Phoenician is not mere Hebrew; it has its own genius, its idioms, its characteristics. The definite article, so constantly recurring in Hebrew, is in Phoenician, comparatively speaking, rare. The quiescent letters, which in Hebrew ordinarily accompany the long vowels, are in Phoenician for the most part absent. The employment of the participle for the definite tenses of the verb is much more common in Phoenician than in Hebrew, and the Hebrew prefix m is wanting. The ordinary termination of feminine singular nouns is -th, not -h. Peculiar forms occur, as ash for asher, 'amath for 'am ("people"), zan for zah ("this"), &c. Words which in Hebrew are confined to poetry pass among the Phoenicians into ordinary use, as pha'al ({...}, Heb. {...}), "to make," which replaces the Hebrew {...}.1311

"It is strange," says M. Renan, "that the people to which all antiquity attributes the invention of writing, and which has, beyond all doubted, transmitted it to the entire civilised world, has scarcely left us any literature."1312 Certainly it is difficult to give the name of literature either to the fragments of so-called Phoenician works preserved to us in Greek translations, or to the epigraphic remains of actual Phoenician writing which have come down to our day. The works are two, and two only, viz. the pretended "Phoenician History" of Sanchoniathon, and the "Periplus" of Hanno. Of the former, it is perhaps sufficient to say that we have no evidence of its genuineness. Philo of Byblus, who pretends that he translated it from a Phoenician original, though possibly he had Phoenician blood in his veins, was a Greek in language, in temperament, and in tone of thought, and belonged to the Greece which is characterised by

Juvenal as "Græcia mendax." It is impossible to believe that the Euemerism in which he indulges, and which was evidently the motive of his work, sprang from the brain of Sanchoniathon nine hundred years before Euemerus existed. One is tempted to suspect that Sanchoniathan himself was a myth—an "idol of the cave," evolved out of the inner consciousness of Philo. Philo had a certain knowledge of the Phoenician language, and of the Phoenician religious system, but not more than he might have gained by personal communication with the priests of Byblus and Aphaca, who maintained the old worship in, and long after, his day. It is not clear that he drew his statements from any ancient authorities, or from books at all. So far as the extant fragments go, a smattering of the language, a very moderate acquaintance with the religion, and a little imagination might readily have produced them.

A few extracts from the remains must be given to justify this judgement:—"The beginning of all things," Philo says,1313 "was a dark and stormy air, or a dark air and a turbid chaos, resembling Erebus; and these were at first unbounded, and for a long series of ages had no limit. But after a time this wind became enamoured of its own first principles, and an intimate union took place between them, a connection which was called Desire {pothos}: and this was the beginning of the creation of all things. But it (i.e. the Desire) had no consciousness of its own creation: however, from its embrace with the wind was generated Môt, which some call watery slime, and others putrescence of watery secretion. And from this sprang all the seed of creation, and the generation of the universe. And first there were certain animals without sensation, from which intelligent animals were produced, and these were called 'Zopher-Sêmin,' i.e. 'beholders of the heavens;' and they were made in the shape of an egg, and from Môt shone forth the sun, and the moon, and the lesser and the greater stars. And when the air began to send forth light, by the conflagration of land and sea, winds were produced, and clouds, and very great downpours, and effusions of the heavenly waters. And when these were thus separated, and carried, through the heat of the sun, out of their proper places, and all met again in the air, and came into collision, there ensued thunderings and lightnings; and through the rattle of the thunder, the intelligent animals, above mentioned, were woke up, and, startled by the noise, began to move about both in the sea and on the land, alike such as were male and such as were female. All these things were found in the cosmogony of Taaut (Thoth), and in his Commentaries, and were drawn from his conjectures, and from the proofs which his intellect discovered, and which he made clear to us."

Again, "From the wind, Colpia, and his wife Bahu (Heb. {...}), which is by interpretation 'Night,' were born Æon and Protogonus, mortal men so named; of whom one, viz. Æon, discovered that life might be sustained by the fruits of trees. Their immediate descendants were called Genos and Genea, who lived in Phoenicia, and in time of drought stretched forth their hands to heaven towards the sun; for him they regarded as the sole Lord of Heaven, and called him Baal-samin, which means 'Lord of Heaven' in the Phoenician tongue, and is equivalent to Zeus in Greek. And from Genos, son of Æon and Protogonus, were begotten mortal children, called Phôs, and Pyr, and Phlox (i.e. Light, Fire, and Flame). These persons invented the method of producing fire by rubbing two pieces of wood together, and taught men to employ it. They begat sons of surprising size and stature, whose names were given to the mountains whereof they had obtained possession, viz. Casius, and Libanus, and Antilibanus, and Brathy. From them were produced Memrumus and Hypsuranius, who took their names from their mothers, women in those days yielding themselves without shame to any man whom they happened to meet. Hypsuranius lived at Tyre, and invented the art of building huts with reeds and rushes and the papyrus plant. He quarrelled with his brother, Usôus, who was the first to make clothing for the body out of the skins of the wild beasts which he slew. On one occasion, when there was a great storm of rain and wind, the trees in the neighbourhood of Tyre so rubbed against each other that they took fire, and the whole forest was burnt; whereupon Usôus took a tree, and having cleared it of its boughs, was the first to venture on the sea in a boat. He also consecrated two pillars to Fire and Wind, and worshipped them, and poured upon them the blood of the animals which he took by hunting. And when the two brothers were dead, those who remained alive consecrated rods to their memory, and continued to worship the pillars, and to hold a festival in their honour year by year."1314

Once more—"It was the custom among the ancients, in times of great calamity and danger, for the rulers of the city or nation to avert the ruin of all by sacrificing to the avenging deities the best beloved of their children as the price of redemption; and such as were thus devoted were offered with mystic ceremonies. Kronus, therefore, who was called El by the Phoenicians, and who, after his death, was deified and attached to the planet which bears his name, having an only son by a nymph of the country, who was called Anobret, took his son, whose name was Ieoud, which means 'only son' in Phoenician, and when a great danger from war impended over the land, adorned him with the ensigns of royalty, and, having prepared an altar for the purpose, voluntarily sacrificed him."1315

It will be seen from these extracts that the literary value of Philo's work was exceedingly small. His style is complicated and confused; his matter, for the most part, worthless, and his mixture of Greek, Phoenician, and Egyptian etymologies absurd. If we were bound to believe that he translated a real Phoenician original, and that that original was a fair specimen of Phoenician literary talent, the only conclusion to which we could come would be, that the literature of the nation is beneath contempt.

But the "Periplus" of Hanno will lead us to modify this judgment. It is so short a work that we venture to give it entire from the translation of Falconer,1316 with a few obvious corrections. The voyage of Hanno, King of the Carthaginians, round the parts of Libya beyond the Pillars of Hercules, which he deposited in the Temple of Kronos.

"It was decreed by the Carthaginians that Hanno should undertake a voyage beyond the Pillars of Hercules, and there found Liby-Phoenician cities. He sailed accordingly with sixty ships of fifty oars each, and a body of men and women, to the number of thirty thousand, and provisions, and other necessaries.

"When we had weighed anchor, and passed the Pillars, and sailed beyond them for two days, we founded the first city, which we named Thymiaterium. Below it lay an extensive plain. Proceeding thence towards the west, we came to Soloeis, a promontory of Libya thickly covered with trees, where we erected a temple to Neptune (Poseidon), and again proceeded for the space of half a day towards the east, until we arrived at a lake lying not far from the sea, and filled with abundance of large reeds. Here elephants and a great number of other wild animals were feeding.

"Having passed the lake about a day's sail, we founded cities near the sea, called Caricon-Teichos, and Gytta, and Acra, and Melitta, and Arambys. Thence we came to the great river Lixus, which flows from Libya. On its banks the Lixitæ, a wandering tribe, were feeding flocks, amongst whom we continued some time on friendly terms. Beyond the Lixitæ dwelt the inhospitable Ethiopians, who pasture a wild country intersected by large mountains, from which they say the river Lixus flows. In the neighbourhood of the mountains lived the Troglodytes, men of various appearances, whom the Lixitæ described as swifter in running than horses. Having procured interpreters from them, we coasted along a desert country towards the south for two days; and thence again proceeded towards the east the course of a day. Here we found in the recess of a certain bay a small island, having a circuit of five stadia, where we settled a colony, and called it Cerne. We judged from our voyage that this place lay in a direct line with Carthage; for the length of our voyage from Carthage to the Pillars was equal to that from the Pillars to Cerne. We then came to a cape, which we reached by sailing up a large river called Chrete. The lake had three islands larger than Cerne; from which, proceeding a day's sail, we came to the extremity of the lake. This was overhung by huge mountains, inhabited by savage men, clothed in skins of wild beasts, who drove us away by throwing stones, and hindered us from landing. Sailing thence, we came to another river, that was deep and broad, and full of crocodiles and river horses (hippopotami), whence returning back, we came again to Cerne. Thence we sailed towards the south for twelve days, coasting along the shore, the whole of which is inhabited by Ethiopians, who would not wait our approach, but fled from us. Their language was unintelligible, even to the Lixitæ who were with us. On the last day we approached some large mountains covered with trees, the wood of which was sweet-scented and variegated. Having sailed by these mountains for two days, we came to an immense opening of the sea; on each side of which, towards the continent, was a plain; from which we saw by night fire arising at intervals, either more or less.

"Having taken in water there, we sailed forward during five days near the land, until we came to a large bay, which our interpreter informed us was called 'the Western Horn.' In this was a large island, and in the island a salt-water lake, and in this another island, where, when we had landed, we could discover nothing in the daytime except trees; but in the night we saw many fires burning, and heard the sound of pipes, cymbals, drums, and confused shouting. We were then afraid, and our diviners ordered us to abandon the island. Sailing quickly away thence, we passed by a country burning with fires and perfumes; and streams of fire supplied thence fell into the sea. The country was untraversable on account of the heat. So we sailed away quickly from there also, being much terrified; and, passing on for four days, we observed at night a country full of flames. In the middle was a lofty fire, larger than the rest, which seemed to touch the stars. When day came, we discovered it to be a huge hill, called 'the Chariot of the Gods.' On the third day after our departure thence, after sailing by streams of fire, we arrived at a bay, called 'the Southern Horn;' at the bottom of which lay an island like the former one, having a lake, and in the lake another island full of savage people, far the greater part of whom were women, whose bodies were hairy, and whom our interpreters called 'gorillæ.' Though we pursued the men, we could not catch any of them; but all escaped us, climbing over the precipices, and defending themselves with stones. Three women were, however, taken; but they attacked their conductors with their teeth and nails, and could not be prevailed upon to accompany us. So we killed them, and flayed them, and brought their skins with us to Carthage. We did not sail further on, our provisions failing us."

The style of this short work, though exceedingly simple and inartificial, is not without its merits. It has the directness, the perspicuity, and the liveliness of Cæsar's Commentaries or of the Duke of Wellington's Despatches. Montesquieu1317 says of it:—"Hanno's Voyage was written by the very man who performed it. His recital is not mingled with ostentation. Great commanders write their actions with simplicity, because they receive more honour from facts than words." If we may take the work as a specimen of the accounts which Phoenician explorers commonly gave of their travels in unknown regions, we must regard them as having set a pattern which modern travellers would do well to follow. Hanno gives us facts, not speculations—the things which he has observed, not those of which he has dreamt; and he delivers his facts in the fewest possible words, and in the plainest possible way. He does not cultivate flowers of rhetoric; he does not unduly spin out his narrative. It is plain that he is especially bent on making his meaning clear, and he succeeds in doing so.

The epigraphic literature of the Phoenicians, which M. Renan considers to supply fairly well the almost complete loss of their books,1318 scarcely deserves to be so highly rated. It consists at present of five or six moderately long, and some hundreds of exceedingly short, inscriptions; the longer ones being, all of them, inscribed on stones, the shorter on stones, vases, pateræ, gems, coins, and the like. The longest of all is that engraved on the sarcophagus of Esmunazar, king of Sidon, discovered near the modern Saida in the year 1855, and now in the museum of the Louvre. This has a length of twenty-two long lines, and contains 298 words.1319 It is fairly legible throughout; and the sense is, for the most part, fairly well ascertained, though the meaning of some passages remains still more or less doubtful. The following is the translation of M. Renan:—

"In the month of Bul (October), in the fourteenth year of the reign of King Esmunazar, king of the Sidonians, son of King Tabnit, king of the Sidonians, King Esmunazar, king of the Sidonians, spake, saying—I am snatched away before my time, the child of a few days, the orphan son of a widow; and lo! I am lying in this coffin, and in this tomb, in the place which I have built. I adjure every royal personage and every man whatsoever, that they open not this my chamber, and seek not for treasures there, since there are here no treasures, and that they remove not the coffin from my chamber, nor build over this my chamber any other funeral chamber. Even if men speak to thee, listen not to their words; since every royal personage and every other man who shall open this funeral chamber, or remove the coffin from this my chamber, or build anything over this chamber—may they have no funeral chamber with the departed, nor be buried in tombs, nor have any son or descendant to succeed to their place; but may the Holy Gods deliver them into the hand of a mighty king who shall reign over them, and destroy the royal personage or the man who shall open this my funeral chamber, or remove this coffin, together with the offspring of the royal personage or other man, and let them not have either root below, or any fruit above, or glory among such as live beneath the sun. Since I am snatched away before my time, the child of a few days, the orphan son of a widow, even I.

"For I am Esmunazar, king of the Sidonians, the son of King Tabnit, king of the Sidonians, and the grandson of Esmunazar, king of the Sidonians, and my mother is Am-Ashtoreth, priestess of our lady Ashtoreth, the queen, the daughter of King Esmunazar, king of the Sidonians—and it is we who have built the temples of the gods, the temple of Ashtoreth in Sidon on the shore of the sea, and have placed Ashtoreth in her temple to glorify her; and we too have built the temple of Esmun, and set the sacred grove, En Yidlal, in the mountain, and made him (Esmun) dwell there to glorify him; and it is we who have built temples to the [other] deities of the Sidonians, in Sidon on the shore of the sea, as the temple of Baal-Sidon, and the temple of Asthoreth, who bears the name of Baal. And for this cause has the Lord of Kings given us Dor and Joppa, and the fertile cornlands which are in the plains of Sharon, as a reward for the great things which I have done, and added them to the boundaries of the land, that they may belong to the Sidonians for ever. I adjure every royal personage, and every man whatsoever, that they open not this my chamber, nor empty my chamber, nor build aught over this my chamber, nor remove the coffin from this my chamber, lest the Holy Gods deliver them up, and destroy the royal personage, or the men [who shall do so], and their offspring for ever."[1320]

The inscription on the tomb of Tabnit, Esmunazar's father, found near Beyrout in 1886, is shorter, but nearly to the same effect. It has been thus translated:—"I, Tabnit, priest of Ashtoreth, and king of Sidon, lying in this tomb, say—I adjure every man, when thou shalt come upon this sepulchre, open not my chamber, and trouble me not, for there is not with me aught of silver, nor is there with me aught of gold, there is not with me anything whatever of spoil, but only I myself who lie in this sepulchre. Open not my chamber, and trouble me not; for it would be an abomination in the sight of Ashtoreth to do such an act. And if thou shouldest open my chamber, and trouble me, mayest thou have no posterity all thy life under the sun, and no resting-place with the departed."[1321]

A stelé of a Byblian king, Jehavmelek, probably somewhat more ancient than these,[1322] bears an inscription of a different kind, since it is attached to a votive offering and not to a sepulchre. The king represents himself in a bas-relief as making an offering to Beltis or Ashtoreth, and then appends an epigraph, which runs to fifteen long lines,[1323] and is to the following effect:—"I am Jehavmelek, king of Gebal, the son of Jahar-baal, and the grandson of Adom-melek, king of Gebal, whom lady Beltis of Gebal has made king of Gebal; and I invoke my lady Beltis of Gebal, because she has heard my voice. And I have made for my lady Beltis of Gebal the brazen altar which is in this temple, and the golden carving which is in front of this my carving, and the uræus of gold which is in the middle of the stone over the golden carving. And I have made this portico, with its columns, and the capitals that are upon the columns, and the roof of the temple also, I, Jehavmelek, king of Gebal, have made for my lady Beltis of Gebal, because, whenever I have invoked my lady Beltis of Gebal, she has heard my voice, and been good to me. May Beltis of Gebal bless Jehavmelek, king of Gebal, and grant him life, and prolong his days and his years over Gebal, because he is a just king; and may the lady Beltis of Gebal obtain him favour in the sight of the Gods, and in the sight of the people of foreign lands, for ever! Every royal personage and every other man who shall make additions to this altar, or to this golden carving, or to this portico, I, Jehavmelek, king of Gebal, set may face against him who shall so do, and I pray my lady Beltis of Gebal to destroy that man, whoever he be, and his seed after him."1324

The inscription of Marseilles, if it had been entire, would have been as valuable and interesting as any of these; but, unfortunately, its twenty-one lines are in every case incomplete, being broken off, or else illegible, towards the left. It appears to have been a decree emanating from the authorities of Carthage, and prescribing the amount of the payments to be made in connection with the sacrifices and officials of a temple of Baal which may have existed either at Marseilles or at Carthage itself. To translate it is impossible without a vast amount of conjecture; but M. Renan's version1325 seems to deserve a place in the present collection.

INSCRIPTION OF MARSEILLES

"The temple of Baal . . . Account of the payments fixed by those set over the payments, in the time of our lords, Halats-Baal, the Suffes, the son of Abd-Tanith, the son of Abd-Esmun, and of Halats-Baal, the Suffes, the son of Abd-Esmun, the son of Halts-Baal, and of their colleagues:—For an ox, whether as burnt sacrifice, or expiatory offering, or thank offering, to the priests [shall be given] ten [shekels] of silver on account of each; and, if it be a burnt sacrifice, they shall have besides this payment three hundred weight of the flesh; and if the sacrifice be expiatory, [they shall have] the fat and the additions, and the offerer of the sacrifice shall have the skin, and the entrails, and the feet, and the rest of the flesh. For a calf without horns and entire, or for a ram, whether as burnt sacrifice, or expiatory offering, or thank offering, to the priests [shall be given] five [shekels] of silver on account of each; and if it be a burnt sacrifice, they shall have, besides this payment, a hundred weight and a half of the flesh; and if the sacrifice be expiatory, they shall have the fat and the additions, and the skin, and entrails, and feet, and the rest of the flesh shall be given to the offerer of the sacrifice. For a he-goat, or a she-goat, whether as a burnt sacrifice, or expiatory offering, or thank offering, to the priests [shall be given] one [shekel] and two zers of silver on account of each; and if it be an expiatory sacrifice, they shall have, besides this payment, the fat and the additions; and the skin, and entrails, and feet, and the rest of the flesh shall be given to the offerer of the sacrifice. For a sheep, or a kid, or a fawn (?), whether as burnt sacrifice, or expiatory offering, or thank offering, to the priests [shall be given] three-fourths of a shekel of silver and . . . zers, on account of each; and if it be an expiatory sacrifice, they shall have, besides this payment, the fat and the additions; and the skin, and the entrails, and the feet, and the rest of the flesh [13shall be given] to the offerer of the sacrifice. For a bird, domestic or wild, whether as thank offering, or for augury, or for divination, to the priests [shall be given] three-fourths of a shekel of silver and two zers on account of each, and the flesh shall be for the offerer of the sacrifice. For a bird, or for the holy first-fruits, or for the offering of a cake, or for an offering of oil, to the priests [shall be given] ten zers of silver on account of each, and . . . In every expiatory sacrifice that shall be offered before the deities, to the priests [shall be given] the fat and the additions, and in the sacrifice of . . . For a meat offering, or for milk, or for fat, or for any sacrifice which any man shall offer as an oblation, to the priests [there shall be given] . . . For every offering that a man shall offer who is poor in sheep, or poor in birds, [there shall be given] to the priests nothing at all. Every native, and every inhabitant, and every feaster at the table of the gods, and all the men who sacrifice . . . those men shall make a payment for every sacrifice, according to that which is prescribed in [this] writing . . . Every payment which is not prescribed in this tablet shall be made proportionally to the rate fixed by those set over the payments in the time of our lords, Halats-Baal, the son of Abd-Tanith, and Halats-Baal, the son of Abd-Esmun, and their colleagues. Every priest who takes a payment beyond the amount prescribed in this tablet shall be fined . . . And every offerer of a sacrifice who shall not pay [the amount] prescribed, beyond the payment which [is here fixed, he shall pay] . . ."

Of the shorter inscriptions of the Phoenicians, by far the greater number were attached either to votive offerings or to tombs. Some hundreds have been found of both classes, but they are almost wholly without literary merit, being bald and jejune in the extreme, and presenting little variety. The depositor of a votive offering usually begins by mentioning the name and title, or titles, of the deity to whom he dedicates it. Then he appends his own name, with the names of his father and grandfather. Occasionally, but rarely, he describes his offering, and states the year in which it was set up. Finally, he asks the deity to bless him. The following are examples:—

INSCRIPTION OF UM-EL-AWAMID

"To the lord Baal-Shamaïm, [the vow] which was vowed by Abdelim, son of Mattan, son of Abdelim, son of Baal-Shomar, of the district of Laodicea. This gateway and doors did I make in fulfilment of it. I built it in the 180th year of the Lord of Kings, and in the 143rd year of the people of Tyre, that it might be to me a memorial and for a good name beneath the feet of my lord, Baal-Shamaïm, for ever. May he bless me!"1326

INSCRIPTION ON A CIPPUS FROM CARTHAGE

"To the lady Tanith, and to our master, the lord Baal-Hammon; the offerer is Abd-Melkarth, the Suffes, son of Abd-Melkarth, son of Hanno."1327

INSCRIPTION ON A CIPPUS FOUND IN MALTA

"To our lord Melkarth, the lord of Tyre. The offerer is thy servant, Abd-Osiri, and my brother, Osiri-Shomar, both [of us] sons of Osiri-Shomar, the son of Abd-Osiri. In hearing their voice, may he bless them."1328

INSCRIPTION ON A MARBLE ALTAR, BROUGHT FROM LARNAKA

"On the sixth day of the month Bul, in the twenty-first year of King Pumi-yitten, king of Citium and Idalium, and Tamasus, son of King Melek-yitten, king of Citium and Idalium, this altar and these two lions were given by Bodo, priest of Reseph-hets, son of Yakun-shalam, son of Esmunadon, to his lord Reseph-hets. May he bless [him]."1329

INSCRIPTION ON A MARBLE TABLET FOUND IN CYPRUS

"On the seventh day of the month . . . in the thirty-first year of the Lord of Kings, Ptolemæus, son of Ptolemæus . . . which was the fifty-seventh year of the Citians, when Amarat-Osiri, daughter of . . . son of Abd-Susim, of Gad'ath, was canephora of Asinoë Philadelphus, these statues were set up by Bathshalun, daughter of Maryichai, son of Esmunadon, to the memory of his grandsons, Esmunadon, Shallum, and Abd-Reseph, the three sons of Maryichai, son of Esmunadon, according to the vow which their father, Maryichai, vowed, when he was still alive, to their lord, Reseph-Mikal. May he bless them!"1330

There is a little more variety in the inscriptions on tombstones. The great majority, indeed, are extremely curt and dry, containing scarcely anything beyond the name of the person who is buried in the tomb, or that together with the name of the person by whom the monument is erected; e.g. "To Athad, the daughter of Abd-Esmun, the Suffes, and wife of Ger-Melkarth, the son of Ben-hodesh, the son of Esmunazar"1331; or "This monument I, Menahem, grandson of Abd-Esmun, have erected to my father, Abd-Shamash, son of Abd-Esmun"1332; or "I, Abd-Osiri, the son of Abd-Susim, the son of Hur, have erected this monument, while I am still alive, to myself, and to my wife, Ammat-Ashtoreth, daughter of Taam, son of Abd-melek, [and have placed it] over the chamber of my tomb, in perpetuity."1333 But, occasionally, we get a glimpse, beyond the mere dry facts, into the region of thought; as where the erector of a monument appends to the name of one, whom we may suppose to have been a miser, the remark, that "the reward of him who heaps up riches is contempt;"1334 or where one who entertains the hope that his friend is happier in another world than he was upon earth, thus expresses himself—"In memory of Esmun. After rain, the sun shines forth;"1335 or, again, where domestic affection shows itself in the declaration concerning the departed—"When he entered into the house that is so full [of guests], there was grief for the memory of the sage, the man that was hard as adamant, that bore calamities of every sort, that was a widower through the death of my mother, that was like a pellucid fountain, and had a name pure from crime.

Erected in affection by me his son to my father."1336

With respect to the extent and range of the Phoenician book literature, the little that can be gathered from the notices remaining to us in the Greek and Roman writers is the following. In Phoenicia Proper there were historical writers at least from the time of Hiram, the contemporary of David, who wrote the annals of their country in a curt dry form somewhat resembling that of Kings and Chronicles.1337 The names of the kings and the length of their reigns were carefully recorded, together with some of the more remarkable events belonging to each reign; but there was no attempt at the philosophy of history, nor at the graces of composition. In some places, especially at Sidon, philosophy and science were to a certain extent cultivated. Mochus, a Sidonian, wrote a work on the atomic theory at a very early date, though scarcely, as Posidonius maintained,1338 one anterior to the Trojan war. Later on, the Sidonian school specially affected astronomy and arithmetic, in which they made so much progress that the Greeks acknowledged themselves their debtors in those branches of knowledge.1339 It is highly probable, though not exactly capable of proof, that the Tyrian navigators from a very remote period embodied in short works the observations which they made in their voyages, on the geography, hydrography, ethology, and natural history of the counties, which were visited by them. Hanno's "Periplus" may have been composed on a model of these earlier treatises, which at a later date furnished materials to Marinus for his great work on geography. It was, however, in the Phoenician colony of Carthage that authorship was taken up with most spirit and success. Hiempsal, Hanno, Mago, Hamilcar, and others, composed works, which the Romans valued highly, on the history, geography, and "origines" of Africa, and also upon practical agriculture.1340 Mago and Hamilcar were regarded as the best authorities on the latter subject both by the Greeks and Romans, and were followed, among the Greeks by Mnaseas and Paxamus,1341 among the Romans by Varro and Columella.1342 So highly was the work of Mago, which ran to twenty-eight books, esteemed, that, on the taking of Carthage, it was translated into Latin by order of the Roman Senate.1343 After the fall of Carthage, Tyre and Sidon once more became seats of learning; but the Phoenician language was discarded, and Greek adopted in its place. The Tyrian, Sidonian, Byblian and Berytian authors, of whom we hear, bear Greek names:1344 and it is impossible to say whether they belonged, in any true sense, to the Phoenician race. Philo of Byblus and Marinus of Tyre are the only two authors of this later period who held to Phoenician traditions, and, presumably, conveyed on to later ages Phoenician ideas and accumulations. If neither literature nor science gained much from the work of the former, that of the latter had considerable value, and, as the basis of the great work of Ptolemy, must ever hold an honourable place in the history of geographical progress.

CHAPTER XIV—POLITICAL HISTORY

1. Phoenicia, before the establishment of the hegemony of Tyre.

Separate autonomy of the Phoenician cities—No marked predominance of any one or more of them during the Egyptian period, B.C. 1600-1350—A certain pre-eminence subsequently acquired by Aradus and Sidon—Sidonian territorial ascendancy—Great proficiency of Sidon in the arts—Sidon's

war with the Philistines—Her early colonies—Her advances
in navigation—Her general commercial honesty—Occasional
kidnapping—Stories of Io and Eumæus—Internal government—
Relations with the Israelites.

When the Phoenician immigrants, in scattered bands, and at longer or shorter intervals, arrived upon the Syrian coast, and finding it empty occupied it, or wrested it from its earlier possessors, there was a decided absence from among them of any single governing or controlling authority; a marked tendency to assert and maintain separate rule and jurisdiction. Sidon, the Arkite, the Arvadite, the Zemarite, are separately enumerated in the book of Genesis;0141 and the Hebrews have not even any one name under which to comprise the commercial people settled upon their coast line,0142 until we come to Gospel times, when the Greeks have brought the term "Syro-Phoenician" into use.0143 Elsewhere we hear of "them of Sidon," "them of Tyre,"0144 "the Giblites,"0145 "the men of Arvad,"0146 "the Arkites," "the Sinites," "the Zemarites,"0147 "the inhabitants of Accho, of Achzib, and Aphek,"0148 but never of the whole maritime population north of Philistia under any single ethnic appellation. And the reason seems to be, that the Phoenicians, even more than the Greeks, affected a city autonomy. Each little band of immigrants, as soon as it had pushed its way into the sheltered tract between the mountains and the sea, settled itself upon some attractive spot, constructed habitations, and having surrounded its habitations with walls, claimed to be—and found none to dispute the claim—a distinct political entity. The conformation of the land, so broken up into isolated regions by strong spurs from Lebanon and Bargylus, lent additional support to the separatist spirit, and the absence in the early times of any pressure of danger from without permitted its free indulgence without entailing any serious penalty. It is difficult to say at what time the first settlements took place; but during the period of Egyptian supremacy over Western Asia, under the eighteenth and nineteenth dynasties (ab. B.C. 1600-1350), we seem to find the Phoenicians in possession of the coast tract, and their cities severally in the enjoyment of independence and upon a quasi-equality. Tyre, Sidon, Gebal, Aradus, Simyra, Sarepta, Berytus, and perhaps Arka, appear in the inscriptions of Thothmes III,0149 and in the "Travels of a Mohar,"1410 without an indication of the pre-eminence, much less the supremacy, of any one of them. The towns pursued their courses independently one of another, submitting to the Egyptians when hard pressed, but always ready to reassert themselves, and never joining, so far as appears, in any league or confederation, by which their separate autonomy might have been endangered. During this period no city springs to any remarkable height of greatness or prosperity; material progress is, no doubt, being made by the nation; but it is not very marked, and it does not excite any particular attention.

But with the decline of the Egyptian power, which sets in after the death of the second Rameses, a change takes place. External pressure being removed, ambitions begin to develop themselves. In the north Aradus (Arvad), in the south Sidon, proceed to exercise a sort of hegemony over several neighbouring states. Sidon becomes known as "Great Zidon."1411 Not content with her maritime ascendancy, which was already pushing her into special notice, she aspired to a land dominion, and threw out offshoots from the main seat of her power as far as Laish, on the head-waters of the Jordan.1412 It was her support, probably, which enabled the inhabitants of such comparatively weak cities as Accho and Achzib and Aphek to resist the invasion of the Hebrews, and maintain themselves, despite all attempts made to reduce them.1413 At the same time she gradually extended her influence over the coast towns in her neighbourhood, as Sarepta, Heldun, perhaps Berytus, Ecdippa, and Accho. The period which succeeds that of Egyptian preponderance in Western Asia may be distinguished as that of Sidonian ascendancy, or of such ascendancy slightly modified by an Aradian hegemony in the north over the settlements intervening between Mount Casius and the northern roots of Lebanon.1414 During this period Sidon came to the front, alike in arts, in arms, and in navigation. Her vessels were found by the earliest Greek navigators in all parts of the Mediterranean into which they themselves ventured, and were known to push themselves into regions where no Greek dared to follow them. Under her fostering care Phoenician colonisation had spread over the whole of the Western Mediterranean, over the Ægean, and into the Propontis. She had engaged in war with the powerful nation of the Philistines, and, though worsted in the encounter, had obtained a reputation for audacity. By her wonderful progress in the arts, her citizens had acquired the epithet of {poludaidaloi},1415 and had come to be recognised generally as the foremost artificers of the world in almost every branch of industry. Sidonian metal-work was particularly in repute. When Achilles at the funeral of Patroclus desired to offer as a prize to the fastest runner the most beautiful bowl that was to be found in all the world, he naturally chose one which had been deftly made by highly-skilled Sidonians, and which Phoenician sailors had conveyed in one of their hollow barks across the cloud-shadowed sea.1416 When Menelaus proposed to present Telemachus, the son of his old comrade Odysseus, with what was at once the most beautiful and the most valuable of all his possessions, he selected a silver bowl with a golden rim, which in former days he had himself received as a present from Phædimus, the Sidonian king.1417 The sailors who stole Eumæus from Ortygia, and carried him across the sea to Ithica, obtained their prize by coming to his father's palace, and bringing with them, among other wares,

 . . . a necklace of fine gold to sell,
 With bright electron linked right wondrously and well.1418

Sidon's pre-eminence in the manufacture, the dyeing, and the embroidery of textile fabrics was at the same time equally unquestionable. Hecuba, being advised to offer to Athêné, on behalf of her favourite son, the best and loveliest of all the royal robes which her well-stored dress-chamber could furnish—

 She to her fragrant wardrobe bent her way,
 Where her rich veils in beauteous order lay;
 Webs by Sidonian virgins finely wrought,
 From Sidon's woofs by youthful Paris brought,
 When o'er the boundless main the adulterer led
 Fair Helen from her home and nuptial bed;
 From these she chose the fullest, fairest far,
 With broidery bright, and blazing as a star.1419

Already, it would seem, the precious shell-fish, on which Phoenicia's commerce so largely rested in later times, had been discovered; and it was the dazzling hue of the robe which constituted its especial value. Sidon was ultimately eclipsed by Tyre in the productions of the loom; and the unrivalled dye has come down to us, and will go down to all future ages, as "Tyrian purple;" but we may well believe that in this, as in most other matters on which prosperity and success depended, Tyre did but follow in the steps of her elder sister Sidon, perfecting possibly the manufacture which had been Sidon's discovery in the early ages. According to Scylax of Cadyanda, Dor was a Sidonian colony.1420 Geographically it belonged rather to Philistia than to Phoenicia; but its possession of large stores of the purple fish caused its sudden seizure and rapid fortification at a very remote date, probably by the Phoenicians of Sidon.1421 It is quite possible that this aggression may have provoked that terrible war to which reference has already been made, between the Philistines under the hegemony of Ascalon and the first of the Phoenician cities. Ascalon attacked the Sidonians by land, blockaded the offending town, and after a time compelled a surrender; but the defenders had a ready retreat by sea, and, when they could no longer hold out against their assailants, took ship, and removed themselves to Tyre, which at the time was probably a dependency.1422

In navigation also and colonisation Sidon took the lead. According to some, she was the actual founder of Aradus, which was said to have owed its origin to a body of Sidonian exiles, who there settled themselves.1423 Not much reliance, however, can be placed on this tradition, which first appears in a writer of the Augustan age. With more confidence we may ascribe to Sidon the foundation of Citium in Cyprus, the colonisation of the islands in the Ægean, and of those Phoenician settlements in North Africa which were anterior to the founding of Carthage. It has even been supposed that the Sidonians were the first to make a settlement at Carthage itself,1424 and that the Tyrian occupation under Dido was a recolonisation of an already occupied site. Anyhow, Sidon was the first to explore the central Mediterranean, and establish commercial relations with the barbarous tribes of the mid-African coast, Cabyles, Berbers, Shuloukhs, Tauriks, and others. She is thought to claim on a coin to be the mother-city of Melita, or Malta, as well as of Citium and Berytus;1425 and, if this claim be allowed, we can scarcely doubt that she was also the first to plant colonies in Sicily. Further than this, it would seem, Sidonian enterprise did not penetrate. It was left for Tyre to discover the wealth of Southern Spain, to penetrate beyond the Straits of Gibraltar, and to affront the perils of the open ocean.

But, within the sphere indicated, Sidonian rovers traversed all parts of the Great Sea, penetrated into every gulf, became familiar sights to the inhabitants of every shore. From timid sailing along the coast by day, chiefly in the summer season, when winds whispered gently, and atmospheric signs indicated that fair weather had set in, they progressed by degrees to long voyages, continued both by night and day,1426 from promontory to promontory, or from island to island, sometimes even across a long stretch of open sea, altogether out of sight of land, and carried on at every season of the year except some few of special danger. To Sidon is especially ascribed the introduction of the practice of sailing by night,1427 which shortened the duration of voyages by almost one-half, and doubled the number of trips that a vessel could accomplish in the course of a year. For night sailing the arts of astronomy and computation had to be studied;1428 the aspect of the heavens at different seasons had to be known; and among the shifting constellations some fixed point had to be found by which it would be safe to steer. The last star in the tail of the Little Bear—the polar star of our own navigation books—was fixed upon by the Phoenicians, probably by the Sidonians, for this purpose,1429 and was practically employed as the best index of the true north from a remote period. The rate of a ship's speed was, somehow or other, estimated; and though it was long before charts were made, or the set of currents taken into account, yet voyages were for the most part accomplished with very tolerable accuracy and safety. An ample commerce grew up under Sidonian auspices. After the vernal equinox was over a fleet of white-winged ships sped forth from the many harbours of the Syrian coast, well laden with a variety of wares— Phoenician, Assyrian, Egyptian1430—and made for the coasts and islands of the Levant, the Ægean, the Propontis, the Adriatic, the mid-Mediterranean, where they exchanged the cargoes which they had brought with them for the best products of the lands whereto they had come. Generally, a few weeks, or at most a month or two, would complete the transfer the of commodities, and the ships which left Sidon in April or May would return about June or July, unload, and make themselves ready for a second voyage. But sometimes, it appears, the return cargo was not so readily procured, and vessels had to remain in the foreign port, or roadstead, for the space of a whole year.1431

The behaviour of the traders must, on the whole, have been such as won the respect of the nations and tribes wherewith they traded. Otherwise, the markets would soon have been closed against them, and, in lieu of the peaceful commerce which the Phoenicians always affected, would have sprung up along the shores of the Mediterranean a general feeling of distrust and suspicion, which would have led on to hostile encounters, surprises, massacres, and then reprisals. The entire history of Phoenician commerce shows that such a condition of things never existed. The traders and their customers were bound together by the bonds of self-interest, and, except in rare instances, dealt by each other fairly and honestly. Still, there were occasions when, under the stress of temptation, fair-dealing was lost sight of, and immediate prospect of gain was allowed to lead to the commission of acts destructive of all feeling of security, subversive of commercial morals, and calculated to effect a rupture of commercial relations, which it may often have taken a long term of years to re-establish. Herodotus tells us that, at a date considerably anterior to the Trojan war, when the ascendancy over the other

Phoenician cities must certainly have belonged to Sidon, an affair of this kind took place on the coast of Argolis, which was long felt by the Greeks as an injury and an outrage. A Phoenician vessel made the coast near Argos, and the crew, having effected a landing, proceeded to expose their merchandise for sale along the shore, and to traffic with the natives, who were very willing to make purchases, and in the course of five or six days bought up almost the entire cargo. At length, just as the traders were thinking of re-embarking and sailing away, there came down to the shore from the capital a number of Argive ladies, including among them a princess, Io, the daughter of Inachus, the Argive king. Hereupon, the trafficking and the bargaining recommenced; goods were produced suited to the taste of the new customers; and each strove to obtain what she desired most at the least cost. But suddenly, as they were all intent upon their purchases, and were crowding round the stern of the ship, the Phoenicians, with a general shout, rushed upon them. Many—the greater part, we are told—made their escape; but the princess, and a certain number of her companions, were seized and carried on board. The traders quickly put to sea, and hoisting their sails, hurried away to Egypt.1432

Another instance of kidnapping, accomplished by art rather than by force, is related to us by Homer.1433 Eumæus, the swineherd of Ulysses, was the son of a king, dwelling towards the west, in an island off the Sicilian coast. A Phoenician woman, herself kidnapped from Sidon by piratical Taphians, had the task of nursing and tending him assigned to her, and discharged it faithfully until a great temptation befell her. A Sidonian merchant-ship visited the island, laden with rich store of precious wares, and proceeded to open a trade with the inhabitants, in the course of which one of the sailors seduced the Phoenician nurse, and suggested that when the vessel left, she should allow herself to be carried off in it. The woman, whose parents were still alive at Sidon, came into the scheme, and being apprised of the date of the ship's departure, stole away from the palace unobserved, taking with her three golden goblets, and also her master's child, the boy of whom she had charge. It was evening, and all having been prepared beforehand, the nurse and child were hastily smuggled on board, the sails were hoisted, and the ship was soon under weigh. The wretched woman died ere the voyage was over, but the boy survived, and was carried by the traders to Ithaca, and there sold for a good sum to Laërtes.

It is not suggested that these narratives, in the form in which they have come down to us, are historically true. There may never have been an "Io, daughter of Inachus," or an "Eumæus, son of Ctesius Ormenides," or an island, "Syria called by name, over against Ortygia," or even a Ulysses or a Laërtes. But the tales could never have grown up, have been invented, or have gained acceptance, unless the practice of kidnapping, on which they are based, had been known to be one in which the Phoenicians of the time indulged, at any rate occasionally. We must allow this blot on the Sidonian escutcheon, and can only plead, in extenuation of their offence, first, the imperfect morality of the age, and secondly, the fact that such deviations from the line of fair-dealing and honesty on the part of the Sidonian traders must have been of rare occurrence, or the flourishing and lucrative trade, which was the basis of all the glory and prosperity of the people, could not possibly have been established. Successful commerce must rest upon the foundation of mutual confidence; and mutual confidence is impossible unless the rules of fair dealing are observed on both sides, if not invariably, yet, at any rate, so generally that the infraction of them is not contemplated on either side as anything but the remotest contingency.

Of the internal government of Sidon during this period no details have come down to us. Undoubtedly, like all the Phoenician cities in the early times,1434 she had her own kings; and we may presume, from the almost universal practice in ancient times, and especially in the East,1435 that the monarchy was hereditary. The main duties of the king were to lead out the people to battle in time of war, and to administer justice in time of peace.1436 The kings were in part supported, in part held in check, by a powerful aristocracy—an aristocracy which, we may conjecture, had wealth, rather than birth, as its basis. It does not appear that any political authority was possessed by the priesthood, nor that the priesthood was a caste, as in India, and (according to some writers) in Egypt. The priestly office was certainly not attached by any general custom to the person of the kings, though kings might be priests, and were so occasionally.1437

We do not distinctly hear of Sidon has having been engaged in any war during the period of her ascendancy, excepting that with the Philistines. Still as "the Zidonians" are mentioned among the nations which "oppressed Israel" in the time of the Judges,1438 we must conclude that differences arose between them and their southern neighbours in some portion of this period, and that, war having broken out between them, the advantage rested with Sidon. The record of "Judges" is incomplete, and does not enable us even to fix the date of the Sidonian "oppression." We can only say that it was anterior to the judgeship of Jephthah, and was followed, like the other "oppressions," by a "deliverance."

The war with the Philistines brought the period of Sidonian ascendancy to an end, and introduces us to the second period of Phoenician history, or that of the hegemony of Tyre. The supposed date of the change is B.C. 1252.1439

2. Phoenicia under the hegemony of Tyre (B.C. 1252-877)

Influx of the Sidonian population raises Tyre to the first place among the cities (about B.C. 1252)—First notable result, the colonisation of Gades (B.C. 1130)—Other colonies of about this period—Extension of Phoenician commerce—Tyre ruled by kings—Abi-Baal—Hiram—Hiram's dealings with Solomon—His improvement of his own capital— His opinion of "the land of Cabul"—His joint trade with the Israelites—His war with Utica—Successors of Hiram—Time of disturbance—Reign of Ithobal—of Badezor—of Matgen—of Pygmalion—Founding of Carthage—First contact of Phoenicia with Assyria—Submission of Phoenicia, B.C. 877.

Tyre was noted as a "strong city" as early as the time of Joshua,1440 and was probably inferior only to Sidon, or to Sidon and Aradus, during the period of Sidonian ascendancy. It is mentioned in the "Travels of a Mohar" (about B.C. 1350) as "a port, richer in fish than in sands."1441 The tradition was, that it acquired its predominance and pre-eminence from the accession of the Sidonian population, which fled thither by sea, when no longer able to resist the forces of Ascalon.1442 We do not find it, however, attaining to any great distinction or notoriety, until more than a century later, when it distinguishes itself by the colonisation of Gades (about B.C. 1130), beyond the Pillars of Hercules, on the shores of the Atlantic. We may perhaps deduce from this fact, that the concentration of energy caused by the removal to Tyre of the best elements in the population of Sidon gave a stimulus to enterprise, and caused longer voyages to be undertaken, and greater dangers to be affronted by the daring seamen of the Syrian coast than had ever been ventured on before. The Tyrian seamen were, perhaps, of a tougher fibre than the Sidonian, and the change of hegemony is certainly accompanied by a greater display of energy, a more adventurous spirit, a wider colonisation, and a more wonderful commercial success, than characterise the preceding period of Sidonian leadership and influence.

The settlements planted by Tyre in the first burst of her colonising energy seem to have been, besides Gades, Thasos, Abdera, and Pronectus towards the north, Malaca, Sexti, Carteia, Belon, and a second Abdera in Spain, together with Caralis in Sardinia,1443 Tingis and Lixus on the West African coast, and in North Africa Hadrumetum and the lesser Leptis.1444 Her aim was to throw the meshes of her commerce wider than Sidon had ever done, and so to sweep into her net a more abundant booty. It was Tyre which especially affected "long voyages,"1445 and induced her colonists of Gades to explore the shores outside the Pillars of Hercules, northwards as far as Cornwall and the Scilly Isles, southwards to the Fortunate Islands, and north-eastwards into the Baltic. It is, no doubt, uncertain at what date these explorations were effected, and some of them may belong to the later hegemony of Tyre, ab. B.C. 600; but the forward movement of the twelfth century seems to have been distinctly Tyrian, and to have been one of the results of the new position in which she was placed by the sudden collapse of her elder sister, Sidon.

According to some,1446 Tyre, during the early period of her supremacy, was under the government of shôphetim, or "judges;" but the general usage of the Phoenician cities makes against this supposition. Philo in his "Origines of Phoenicia" speaks constantly of kings,1447 but never of judges. We hear of a king, Abd-Baal, at Berytus1448 about B.C. 1300. Sidonian kings are mentioned in connection with the myth of Europa.1449 The cities founded by the Phoenicians in Cyprus are always under monarchical rule.1450 Tyre itself, when its history first presents itself to us in any detail, is governed by a king.1451 All that can be urged on the other side is, that we know of no Tyrian king by name until about B.C. 1050; and that, if there had been earlier kings, it might have been expected that some record of them would have come down to us. But to argue thus is to ignore the extreme scantiness and casual character of the notices which have reached us bearing upon the early Phoenician history. No writer has left us any continuous history of Phoenicia, even in the barest outline.1452 Native monumental annals are entirely wanting. We depend for the early times upon the accident of Jewish monarchs having come into contact occasionally with Phoenician ones, and on Jewish writers having noted the occasions in Jewish histories. Scripture and Josephus alone furnish our materials for the period now under consideration, and the materials are scanty, fragmentary, and sadly wanting in completeness.

It is towards the middle of the eleventh century B.C. that these materials become available. About the time when David was acclaimed as king by the tribe of Judah at Hebron, a Phoenician prince mounted the throne of Tyre, by name Abibalus, or Abi-Baal.1453 We do not know the length of his reign; but, while the son of Jesse was still in the full vigour of life, Abi-Baal was succeeded on the Tyrian throne by his son, Hiram or Hirôm, a prince of great energy, of varied tastes, and of an unusually broad and liberal turn of mind. Hiram, casting his eye over the condition of the states and kingdoms which were his neighbours, seems to have discerned in Judah and David a power and a ruler whose friendship it was desirable to cultivate with a view to the establishment of very close relations. Accordingly, it was not long after the Jewish monarch's capture of the Jebusite stronghold on Mount Zion that the Tyrian prince sent messengers to him to Jerusalem, with a present of "timber of cedars," and a number of carpenters, and stone-hewers, well skilled in the art of building.1454 David accepted their services, and a goodly palace soon arose on some part of the Eastern hill, of which cedar from Lebanon was the chief material,1455 and of which Hiram's workmen were the constructors. At a later date David set himself to collect abundant and choice materials for the magnificent Temple which Solomon his son was divinely commissioned to build on Mount Moriah to Jehovah; and here again "the Zidonians and they of Tyre," or the subjects of Hiram, "brought much cedar wood to David."1456 The friendship continued firm to the close of David's reign;1457 and when Solomon succeeded his father as king of Israel and lord of the whole tract between the middle Euphrates and Egypt, the bonds were drawn yet closer, and an alliance concluded which placed the two powers on terms of the very greatest intimacy. Hiram had no sooner heard of Solomon's accession than he sent an embassy to congratulate him;1458 and Solomon took advantage of the opening which presented itself to announce his intention of building the Temple which his father had designed, and to request Hiram's aid in the completion of the work. Copies of letters which passed between the two monarchs were preserved both in the Tyrian and the Jewish archives, and the Tyrian versions are said to have been still extant in the public record office of the city in the first century of the Christian era.1459 These documents ran as follows:—

"Solomon to King Hiram [sends greeting]:—Know that my father David was desirous of building a temple to God, but was prevented by his wars and his continual expeditions; for he did not rest from subduing his adversaries, until he had made every one of them tributary to him. And now I for my part return thanks to God for the present time of peace, and having rest thereby I purpose to build the house; for God declared to my father that it should be built by me. Wherefore I beseech thee to send some of thy servants with my servants to Mount Lebanon, to cut wood there, for none among us can skill to hew timber like unto the Sidonians. And I will pay the wood-cutters their hire at whatsoever rate thou shalt determine."

"King Hiram to King Solomon [sends greeting]:—Needs must I praise God, that hath given thee to sit upon thy father's throne, seeing that thou art a wise man, and possessed of every virtue. And I, rejoicing at these things, will do all that thou hast desired of me. I will by my servants cut thee in abundance timber of cedar and timber of cypress, and will bring them down to the sea, and command my servants to construct of them a float, or raft, and navigate it to whatever point of thy coast thou mayest wish, and there discharge them; after which thy servants can carry them to Jerusalem. But be it thy care to provide me in return with a supply of food, whereof we are in want as inhabiting an island."1460

The result was an arrangement by which the Tyrian monarch furnished his brother king with timber of various kinds, chiefly cedar, cut in Lebanon, and also with a certain number of trained artificers, workers in metal, carpenters, and masons, while the Israelite monarch on his part made a return in corn, wine, and oil, supplying Tyre, while the contract lasted, with 20,000 cors of wheat, the same quantity of barley, 20,000 baths of wine, and the same number of oil, annually.1461 Phoenicia always needed to import supplies of food for its abundant population,1462 and having an inexhaustible store of timber in Lebanon, was glad to find a market for it so near. Thus the arrangement suited both parties. The hillsides of Galilee and the broad and fertile plains of Esdraelon and Sharon produced a superabundance of wheat and barley, whereof the inhabitants had to dispose in some quarter or other, and the highlands of Sumeria and Judæa bore oil and wine far beyond the wants of those who cultivated them. What Phoenicia lacked in these respects from the scantiness of its cultivable soil, Palestine was able and eager to supply; while to Phoenicia it was a boon to obtain, not only a market for her timber, but also employment for her surplus population, which under ordinary circumstances was always requiring to be carried off to distant lands, from the difficulty of supporting itself at home.

A still greater advantage was it to the rude Judæans to get the assistance of their civilised and artistic neighbours in the design and execution, both of the Temple itself and of all those accessories, which in ancient times a sacred edifice on a large scale was regarded as requiring. The Phoenicians, and especially the Tyrians, had long possessed, both in their home and foreign settlements, temples of some pretension, and Hiram had recently been engaged in beautifying and adorning, perhaps in rebuilding, some of these venerable edifices at Tyre.1463 A Phoenician architectural style had thus been formed, and Hiram's architects and artificers would be familiar with constructive principles and ornamental details, as well as with industrial processes, which are very unlikely to have been known at the time to the Hebrews. The wood for the Jewish Temple was roughly cut, and the stones quarried, by Israelite workmen;1464 but all the delicate work, whether in the one material or the other, was performed by the servants of Hiram. Stone-cutters from Gebal (Byblus) shaped and smoothed the "great stones, costly stones" employed in the substructions of the "house;"1465 Tyrian carpenters planed and polished the cedar planks used for the walls, and covered them with representations of cherubs and palms and gourds and opening flowers.1466 The metallurgists of Sidon probably supplied the cherubic figures in the inner sanctuary,1467 as well as the castings for the doors,1468 and the bulk of the sacred vessels. The vail which separated between the "Holy Place" and the Holy of Holies—a marvellous fabric of blue, and purple, and crimson, and white, with cherubim wrought thereon1469—owed its beauty probably to Tyrian dyers and Tyrian workers in embroidery. The master-workman lent by the Tyrian monarch to superintend the entire work—an extraordinary and almost universal genius— "skilful to work in gold and in silver, in brass, in iron, in stone, and in timber; in purple, in blue, in fine linen, and in crimson; also to grave any manner of graving"1470—who bore the same name with the king,1471 was the son of an Israelite mother, but boasted a Tyrian father,1472 and was doubtless born and bred up at Tyre. Under his special direction were cast in the valley of the Jordan, between Succoth and Zarthan,1473 those wonderful pillars, known as Jachin and Boaz, which have already been described, and which seem to have had their counterparts in the sacred edifices both of Phoenicia and Cyprus.1474 To him also is specially ascribed the "molten sea," standing on twelve oxen,1475 which was perhaps the most artistic of all the objects placed within the Temple circuit, as are also the lavers upon wheels,1476 which, if less striking as works of art, were even more curious.

The partnership established between the two kingdoms in connection with the building and furnishing of the Jewish Temple, which lasted for seven years,1477 was further continued for thirteen more1478 in connection with the construction of Solomon's palace. This palace, like an Assyrian one, consisted of several distinct edifices. "The chief was a long hall which, like the Temple, was encased in cedar; whence probably its name, 'The House of the Forest of Lebanon.' In front of it ran a pillared portico. Between this portico and the palace itself was a cedar porch, sometimes called the Tower of David. In this tower, apparently hung over the walls outside, were a thousand golden shields, which gave to the whole place the name of the Armoury. With a splendour that outshone any like fortress, the tower with these golden targets glittered far off in the sunshine like the tall neck, as it was thought, of a beautiful bride, decked out, after the manner of the East, with strings of golden coins. This porch was the gem and centre of the whole empire; and was so much thought of that a smaller likeness to it was erected in another part of the precinct for the queen. Within the porch itself was to be seen the king in state. On a throne of ivory, brought from Africa or India, the throne of many an Arabian legend, the kings of Judah were solemnly seated on the day of their accession. From its lofty seat, and under that high gateway, Solomon and his successors after him delivered their solemn judgments. That 'porch' or 'gate of justice' still kept alive the likeness of the old patriarchal custom of sitting in judgment at the gate; exactly as the 'Gate of Justice' still recalls it to us at Granada, and the Sublime Porte—'the Lofty Gate'—at Constantinople. He sate on the back of a golden bull, its head turned over its shoulder, probably the ox or bull of Ephraim; under his feet, on each side of the steps, were six golden lions, probably the lions of Judah. This was 'the seat of Judgment.' This was 'the throne of the House of David.'"1479

We have dwelt the longer upon these matters because it is from the lengthy and elaborate descriptions which the Hebrew writers give of these Phoenician constructions at Jerusalem that we must form our conceptions, not only of the state of Phoenician art in Hiram's time, but also of the works wherewith he adorned his own capital. He came to the throne at the age of nineteen,1480 on the decease of his father, and immediately set to work to improve, enlarge, and beautify the city, which in his time claimed the headship of, at any rate, all Southern Phoenicia. He found Tyre a city built on two islands, separated the one from the other by a narrow channel, and so cramped for room that the inhabitants had no open square, or public place, on which they could meet, and were closely packed in overcrowded dwellings.1481 The primary necessity was to increase the area of the place; and this Hiram effected, first, by filling up the channel between the two islands with stone and rubbish, and so gaining a space for new buildings, and then by constructing huge moles or embankments towards the east, and towards the south, where the sea was shallowest, and thus turning what had been water into land. In this way he so enlarged the town that he was able to lay out a "wide space" (Eurychôrus)1482 as a public square, which, like the Piazza di San Marco at Venice, became the great resort of the inhabitants for business and pleasure. Having thus provided for utility and convenience, he next proceeded to embellishment and ornamentation. The old temples did not seem to him worthy of the renovated capital; he therefore pulled them down and built new ones in their place. In the most central part of the city1483 he erected a fane for the worship of Melkarth and Ashtoreth, probably retaining the old site, but constructing an entirely new building—the building which Herodotus visited,1484 and in which Alexander insisted on sacrificing.1485 Towards the south-west,1486 on what had been a separate islet, he raised a temple to Baal, and adorned it with a lofty pillar of gold,1487 or at any rate plated with gold. Whether he built himself a new palace is not related; but as the royal residence of later times was situated on the southern shore,1488 which was one of Hiram's additions to his capital, it is perhaps most probable that the construction of this new palace was due to him. The chief material which he used in his buildings, was, as in Jerusalem, cedar. The substructions alone were of stone. They were probably not on so grand a scale as those of the Jewish Temple, since the wealth of Hiram, sovereign of a petty kingdom, must have fallen very far short of Solomon's, ruler of an extensive empire.

At the close of the twenty years during which Hiram had assisted Solomon in his buildings, the Israelite monarch deemed it right to make his Tyrian brother some additional compensation beyond the corn, and wine, and oil with which, according to his contract, he had annually supplied him. Accordingly, he voluntarily ceded to him a district of Galilee containing twenty cities, a portion of the old inheritance of Asher,1489 conveniently near to Accho, of which Hiram was probably lord, and not very remote from Tyre. The tract appears to have been that where the modern Kabûl now stands, which is a rocky and bare highland,1490—part of the outlying roots of Lebanon—overlooking the rich plain of Akka or Accho, and presenting a striking contrast to its fertility. Hiram, on the completion of the cession, "came out from Tyre to see the cities which Solomon had given him," and was disappointed with the gift. "What cities are these," he said, "which thou hast given me, my brother? And he called them the land of Cabul"—"rubbish" or "offscourings"—to mark his disappointment.1491

But this passing grievance was not allowed in any way to overshadow, or interfere with, the friendly alliance and "entente cordiale" (to use a modern phrase) which existed between the two nations. Solomon, according to one authority,1492 paid a visit to Tyre, and gratified his host by worshipping in a Sidonian temple. According to another,1493 Hiram gave him in marriage, as a secondary wife, one of his own daughters—a marriage perhaps alluded to by the writer of Kings when he tells us that "King Solomon loved many strange women together with the daughter of Pharaoh, women of the Moabites, Ammonites, Edomites, Zidonians, and Hittites."1494 The closest commercial relations were established between the two countries, and the hope of them was probably one of the strongest reasons which attracted both parties to the alliance. The Tyrians, on their part, possessed abundant ships; their sailors had full "knowledge of the sea,"1495 and the trade of the Mediterranean was almost wholly in their hands. Solomon, on his side, being master of the port of Ezion-Geber on the Red Sea, had access to the lucrative traffic with Eastern Africa, Arabia, and perhaps India, which had hitherto been confined to the Egyptians and the Arabs. He had also, by his land power, a command of the trade routes along the Coele-Syrian valley, by Aleppo, and by Tadmor, which enabled him effectually either to help or to hinder the Phoenician land traffic. Thus either side had something to gain from the other, and a close commercial union might be safely counted on to work for the mutual advantage of both. Such a union, therefore, took place. Hiram admitted Solomon to a participation in his western traffic; and the two kings maintained a conjoint "navy of Tarshish,"1496 which, trading with Spain and the West coast of Africa, brought to Phoenicia and Palestine "once in three years" many precious and rare commodities, the chief of them being "gold, and silver, ivory, and apes, and peacocks." Spain would yield the gold and the silver, for the Tagus brought down gold,1497 and the Spanish silver-mines were the richest in the world.1498 Africa would furnish in abundance the ivory and the apes; for elephants were numerous in Mauritania,1499 and on the west coast,14100 in ancient times; and the gorilla14101 and the Barbary ape are well-known African products. Africa may also have produced the "peacocks," if tukkiyim are really "peacocks," though they are not found there at the present day. Or the tukkiyim may have been Guinea-fowl—a bird of the same class with the peacock.

In return, Solomon opened to Hiram the route to the East by way of the Red Sea. Solomon, doubtless by the assistance of shipwrights furnished to him from Tyre, "made a navy of ships at Ezion-Geber, which is beside Eloth, on the shore of the Red Sea, in the land of Edom,"14102 and the sailors of the two nations conjointly manned the ships, and performed the voyage to Ophir, whence they brought gold, and "great plenty of almug-trees," and precious stones.14103 The position of Ophir has been much disputed, but the balance of argument is in favour of the theory which places it in Arabia, on the south-eastern coast, a little outside the Straits of Bab-el-Mandeb.14104 It is possible that the fleet did not confine itself to trade with Ophir, but, once launched on the Indian Ocean, proceeded along the Atlantic coast to the Persian Gulf and the peninsula of Hindustan. Or Ophir may have been an Arab emporium for the Indian trade, and the merchants of Syria may have found there the Indian commodities, and the Indian woods,14105 which they seem to have brought back with them to their own country. A most lucrative traffic was certainly established by the united efforts of the two kings; and if the lion's share of the profit fell to Solomon and the Hebrews,14106 still the Phoenicians and Hiram must have participated to some considerable extent in the gains made, or the arrangement would not have continued.

It is thought that Hiram was engaged in one war of some importance. Menander tells us, according to the present text of Josephus,14107 that the "Tityi" revolted from him, and refused any longer to pay him tribute, whereupon he made an expedition against them, and succeeded in compelling them to submit to his authority. As the "Tityi" are an unknown people, conjecture has been busy in suggesting other names,14108 and critics are now of the opinion that the original word used by Menander was not "Tityi," but "Itykæi." The "Itykæi" are the people of Utica: and, if this emendation be accepted,14109 we must regard Hiram as having had to crush a most important and dangerous rebellion. Utica, previously to the foundation of Carthage, was by far the most important of all the mid-African colonies, and her successful revolt would probably have meant to Tyre the loss of the greater portion, if not the whole, of those valuable settlements. A rival to her power would have sprung up in the West, which would have crippled her commerce in that quarter, and checked her colonising energy. She would have suffered thus early more than she did four hundred years later by the great development of the power of Carthage; would have lost a large portion of her prestige; and have entered on the period of her decline when she had but lately obtained a commanding position. Hiram's energy diverted these evils: he did not choose that his kingdom should be dismembered, if he could anyhow help it; and, offering a firm and strenuous opposition to the revolt, he succeeded in crushing it, and maintaining the unity of the empire.

The brilliant reign of Hiram, which covered the space of forty-three years, was not followed, like that of Solomon, by any immediate troubles, either foreign or domestic. He had given his people, either at home or abroad, constant employment; he had consulted their convenience in the enlargement of his capital; he had enriched them, and gratified their love of adventure, by his commercial enterprises; he had maintained their prestige by rivetting their yoke upon a subject state; he had probably pleased them by the temples and other public buildings with which he had adorned and beautified their city. Accordingly, he went down to the grave in peace; and not only so, but left his dynasty firmly established in power. His son, Baal-azar or Baleazar, who was thirty-six years of age, succeeded him, and held the throne for seven years, when he died a natural death.14110 Abd-Ashtoreth (Abdastartus), the fourth monarch of the house, then ascended the throne, at the age of twenty, and reigned for nine years before any troubles broke out. Then, however, a time of disturbance supervened. Four of his foster-brothers conspired against Abd-Ashtoreth, and murdered him. The eldest of them seized the throne, and maintained himself upon it for twelve years, when Astartus, perhaps a son of Baal-azar, became king, and restored the line of Hiram. He, too, like his predecessor, reigned twelve years, when his brother, Aserymus, succeeded him. Aserymus, after ruling for nine years, was murdered by another brother, Pheles, who, in his turn, succumbed to a conspiracy headed by the High Priest, Eth-baal, or Ithobal.14111 Thus, while the period immediately following the death of Hiram was one of tranquillity, that which supervened on the death of Abd-Astartus, Hiram's grandson, was disturbed and unsettled. Three monarchs met with violent deaths within the space of thirty-four years, and the reigning house was, at least, thrice changed during the same interval.

At length with Ithobal a more tranquil time was reached. Ithobal, or Eth-baal, was not only king, but also High Priest of Ashtoreth, and thus united the highest sacerdotal with the highest civil authority. He was a man of decision and energy, a worthy successor of Hiram, gifted like him with wide-reaching views, and ambitious of distinction. One of his first acts was to ally himself with Ahab, King of Israel, by giving him his daughter, Jezebel, in marriage,14112 thus strengthening his land dominion, and renewing the old relations of friendship with the Hebrew people. Another act of vigour assigned to him is the foundation of Botrys, on the Syrian coast, north of Gebal, perhaps a defensive movement against Assyria.14113 Still more enterprising was his renewal of the African colonisation by his foundation of Aüza in Numidia,14114 which became a city of some importance. Ithobal's reign lasted, we are told, thirty-two years. He was sixty-eight years of age at his death, and was succeeded by his son, who is called Badezor, probably a corruption of Balezor, or Baal-azar14115—the name given by Hiram to his son and successor. Of Badezor we know nothing, except that he reigned six years, and was succeeded by his son Matgen, perhaps Mattan,14116 a youth of twenty-three.

With Matgen, or Mattan, whichever be the true form of the name, the internal history of Tyre becomes interesting. It appears that two parties already existed in the state, one aristocratic, and the other popular.14117 Mattan, fearing the ascendancy of the popular party, married his daughter, Elisa, whom he intended for his successor, to her uncle and his own brother, Sicharbas, who was High Priest of Melkarth, and therefore possessed of considerable authority in his own person. Having effected this marriage, and nominated Elisa to succeed him, Mattan died at the early age of thirty-two, after a reign of only nine years.14118 Besides his daughter, he had left behind him a son, Pygmalion, who, at his decease, was but eight or nine years old. This child the democratic party contrived to get under their influence, proclaimed him king, young as he was, and placed him upon the throne. Elisa and her husband retired into private life, and lived in peace for seven years, but Pygmalion, being then grown to manhood, was not content to leave them any longer unmolested. He murdered Sicharbas, and endeavoured to seize his riches. But the ex-Queen contrived to frustrate his design, and having possessed herself of a fleet of ships, and taken on board the greater number of the nobles, sailed away, with her husband's wealth untouched, to Cyprus first, and then to Africa.14119 Here, by agreement with the inhabitants, a site was obtained, and the famous settlement founded, which became known to the Greeks as "Karchêdon," and to the Romans as "Carthago," or Carthage. Josephus places this event in the hundred and forty-fourth year after the building of the Temple of Solomon,14120 or about B.C. 860. This date, however, is far from certain.

It appears to have been in the reign of Ithobal that the first contact took place between Phoenicia and Assyria. About B.C. 885, a powerful and warlike monarch, by name Asshur-nazir-pal, mounted the throne of Nineveh, and shortly engaged in a series of wars towards the south, the east, the north, and the north-west.14121 In the last-named direction he crossed the Euphrates at Carchemish (Jerablus) and, having overrun the country between that river and the Orontes, he proceeded to pass this latter stream also, and to carry his arms into the rich tract which lay between the Orontes and the Mediterranean. "It was a tract," says M. Maspero,14122 "opulent and thickly populated, at once full of industries and commercial; the metals, both precious and ordinary, gold, silver, copper, tin (?), iron, were abundant; traffic with Phoenicia supplied it with the purple dye, and with linen stuffs, with ebony and with sandal-wood. Asshur-nazir-pal's attack seems to have surprised the chief of the Hittites in a time of profound peace. Sangar, King of Carchemish, allowed the passage of the Euphrates to take place without disputing it, and opened to the Assyrians the gates of his capital. Lubarna, king of Kunulua, alarmed at the power of the enemy, and dreading the issue of a battle, came to terms with him, consenting to make over to him twenty talents of gold, a talent of silver, two hundred talents of tin, a hundred of iron, 2,000 oxen, 10,000 sheep, a thousand garments of wool or linen, together with furniture, arms, and slaves beyond all count. The country of Lukhuti resisted, and suffered the natural consequences—all the cities were sacked, and the prisoners crucified. After this exploit, Asshur-nazir-pal occupied both the slopes of Mount Lebanon, and then descended to the shores of the Mediterranean. Phoenicia did not await his arrival to do him homage: the kings of Tyre, Sidon, Gebal, and Arvad, 'which is in the midst of the sea,' sent him presents. The Assyrians employed their time in cutting down cedar trees in Lebanon and Amanus, together with pines and cypresses, which they transported to Nineveh to be used in the construction of a temple to Ishtar."

The period of the Assyrian subjection, which commenced with this attack on the part of Asshur-nazir-pal, will be the subject of the next section. It only remains here briefly to recapitulate the salient points of Phoenician history under Tyre's first supremacy. In the first place, it was a time of increased daring and enterprise, in which colonies were planted upon the shores of the Atlantic Ocean, and trade extended to the remote south, the more remote north, and the still more remote north-east, to the Fortunate Islands, the Cassiterides, and probably the Baltic. Secondly, it was a time when the colonies on the North African coast were reinforced, strengthened, and increased in number; when the Phoenician yoke was rivetted on that vast projection into the Mediterranean which divides that sea into two halves, and goes far to give the power possessing it entire command of the Mediterranean waters. Thirdly, it was a time of extended commerce with the East, perhaps the only time when Phoenician merchant vessels were free to share in the trade of the Red Sea, to adventure themselves in the Indian Ocean, and to explore the distant coasts of Eastern Africa, Southern Arabia, Beloochistan, India and Ceylon. Fourthly, it was a time of artistic vigour and development, when Tyre herself assumed that aspect of splendour and magnificence which thenceforth characterised her until her destruction by Alexander, and when she so abounded in æsthetic energy and genius that she could afford to take the direction of an art movement in a neighbouring country, and to plant her ideas on that conspicuous hill which for more than a thousand years drew the eyes of men almost more than any other city of the East, and was only destroyed because she was felt by Rome to be a rival that she could not venture to spare. Finally, it was a time when internal dissensions, long existing, came to a head, and the state lost, through a sudden desertion, a considerable portion of its strength, which was transferred to a distant continent, and there steadily, if not rapidly, developed itself into a power, not antagonistic indeed, but still, by the necessity of its position, a rival power—a new commercial star, before which all other stars, whatever their brightness had been, paled and waned—a new factor in the polity of nations, whereof account had of necessity to be taken; a new trade-centre, which could not but supersede to a great extent all former trade-centres, and which, however unwillingly, as it rose, and advanced, and prospered, tended to dim, obscure, and eclipse the glories of its mother-city.

3. Phoenicia during the period of its subjection to Assyria (B.C.

877-635)
Phoenicia conquered by the Assyrians (about B.C. 877)—
Peaceful relations established (about B.C. 839)—Time of
quiet and prosperity—Harsh measures of Tiglath-pileser II.
(about B.C. 740)—Revolt of Simyra—Revolt of Tyre under

Elulæus—Wars of Elulæus with Shalmaneser IV. and with
Sennacherib—Reign of Abdi-Milkut—His war with Esarhaddon—
Accession of Baal—His relations with Esarhaddon and Asshur-
bani-pal—Revolt and reduction of Arvad, Hosah, and Accho—
Summary.

The first contact of Phoenicia with Assyria took place, as above observed, in the reign of
Asshur-nazir-pal, about the year B.C. 877. The principal cities, on the approach of the great
conquering monarch, with his multitudinous array of chariots, his clouds of horse, and his
innumerable host of foot soldiers, made haste to submit themselves, sought to propitiate the
invader by rich gifts, and accepted what they hoped might prove a nominal subjection. Arvad,
which, as the most northern, was the most directly threatened, Gebal, Sidon, and even the
comparatively remote Tyre, sent their several embassies, made their offerings, and became, in
name at any rate, Assyrian dependencies. But the real subjection of this country was not
effected at this time, nor without a struggle. Asshur-nazir-pal's yoke lay lightly upon his
vassals, and during the remainder of his long reign—from B.C. 877 to B.C. 860—he seems to
have desisted from military expeditions,14123 and to have exerted no pressure on the
countries situated west of the Euphrates. It was not until the reign of his son and successor,
Shalmaneser II., that the real conquest of Syria and Phoenicia was taken in hand, and pressed
to a successful issue by a long series of hard-fought campaigns and bloody battles. From his
sixth to his twenty-first year Shamaneser carried on an almost continuous war in Syria,14124
where his adversaries were the monarchs of Damascus and Hamath, and "the twelve kings
beside the sea, above and below,"14125 one of whom is expressly declared to have been
"Mattan-Baal of Arvad."14126 It was not until the year B.C. 839 that this struggle was
terminated by the submission of the monarchs engaged in it to their great adversary, and the
firm establishment of a system of "tribute and taxes."14127 The Phoenician towns agreed to
pay annually to the Assyrian monarch a certain fixed sum in the precious metals, and further to
make him presents from time to time of the best products of their country. Among these are
mentioned "skins of buffaloes, horns of buffaloes, clothing of wool and linen, violet wool,
purple wool, strong wood, wood for weapons, skins of sheep, fleeces of shining purple, and
birds of heaven."14128

The relations of Phoenicia towards the Assyrian monarchy continued to be absolutely peaceful
for above a century. The cities retained their native monarchs, their laws and institutions, their
religion, and their entire internal administration. So long as they paid the fixed tribute, they
appear not to have been interfered with in any way. It would seem that their trade prospered.
Assyria had under her control the greater portion of those commercial routes across the
continent of Asia,14129 which it was of the highest importance to Phoenicia to have open and
free from peril. Her caravans could traverse them with increased security, now that they were
safeguarded by a power whereof she was a dependency. She may even have obtained through
Assyria access to regions which had been previously closed to her, as Media, and perhaps
Persia. At any rate Tyre seems to have been as flourishing in the later times of the Assyrian
dominion as at almost any other period. Isaiah, in denouncing woe upon her, towards the close
of the dominion, shows us what she had been under it:—

Be silent (he says), ye inhabitants of the island,
Which the merchants of Zidon, that pass over the sea, have
    replenished.
The corn of the Nile, on the broad waters,
The harvest of the River, has been her revenue:
She has been the mart of nations . . .
She was a joyful city,
Her antiquity was of ancient days . . .
She was a city that dispensed crowns;
Her merchants were princes,

And her traffickers the honourable of the earth.14130

A change in the friendly feelings of the Phoenician cities towards Assyria first began after the rise of the Second or Lower Assyrian Empire, which was founded, about B.C. 745, by Tiglath-pileser II.14131 Tiglath-pileser, after a time of quiescence and decay, raised up Assyria to be once more a great conquering power, and energetically applied himself to the consolidation and unification of the empire. It was the Assyrian system, as it was the Roman, to absorb nations by slow degrees—to begin by offering protection and asking in return a moderate tribute; then to draw the bonds more close, to make fresh demands and enforce them; finally, to pick a quarrel, effect a conquest, and absorb the country, leaving it no vestige of independence. Tiglath-pileser began this process of absorption in Northern Syria about the year B.C. 740. He rearranged the population in the various towns, taking from some and giving to others,14132 adding also in most cases an Assyrian element, appointing Assyrian governors,14133 and requiring of the inhabitants "the performance of service like the Assyrians."14134 Among the places thus treated between the years B.C. 740 and B.C. 738, we find the Phoenician cities of Zimirra, or Simyra, and Arqa, or Arka. Zimirra was in the plain between the sea and Mount Bargylus, not very far from the island of Aradus, whereof it was a dependency. Arqa was further to the south, beyond the Eleutherus, and belonged properly to Tripolis, if Tripolis had as yet been founded, or else to Botrys. Both of them were readily accessible from the Orontes valley along the course of the Eleutherus, and, being weak, could offer no resistance. Tiglath-pileser carried out his plans, rearranged the populations, and placed the cities under Assyrian governors responsible to himself. There was no immediate outbreak; but the injury rankled. Within twenty years Zimirra joined a revolt, to which Hamath, Arpad, Damascus, and Samaria were likewise parties, and made a desperate attempt to shake off the Assyrian yoke.14135 The attempt failed, the revolt was crushed, and Zimirra is heard of no more in history.

But this was not the worst. The harsh treatment of Simyra and Arka, without complaint made or offence given, after a full century of patient and quiet submission, aroused a feeling of alarm and indignation among the Phoenician cities generally, which could not fail to see in what had befallen their sisters a foreshadowing of the fate that they had to expect one day themselves. Beginning with the weakest cities, Assyria would naturally go on to absorb those which were stronger, and Tyre herself, the "anointed cherub,"14136 could look for no greater favour than, like Ulysses in the cave of Polyphemus, to be devoured last. Luliya, or Elulæus, the king of Tyre at the time,14137 endeavoured to escape this calamity by gathering to himself a strength which would enable him to defy attack. He contrived to establish his dominion over almost the whole of Southern Phoenicia—over Sidon, Accho, Ecdippa, Sarepta, Hosah, Bitsette, Mahalliba, &c.14138—and at the same time over the distant Cyprus,14139 where the Cittæans, or people of Citium, held command of the island. After a time the Cittæans revolted from him, probably stirred up by the Assyrians. But Elulæus, without delay, led an expedition into Cyprus, and speedily put down the rebellion. Hereupon the Assyrian king of the time, Shalmaneser IV., the successor and probably the son of Tiglath-pileser II., led a great expedition into the west about B.C. 727, and "overran all Syria and Phoenicia."14140 But he was unable to make any considerable impression. Tyre and Aradus were safe upon their islands; Sidon and the other cities upon the mainland, were protected by strong and lofty walls. After a single campaign, the Great King found it necessary to offer terms of peace, which proved acceptable, and the belligerents parted towards the close of the year, without any serious loss or gain on either side.14141

It seemed necessary to adopt some different course of action. Shalmaneser had discovered during his abortive campaign that there were discords and jealousies among the various Phoenician cities; that none of them submitted without repugnance to the authority of Tyre, and that Sidon especially had an ancient ground of quarrel with her more powerful sister, and always cherished the hope of recovering her original supremacy. He had seen also that the greater number of the Phoenician towns, if he chose to press upon them with the full force of his immense military organisation, lay at his mercy. He had only to invest each city on the land side, to occupy its territory, to burn its villas, to destroy its irrigation works, to cut down its fruit trees, to interfere with its water-supply, and in the last instance to press upon it, to batter down its walls, to enter its streets, slaughter its population, or drive it to take refuge in its ships,14142 and he could become absolute master of the whole Phoenician mainland. Only Tyre and Aradus could escape him. But might not they also be brought into subjection by the naval forces which their sister cities, once occupied, might be compelled to furnish, and to man, or, at any rate, to assist in manning? Might not the whole of Phoenicia be in this way absorbed into the empire? The prospect was pleasing, and Shalmaneser set to work to convert the vision into a reality. By his emissaries he stirred up the spirit of disaffection among the Tyrian subject towns, and succeeded in separating from Tyre, and drawing over to his own side, not only Sidon and Acre and their dependencies, but even the city of Palæ-Tyrus itself,14143 or the great town which had grown up opposite the island Tyre upon the mainland. The island Tyre seems to have been left without support or ally, to fight her own battle singly. Shalmaneser called upon his new friends to furnish him with a fleet, and they readily responded to the call, placing their ships at his disposal to the number of sixty, and supplying him further with eight hundred skilled oarsmen, not a sufficient number to dispense with Assyrian aid, but enough to furnish a nucleus of able seamen for each vessel. The attack was then made. The Assyro-Phoenician fleet sailed in a body from some port on the continent, and made a demonstration against the Island City, which they may perhaps have expected to frighten into a surrender. But the Tyrians were in no way alarmed. They knew, probably, that their own countrymen would not fight with very much zeal for their foreign masters, and they despised, undoubtedly, the mixed crews, half skilled seamen, half tiros and bunglers, which had been brought against them. Accordingly they thought it sufficient to put to sea with just a dozen ships—one to each five of the enemy, and making a sudden attack with these upon the adverse fleet, they defeated it, dispersed it, and took five hundred prisoners. Shalmaneser saw that he had again miscalculated; and, despairing of any immediate success, drew off his ships and his troops, and retired to his own country. He left behind him, however, on the mainland opposite the island Tyre, a certain number of his soldiers, with orders to prevent the Tyrians from obtaining, according to their ordinary practice, supplies of water from the continent. Some were stationed at the mouth of the river Leontes (the Litany), a little to the north of Tyre, a perennial stream bringing down a large quantity of water from Coele-Syria and Lebanon; others held possession of the aqueducts on the south, built to convey the precious fluid across the plain from the copious springs of Ras el Ain14144 to the nearest point of the coast opposite the city. The continental water supply was thus effectually cut off; but the Tyrians were resolute, and made no overtures to the enemy. For five years, we are told,14145 they were content to drink such water only as could be obtained in their own island from wells sunk in the soil, which must have been brackish, unwholesome, and disagreeable. At the end of that time a revolution occurred at Nineveh. Shalmaneser lost his throne (B.C. 722), and a new dynasty succeeding, amid troubles of various kinds, attention was drawn away from Tyre to other quarters; and Elulæus was left in undisturbed possession of his island city for nearly a quarter of a century.

It appears that, during this interval, Elulæus rebuilt the power which Shalmaneser had shattered and brought low, repossessing himself of Cyprus, or, at any rate, of some portion of it,14146 and re-establishing his authority over all those cities of the mainland which had previously acknowledged subjection to him. These included Sidon, Bit-sette, Sarepta, Mahalliba, Hosah, Achzib or Ecdippa, and Accho (Acre). There is some ground for thinking that he transferred his own residence to Sidon,14147 perhaps for the purpose of keeping closer watch upon the town which he most suspected of disaffection. The policy of Sargon seems to have been to leave Phoenicia alone, and content himself with drawing the tribute which the cities were quite willing to pay in return for Assyrian protection. His reign lasted from B.C. 722 to B.C. 705, and it was not until Sennacherib, his son and successor, had been seated for four years upon the throne that a reversal of this policy took place, and war à outrance was declared against the Phoenician king, who had ventured to brave, and had succeeded in baffling, Assyria more than twenty years previously. Sennacherib entertained grand designs of conquest in this quarter, and could not allow the example of an unpunished and triumphant rebellion to be flaunted in the eyes of a dozen other subject states, tempting them to throw off their allegiance. He therefore, as soon as affairs in Babylonia ceased to occupy him, marched the full force of the empire towards the west, and proclaimed his intention of crushing the Phoenician revolt, and punishing the audacious rebel who had so long defied the might of Assyria. The army which he set in motion must have numbered more than 200,000 men;14148 its chariots were numerous,14149 its siege-train ample and well provided.14150 Such terror did it inspire among those against whom it was directed that Elulæus was afraid even to await attack, and, while Sennacherib was still on his march, took ship and removed himself to the distant island of Cyprus,14151 where alone he could feel safe from pursuit and capture. But, though deserted by their sovereign, his towns seem to have declined to submit themselves. No great battle was fought; but severally they took arms and defended their walls. Sennacherib tells us that he took one after another—"by the might of the soldiers of Asshur his lord"14152—Great Sidon, Lesser Sidon, Bit-sette, Zarephath or Sarepta, Mahalliba, Hosah, Achzib or Ecdippa, and Accho—"strong cities, fortresses, walled and enclosed, Luliya's castles."14153 He does not claim, however, to have taken Tyre, and we may conclude that the Island City escaped him. But he made himself master of the entire tract upon the continent which had constituted Luliya's kingdom, and secured its obedience by placing over it a new king, in whom he had confidence, a certain Tubaal14154 (Tob-Baal), probably a Phoenician. At the same time he rearranged the yearly tribute which the cities had to pay to Assyria,14155 probably augmenting it, as a punishment for the long rebellion.

We hear nothing more of Phoenicia during the reign of Sennacherib, except that, shortly after his conquest of the tract about Sidon, he received tribute, not only from the king whom he had just set over that town, but also from Uru-melek, king of Gebal (Byblus), and Abd-ilihit, king of Arvad.14156 The three towns represent, probably, the whole of Phoenicia, Aradus at this time exercising dominion over the northern tract, or that extending from Mount Casius to the Eleutherus, Gebal or Byblus over the central tract from the Eleutherus to the Tamyras, and Sidon, in the temporary eclipse of Tyre, ruling the southern tract from the Tamyrus to Mount Carmel. It appears further,14157 that at some date between this tribute-giving (B.C. 701) and the death of Sennacherib (B.C. 681) Tubaal must have been succeeded in the government of Sidon by Abdi-Milkut, or Abd-Melkarth14158 ({...}), but whether this change was caused by a revolt, or took place in the ordinary course, Tubaal dying and being succeeded by his son, is wholly uncertain.

All that we know is that Esarhaddon, on his accession, found Abd-Melkarth in revolt against his authority. He had formed an alliance with a certain Sanduarri, king of Kundi and Sizu,14159 a prince of the Lebanon, and had set up as independent monarch, probably during the time of the civil way which was waged between Esarhaddon and two of his brothers who disputed his succession after they had murdered his father.14160 As soon as this struggle was over, and the Assyrian monarch found himself free to take his own course, he proceeded at once (B.C. 680) against these two rebels. Both of them tried to escape him. Abd-Melkarth, quitting his capital, fled away by sea, steering probably either for Aradus or for Cyprus. Sanduarri took refuge in his mountain fastnesses. But Esarhaddon was not to be baffled. He caused both chiefs to be pursued and taken. "Abd-Melkarth," he says,14161 "who from the face of my solders into the middle of the sea had fled, like a fish from out of the sea, I caught, and cut off his head . . . Sanduarri, who took Abd-Melkarth for his ally, and to his difficult mountains trusted, like a bird from the midst of the mountains, I caught and cut off his head." Sidon was very severely punished. Esarhaddon boasts that he swept away all its subject cities, uprooted its citadel and palace, and cast the materials into the sea, at the same time destroying all its habitations. The town was plundered, the treasures of the palace carried off, and the greater portion of the population deported to Assyria. The blank was filled up with "natives of the lands and seas of the East"—prisoners taken in Esarhaddon's war with Babylon and Elam, who, like the Phoenicians themselves at a remote time, exchanged a residence on the shores of the Persian Gulf for one on the distant Mediterranean. An Assyrian general was placed as governor over the city, and its name changed from Sidon to "Ir-Esarhaddon."

It seems to have been in the course of the same year that Esarhaddon held one of those courts, or durbars, in Syria, which all subject monarchs were expected to attend, and whereat it was the custom that they should pay homage to their suzerain. Hither flocked almost all the neighbouring monarchs14162—Manasseh, king of Judah, Qavus-gabri, king of Ammon, Zilli-bel, king of Gaza, Mitinti of Askelon, Ikasamsu of Ekron, Ahimelek of Ashdod, together with twelve kings of the Cyprians, and three Phoenician monarchs, Baal, king of Tyre, Milki-asaph, king of Gebal, and Mattan-baal, king of Arvad. Tribute was paid, home rendered, and after a short sojourn at the court, the subject-monarchs were dismissed. The foremost position in Esarhaddon's list is occupied by "Baal, king of Tyre;" and this monarch appears to have been received into exceptional favour. He had perhaps been selected by Esarhaddon to rule Southern Phoenicia on the execution of Abd-Melkarth. At any rate, he enjoyed for some time the absolute confidence and high esteem of his suzerain. If we may venture to interpret a mutilated inscription,14163 he furnished Esarhaddon with a fleet, and manned it with his own sailors. Certainly, he received from Esarhaddon a considerable extension of his dominions. Not only was his authority over Accho recognised and affirmed, but the coast tract south of Carmel, as far as Dor, the important city Gebal, and the entire region of Lebanon, were placed under his sovereignty.14164 The date assigned to these events is between B.C. 680 and B.C. 673. It was in this latter year that the Assyrian monarch resolved on an invasion of Egypt. For fifty years the two countries had been watching each other, counteracting each other's policy, lending support to each other's enemies, coming into occasional collision the one with the other, not, however, as principals, but as partakers in other persons' quarrels. Now, at length there was to be an end of subterfuge and pretences. Esarhaddon, about B.C. 673, resolved to attempt the conquest of Egypt. He "set his face to go to the country of Magan and Milukha."14165 He let his intention be generally known. No doubt he called on his subject allies for contingents of men, if not for supplies of money. To Tyre he must naturally have looked for no niggard or grudging support. What then must have been his disgust and rage at finding that, at the critical moment, Tyre had gone over to the enemy? Notwithstanding the favours heaped on him by his suzerain, "Baal, king of Tyre, to Tirhakah, king of Ethiopia, his country entrusted, and the yoke of Asshur threw off and made defiance."14166 Esarhaddon was too strongly bent on his Egyptian expedition to be diverted from it by this defection; but in the year B.C. 672, as he marched through Syria and Palestine on his way to attack Tirhakah, he sent a detachment against Tyre, with orders to his officers to repeat the tactics of Shalmaneser, by occupying points of the coast opposite to the island Tyre, and "cutting off the supplies of food and water."14167 Baal was by this means greatly distressed, and it would seem that within a year or two he made his submission, surrendering either to Esarhaddon or to his son Asshur-bani-pal, in about the year of the latter's accession (B.C. 668). It is surprising to find that he was not deposed from his throne; but as the circumstances seem to have been such as made it imperative on the Assyrian king to condone minor offences in order to accomplish a great enterprise—the restoration of the Assyrian dominion over the Nile valley. Esarhaddon had effected the conquest of Egypt in about the year B.C. 670, and had divided the country into twenty petty principalities;14168 but within a year his yoke had been thrown off, his petty princes expelled, and Tirhakah reinstated as sole monarch over the "Two Regions."14169 It was the determination of Asshur-bani-pal, on becoming king, to strain every nerve and devote his utmost energy to the re-conquest of the ancient kingdom, so lightly won and so lightly lost by his father. Baal's perfidy was thus forgiven or overlooked. A great expedition was prepared. The kings of Phoenicia, Palestine, and Cyprus were bidden once more to assemble, to bring their tribute, and pay homage to their suzerain as he passed on his way at the head of his forces towards the land of the Pharaohs. Baal came, and again holds the post of honour;14170 with him were the king of Judah—doubtless Manasseh, but the name is lost—the kings of Edom, Moab, Gaza, Askelon, Ekron, Gebal, Arvad, Paphos, Soli, Curium, Tamassus, Ammochosta, Lidini, and Aphrodisias, with probably those also of Ammon, Ashdod, Idalium, Citium, and Salamis.14171 Each in turn prostrated himself at the foot of the Great Monarch, paid homage, and made profession of fidelity. Asshur-bani-pal then proceeded on his way, and the kings returned to their several governments.

It is about four years after this, B.C. 664, that we find Baal attacked and punished by the Assyrian monarch. The subjugation of Egypt had been in the meantime, though not without difficulty, completed. Asshur-bani-pal's power extended from the range of Niphates to the First Cataract. Whether during the course of the four years' struggle, by which the reconquest of Egypt was effected, the Tyrian prince had given fresh offence to his suzerain, or whether it was the old offence, condoned for a time but never forgiven, that was now avenged, is not made clear by the Assyrian Inscriptions. Asshur-bani-pal simply tells us that, in his third expedition, he proceeded against Baal, king of Tyre, dwelling in the midst of the sea, who his royal will disregarded, and did not listen to the words of his lips. "Towers round him," he says, "I raised, and over his people I strengthened the watch; on sea and land his forts I took; his going out I stopped. Water and sea-water, to preserve their lives, their mouths drank. By a strong blockade, which removed not, I besieged them; their works I checked and opposed; to my yoke I made them submissive. The daughter proceeding from his body, and the daughters of his brothers, for concubines he brought to my presence. Yahi-milki, his son, the glory of the country, of unsurpassed renown, at once he sent forward, to make obeisance to me. His daughter, and the daughters of his brothers, with their great dowries, I received. Favour I granted him, and the son proceeding from his body, I restored, and gave him back."14172

Thus Baal once more escaped the fate he must have expected. Asshur-bani-pal, who was far from being of a clement disposition, suffered himself to be appeased by the submission made, restored Baal to his favour, and allowed him to retain possession of his sovereignty.

Another Phoenician monarch also was, about the same time, threatened and pardoned. This was Yakinlu, the king of Arvad, probably the son and successor of Mattan-Baal, the contemporary of Esarhaddon.14173 He is accused of having been wanting in submission to Asshur-bani-pal's fathers;14174 but we may regard it as probable that his real offence was some failure in his duties towards Asshur-bani-pal himself. Either he had openly rebelled, and declared himself independent, or he had neglected to pay his tribute, or he had given recent offence in some other way. The Phoenician island kings were always more neglectful of their duties than others, since it was more difficult to punish them. Assyria did not even now possess any regular fleet, and could only punish a recalcitrant king of Arvad or Tyre by impressing into her service the ships of some of the Phoenician coast-towns, as Sidon, or Gebal, or Accho. These towns were not very zealous in such a service, and probably did not maintain strong navies, having little use for them. Thus Yakinlu may have expected that his neglect, whatever it was, would be overlooked. But Asshur-bani-pal was jealous of his rights, and careful not to allow any of them to lapse by disuse. He let his displeasure be known at the court of Yakinlu, and very shortly received an embassy of submission. Like Baal, Yakinlu sent a daughter to take her place among the great king's secondary wives, and with her he sent a large sum of money, in the disguise of a dowry.14175 The tokens of subjection were accepted, and Yakinlu was allowed to continue king of Arvad. When, not long afterwards, he died,14176 and his ten sons sought the court of Nineveh to prefer their claims to the succession, they were received with favour. Azi-Baal, the eldest, was appointed to the vacant kingdom, while his nine brothers were presented by Asshur-bani-pal with "costly clothing, and rings."14177

Two other revolts of two other Phoenician towns belong to a somewhat later period. On his return from an expedition against Arabia, about B.C. 645, Asshur-bani-pal found that Hosah, a small place in the vicinity of Tyre,14178 and Accho, famous as Acre in later times, had risen in revolt against their Assyrian governors, refused their tribute, and asserted independence.14179 He at once besieged, and soon captured, Hosah. The leaders of the rebellion he put to death; the plunder of the town, including the images of its gods, and the bulk of its population, he carried off into Assyria. The people ot Accho, he says, he "quieted." It is a common practice of conquerors "to make a solitude and call it peace." Asshur-bani-pal appears to have punished Accho, first by a wholesale massacre, and then by the deportation of all its remaining inhabitants.

It is evident from this continual series of revolts and rebellions that, however mild had been the sway of Assyria over her Phoenician subjects in the earlier times, it had by degrees become a hateful and a grinding tyranny. Commercial states, bent upon the accumulation of wealth, do not without grave cause take up arms and affront the perils of war, much less do so when their common sense must tell them that success is almost absolutely hopeless, and that failure will bring about their destruction. The Assyrians were a hard race. Such tenderness as they ever showed to any subject people was, we may be sure, in every case dictated by policy. While their power was unsettled, while they feared revolts, and were uncertain as to their consequences, their attitude towards their dependents was conciliating. When they became fully conscious of the immense preponderance of power which they wielded, and of the inability of the petty states of Asia to combine against them in any firm league, they grew careless and confident, reckless of giving offence, ruder in their behaviour, more grasping in their exactions, more domineering, more oppressive. Prudence should perhaps have counselled the Phoenician cities to submit, to be yielding and pliant, to cultivate the arts of the parasite and the flatterer; but the people had still a rough honesty about them. It was against the grain to flatter or submit themselves; constant voyages over wild seas in fragile vessels kept up their manhood; constant encounters with pirates, cannibals, and the rudest possible savages made them brave and daring; exposure to storm, and cold, and heat braced their frames; the nautical life developed and intensified in them a love of freedom. The Phoenician of Assyrian times was not to be coaxed into accepting patiently the lot of a slave. Suffer as he might by his revolts, they won him a certain respect; it is likely that they warded off many an indignity, many an outrage. The Assyrians knew that his endurance could not be reckoned on beyond a certain point, and they knew that in his death-throes he was dangerous. The Phoenicians probably suffered considerably less than the other subject nations under Assyrian rule; and the maritime population, which was the salt of the people, suffered least of all, since it was scarcely ever brought into contact with its nominal rulers.

4. Phoenicia during its struggles with Babylon and Egypt (about B.C.

635-527)

> Decline of Assyria—Scythic troubles—Fall of Nineveh—Union
> of the Phoenician cities under Tyre—Invasion of Syria by
> Neco—Battle of Megiddo—Submission of Phoenicia to Neco—
> Tyrian colony at Memphis—Conquest of Phoenicia by
> Nebuchadnezzar—Reign of Ithobal II. at Tyre—He revolts
> from Nebuchadnezzar but is reduced to subjection—Decline of
> Tyre—General weakness of Phoenicia under Babylon.

It is impossible to fix the year in which Phoenicia became independent of Assyria. The last trace of Assyrian interference, in the way of compulsion, with any of the towns belongs to B.C. 645, when she severely punished Hosah and Accho. The latest sign of her continued domination is found in B.C. 636, when the Assyrian governor of a Phoenician town, Zimirra, appears in the list of Eponyms.14180 It must have been very soon after this that the empire became involved in those troubles and difficulties which led on to its dissolution. According to Herodotus,14181 Cyaxares, king of Media, laid siege to Nineveh in B.C. 633, or very soon afterwards. His attack did not at once succeed; but it was almost immediately followed by the irruption into South-western Asia of Scythic hordes from beyond the Caucasus, which overran country after country, destroying and ravaging at their pleasure.14182 The reality of this invasion is now generally admitted. "It was the earliest recorded," says a modern historian, "of those movements of the northern populations, hid behind the long mountain barrier, which, under the name of Himalaya, Caucasus, Taurus, Hæmus, and the Alps, has been reared by nature between the civilised and uncivilised races of the old world. Suddenly, above this boundary, appeared those strange, uncouth, fur-clad forms, hardly to be distinguished from their horses and their waggons, fierce as their own wolves or bears, sweeping towards the southern regions, which seemed to them their natural prey. The successive invasions of Parthians, Turks, Mongols in Asia, of Gauls, Goths, Vandals, Huns in Europe, have, it is well said, 'illustrated the law, and made us familiar with its operations. But there was a time in history before it had come into force, and when its very existence must have been unsuspected. Even since it began to operate, it has so often undergone prolonged suspension that the wisest may be excused if they cease to bear it in mind, and are as much startled when a fresh illustration of it occurs, as if the like had never happened before.'14183 No wonder that now, when the veil was for the first time rent asunder, all the ancient monarchies of the South— Assyria, Babylon, Media, Egypt, even Greece and Asia Minor—stood aghast at the spectacle of these savage hordes rushing down on the seats of luxury and power."14184 Assyria seems to have suffered from the attack almost as much as any other country. The hordes probably swarmed down from Media through the Zagros passes into the most fruitful portion of the empire—the flat country between the mountains and the Tigris. Many of the old cities, rich with the accumulated stores of ages, were besieged, and perhaps taken, and their palaces wantonly burnt by the barbarous invaders. The tide then swept on. Wandering from district to district, plundering everywhere, settling nowhere, the clouds of horse passed over Mesopotamia, the force of the invasion becoming weaker as it spread itself, until in Syria it reached its term through the policy of the Egyptian king, Psamatik I. That monarch bribed the nomads to advance no further,14185 and from this time their power began to wane. Their numbers must have been greatly thinned in the long course of battles, sieges, and skirmishes wherein they were engaged year after year; they suffered also through their excesses;14186 and perhaps through intestine dissensions. At last they recognised that their power was broken. Many bands probably returned across the Caucasus into the Steppe country. Others submitted and took service under the native rulers of Asia.14187 Great numbers were slain, and, except in a province of Armenia, which thenceforward became known as Sacasêné,14188 and perhaps in one Syrian town, which acquired the name of Scythopolis,14189 the invaders left no permanent trace of their brief but terrible inroad.

The shock of the Scythian irruption cannot but have greatly injured and weakened Assyria. The whole country had been ravaged and depopulated; the provinces had been plundered, many of the towns had been taken and sacked, the palaces of the old kings had been burnt,14190 and all the riches that had not been hid away had been lost. Assyria, when the Scythian wave had passed, was but the shadow of her former self. Her prestige was gone, her armed force must have been greatly diminished, her hold upon the provinces, especially the more distant ones, greatly weakened. Phoenicia is likely to have detached herself from Assyria at latest during the time that the Scyths were dominant, which was probably from about B.C. 630 to B.C. 610. When Assyrian protection was withdrawn from Syria, as it must have been during this period, and when every state and town had to look solely to itself for deliverance from a barbarous and cruel enemy, the fiction of a nominal dependence on a distant power could scarcely be maintained. Without any actual revolt, the Phoenician cities became their own masters, and the speedy fall of Assyria before the combined attack of the Medes and Babylonians,14191 after the Scythians had withdrawn, prevented for some time any interference with their recovered independence.

A double danger, however, impended. On the one side Egypt, on the other Babylon, might be confidently expected to lay claim to the debatable land which nature had placed between the seats of the great Asiatic and the great African power, and which in the past had almost always been possessed by the one or the other of them. Egypt was the nearer of the two, and probably seemed the most to be feared. She had recently fallen under the power of an enterprising native monarch, who had already, before the fall of Assyria, shown that he entertained ambitious designs against the Palestinian towns, having begun attacks upon Ashdod soon after he ascended the throne.14192 Babylon was, comparatively speaking, remote and had troublesome neighbours, who might be expected to prevent her from undertaking distant expeditions. It was clearly the true policy for Phoenicia to temporise, to enter into no engagements with either Babylon or Egypt, to strengthen her defences, to bide her time, and, so far as possible, to consolidate herself. Something like a desire for consolidation would seem to have come over the people; and Tyre, the leading city in all but the earliest times, appears to have been recognised as the centre towards which other states must gravitate, and to have risen to the occasion. If there ever was such a thing as a confederation of all the Phoenician cities, it would seem to have been at this period. Sidon forgot her ancient rivalry, and consented to furnish the Tyrian fleet with mariners.14193 Arvad gave not only rowers to man the ships, but also men-at-arms to help in guarding the walls.14194 The "ancients of Gebal" lent their aid in the Tyrian dockyards.14195 The minor cities cannot have ventured to hold aloof. Tyre, as the time approached for the contest which was to decide whether Egypt or Babylon should be the great power of the East, appears to have reached the height of her strength, wealth, and prosperity. It is now that Ezekial says of her—"O Tyrus, thy heart is lifted up, and thou hast said, I am a God, I sit in the seat of God in the midst of the seas—Behold, thou art wiser than Daniel, there is no secret that they can hide from thee: from thy wisdom and with thine understanding hast thou gotten thee riches, and hast gotten gold and silver into thy treasures: by thy great wisdom and by thy traffick thou hast increased thy riches, and thy heart is lifted up because of thy riches"14196; and again, "O thou that are situated at the entry of the sea, which art the merchant of the peoples unto many isles, thus saith the Lord God, Thou, O Tyre, hast said, I am perfect in beauty. Thy borders are in the heart of the sea; thy builders have perfected thy beauty. They have made all thy planks of fir-trees from Senir; they have taken from Lebanon cedars to make masts for thee; of the oaks of Bashan have they made thine oars; they have made thy benches of ivory, inlaid in boxwood, from the isles of Kittim . . . The ships of Tarshish were thy caravans for thy merchandise; and thou wast replenished, and made very glorious in the heart of the sea."14197

The first to strike of the two great antagonists was Egypt. Psamatik I., who was advanced in years at the time of Assyria's downfall,14198 died about B.C. 610, and was succeeded by a son still in the full vigour of life, the brave and enterprising Neco. Neco, in B.C. 608, having made all due preparations, led a great expedition into Palestine,14199 with the object of bringing under his dominion the entire tract between the River of Egypt (Wady el Arish) and the Middle Euphrates. Already possessed of Ashdod14200 and perhaps also of Gaza14201 and Askelon,14202 he held the keys of Syria, and could have no difficulty in penetrating along the coast route, through the rich plain of Sharon, to the first of the mountain barriers which are interposed between the Nile and the Mesopotamian region. His famous fleet14203 would support him along the shore, at any rate as far Carmel; and Dor and Accho would probably be seized, and made into depôts for his stores and provisions. The powerful Egyptian monarch marching northward with his numerous and well-disciplined army, partly composed of native troops, partly of mercenaries from Asia Minor, Greeks and Carians, probably did not look to meet with any opposition, till, somewhere in Northern Syria, he should encounter the forces of Babylonia, which would of course be moved westward to meet him. What then must have been his surprise when he found the ridge connecting Carmel with the highland of Samaria occupied by a strong body of troops, and his further progress barred by a foe who had appeared to him too insignificant to be taken into account? Josiah, the Jewish monarch of the time, grandson of Manasseh and great-grandson of Hezekiah, who, in the unsettled state of Western Asia, had united under his dominion the entire country of the twelve tribes,14204 had quitted Jerusalem, and thrown himself across the would-be conqueror's path in the strong and well-known position of Megiddo. Here, in remote times, had the great Thothmes met and defeated the whole force of Syria and Mesopotamia under the king of Kadesh;14205 here had Deborah and Barak, the son of Abinoam, utterly destroyed the mighty army of Jabin, king of Canaan, under Sisera.14206 Here now the gallant, if rash, Judæan king elected to take his stand, moved either by a sense of duty, because he regarded himself as a Babylonian feudatory, or simply determined to defend the Holy Land against any heathen army that, without permission, trespassed on it. In vain did Neco seek to induce Josiah to retire and leave the way open, by assuring him that he had no hostile intentions against Judæa, but was marching on Carchemish by the Euphrates, there to contend with the Babylonians.14207 The Jewish king persisted in his rash enterprise, and Neco was forced to brush him from his path. His seasoned and disciplined troops easily overcame the hasty levies of Josiah; and Josiah himself fell in the battle.

We have no details with respect to the remainder of the expedition. Neco, no doubt, pressed forward through Galilee and Coele-Syria towards the Euphrates. Whether he had to fight any further battles we are not informed. It is certain that he occupied Carchemish,14208 and made it his headquarters, but whether it submitted to him, or was besieged and taken, is unknown. All Syria, Phoenicia, and Palestine were overrun, and became temporarily Egyptian possessions.14209 But Phoenicia does not appear to have been subdued by force. Tyrian prosperity continued, and the terms on which Phoenicia stood towards Egypt during the remainder of Neco's reign were friendly. Phoenicians at Neco's request accomplished the circumnavigation of Africa;14210 and we may suspect that it was Neco who granted to Tyre the extraordinary favour of settling a colony in the Egyptian capital, Memphis.14211 Probably Phoenicia accepted at the hands of Neco the same sort of position which she had at first occupied under Assyria, a position, as already explained, satisfactory to both parties.

But the glory and prosperity which Egypt had thus acquired were very short-lived. Within three years Babylonia asserted herself. In B.C. 605, the crown prince, Nebuchadnezzar, acting on behalf of his father, Nabopolassar, who was aged and infirm,14212 led the forces of Babylon against the audacious Pharaoh, who had dared to affront the "King of kings," "the Lord of Sumir and Accad," had taken him off his guard, and deprived him of some of his fairest provinces. Babylonia, under Nabopolassar and Nebuchadnezzar, was no unworthy successor of the mighty power which for seven hundred years had held the supremacy of Western Asia. Her citizens were as brave; her armies as well disciplined; her rulers as bold, as sagacious, and as unsparing. Habakkuk's description of a Babylonian army belongs to about this date, and is probably drawn from the life—"Lo, I raise up the Chaldæans, that bitter and hasty nation, which shall march through the breadth of the land, to possess the dwelling-places that are not theirs. They are terrible and dreadful; from them shall proceed judgment and captivity; their horses are swifter than leopards, and are more fierce than the evening wolves; and their horsemen shall spread themselves, and their horsemen shall come from far; they shall fly as the eagle that hasteth to eat. They shall come all for violence; their faces shall sup as the east wind, and they shall gather the captivity as the sand. And they shall scoff at kings, and princes shall be a scorn unto them; they shall deride every stronghold; for they shall heap dust, and take it."14213 Early in the year B.C. 605 the host of Nebuchadnezzar appeared on the right bank of the Euphrates, moving steadily along its reaches, and day by day approaching nearer and nearer to the great fortress in and behind which lay the army of Neco, well ordered with shield and buckler, its horses harnessed, and its horsemen armed with spears that had been just furbished, and protected by helmets and brigandines.14214 One of the "decisive battles of the world" was impending. If Egypt conquered, Oriental civilisation would take the heavy immovable Egyptian type; change, advance, progress would be hindered; sacerdotalism in religion, conventionalism in art, pure unmitigated despotism in government would generally prevail; all the throbbing life of Asia would receive a sudden and violent check; Semitism would be thrust back; Aryanism, just pushing itself to the front, would shrink away; the monotonous Egyptian tone of thought and life would spread, like a lava stream, over the manifold and varied forms of Asiatic culture; crushing them out, concealing them, making them as though they had never been. The victory of Babylon, on the other hand, would mean room for Semitism to develop itself, and for Aryanism to follow in its wake; fresh stirs of population and of thought in Asia; further advances in the arts; variety, freshness, growth; the continuance of the varied lines of Oriental study and investigation until such time as would enable Grecian intellect to take hold of them, sift them, and assimilate whatever in them was true, valuable, and capable of expansion.

We have no historical account of the great battle of Carchemish. Jeremiah, however, beholds it in vision. He sees the Egyptians "dismayed and turned away back—their mighty ones are beaten down, and are fled apace, and look not back, since fear is round about them."14215 He sees the "swift flee away," and the "mighty men" attempting to "escape;" but they "stumble and fall toward the north by the river Euphrates."14216 "For this is the day of the Lord God of hosts, a day of vengeance, that He may avenge Him of His adversaries; and the sword devours, and it is satiate and made drunk with their blood, for the Lord God of hosts hath a sacrifice in the north country by the river Euphrates."14217 The "valiant men" are "swept away"—"many fall—yea, one falls upon another, and they say, Arise and let us go again to our own people, and to the land of our nativity from the oppressing sword."14218 Nor do the mercenaries escape. "Her hired men are in the midst of her, like fatted bullocks; for they also are turned back, and are fled away together; they did not stand because the day of their calamity was come upon them, and the time of their visitation."14219 The defeat was, beyond a doubt, complete, overwhelming. The shock of it was felt all over the Delta, at Memphis, and even at distant Thebes.14220 The hasty flight of the entire Egyptian host left the whole country open to the invading army. "Like a whirlwind, like a torrent, it swept on. The terrified inhabitants retired into the fortified cities,"14221 where for the time they were safe. Nebuchadnezzar did not stop to commence any siege. He pursued Neco up to the very frontier of Egypt, and would have continued his victorious career into the Nile valley, had not important intelligence arrested his steps. His aged father had died at Babylon while he was engaged in his conquests, and his immediate return to the capital was necessary, if he would avoid a disputed succession.14222 Thus matters in Syria had to be left in a confused and unsettled state, until such time as the Great King could revisit the scene of his conquests, and place them upon some definite and satisfactory footing.

On the whole, the campaign had, apparently, the effect of drawing closer the links which united Phoenicia with Egypt.14223 Babylon had shown herself a fierce and formidable enemy, but had disgusted men more than she had terrified them. It was clear enough that she would be a hard mistress, a second and crueller Assyria. There was thus, on Nebuchadnezzar's departure, a general gravitation of the Syrian and Palestinian states towards Egypt, since they saw in her the only possible protector against Babylon, and dreaded her less than they did the "bitter and hasty nation."14224 Neco, no doubt, encouraged the movement which tended at once to strengthen himself and weaken his antagonist; and the result was that, in the course of a few years, both Judæa and Phoenicia revolted from Nebuchadnezzar, and declared themselves independent. Phoenicia was still under the hegemony of Tyre, and Tyre had at its head an enterprising prince, a second Ithobal,14225 who had developed its resources to the uttermost, and was warmly supported by the other cities.14226 His revolt appears to have taken place in the year B.C. 598, the seventh year of Nebuchadnezzar.14227 Nebuchadnezzar at once marched against him in person. The sieges of Tyre, Sidon, and Jerusalem were formed. Jerusalem submitted almost immediately.14228 Sidon was taken after losing half her defenders by pestilence;14229 but Tyre continued to resist for the long space of thirteen years.14230 The continental city was probably taken first. Against this Nebuchadnezzar could freely employ his whole force—his "horses, his chariots, his companies, and his much people"—he could bring moveable forts close up to the walls, and cast up banks against them, and batter them with his engines, or undermine them with spade and mattock. When a breach was effected, he could pour his horse into the streets, and ride down all opposition. It is the capture of the continental city which Ezekiel describes when he says:14231 "Thus saith the Lord God: Behold, I will bring upon Tyrus Nebuchadnezzar, king of Babylon, a king of kings, from the north, with horses and with chariots, and with horsemen, and companies, and much people. He shall slay with the sword thy daughters in the field; and he shall make a fort against thee, and cast a mount against thee, and lift up the buckler against thee. And he shall set engines of war against thy walls, and with his axes he shall break down thy towers. By reason of the abundance of his horses, their dust shall cover thee; thy walls shall shake at the noise of the horseman, and of the wheels and of the chariots, when he shall enter into thy gates, as men enter into a city wherein is made a breach. With the hoofs of his horses shall he tread down all thy streets: he shall slay thy people by the sword, and thy strong garrisons shall go down to the ground. And they shall make a spoil of thy riches, and make a prey of thy merchandise; and they shall break down thy walls, and destroy thy pleasant houses: and they shall lay thy stones and thy timber and thy dust in the midst of the water." But the island city did not escape. When continental Phoenicia was reduced, it was easy to impress a fleet from maritime towns; to man it, in part with Phoenicians, in part with Babylonians, no mean sailors,14232 and then to establish a blockade of the isle. Tyre may more than once have crippled and dispersed the blockading squadron; but by a moderate expenditure fresh fleets could be supplied, while Tyre, cut off from Lebanon, would find it difficult to increase or renew her navy. There has been much question whether the island city was ultimately captured by Nebuchadnezzar or no; but even writers who take the negative view14233 admit that it must have submitted and owned the suzerainty of its assailant. The date of the submission was B.C. 585.

Thus Tyre, in B.C. 585, "fell from her high estate." Ezekiel's prophecies were fulfilled. Ithobal II., the "prince of Tyrus" of those prophecies,14234 whose "head had been lifted up," and who had said in his heart, "I am a God, I sit in the seat of God, in the midst of the waters," who deemed himself "wiser than Daniel," and thought that no secret was hid from him, was "brought down to the pit," "cast to the ground," "brought to ashes upon the earth in the sight of all them that beheld him."14235 Tyre herself was "broken in the midst of the seas."14236 A blight fell upon her. For many years, Sidon, rather than Tyre, became once more the leading city of Phoenicia, was regarded as pre-eminent in naval skill,14237 and is placed before Tyre when the two are mentioned together.14238 Internal convulsion, moreover, followed upon external decline. Within ten years of the death of Ithobal, the monarchy came to an end by a revolution,14239 which substituted for Kings Suffetes or Shophetim, "judges," officers of an inferior status, whose tenure of office was not very assured. Ecnibal, the son of Baslach, the first judge, held the position for no more than two months; Chelbes, the son of Abdæus, who followed him, ruled for ten months; Abbarus, a high priest, probably of Melkarth, for three months. Then, apparently to weaken the office, it was shared between two, as at Carthage, and Mytgon (perhaps Mattan), together with Ger-ashtoreth, the son of Abd-elim, judged Tyre for six years. But the partisans of monarchy were now recovering strength; and the reign of a king, Balator, was intruded at some point in the course of the six years' judgeship. Judges were then abolished by a popular movement, and kings of the old stock restored. The Tyrians sent to Babylon for a certain Merbal, who must have been either a refugee or a hostage at the court of Neriglissar. He was allowed to return to Tyre, and, being confirmed in the sovereignty, reigned four years. His brother, Eirom, or Hiram, succeeded him, and was still upon the throne when the Empire of Babylon came to an end by the victory of Cyrus over Nabonidus (B.C. 538).

Phoenicia under the Babylonian rule was exceptionally weak. She had to submit to attacks from Egypt under Apries, which fell probably in the reign of Baal over Tyre, about B.C. 565. She had also to submit to the loss of Cyprus under Amasis,14240 probably about B.C. 540, or a little earlier, when the power of Babylon was rapidly declining. She had been, from first to last, an unwilling tributary of the Great Empire on the Lower Euphrates, and was perhaps not sorry to see that empire go down before the rising power of Persia. Under the circumstances she would view any chance as likely to advance her interests, and times of disturbance and unsettlement gave her the best chance of obtaining a temporary independence. From B.C. 538 to B.C. 528 or 527 she seems to have enjoyed one of these rare intervals of autonomy. Egypt, content with having annexed Cyprus, did not trouble her; Persia, engaged in wars in the far East,14241 made as yet no claim to her allegiance. In peace and tranquillity she pursued her commercial career, covered the seas with her merchant vessels, and the land-routes of trade with her caravans, repaired the damages inflicted by Nebuchadnezzar on her cities; maintained, if she did not even increase, her naval strength, and waited patiently to see what course events would take now that Babylon was destroyed, and a new and hitherto unknown power was about to assume the first position among the nations of the earth.

5. Phoenicia under the Persians (B.C. 528-333)

Phoenicia not claimed by Cyrus—Submits willingly to
Cambyses—Takes part in his invasion of Egypt—Refuses to
proceed against Carthage—Exceptional privileges enjoyed by
the Phoenicians under the Persians—Government system of
Darius advantageous to them—Their conduct in the Ionian
revolt—In the expeditions of Mardonius and Datis—In the
great expedition of Xerxes—-Interruption of the friendly
relations between Phoenicia and Persia—Renewal of amity—
Services rendered to Persia between B.C. 465 and 392—
Amicable relations with Athens—Phoenicia joins in revolt of
Evagoras—Supports Tachos, king of Egypt—Declares herself
independent under Tennes—Conquered and treated with great
severity of Ochus—Sidonian dynasty of the Esmunazars.

The conquest of Babylon by Cyrus gave him, according to Oriental notions generally, a claim to succeed to the inheritance of the entire Babylonian empire; but the claim would remain dormant until it was enforced. The straggling character of the territory, which was shaped like a Greek {L}, ascending from Babylon along the course of the Euphrates to the Armenian mountains, and then descending along the line of the Mediterranean coast as far as Gaza or Raphia, rendered the enforcement of the claim a work of difficulty, more especially in the remote West, which was distant fifteen hundred miles from Persia Proper, and more than a thousand miles from Babylon. Cyrus, moreover, was prevented, first by wars in his immediate neighbourhood,14242 and later on by a danger upon his north-eastern frontier,14243 from taking the steps usually taken by a conqueror to establish his dominion in a newly-annexed region, and thus he neither occupied Syria with troops, nor placed it under the administration of Persian governors. The only step which, so far as we know, he took, implying that his authority reached so far, was the commission which he gave to Zerubbabel and the other chiefs of the Jewish nation to proceed from Babylonia to Judæa, and re-establish themselves, if they could, on the site of the destroyed Jerusalem.14244 The return from the Captivity which followed was in some sense the occupation of a portion of the extreme West by a Persian garrison, and may be viewed as a step intended to be "preparatory towards obtaining possession of the entire sea-coast;"14245 but it appears to have been an isolated movement, effected without active Persian support, and one whereby the neighbouring countries were only slightly affected.

That Phoenicia retained her independence until the reign of Cambyses is distinctly implied, if not actually asserted, by Herodotus.14246 She saw without any displeasure the re-establishment in her neighbourhood of a nation with which her intercourse had always been friendly, and sometimes close and cordial. Tyre and Sidon vied with each other in their readiness to supply the returned exiles with the timber which they needed for the rebuilding of their temple and city; and once more, as in the days of Solomon, the Jewish axes were heard amid the groves of Lebanon, and the magnificent cedars of that favoured region were cut down, conveyed to the coast, and made into floats or rafts, which Phoenician mariners transported by sea to Joppa, the nearest seaport to Jerusalem.14247 In return, the Jews willingly rendered to the Phoenicians such an amount of corn, wine, and oil as was equivalent in value to the timber received from them,14248 and thus the relations between the two peoples were replaced on a footing which recalled the time of their closest friendship, nearly five hundred years previously.

On the death of Cyrus, and the accession of his son Cambyses, B.C. 529, the tranquillity which South-western Asia had enjoyed since the time of the wars of Nebuchadnezzar came to an end. Cyrus had, it is said, designed an expedition against Egypt,14249 as necessary to round off his conquests, and Cambyses naturally inherited his father's projects. He had no sooner mounted the throne than he commenced preparations for an attack upon the ancient kingdom of the Pharaohs, which, under the dynasty of the Psamatiks, had risen to something of its early greatness, and had been especially wealthy and prosperous under the usurper Amasis.14250 It was impossible to allow an independent and rival monarchy so close upon his borders, and equally impossible to shrink from an enterprise which had been carried to a successful issue both by Assyria and by Babylon. Persian prestige required the subjugation and absorption of a country which, though belonging geographically to Africa, was politically and commercially an integral part of that Western Asia over which Persia claimed a complete and absolute supremacy.

The march upon Egypt implied and required the occupation of the Mediterranean seaboard. No armies of any considerable size have ever attempted to traverse the almost waterless desert which separates the Lower Euphrates valley from the delta of the Nile. Light corps d'armée have no doubt occasionally passed from Circesium by way of Tadmor to Damascus, and vice versâ;14251 but the ordinary line of route pursued by conquerors follows the course of the Euphrates to Carchemish, then strikes across the chalky upland in the middle of which stands the city of Aleppo, and finally descends upon Egypt by way of the Orontes, the Coele-Syrian valley, and the plains of Sharon and Philistia.14252 This was undoubtedly the line followed by Cambyses,14253 and it necessarily brought him into contact with the Phoenicians. The contact was not an hostile one. It would have been madness on the part of the Phoenicians to have attempted any resistance to the vast host with which Cambyses, we may be sure, made his invasion, and it would have been folly on the part of Cambyses to employ force when he could better obtain his object by persuasion. It must have been a very special object with him to obtain the hearty co-operation of the Phoenician naval forces in the attack which he was meditating, since he would otherwise have had no fleet at all capable of coping with the fleet of Egypt. Neco had made Egypt a strong naval power;14254 Apries had contented for naval supremacy in the Eastern Mediterranean with Tyre;14255 Amasis had made an expedition by sea against Cyprus, had crushed whatever resistance the Cyprians were able to offer, had permanently occupied the island,14256 and added the Cyprian fleet to his own. Cambyses had as yet no ships, except such as he could procure from the Greek cities of Asia Minor, which were not likely to be very zealous in his service, since they had friends engaged upon the other side.14257 Accordingly, the Persian monarch seems to have made friendly overtures to the Phoenician states, which were received with favour, and led to an arrangement satisfactory to both parties. Phoenicia surrendered the independence which it was impossible for her to maintain, and placed her fleet at the disposal of Persia.14258 Persia spared her cities any occupation, imposed on her a light tribute, and allowed her that qualified independence which is implied in the retention of her native princes. From first to last under the Persian régime, Phoenician monarchs bear rule in the Phoenician cities,14259 and command the contingents which the cities furnish to any combined Persian fleet.

The friendly arrangement concluded between Phoenicia and Persia was followed, very naturally, by a further accession to the Persian power. Cyprus, whose population was in great part Phoenician, had for centuries been connected politically in the closest manner with the Phoenician towns on the Asiatic mainland, especially with Tyre and Sidon. Her enslavement by Amasis must have been hateful to her, and she must have been only too glad to see an opportunity of shaking off the Egyptian yoke. Accordingly, no sooner did the Phoenicians of the mainland conclude the arrangement by which they became part and parcel of the Persian Empire than the Cyprians followed their example, and, revolting from Egypt, offered themselves of their own free will to Persia.14260 Cambyses, it is needless to say, readily accepted them as his subjects.

The invasion of Egypt could now be taken in hand with every prospect of a successful issue. The march of the land army along the shore would be supported by a parallel movement on the part of a powerful fleet, which would carry its provisions and its water, explore the country in front, and give notice of the movements of the enemy, and of the place where they proposed to make a stand in force. When Egypt was reached the fleet would command all the navigable mouths of the Nile, would easily establish a blockade of all ports, and might even mount the Nile and take a part in the siege of Memphis. It would seem that all these services were rendered to the Persian monarch by the great fleet which he had collected, of which the Phoenician ships were recognised as the main strength. The rapid conquest of Egypt was in this way much facilitated, and Cambyses within a twelvemonth found himself in possession of the entire country within its recognised limits of the Mediterranean and "the tower of Syêné."14261

But the Great King was not satisfied with a single, albeit a magnificent, achievement. He had accomplished in one short campaign what it took the Assyrians ten years, and Nebuchadnezzar eighteen years, to effect. But he now set his heart on further conquests. "He designed," says Herodotus,14262 "three great expeditions. One was to be against the Carthaginians, another against the Ammonians, and a third against the long-lived Ethopians, who dwelt in that part of Lybia which borders upon the southern sea." The expedition against the Carthaginians is the only one of the three which here concerns us: it was to be entrusted to the fleet. Instead of conducting, or sending, a land force along the seaboard of North Africa, which was probably known to be for the most part barren and waterless, Cambyses judged that it would be sufficient to dispatch his powerful navy against the Liby-Phoenician colony, which he supposed would submit or else be subjugated. But on broaching this plan to the leaders of the fleet he was met with a determined opposition. The Phoenicians positively refused to proceed against their own colonists. They urged that they were bound to the Carthaginians by most solemn oaths, and that it would be as wicked and unnatural for them to execute the king's orders as for parents to destroy their own children.14263 It was a bold act to run counter to the will of a despotic monarch, especially of one so headstrong and impetuous as Cambyses. But the Phoenicians were firm, and the monarch yielded. "He did not like," Herodotus says, "to force the war upon the Phoenicians, because they had surrendered themselves to the Persians, and because on the Phoenicians his entire sea-service depended." He therefore allowed their opposition to prevail, and desisted from his proposed undertaking.14264

This acquiescence in their wishes on the part of the Great King, and his abstinence from any attempt at compulsion, would seem to have paved the way for that thoroughly good understanding between the suzerain power and her dependency which characterises the relations of the two for the next century and a half, with the single exception of one short interval. "The navy of Phoenicia became a regular and very important part of the public power"14265 of the Persian state. Complete confidence was felt by their Persian masters in the fidelity, attachment, and hearty good-will of the Phoenician people. Exceptional favour was shown them. Not only were they allowed to maintain their native kings, their municipal administration, their national laws and religion, but they were granted exceptional honours and exceptional privileges and immunities. The Great King maintained a park and royal residence in some portion of Phoenicia,14266 probably in the vicinity of Sidon,14267 and no doubt allowed his faithful subjects to bask occasionally in the sunshine of his presence. When the internal organisation of the empire was taken in hand, and something approaching to a uniform system of government established for revenue purposes, though Phoenicia could not be excused from contributing to the taxation of the empire, yet the burden laid upon her seems to have been exceptionally light. United in a satrapy—the fifth—with Syria, Cyprus, and Palestine, and taxed according to her population rather than according to her wealth, she paid a share—probably not more than a third or a fourth—of 350 talents,14268 or an annual contribution to the needs of the empire amounting to no less than 30,000l. Persia, moreover, encouraged Phoenicia to establish an internal organisation of her own, and, under her suzerainty, Tyre, Sidon, and Aradus were united by federal bonds, and had a common council, which met at Tripolis, probably of three hundred members.14269 This council debated matters in which Phoenicia generally was interested, and, in times of disturbance, decided questions of peace and war.

The reign of Darius Hystaspis (B.C. 521-486), the successor of Cambyses upon the Persian throne, introduced several changes into the Persian governmental system which were of advantage to the Phoenicians. Darius united the most distant parts of his empire by postal routes, along which at moderate intervals were maintained post-houses, with relays of horses,14270 primarily for the use of the government, but at the service of the traveller or private trader when not needed for business of state. Phoenician commerce must have been much helped by these arrangements, which facilitated rapid communication, gave security to lines of route which had been previously infested with robbers, and provided resting-places for the companies of merchants and traders, not unlike the caravanserai of modern Turkey and Persia.

Darius also established throughout his vast empire a uniform coinage, based apparently on that which had previously prevailed in Lydia. His "darics," as they were called by the Greeks, were, in the first instance, gold coins of a rude type, a little heavier than our sovereigns, weighing between 123 and 124 grains troy.14271 They bore the figure of an archer on the obverse, and on the reverse a very rough and primitive quadratum incusum. Darius must have coined them in vast abundance, since early in the reign of his successor a single individual of no great eminence had accumulated as many as 3,993,000 of them.14272 Subsequently to the introduction of the gold darics, a silver coinage was issued, originally (we are told) in Egypt by a Persian satrap called Aryandes,14273 but afterwards by the central government. The name of "daric" was extended to these coins also, which, however, were much larger and heavier than the gold coins, weighing as much as 235 grains, and corresponding to the Greek tetradrachm, and (nearly) to the Hebrew shekel. The establishment of this excellent circulating medium, and the wide extension which it almost immediately attained, must have given an enormous stimulus to trade, and have been found of the greatest convenience by the Phoenician merchants, who had no longer to carry with them the precious metal in bars or ingots, and to weigh their gold and silver in the balance in connection with every purchase that they made, but could effect both sales and purchases in the simple and commodious manner still in use among all civilised nations at the present day.

Under these circumstances we can well understand that the Phoenicians were thoroughly satisfied with the position which they occupied under the earlier Persian kings, and strove zealously to maintain and extend the empire to which they owed so much. Their fidelity was put to a crucial test after they had been subjects of Darius Hystaspis for a little more than twenty years, and had had about fourteen or fifteen years' experience of the advantages of his governmental system. Aristagoras of Miletus, finding himself in a position of difficulty, had lighted up the flames of war in Asia Minor, and brought about a general revolt of the Greeks in those parts against the Persian power—a revolt which spread on from the Greeks to the native Asiatics, and in a short time embraced, not only Ionia and Æolis, but Caria, Caunus, and almost the whole of Cyprus.14274 The bulk of the Cyprian cities were Phoenician colonies, and the political connection between these cities and Phoenicia was so close and of such ancient date that the Phoenicians can scarcely have failed to be moved by their example and by their danger. A wave of sympathy might have been expected to sweep across the excitable people, and it would not have been surprising had they rushed headlong into rebellion with the same impetuosity as their Cyprian brethren. Had they done so the danger to Persia would have been very great, and the course of the world's history might perhaps have been differently shaped. The junction of the Phoenician fleet with the navies of Cyprus, Ionia, Caria, and Æolis would have transferred the complete sovereignty of the Eastern Mediterranean to the side of the rebels.14275 The contagion of revolt would probably have spread. Lycia and Cilicia, always eager for independence,14276 would probably have joined the malcontents; Pamphylia, which lay between them, would have followed their example; the entire seaboard of Asia Minor and Syria would have been lost; Egypt would, most likely, have seen in the crisis her opportunity, and have avenged the cruelties and insults of Cambyses14277 by the massacre of her Persian garrison. Persia's prosperity would have received a sudden check, from which it might never have recovered; Greece would have escaped the ordeal of the invasion of Xerxes; and the character of the struggle between Europe and Asia would have been completely altered.

But the view which the Phoenicians took of their duties, or of their interests, led them to act differently. When the Persians, anxious to recover Cyprus, applied to the Phoenician cities for a naval force, to transport their army from Cilica to the island, and otherwise help them in the war, their request was at once complied with. Ships were sent to the Cilician coast without any delay;14278 the Persian land force was conveyed in safety across the strait and landed on the opposite shore; the ships then rounded Cape St. Andreas and anchored in the bay opposite Salamis, where the Ionian fleet was drawn up in defence of the town.14279 An engagement followed—the first, so far as we know, between Phoenicians and Greeks—wholly to the advantage of the latter.14280 No complaint, however, is made of any lukewarmness, or want of zeal, on the part of the Phoenicians, who seem to have been beaten in fair fight by an enemy whom they had perhaps despised. Their ill fortune did not lead to any very serious result, since the Persian land force defeated the Cyprians, and thus Persia once more obtained possession of the island.

A year or two later the Phoenicians recovered their lost laurels. In B.C. 495 the Persians, having trampled out the flames of revolt in Cyprus, Caria, and Caunus, resolved on a great effort to bring the war to a close by attacking the Ionian Greeks in their own country, and crushing the head and front of the rebellion, which was the great and flourishing city of Miletus. Miletus lay on the southern shore of a deep bay—the Sinus Latmicus—which penetrated the western coast of Asia Minor in about Lat. 37° 30′, but which the deposits of the Mæander have now filled up.14281 North-west of the town, at the distance of about a mile, was the small island of Ladé, now a mere hillock on the flat alluvial plain. While the Persian land force advanced along the shore, and invested Milestus on the side towards the continent, a combined fleet of six hundred vessels14282 proceeded to block the entrance to the bay, and to threaten the doomed city from the sea. This fleet was drawn from four only of the countries subject to Persia—viz. Phoenicia, Cilicia, Cyprus, and Egypt—whereof Phoenicia, we are told, "showed the greatest zeal,"14283 and we may presume furnished by far the larger number of ships. On their arrival in Milesian waters the captains found a strong naval force collected to meet them, which rested upon the island of Ladé, and guarded the approaches to the town. Miletus had summoned to her aid the contingents of her various allies—Chios, Lesbos, Samos, Teos, Priene, Erythræ, Phocæa, Myus—and had succeeded in gathering together a fleet amounting to above three hundred and fifty vessels.14284 This time Phoenicia did not despise her foe. Before engaging, every effort was made to sow discord and dissension among the confederates, and induce the Greek captains to withdraw their squadrons, or at any rate to remain neutral in the battle.14285 Considerable effect was produced by these machinations; and when at last the attack was made, two of the principal of the Greek allies14286 drew off, and sailed homewards, leaving the rest of the confederates to their fate. Yet, notwithstanding this defection, the battle was stoutly contested by the ships which remained, especially those of the Chians,14287 and though a very decisive and complete victory was ultimately gained by the Phoenicians and their allies, the cost of the victory was great. Persia regained her naval supremacy in the Eastern Mediterranean; Phoenicia re-established her claim to be considered the great sea power of the time; but she lost a large number of her best vessels and seamen, and she was taught the lesson that, to cope with Greeks, she must have a vast superiority of force upon her side—a superiority of not much less than three to one.

Miletus soon fell after the victory of Ladé, and the Phoenician fleet was then employed for some time in chastising the islanders who had taken part in the revolt, and in reducing various towns upon the European shores of the Hellespont, the Propontis, and the Bosphorus, including Perinthus, Selymbria, and Byzantium.14288 Miltiades, the destined hero of Marathon, narrowly escaped capture at the hands of the Phoenicians at this time, as he fled from his government in the Thracian Chersonese to Athens. The vessel which bore him just escaped into the harbour of Imbrus; but his son, Metiochus, who was on board a worse sailer, was less fortunate. The Phoenicians captured him, and, learning who he was, conveyed him to Darius at Susa, where he was well treated and became a naturalised Persian.14289

After the Ionian revolt had been completely put down and avenged, the states subject to Persia, and the Phoenicians among them, enjoyed a brief period of repose. But soon the restless spirit which possessed all the earlier Persian monarchs incited Darius to carry his warlike enterprises into "fresh fields and pastures new." From the eastern coast of the Ægean Sea he looked out towards a land possessing every attraction that soil or clime could offer, fertile, rich in minerals, and with many excellent harbours, well watered, abounding in corn and wine and oil, in wooded hillsides, and in productive plains. According to Herodotus,14290 he had already explored the strength and weakness of the region by means of a commission of Persian nobles, who had surveyed all the shores of Greece from the decks of Phoenician ships. The result was that he coveted the possession of the land thus made known to him, and came to a fixed resolution that he would add it to his territories.

There were two modes by which Greece might be approached from Asia. Bridges of boats could be thrown across the Bosphorus or the Hellespont, mere salt rivers, scarcely more formidable than the streams of the Euphrates and the Tigris. In this way Europe could be invaded in force, and the army sent across the straits, could pursue its way along the shore till it reached the rich plains of Thessaly, and from Thessaly passed into Boetia, Attica, and the Peloponnese. Or a fleet, with a land force on board, might proceed from Asia Minor across the Ægean, where the numerous islands, scattered at short intervals, seemed to have been arranged by nature as stepping-stones, whereby the adventurous denizens of either continent might cross easily into the other; and a landing might be suddenly effected near the very heart of Greece without a tenth part of the trouble that must be taken if the other line of route were pursued. In either case the attendance of a fleet would be necessary. If the more circuitous route were pursued, a powerful squadron must attend the march of the army along the shore, to convey its supplies; if the direct route were preferred, a still larger fleet would be necessary for the conveyance, not only of the supplies, but of the army itself. Darius gave a trial to each of the two plans. In the year B.C. 492 he sent a fleet and army under Mardonius by way of the Hellespont and the European coast; but this expedition met with severe disasters, the fleet being shattered by a storm off Mount Athos, and the land force greatly damaged by a night attack on the part of the Thracians.14291 Two years later he dispatched the famous expedition under Datis and Artaphernes, which took its course through the islands, and landed perhaps 200,000 men on the plain of Marathon,14292 but being there defeated by Miltiades, returned hastily to Asia by the sea route. The fleets employed on both these occasions were numerous,14293 and appear to have been collected from several of the Persian maritime states;14294 the proportion which the several contingents bore one to another is not stated, but there can be little doubt that the Phoenicians contributed the greater number. We have no details of the conduct of the Phoenicians on either occasion, beyond a casual notice that in the expedition of Datis and Artaphernes one of their vessels plundered the temple of Delium on the Boeotian coast opposite Chalcis, carrying off from it an image of Apollo plated with gold.14295 The superstition of Datis deprived them of this valuable booty; but we may safely conclude from the anecdote that, while rendering service to Persia, the keen-witted mariners took care not to neglect their own material interests.

In the third and greatest of the expeditions conducted by Persia against Greece, the Phoenicians are found to have played a very important and prominent part. Even before the expedition commenced, a call was made upon them in connection with it for services of an unusual character. The loss of the fleet of Mardonius off Mount Athos induced Xerxes to determine on cutting a ship-canal through the isthmus which joins Athos to the mainland; and his passion for great and striking achievements caused him to project the construction of a double bridge of boats across the Hellespont. Phoenician technical skill was invoked for the furtherance of both objects. At Athos they worked in conjunction with the maritime states generally, but showed an amount of engineering knowledge far in advance of their fellow-labourers. The others attempted to give perpendicular sides to their portions of the excavation, but found the sides continually fall in, and so (as Herodotus observes) "had double labour."14296 The Phoenicians alone knew that the sides must be sloped at an angle, and, calculating the proper slope aright, performed their share of the task without mishap. At the Hellespont the Phoenicians had for co-partners the Egyptians only, and the two nations appear to have displayed an equal ability.14297 Cables were passed from shore to shore, made taut by capstans and supported by an almost continuous line of boats; planks were then laid upon the cables, and covered with brushwood, while a thick layer of earth was placed upon the top. A solid causeway was thus formed, which was guarded on either side by bulwarks of such a height that the horses which crossed the bridge could not see over them; and thus the cavalry and the sumpter beasts passed from one continent to the other without a suspicion that they had ever had anything but terra firma under them. The structure served its purpose, but was not found strong enough to defy even for a year the forces of the winds and waves. Before the return of Xerxes, towards the close of B.C. 480, the autumnal gales had broken it up; and the army which accompanied him had to re-cross the strait in a number of separate ships.14298 The fleet which Xerxes collected to accompany his land army and take part in his great expedition amounted, it is said, to a total of 1207 vessels.14299 Of these the Phoenician triremes were at once the most numerous and the best. While Egypt furnished 200 ships, Cyprus 150, Cilicia, Ionia, and the Hellespontine Greeks 100 each, and the other maritime nations, all together, 257, Phoenicia singly contributed no fewer than 300.14300 The superiority of the Phoenician vessels was sufficiently shown, first by the regatta at Abydos, which was won by a Sidonian trireme;14301 next, by the preference of Xerxes for Phoenician over other vessels;14302 and, thirdly, by the position assigned them at Salamis, where care was taken to pit them against the Athenians,14303 who were recognised as superior at sea to all the other Greeks. If the Phoenician prowess and naval skill did not succeed in averting defeat from the Persians, we must ascribe it first to the narrowness of the seas in which they had to engage the enemy; and, secondly, to the still greater prowess and skill of their principal antagonists, the Athenians, the Eginetans, and the Corinthians.

In the naval combats at Artemisium, the Egyptians, according to Herodotus,14304 were considered to have borne off the palm on the Persian side; but Diodorus assigns that honour to the Sidonians.14305 At Salamis the brunt of the conflict fell on the Phoenician contingent, which began the battle,14306 and for some time forced the Athenian squadron to beat a retreat, but was ultimately overpowered and forced to take to flight, after suffering great losses. A large number of the ships were sunk; several were taken by the Greeks;

comparatively few escaped from the battle without serious injury.14307 Xerxes, however, who from his silver-footed throne on Mount Ægaleos surveyed the scene,14308 but, amid the general turmoil and confusion, could ill distinguish the conduct of the several contingents, enraged at the loss of the battle, and regarding the Phoenicians as answerable for the unhappy result, since they formed the nucleus and chief strength of the fleet, laid the whole blame of the failure upon them, and, on some of the captains appearing before him to excuse themselves, had them beheaded upon the spot.14309 At the same time he also threatened the other Phoenician commanders with his vengeance, and so alarmed them that, according to Diodorus,14310 they quitted the fleet and sailed away to Asia.

This harsh and unjust treatment seems to have led to an estrangement between the Persians and the foremost of the naval nations subject to them, which lasted for fifteen years. The Persians naturally distrusted those whom they had injured, and were unwilling to call them in to their aid. The Phoenicians probably brooded over their wrongs, and abstained from volunteering an assistance which they were not asked to furnish. The war between Persia and Greece continued, and was transferred from Europe to Asia, but no Phoenicians are mentioned as taking part in it. The Phoenician ships retired from Samos on the approach of the Greek fleet under Leotychides.14311 No Phoenicians fought at Mycale. None are heard of as engaged at Sestos, or Byzantium, or Eïon, or Doriscus, or even Phaselis. It was not until—in B.C. 465—the war passed from the Ægean to the southern coast of Asia Minor, and their dependency, Cyprus, was threatened, that the Phoenicians again appeared upon the scene, and mustered in strength to the support of their Persian suzerain.

The Persian fleet which fought at the Eurymedon is said to have consisted of three hundred and forty vessels, drawn from the three subject nations of the Phoenicians, the Cyprians, and the Cilicians.14312 It was under the command of Tithraustes, a son of Xerxes. Cimon, who led the fleet of the Athenians and their allies, attacked it with a force of 250 triremes, of which Athens had furnished the greater number. The battle was contested with extreme obstinacy on both sides; but at length the Athenians prevailed, and besides destroying a large number of the enemy's vessels, took as many as a hundred with their crews on board. At the same time a land victory was gained over the Persian troops. The double exploit was regarded as one of the most glorious in the annals of Greece, and was commemorated at Delos by a tablet with the following inscription:—14313

Since first the sea Europe from Asia severed,
\   And Mars to rage 'mid humankind began,
Never was such a blow as this delivered
\   On land and sea at once by mortal man.
These heroes did to death a host of Medes
\   Near Cyprus, and then captured with their crews
\   Five score Phoenician vessels; at the news
All Asia groaned, hard hit by such brave deeds.

It is scarcely necessary to follow further in detail the services which Phoenicia rendered to Persia as her submissive and attached ally. For the space of about seventy-five years from the date of the engagement at the Eurymedon (B.C. 465-390), the Phoenicians continued to hold the first place among the Persian naval states, and to render their mistress effective help in all her naval enterprises. They protected Cyprus and Egypt from the Athenian attacks, bore their part in the war with Amyrtæus and Inaros, and more than once inflicted severe blows upon the Athenian navy.14314 It was his command of a Phoenician fleet amounting to nearly a hundred and fifty triremes which enabled Tissaphernes to play so influential a part in Asia Minor during the later years of the Peloponnesian war. It was the presence of their ships at Cnidus which, in B.C. 394, turned the scale between Athens and Sparta, enabling the Athenians to recover the naval supremacy which they had lost at Ægos-Potami. It was the appearance of a Phoenician fleet in Greek waters14315 which, in the following year, gave an opportunity to the Athenians to rebuild their "Long Walls," alarmed Sparta for her own safety, and extorted from her fears—in B.C. 387—the agreement known as "the Peace of Antalcidas." Persia owed to her Phoenician subjects the glory of recovering complete possession of Asia Minor, and of being accepted as a sort of final arbiter in the quarrels of the Grecian states. From B.C. 465 to B.C. 392 Phoenicia served Persia with rare fidelity, never hesitating to lend her aid, and never showing the least inclination to revolt.

It was probably under these circumstances, when Athens owed the recovery of her greatness in no small measure to the Phoenicians, that those relations of friendship and intimacy were established between the two peoples of which we have evidence in several inscriptions, Phoenicians settled in Attica, particularly at Phalerum and the Piræus, and had their own places of worship and interment. Six sepulchral inscriptions have been found, either in Athens itself or at the Piræus,14316 five of them bilingual,14317 which mark the interment in Attic soil of persons whose nationality was Phoenician. They had monuments erected over them, generally of some pretension, which must have obtained as much respect as the native tombstones, since otherwise they could not have endured to our day. There is also at the Piræus an altar,14318 which a Phoenician must have erected and dedicated to a Phoenician god, whom he worshipped on Attic soil apparently without let or hindrance. The god's name is given as "Askum-Adar," a form which does not elsewhere recur, but which is thought to designate the god elsewhere called Sakon, who corresponded to the Grecian Hermes.14319 Moreover, there is evidence of the Phoenicians having worshipped two other deities in their Attic abodes, one a god who corresponded to the Greek Poseidon and the Roman Neptune, the other the Babylonian and Assyrian Nergal. Among the lost orations of Deniarchus was one delivered by that orator on the occasion of the suit between the people of Phalerum and the Phoenician inhabitants of the place with respect to the priesthood of Poseidon;14320 and a sepulchral monument at the Piræus was erected to Asepta, daughter of Esmun-sillem, of Sidon, by Itten-bel, son of Esmun-sibbeh, high priest of the god Nergal.14321 It appears further from the Greek inscription, edited by Böckh,14322 that about this time (B.C. 390-370) a decree was promulgated by the Council {bonle} of Athens whereby the relation of Proxenia was established between Strato (Abd-astartus), king of Sidon, and the Athenian people, and all Sidonians sojourning in Attica were exempted from the tax usually charged upon foreign settlers, from the obligation of the Choregia, and from all other contributions to the state.

The power of Persia began about this time to decline, and the Phoenicians seem to have wavered in their allegiance. In B.C. 406 or 405 Egypt shook off the Persian yoke, and established her independence under a native sovereign.14323 Soon afterwards, probably in B.C. 392 or 391, Evagoras, a Cypriot Greek, who claimed descent from Teucer, inaugurated a revolution at Salamis in Cyprus, where he slew the Phoenician monarch, Abdemon, who held his throne under Persia, and, himself mounting the throne, proceeded to reduce to subjection the whole island.14324 Vast efforts were made to crush him, but for ten years he defied the power of Persia, and maintained himself as an independent monarch.14325 Even when finally he made his submission, it was under an express stipulation that he should retain his royal dignity, and be simply bound to pay his tribute regularly, and to render such obedience as subject kings commonly paid to their suzerain.14326

In the course of his resistance to Persia, it is beyond question that Evagoras received a certain amount of support from Phoenicia; but the circumstances under which the support was given was doubtful. According to Isocrates,14327 he equipped a large fleet, and attacked the Phoenicians on the mainland with so much vigour as even to take the great city of Tyre by assault; but Diodorus says nothing of the attack, and it is conjectured that the contagion of revolt, which certainly affected, more or less, Cyprus, Cilicia, Caria, and some of the Syrian Arabs,14328 spread also thus early to Phoenicia, and that "the surrender of Tyre was a voluntary defection."14329 In that case, we must view Phoenicia, or at any rate a portion of it, as having detached itself from Persia, about B.C. 390, sixty years before the final break-up of the Empire.

But the disaffection of Phoenicia does not become open and patent until about thirty years later. The decline of Persia had continued. In B.C. 375 an attempt to recover Egypt, for which a vast armament had been collected under Pharnabazus and Iphicrates, completely failed.14330 Nine years afterwards, in B.C. 366, the revolt of the satraps began. First Ariobarzanes, satrap of Phrygia, renounced his allegiance, and defended himself with success against Autophradutes, satrap of Lydia, and Mausolus, native king of Caria under Persia. Then Aspis, who held a part of Cappadocia, revolted and maintained himself by the help of the Pisidians, until he was overpowered by Datames. Next Datames himself, satrap of the rest of Cappadocia, understanding that the mind of the Persian king was poisoned against him, made a treaty with Ariobarzanes, and assumed an independent attitude in his own province. Finally, in B.C. 362, there seems to have been something like a general revolt of the western provinces, in which the satraps of Mysia, Phrygia, and Lydia, Mausolus prince of Caria, and the peoples of Lycia, Pisidia, Pamphylia, Cilicia, and Syria participated.14331 Then, if not earlier, Phoenicia openly threw in her lot with the disaffected;14332 refused her tribute like the others, and joined her forces with theirs. Nor, when the rebellion collapsed, did she at once return to her allegiance. When Tachos, native king of Egypt, in B.C. 361, having secured the services of Agesilaus and Chabrias, advanced boldly into Syria, with the object of enlarging his own dominions at the expense of Persia, he was received with favour by the Phoenicians, who were quite willing to form a portion of his empire. But the rebellion of Nectanebo forced Tachos to relinquish his projects,14333 and the dominion over the Phoenician cities seems to have reverted to Persia without any effort on her part.

In this condition matters remained till about the year B.C. 351, when Sidon, feeling herself aggrieved by the conduct of the Persian authorities at Tripolis,14334 where the general assembly of the Phoenicians held its meetings, boldly raised the standard of revolt against Persia under Tennes, or Tabnit II., and induced the Phoenicians generally to declare themselves independent. Alliance was at once formed with the Egyptian king, Nekht-nebf, or Nectanebo II., who sent a body of 4,000 Greek mercenaries, under Mentor the Rhodian, to the aid of Tennes.14335 Hostilities commenced by the Phoenicians expelling or massacring the Persian garrisons, devastating the royal park or paradise, and burning the stores of forage collected for the use of the Persian cavalry.14336 An attempt made by two satraps—Belesys of Syria and Mazæus of Cilicia—to crush the revolt was completely defeated by Tennes, with the aid of Mentor and his Greeks, who gained a decisive victory over the satraps, and drove the Persians out of Phoenicia.14337 Cyprus then joined the rebels. The nine principal cities made common cause, expelled the Persians, and declared themselves free states, under their respective native kings.14338 Ochus, the Persian king, was at last roused to exert himself. Collecting an army of 300,000 foot and 30,000 horse, supported by 300 triremes and 500 transports or provision-ships,14339 he proceeded to the west in person, determined to inflict condign punishment on the rebels, and to recover to the empire, not only Cyprus and Phoenicia, but also the long-lost Egypt.

Tennes, on his part, had done his best in the way of preparations for defence. He had collected a fleet of above a hundred ships—triremes and quinqueremes,14340 the latter now heard of for the first time in Asiatic warfare. He had strengthened the fortifications of Sidon, surrounding the town with a triple ditch of great width and depth, and considerably raising the height of the walls.14341 He had hired Greek mercenaries to the number of six thousand, raising thus the number in his service to ten thousand in all, had armed and drilled the most active and athletic of the citizens, and had collected vast stores of provisions, armour, and weapons. But the advance of the Persian monarch at the head of so large a force filled Tennes with dismay and despair. Successful resistance was, he thought, impossible; and with a selfishness and a cowardice that must ever make him rank among the most infamous of men, he resolved, if possible, to purchase his own pardon of the King by delivering to his vengeance the entire body of his fellow-countrymen. Accordingly, after handing over to him a hundred of the principal citizens, who were immediately transfixed with javelins, he concerted measures with Mentor for receiving the Persians within the walls. While the arrangements were proceeding, five hundred of the remaining citizens issued forth from one of the gates of the town, with boughs of supplication, as a deputation to implore the mercy of Ochus, but only to suffer the same fate as their fellow-townsmen. The Persians were then received within the walls; but the citizens, understanding what their fate was to be, resolved to anticipate it. They had already burnt their ships, to prevent any desertion. Now they shut themselves up, with their wives and children, in their houses, and applying the torch to their dwellings lighted up a general conflagration. More than forty thousand persons perished in the flames. Ochus sold the ruins at a high price to speculators, who calculated on reimbursing themselves by the treasures which they might dig out from among the ashes. As for Tennes, it is satisfactory to find that a just vengeance overtook him. The treachery which he had employed towards others was shown also to himself. Ochus, who had given him a solemn promise that he would spare his life, no sooner found that there was nothing more to be gained by letting him live, than he relentlessly put him to death.14342

No further resistance was made by the Phoenician cities. Ochus marched on against Egypt and effected its reconquest.14343 The Cyprian revolt was put down by the Prince of Caria, Istricus.14344 A calm, prelude to the coming storm, settled down upon Persia; and Phoenicia participated in the general tranquillity. The various communities, exhausted by their recent efforts, and disappointed with the result, laid aside their political aspirations, and fell back upon their commercial instincts. Trade once more flourished. Sidon rose again from her ashes, and recovered a certain amount of prosperity. She held the coast from Leontopolis to Ornithonpolis, and possessed also the dependency of Dor;14345 but she had lost Sarepta to Tyre,14346 which stepped into the foremost place among the cities on her fall, and retained it until destroyed by Alexander. The other towns which still continued to be of some importance were Aradus, and Gebal or Byblus. These cities, like Tyre and Sidon, retained their native kings,14347 who ruled their several states with little interference from the Persians. The line of monarchs may be traced at Sidon for five generations, from the first Esmunazar, who probably reigned about B.C. 460-440, through three generations and four kings, to the second Strato, the contemporary of Alexander.14348 The first Esmunazar was succeeded by his son, Tabnit, about B.C. 440. Tabnit married his sister, Am-Ashtoreth, priestess of Ashtoreth, and had issue, two sons, Esmunazar II., whose tomb was found near Sidon by M. de Vogüé in the year 1855, and Strato I. Esmunazar II. is thought to have died about B.C. 400, and to have been succeeded by his brother Strato, the Proxenus of Athens, who reigned till B.C. 361. On Strato's death, his son, the second Tabnit—known to the Greeks as Tennes—mounted the throne, and reigned till B.C. 345, when he was put to death by Ochus. A second Strato, the son of Tennes, then became king, and retained his sovereignty till after the battle of Issus14349 (B.C. 333).

6. Phoenicia in the time of Alexander the Great (B.C. 333-323)

Alexander's invasion of Asia—Preparations made to resist
it, insufficient—What should have been done—Movements of
Memnon in B.C. 333—His death—Paralysis of the Persian
fleet—Attack on Phoenicia after Issus—Submission of all
the cities but Tyre—Siege of Tyre—Fall of the city—Cruel
treatment of the inhabitants.

The invasion of Asia by Alexander the Great, though it found the Persians unready, was by no means of the nature of a surprise. The design had been openly proclaimed by Philip in the year B.C. 338, when he forced the Grecian States to appoint him generalissimo of their armies, which he promised to lead to the conquest of the East.14350 Darius Codomannus had thus ample warning of what he had to expect, and abundant opportunity to make the fullest preparations for defence. During the years B.C. 338 and 337, while Philip was still alive, he did do something towards organising defensive measures, collected troops and ships, and tried to foment discontent and encourage anti-Macedonian movements in Greece.14351 But the death of Philip by the dagger of Pausanias caused him most imprudently to relax his efforts, to consider the danger past, and to suspend the operations, which he had commenced, until he should see whether Alexander had either the will or the power to carry into effect his father's projects. The events of the years B.C. 336 and 335, the successes of Alexander in Thrace, Illyria, and Boeotia,14352 woke him from his fool's paradise to some sense of the realities of the situation. In B.C. 335 the preparations for defence were resumed. Orders were issued to the satraps of Phrygia and Lydia to draw together their troops towards the north-western corner of Asia Minor, and to take the offensive against the Macedonian force which had crossed the straits before Philip's death. The Persian garrisons in this quarter were strongly reinforced with troops of a good quality, drawn from the remoter provinces of the empire, as from Persia Proper, Media, Hyrcania, and Bactria. Notice was given to the Phoenicians to prepare a considerable fleet, and hold it in readiness for active service. Above all, Memnon the Rhodian was given a command on the Asiatic seaboard, and entrusted with a body of five thousand Greek mercenaries, which he was empowered to use at his discretion.14353

But these steps, though in the right direction, were quite inadequate under the circumstances. Everything that was possible should have been done to prevent Alexander from crossing to Asia in force. The fleet should not only have been commanded to hold itself in readiness, but should have been brought up. Four hundred or five hundred vessels,14354 from Phoenicia, Cyprus, Egypt, Lycia, and Cilicia, should have been moved into the northern Egean and the Propontis, and have kept watch on every Grecian port. Alexander was unable to muster for the transport of his army across the Straits a larger number than 160 triremes.14355 Persia should have met them with a fleet three times as large. Had Memnon been given from the first a free hand at sea, instead of satrapial power on land, it is quite conceivable that the invasion of Asia by Alexander might have proved as abortive an enterprise as the contemplated invasion of England by Napoleon.

As it was, the fleet of Persia, composed mainly of Phoenician vessels, did not appear in the northern Egean waters until some weeks after Alexander had transported his grand army into Asia, and fought at the Granicus, so that when it arrived it was of comparatively little service. Too late even to save Miletus, it had to be a tame spectator of the siege and capture of that important town.14356 It was then withdrawn to Halicarnassus, where its presence greatly helped the defence, but not to the extent of wholly baffling the besiegers. Halicarnassus fell, like Miletus, after a while, being entered from the land side; but the fleet saved the troops, the stores, and the inhabitants.14357

During the early part of the ensuing year, B.C. 333, while Alexander was engaged in conquering the interior of Asia Minor, the Persian fleet under Memnon at last took the aggressive, and, advancing northwards, employed itself in establishing Persian influence over the whole of the Egean, and especially in reducing the important islands of Chios and Lesbos.14358 Memnon was now in full command. Fortune smiled on him; and it seemed more than probable that the war would be, at least partially, transferred into Greece, where the Spartans only waited for Memnon's appearance to commence an anti-Macedonian movement. The presence of a powerful fleet in Greek waters, and Memnon's almost unlimited command of Persian gold, might in a short time have raised such a flame in Greece as to necessitate Alexander's return in order to extinguish it.14359 The invasion of Asia might have been arrested in mid course; Alexander might have proved as powerless as Agesilaus to effect any great change in the relations of the two continents; but, at the critical moment, the sudden and unexpected death of the Rhodian chief cast all these hopes to the ground,14360 and deprived Persia of her last chance of baffling the invader.

Thus, first by mismanagement and then by an unhappy accident, the Phoenicians were precluded from rendering Persia any effective service in the time of her great necessity. Wiser than Napoleon, Alexander would not contest the sovereignty of the seas with the great naval power of the day, and he even, when he once felt himself strongly lodged in Asia, disbanded his naval force,14361 that so it might be impossible for disaster at sea to tarnish his prestige. He was convinced that Asia could be won by the land force which he had been permitted to disembark on its shores, and probably anticipated the transfer of naval supremacy which almost immediately followed on the victory of Issus. The complete defeat of the great army of Codomannus, and its retirement on the Euphrates,14362 left the entire seaboard of Syria and Phoenicia open to him. He resolved at once to take advantage of the opportunity, and to detach from Persia the three countries of Phoenicia, Egypt, and Cyprus. If he could transfer to himself the navies of these powers, his maritime supremacy would be incontestable. He would render his communications with Macedonia absolutely secure. He would have nothing to fear from revolt or disturbance at home, however deeply he might plunge into the Asiatic continent. If the worst happened to him in Asia, he would have assured himself a safe return.

Accordingly, no sooner was the retreat of Darius upon the line of the Euphrates, and his abandonment of Syria, ascertained, than Alexander, after despatching a detachment of his army to Damascus, marched in person into Phoenicia.14363 The Phoenicians were placed between two dangers. On the one hand, Alexander might ravage their territory, capture and pillage their cities, massacre or sell for slaves the greater portion of their citizens, and destroy their very existence as a people; on the other hand, Darius held as hostages for their fidelity the crews and captains of their triremes, which formed a portion of his fleet, and had on board a large number of their chief men, and even some of their kings.14364 It was impossible, however, to temporise; a choice had necessarily to be made; and when Alexander entered Phoenicia, the cities, in almost every case, decided on submitting to him. First Strato, the son of Ger-astartus, king of Aradus, who was serving on board the Phoenician contingent to the Persian fleet, went out to meet Alexander, and surrendered into his hands the four cities of Aradus, Marathus, Sigon, and Mariamme.14365 Then Byblus, whose king was also absent with the fleet, opened its gates to the Macedonians.14366 Next Sidon, mindful of her recent wrongs, sent envoys to invite Alexander's approach, and joyfully embraced his cause.14367 Even Tyre nominally made submission, and declared itself ready to obey Alexander's commands;14368 and the transfer of Phoenicia to the side of Alexander might have been made without bloodshed, had the Macedonian monarch been content to leave their island city, which was their true capital, and their pride and glory, unmolested. But Alexander could not brook anything that in any degree savoured of opposition to his will. When therefore, on his expressing a wish to sacrifice to Melkarth in their island town, the Tyrians declined to receive him within the walls, and suggested that his pious design might be sufficiently accomplished by his making his intended offering in Palæ-Tyrus, where there was a temple of the same god, which was older (they said) and more venerable than their own, Alexander's pride was touched, and he became violently enraged.14369 Dismissing the envoys with angry threats, he at once began preparations for an attack upon the town.

The Tyrians have been accused of extreme rashness and folly in not making an unqualified submission to the demands preferred by Alexander,14370 but the reproach scarcely appears to be deserved. They had on previous occasions resisted for years the entire power of Assyria, and of Babylon; they naturally deemed themselves only assailable by sea; their fortifications were of immense strength; and they possessed a navy much superior to any of which Alexander could boast at the time when he threatened them. Their own vessels were eighty in number; those of their kinsmen upon the continent were likewise eighty; Cyprus, which for centuries had been closely allied with them, and which was more than half Phoenician in blood, could furnish a hundred and twenty; Carthage, if she chose, could send to their aid, without any difficulty, as many as two hundred.14371 Alexander had never been able to collect from the Greek states which owned his sway a fleet of more than one hundred and sixty sail; and, having disbanded this fleet, he could not readily have mustered from the cities and countries accessible to him, exclusive of Cyprus and Phoenicia, so many as a hundred.14372 The Tyrians, when they took their resolution to oppose Alexander, had a right to expect that their kindred would either assist them, or at any rate not serve against them, and that thus they would be sure to maintain their supremacy at sea. As for Alexander's design to join the island Tyre to the continent by means of a mole, they cannot have had the slightest suspicion of it, since no work of the kind had ever previously been accomplished, or even attempted; for the demonstration of Xerxes against Salamis was not seriously intended.14373 They naturally counted on the struggle being entirely by sea, and may well have thought that on their own element they would not be worsted. Even if the continental towns forsook them and went over to the enemy, why might they not do as they had done in Shalmaneser's time, defeat their unnatural countrymen, and retain their naval supremacy? Moreover, if they made a gallant fight, might not Persia be expected to second their efforts? Would she not attack Alexander from the flanks of Lebanon, intercept his supplies, cut off his foragers, and make his position untenable; the Tyrians could scarcely anticipate that Persia would sit with folded hands, a calm spectator of a seven months' siege, and do absolutely nothing.

Having determined on resistance to the demands of Alexander, the Tyrians lost no time in placing their city in a position to resist attack. They summoned their king, Azemilcus, from the Persian fleet, and required him to hasten home with the entire squadron which he commanded.14374 They collected triremes and lighter vessels from various quarters. They distributed along the walls of the city upon every side a number of engines of war, constructed to hurl darts and stones, and amply provided them with missiles.14375 The skilled workmen and engineers resident in the town were called upon not merely to furnish additional engines of the old type, but to exercise their ingenuity in devising new and unheard of structures.14376 They armed all the young and vigorous among the people, and appointed them their several stations at the walls. Finally, to diminish the number of mouths to be fed, and to save themselves from distracting cares, they sent away to Carthage a number of their aged men, their women, and their children, who were readily received and supported by the rich and friendly colonists.14377

Meantime Alexander had taken his resolution. Either recollecting what Xerxes had threatened to do at Salamis, or prompted merely by his own inventive genius, he determined on the construction of a great mole, or embankment, which should be carried out from the Asiatic mainland across the half-mile of channel to the very walls of the recalcitrant city, and should thus join the island to the Syrian shore. The width of the embankment he fixed at two plethra, or nearly seventy yards.14378 Material for the construction was abundant. The great city of Palæ-Tyrus was close at hand, partly in ruins, and with many of the houses deserted by their inhabitants. Its walls would furnish abundance of stone, mortar, and rubble. Behind Palæ-Tyrus lay the flanks of Lebanon, cultivated in orchards, while beyond were its dense and inexhaustible forests of fir, pine, and cedar. Human labour could be obtained to almost any extent, for the neighbourhood was populous, and Alexander's authority acknowledged by all. Accordingly the work, once commenced, for a while made fair progress. Piles were cut in the mountain, which were driven with much ease into the soft mud of the channel, which was shallow near the shore,14379 and completely under the control of the Macedonians, since the Tyrian vessels could not approach it for fear of sticking in the ooze. Between the piles, towards the edge of the mole, were sunk stones, trunks of trees, and material of the more solid character, while the central part was filled up with rubble and rubbish of every sort and kind. Still, the operation was toilsome and tedious, even from the first, while the further that the mole was advanced into the sea, the more difficult and dangerous became its construction. The channel deepened gradually from a few feet towards the shore to eighteen or twenty,14380 as it approached the island. The Tyrians in their vessels were soon able to act. In small boats at first, and afterwards in their triremes, they attacked and annoyed the workmen, perpetually hindered their work, and occasionally destroyed portions of it.14381 Damage was also inflicted by the wind and waves; and the rate of progress became, in consequence, exceedingly slow. A strong current set through the channel, and this was continually working its way among the interstices of the mole, washing holes in its sides and face, and loosening the interior of the structure. When a storm arose, the surf broke over the top of the work, and did even greater damage, carrying portions of the outer casing into the sea.

To meet the assaults of the Tyrian ships upon the work, the Macedonians constructed two movable towers, well protected against torches and weapons by curtains made of raw hides,14382 and advancing these upon the surface of the mole to the points most threatened, discharged from the engines which the towers contained darts and stones of a large size against the Tyrian sailors. Thus protected, the workmen were able to make sensible progress, and the Tyrians began to fear that, unless they could destroy the towers, the mole would ere long be completed. For the accomplishment of their purpose, they resolved to employ a fire-ship.14383 Selecting one of the largest of their horse-transports, they stowed the hold with dry brushwood and other combustible materials; and erecting on the prow two masters, each with a projecting arm, attached to either a cauldron, filled with bitumen and sulphur, and with every sort of material apt to kindle and nourish flame. By loading the stern of the transport with stones of a large size, they succeeded in depressing it and correspondingly elevating the prow, which was thus prepared to glide over the smooth surface of the mole and bring itself into contact with the towers. In the fore part of the ship were deposited a quantity of torches, resin, and other combustibles. Watching an opportunity when the wind blew strongly from the seaward straight upon the mole, they towed the vessel at their best speed in the direction of the towers, set it on fire, and then, loosing their hawsers, allowed it to dash itself upon the work. The prow slid over the top a certain distance and then stopped. The arms projecting from the masts broke off at the sudden check,14384 and scattered the contents of the cauldrons around. The towers caught fire and were at once in a blaze. The Macedonians found it impossible to extinguish the flames, since the Tyrian triremes, drawing close to the mole, prevented approach by flights of arrows and other missiles. "At the same time, the full naval force of the city, both ships and little boats, was sent forth to land men at once on all parts of the mole. So successful was this attack, that all the Macedonian engines were burnt—the outer woodwork which kept the mole together was torn up in many places—and a large part of the structure came to pieces."14385 A heavy sea, moreover, accompanied the gale of wind which had favoured the conflagration, and penetrating the loosened work, carried the whole into deep waters.14386

Alexander had now seriously to consider what course he should take. Hitherto his attempt had proved an entire failure. Should he relinquish it? To do so would be to acknowledge himself baffled and defeated, to tarnish the prestige which he held so dear, and to cripple the plans that he had formed against Persia. It was simply impossible that Alexander, being the man he was, should so act. No—he must persevere—he must confront and overcome his difficulties—he must repair the damages that he had suffered, restore his lost works, and carry them out on a larger scale, and with more skill than before. He gave orders therefore for an enlargement and alteration of the mole, which he no longer carried across the strait in a direct line, but inclined to the south-west,14387 so that it might meet the force of the prevalent wind, instead of exposing its flank to the violent gusts. He also commanded the construction of fresh towers and fresh engines, stronger and more in number than the former ones.14388 But this alone would not, he felt, be enough. His designs had been frustrated hitherto solely from the fact that the Tyrians were masters of the sea; and it was plain to him that, so long as this state of things remained unaltered, it was next to impossible that he should succeed. The great desideratum—the one condition of success—was the possession of a powerful fleet. Such a fleet must be either built or collected. Leaving therefore the restoration of the mole and the engines to his generals, Alexander went in person to Sidon, and there set himself to gather together as large a fleet as he could. Most opportunely it happened that, either shortly before Alexander's arrival or immediately afterwards, the ships of Sidon, Aradus, and Byblus, which had been serving with the Persian naval force in the Ægean, had been required by their respective commanders to proceed homewards, and, to the number of eighty, had sailed into the harbour of Sidon.14389 The kings had, in fact, deserted the Persian cause on hearing that their cities had submitted to Alexander, and readily placed their respective squadrons at his disposal. Further contingents were received from other quarters—from Rhodes ten triremes, from the seaports of Lycia the same number, from Soli and Mallus three, from Macedonia a single penteconter.14390 The number of the vessels was thus brought up to one hundred and four; but even with such a fleet it would have been rash to engage the Tyrian navy; and Alexander would probably have had to build an additional squadron had he not received, suddenly and unexpectedly, the adhesion of the princes of Cyprus. Cyprus, being an island, was as yet in no danger, and might have been expected at least to remain neutral until the fate of Tyre was decided; but, for reasons that history has not recorded, the petty kings of the island about this time—some months after the battle of Issus—resolved to desert Persia, to detach themselves wholly from Tyre, and to place their navy at the disposal of the Macedonians.14391 The number of their triremes amounted to 120; and Alexander, having now under his command a fleet of 224 sail, could no longer feel any doubt of being able to wrest the supremacy at sea from the unfortunate Tyrians.

Accordingly, after allowing his ships a period of eleven days for nautical practice, and placing on board a number of his bravest soldiers,14392 Alexander sailed out from Sidon at the head of his entire fleet, and made straight for Tyre in order of battle. He himself in person commanded the right wing, the post of danger, since it held the open sea, and had under him the bulk of the Cyprian ships, with their commanders. Pnytagoras of Salamis and Craterus led the left wing, which was composed mainly of the vessels furnished by the Phoenician towns upon the mainland, and held its course at no great distance from the shore. The Tyrians, who had received no intelligence from without, saw with astonishment the great fleet, nearly three times as large as their own,14393 bearing down upon them in orderly array, and challenging them to the combat. They had not now the spirit of ancient times, when no disparity of force dismayed them. Surprised and alarmed, they resolved to decline a battle, to remain within their ports, and to use their ships for blocking the entrances. Alexander, advancing from the north, when he saw the mouth of the Sidonian harbour, which faced northwards, strongly guarded, did not attempt to force it, but anchored his vessels outside, and established a blockade, the maintenance of which he entrusted to the Cyprian squadron. The next day he ordered the Phoenician ships to proceed southwards, and similarly block and watch the southern or Egyptian harbour.14394 For himself, he landed upon the mole, and pitching his tent near the south-western corner, there established himself.14395

The mole had not advanced very much during his absence. Vast efforts had been made to re-establish it, but they had not been attended with any great success.14396 Whole trees, torn up by the roots, and with their branches still adhering to them, had been dragged to the water's edge, and then precipitated into the strait;14397 a layer of stones and mud had been placed upon them, to solidify them into a mass; on the top of this other trees had been placed, and the former process repeated. But the Tyrians had met the new tactics with new methods. They had employed divers to attach hooks to the boughs where they projected into the sea, and by sheer force had dragged the trees out from the superincumbent mass, bringing down in this way large portions of the structure.14398 But with Alexander's coming, and the retirement of the Tyrian fleet, all this was altered. Alexander's workmen were no longer impeded, except from the town, and in a short time the mole was completed across the channel and carried up to the very foot of the defences. The new towers, which had replaced the burnt ones, were brought up close to the walls, and plied the new machines which Cyprian and Phoenician engineers had constructed for their new master.14399 The battering of the wall began. Engines moreover of a large size were placed on horse-transports furnished by Sidon, and on the heavier and clumsier of the triremes, and with these attacks were made upon the town in various places, all round the circuit of the walls, which, if they did nothing else, served to distract the attention of the defenders. To meet such assailants the Tyrians had let down huge blocks of stone into the sea, which prevented the approach of the ships, and hindered those on board from using the battering ram. These blocks the Macedonians endeavoured to weigh up and remove by means of cranes; but their vessels were too unsteady for the purpose, whereupon they proceeded to anchor them. The Tyrians went out in boats well protected, and passing under the stems and sterns of the vessels, cut the cables, whereupon the Macedonians kept an armed watch upon the cables in boats of their own, which the Tyrians did not venture to attack. They were not, however, without resource even yet, since they contrived still to cut the cables by means of divers. At last the Macedonians bethought themselves of using chains for cables instead of ropes; these could not be cut, and the result was that at length they succeeded in dragging the stones away and obtaining access to the foot of the walls wherever they pleased.14400

Under these circumstances, threatened on every side, and feeling almost at the last gasp, the Tyrians resolved on a final desperate effort. They would make a bold attempt to recover the command of the sea. As the Macedonian fleet was divided, part watching the Sidonian and part the Egyptian harbour, they could freely select to contend with which portion they preferred. Their choice fell upon the Cyprian contingent, which was stationed to the north of the mole, keeping guard on the "Portus Sidonius." This they determined to attack, and to take, if possible, by surprise. Long previously they had spread sails along the mouth of the harbour, to prevent their proceedings inside it from being overlooked.14401 They now prepared a select squadron of thirteen ships—three of them quinqueremes, three quadriremes, and seven triremes—and silently placing on board their best sailors and the best and bravest of their men-at-arms, waited till the hour of noon, when the Cyprian crews would be taking their mid-day meal, and Alexander might be expected, according to his general habit, to have retired to his tent on the opposite side of the mole. When noon came, still in deep silence, they issued from the harbour in single file, each crew rowing gently without noise or splash, or a word spoken, either by the boatswains or by anyone else. In this way they came almost close to the Cyprians without being perceived: then suddenly the boatswains gave out their cry, and the men cheered, and all pulled as hard as they could, and with splash and dash they drove their ships against the enemy's, which were inert, lying at anchor, some empty, others hurriedly taking their crews on board. The ships of three Cyprian kings—Pnytagoras, king of Salamis, Androcles, king of Amathus, and Pasicrates, king of Curium14402—were at once run down and sunk.14403 Many others were disabled; the rest fled, pursued by the Tyrians, and sought to reach the shore. All would probably have been lost, had not Alexander returned from his tent earlier than usual, and witnessed the Tyrian attack. With his usual promptitude, he at once formed his plan. As only a portion of the Cyprian fleet had maintained the blockade, while the remainder of their ships were lying off the north shore of the mole with their crews disembarked, he set to work to man these, and sent them off, as each was got ready, to station themselves at the mouth of the harbour, and prevent any more of the Tyrian vessels from sallying forth. He then hurried to the southern side of the mole, where the Greco-Phoenician squadron kept guard, and manning a certain number of the vessels,14404 sailed with them round the western shore of the island into the northern bay, where the Tyrians and the remnant of the Cyprian fleet were still contending. Those in the city perceived the movement, and made every effort to signal it to their sailors, but in vain. The noise and uproar of the battle prevented them from hearing until it was too late. It was not till Alexander had entered the northern bay that they understood, and turned and fled, pursued by his ships, which captured or disabled the greater number. The crews, however, and the men-at-arms, escaped, since they threw themselves overboard, and easily swam into the harbour.14405

This was the last attempt of the Tyrians by sea. They were now invested on every side, and hopelessly shut up within their defences. Still, however, they made a desperate resistance. On the side of the mole the Macedonians, having brought up their towers and battering-ram close to the wall, attacked it with much vigour, hurling against it great masses of stone, and by constant flights of darts and arrows driving the defenders from the battlements.14406 At the same time the battering-rams were actively plied, and every effort made to effect a breach. But the Tyrians deadened the blows of the rams and the force of the stones by letting down from the walls leathern bags filled with sea-weed at the points assailed;14407 while, by wheels which were set in rapid motion, they intercepted the darts and javelins wherewith they were attacked, and broke them or diverted them from their intended courses.14408 When boarding-bridges were thrown from the towers to the top of the walls, and an attempt was made to pass troops into the town across them, they flung grappling hooks among the soldiers on the bridges, which caught in their bodies and lacerated them, or dragged their shields from their hands, or sometimes hauled them bodily into the air, and then dashed them against the wall or against the ground.14409 Further, they made ready masses of red-hot metal, and hurled them against the towers and the scaling-parties.14410 They also heated sand over fires and poured it from the battlements on all who approached the foot of the wall; this, penetrating between the armour and the skin, inflicted such intolerable pain that the sufferers were forced to tear off their coats of mail, whereupon they were easily transfixed by arrows or long lances.14411 With scythes they cut the ropes and thongs by means of which the rams were worked;14412 and at last, armed with hatchets, they sprang from the battlements upon the Macedonian boarding-bridges, and in a hand-to-hand combat defeated and drove back their assailants.14413 Finally, when, despite of all their efforts, the outer wall began to give way, they constructed an inner wall to take its place, broader and stronger than the other.14414 Alexander, after a time, became convinced that his endeavours to take the city from the mole were hopeless, and turned his attention to the sea defences, north and south of the mole, which were far less strong than those which he had hitherto been attacking.14415 He placed his best engines and his boarding-bridges upon ships, and proceeded to batter the sea walls in various places. On the south side, near the Egyptian harbour, he found a weak place, and concentrating his efforts upon it, he succeeded in effecting a large breach.14416 He then gave orders for a general assault.14417 The two fleets were commanded to force simultaneously the entrances to the two harbours; other vessels to make demonstrations against the walls at all approachable points; the army collected on the mole to renew its assaults; while he himself, with his trustiest soldiers, delivered the main attack at the southern breach.14418 Two vessels were selected for the purpose. On one, which was that of Coenus, he embarked a portion of the phalanx; on the other, which was commanded by Admetus, he placed his bodyguard, himself accompanying it. The struggle was short when once the boarding-bridges were thrown across and rested on the battered wall. Fighting under the eye of their king, the Macedonians carried all before them, though not without important losses. Admetus himself, who was the first to step on to the wall, received a spear thrust, and was slain.14419 But the soldiers who were following close behind him maintained their footing, and in a little time got possession of several towers, with the spaces between them. Alexander was among the foremost of those who mounted the breach,14420 and was for a while hotly engaged in a hand-to-hand fight with the enemy. When those who resisted him were slain or driven off, he directed his troops to seize the royal palace, which abutted on the southern wall, and through it make their entrance into the town.14421

Meanwhile, the Greco-Phoenician fleet on the south side of the mole had burst the boom and other obstacles by which the Egyptian harbour was closed, and, attacking the ships within, had disabled some, and driven the rest ashore, thus gaining possession of the southern port and a ready access to the adjacent portion of the city.14422 The Cyprians, moreover, on the north, had forced their way into the Sidonian harbour, which had no boom, and obtained an entrance into the town on that quarter.14423 The defences were broken through in three places, and it might have been expected that resistance would have ceased. But the gallant defenders still would not yield. A large body assembled at the Agenorium, or temple of Agenor, and there made a determined stand, which continued till Alexander himself attacked them with his bodyguard, and slew almost the entire number. Others, mounting upon the roofs of the houses, flung down stones and missiles of all kinds upon the Macedonians in the street. A portion shut themselves up in their homes and perished by their own hands. In the streets and squares there was a terrible carnage. The Macedonians were infuriated by the length of the siege, the stubbornness of the resistance, and the fact that the Tyrians had in the course of the siege publicly executed, probably by way of sacrifice, a number of their prisoners upon the walls. Those who died with arms in their hands are reckoned at eight thousand;14424 two thousand more, who had been made prisoners, were barbarously crucified by command of Alexander round the walls of the city.14425 None of the adult free males were spared, except the few who had taken refuge with Azemilcus the king in the temple of Melkarth, which Alexander professed greatly to revere, and a certain number whom the Sidonians, touched at last with pity, concealed on board their triremes. The women, the children, and the slaves, to the number of thirty thousand,14426 were sold to the highest bidder.

Having worked his will, and struck terror, as he hoped, into the hearts of all who might be thinking of resisting him, Alexander concluded the Tyrian episode of his career by a religious ceremony.14427 Entering the city from the mole in a grand procession, accompanied by his entire force of soldiers, fully armed and arrayed, while his fleet also played its part in the scene, he proceeded to the temple of Melkarth in the middle of the town, and offered his much desired sacrifice to Hercules. A gymnastic contest and a torch race formed a portion of the display. To commemorate his victory, he dedicated and left in the temple the battering-ram which had made the first impression on the southern wall, together with a Tyrian vessel, used in the service of the god, which he had captured when he bore down upon the city from Sidon with his fleet. Over the charred and half-ruined remnants of the city, into which he had introduced a certain number of colonists, chiefly Carians,14428 he placed as ruler a member of a decayed branch of the royal family, a certain Abd-elonim, whom the Greeks called Ballonymos.14429

7. Phoenicia under the Greeks (B.C. 323-65)

The Phoenicians faithful subjects of Alexander—At his death
Phoenicia falls, first to Laomedon, then to Ptolemy Lagi—Is
held by the Ptolemies for seventy years—Passes willingly,
B.C. 198, under the Seleucidæ—Relations with the Seleucid
princes and with the Jews—Hellenisation of Phoenicia—
Continued devotion of the Phoenicians generally to trade and
commerce—Material prosperity of Phoenicia.

Phoenicia continued faithful to Alexander during the remainder of his career. Phoenician vessels were sent across the Ægean to the coast of the Peloponnese to maintain the Macedonian interest in that quarter.14430 Large numbers of the mercantile class accompanied the march of his army for the purposes of traffic. A portion of these, when Alexander reached the Hydaspes and determined to sail down the course of the Indus to the sea, were drafted into the vessels which he caused to be built,14431 descended the river, and accompanied Nearchus in his voyage from Patala to the Persian Gulf. Others still remained with the land force, and marched with Alexander himself across the frightful deserts of Beloochistan, where they collected the nard and myrrh, which were almost its only products, and which were produced in such abundance as to scent the entire region.14432 On Alexander's return to Babylon, Phoenicia was required to supply him with additional vessels, and readily complied with the demand. A fleet of forty-eight ships—two of them quinqueremes, four quadriremes, twelve triremes, and thirty pentaconters, or fifty-oared galleys—was constructed on the Phoenician coast, carried in fragments to Thapsacus on the Euphrates, and there put together and launched on the stream of the Euphrates, down which it sailed to Babylon.14433 Seafaring men from Phoenicia and Syria were at the same time enlisted in considerable numbers, and brought to

Alexander at his new capital to man the ships which he was building there, and also to supply colonists for the coasts of the Persian Gulf and the islands scattered over its surface.14434 Alexander, among his many projects, nourished an intention of adding to his dominions, at any rate, the seaboard of Arabia, and understood that for this purpose he must establish in the Persian Gulf a great naval power, such as Phoenicia alone out of all the countries under his dominion was able to furnish. His untimely death brought all these schemes to an end, and plunged the East into a sea of troubles.

In the division of Alexander's empire, which followed upon his death, Phoenicia was at first assigned, together with Syria, to Laemedon, and the two formed together a separate satrapy.14435 But, after the arrangement of Triparadisus (B.C. 320), Ptolemy Lagi almost immediately attacked Laemedon, dispossessed him of his government, and attached it to his own satrapy of Egypt.14436 Six years later (B.C. 314), attacked in his turn by Antigonus, Ptolemy was forced to relinquish his conquests,14437 none of which offered much resistance excepting Tyre. Tyre, though no more than eighteen years had elapsed since its desolation by Alexander, had, like the fabled phoenix, risen again from its ruins, and through the recuperative energy of commerce had attained almost to its previous wealth and prosperity.14438 Its walls had been repaired, and it was defended by its Egyptian garrison with pertinacity. Antigonus, who was master of the Phoenician mainland, established dockyards at Sidon, Byblus, and Tripolis, set eight thousand sawyers and labourers to cut down timber in Lebanon, and called upon the kings of the coast towns to build him a fleet with the least possible delay.14439 His orders were carried out, and Tyre was blockaded by sea and land for the space of fifteen months, when the provisions failed and the town was forced to surrender itself.14440 The garrison marched out with the honours of war, and Phoenicia became an appendage of the empire (for such it was) of Antigonus.

From Antigonus Phoenicia passed to his son Demetrius, who maintained his hold on it, with some vicissitudes of fortune, till B.C. 287, when it once more passed under the dominion of Ptolemy Lagi.14441 From this time it was an Egyptian dependency for nearly seventy years, and flourished commercially, if it not distinguish itself by warlike exploits. The early Ptolemies were mild and wise rulers. They encouraged commerce, literature, and art. So far as was possible they protected their dominions from external attack, put down brigandage, and ruled with equity and moderation. It was not until the fourth prince of the house of Lagus, Philopator, mounted the throne (B.C. 222) that the character of their rule changed for the worse, and their subjects began to have reason to complain of them. The weakness and profligacy of Philopater14442 tempted Antiochus III. to assume the aggressive, and to disturb the peace which had now for some time subsisted between Syria and Egypt, the Lagidæ and the Seleucidæ. In B.C. 219 he drove the Egyptians out of Seleucia, the port of Antioch,14443 and being joined by Theodotus, the Egyptian governor of the Coelesyrian province, invaded that country and Phoenicia, took possession of Tyre and Accho, which was now called Ptolemaïs, and threatened Egypt with subjugation.14444 Phoenicia once more became the battle-field between two great powers, and for the next twenty years the cities were frequently taken and re-taken. At last, in B.C. 198, by the victory of Antiochus over Scopas,14445 and the surrender of Sidon, Phoenicia passed, with Coelesyria, into the permanent possession of the Seleucidæ, and, though frequently reclaimed by Egypt, was never recovered.

The change of rulers was, on the whole, in consonance with the wishes and feelings of the Phoenicians. Though Alexandria may not have been founded with the definite intention of depressing Tyre, and raising up a commercial rival to her on the southern shore of the Mediterranean;14446 yet the advantages of the situation, and the interests of the Lagid princes, constituted her in a short time an actual rival, and an object of Phoenician jealousy. Phoenicia had been from a remote antiquity14447 down to the time of Alexander, the main, if not the sole, dispenser of Egyptian products to Syria, Asia Minor, and Europe. With the foundation of Alexandria this traffic passed out of her hands. It may be true that what she lost in this way was "more than compensated by the new channels of eastern traffic which Alexander's conquests opened to her, by the security given to commercial intercourse by the establishment of a Greek monarchy in the ancient dominions of the Persian kings, and by the closer union which now prevailed between all parts of the civilised world,"14448 But the balance of advantage and disadvantage does not even now always reconcile traders to a definite and tangible loss; and in the ruder times of which we are writing it was not to be expected that arguments of so refined and recondite a character should be very sensibly felt. Tyre and Sidon recognised in Alexandria a rival from the first, and grew more and more jealous of her as time went on. She monopolised the trade in Egyptian commodities from her foundation. In a short time she drew to herself, not only the direct Egyptian traffic, but that which her rulers diverted from other quarters, and drew to Egypt by the construction of harbours, and roads with stations and watering places.14449 Much of the wealth that had previously flowed into Phoenicia was, in point of fact, diverted to Egypt, and especially to Alexandria, by the judicious arrangements of the earlier Lagid princes. Phoenicia, therefore, in attaching herself to the Seleucidæ, felt that she was avenging a wrong, and though materially she might not be the gainer, was gratified by the change in her position.

The Seleucid princes on their part regarded the Phoenicians with favour, and made a point of conciliating their affections by personal intercourse with them, and by the grant of privileges. At the quinquennial festival instituted by Alexander ere he quitted Tyre, which was celebrated in the Greek fashion with gymnastic and musical contests, the Syrian kings were often present in person, and took part in the festivities.14450 They seem also to have visited the principal cities at other times, and to have held their court in them for many days together.14451 With their consent and permission, the towns severally issued their own coins, which bore commonly legends both in Greek and in Phoenician, and had sometimes Greek, sometimes Phoenician emblems.14452 Both Aradus and Tyre were allowed the privilege of being asylums,14453 from which political refugees could not be demanded by the sovereign.

The Phoenicians in return served zealously on board the Syro-Macedonian fleet, and showed their masters all due respect and honour.14454 They were not afraid, however, of asserting an independence of thought and judgment, even in matters where the kings were personally concerned. On one occasion, when Antiochus Epiphanes was holding his court at Tyre, a cause of the greatest importance was brought before him for decision by the authorities at Jerusalem. The high-priest of the time, Menelaus, who had bought the office from the Syrian king, was accused of having plundered the Temple of a number of its holy vessels, and of having sold them for his own private advantage. The Sanhedrim, who prosecuted Menelaus, sent three representatives to Tyre, to conduct the case, and press the charges against him. The evidence was so clear that the High Priest saw no chance of an acquittal, except by private interest. He therefore bribed an influential courtier, named Ptolemy, the son of a certain Dorymenes, to intercede with Antiochus on his behalf, and, if possible, obtain his acquittal. The affair was not one of much difficulty. Justice was commonly bought and sold at the Syro-Macedonian Court, and Antiochus readily came into the views of Ptolemy, and pronounced the High Priest innocent. He thought, however, that in so grave a matter some one must be punished, and, as he had acquitted Menelaus, he could only condemn his accusers. These unfortunates suffered death at his hands, whereon the Tyrians, compassionating their fate, and to mark their sense of the iniquity of the sentence, decreed to give them an honourable burial. The historian who relates the circumstance evidently feels that it was a bold and courageous act, very creditable to the Tyrian people.14455

It is not always, however, that we can justly praise the conduct of the Phoenicians at this period. Within six years of the time when the Tyrians showed themselves at once so courageous and so compassionate, the nation generally was guilty of complicity in a most unjust and iniquitous design. Epiphanes, having driven the Jews into rebellion by a most cruel religious persecution, and having more than once suffered defeat at their hands, resolved to revenge himself by utterly destroying the people which had provoked his resentment.14456 Called away to the eastern provinces by a pressing need, he left instructions with his general,

Lysias, to invade Judæa with an overwhelming force, and, after crushing all resistance, to sell the surviving population—men, women, and children—for slaves. Lysias, in B.C. 165, marched into Judæa, accompanied by a large army, with the full intention of carrying out to the letter his master's commands. In order to attract purchasers for the multitude whom he would have to sell, he made proclamation that the rate of sale should be a talent for ninety, or less than 3l. a head,14457 while at the same he invited the attendance of the merchants from all "the cities of the sea-coast," who must have been mainly, if not wholly, Phoenicians. The temptation was greater than Phoenician virtue could resist. The historian tells us that "the merchants of the country, hearing the fame of the Syrians, took silver and gold very much, with servants, and came into the Syrian camp to buy the children of Israel for money."14458 The result was a well-deserved disappointment. The Syrian army suffered complete defeat at the hands of the Jews, and had to beat a hasty retreat; the merchants barely escaped with their lives. As for the money which they had brought with them for the purchase of the captives, it fell into the hands of the victorious Jews, and formed no inconsiderable part of the booty which rewarded their valour.14459

After this, we hear but little of any separate action on the part of the Phoenicians, or of any Phoenician city, during the Seleucid period. Phoenicia became rapidly Hellenised; and except that they still remained devoted to commercial pursuits, the cities had scarcely any distinctive character, or anything that marked them out as belonging to a separate nationality. Greek legends became more frequent upon the coins; Greek names were more and more affected, especially by the upper classes; the men of letters discarded Phoenician as a literary language, and composed the works, whereby they sought to immortalize their names, in Greek. Greek philosophy was studied in the schools of Sidon;14460 and at Byblus Phoenician mythology was recast upon a Greek type. At the same time Phoenician art conformed itself more and more closely to Greek models, until all that was rude in it, or archaic, or peculiar, died out, and the productions of Phoenician artists became mere feeble imitations of second-rate Greek patterns.

The nation gave itself mainly to the pursuit of wealth. The old trades were diligently plied. Tyre retained its pre-eminence in the manufacture of the purple dye; and Sidon was still unrivalled in the production of glass. Commerce continued to enrich the merchant princes, while at the same time it provided a fairly lucrative employment for the mass of the people. A new source of profit arose from the custom, introduced by the Syro-Macedonians, of farming the revenue. In Phoenicia, as in Syria generally, the taxes of each city were let out year by year to some of the wealthiest men of the place,14461 who collected them with extreme strictness, and made over but a small proportion of the amount to the Crown. Large fortunes were made in this way, though occasionally foreigners would step in, and outbid the Phoenician speculators,14462 who were not content unless they gained above a hundred per cent. on each transaction. Altogether, Phoenicia may be pronounced to have enjoyed much material prosperity under the Seleucid princes, though, in the course of the civil wars between the different pretenders to the Crown, most of the cities had, from time to time, to endure sieges. Accho especially, which had received from the Lagid princes the name of Ptolemaïs, and was now the most important and flourishing of the Phoenician towns, had frequently to resist attack, and was more than once taken by storm.14463

8. Phoenicia under the Romans (B.C. 65-A.D. 650)

Syria made a Roman province, B.C. 65—Privileges granted by
Rome to the Phoenician cities—Phoenicia profits by the
Roman suppression of piracy, but suffers from Parthian

ravages—The Phoenicians offend Augustus and lose their favoured position, but recover it under later emperors—Mention of the Phoenician cities in the New Testament—Phoenicia accepts Christianity—Phoenician bishops at the early Councils—Phoenician literature at this date—Works of Antipater, Apollonius, Philo, Hermippus, Marinus, Maximus, and Porphyry—School of law at Berytus—Survival of the Phoenician commercial spirit—Survival of the religion—Summary.

The kingdom of the Seleucidæ came to an end through its own internal weakness and corruption. In B.C. 83 their subjects, whether native Asiatics or Syro-Macedonians, were so weary of the perpetual series of revolts, civil wars, and assassinations that they invited Tigranes, the king of the neighbouring Armenia, to step in and undertake the government of the country.14464 Tigranes ruled from B.C. 83 till B.C. 69, when he was attacked by the Romans, to whom he had given just cause of offence by his conduct in the Mithridatic struggle. Compelled by Lucullus to relinquish Syria, he retired to his own dominions, and was succeeded by the last Seleucid prince, Antiochus Asiaticus, who reigned from B.C. 69 to B.C. 65. Rome then at length came forward, and took the inheritance to which she had become entitled a century and a quarter earlier by the battle of Magnesia, and which she could have occupied at any moment during the interval, had it suited her purpose. The combat with Mithridates had forced her to become an Asiatic power; and having once overcome her repugnance to being entangled in Asiatic politics, she allowed her instinct of self-aggrandizement to have full play, and reduced the kingdom of the Seleucidæ into the form of a Roman province.14465

The province, which retained the name of Syria, and was placed under a proconsul,14466 whose title was "Præses Syriæ," extended from the flanks of Amanus and Taurus to Carmel and the sources of the Jordan, and thus included Phoenicia. The towns, however, of Tripolis, Sidon, and Tyre were allowed the position of "free cities," which secured them an independent municipal government, under their own freely elected council and chief magistates. These privileges, conferred by Pompey, were not withdrawn by Julius Cæsar, when he became master of the Roman world; and hence we find him addressing a communication respecting Hyrcanus to the "Magistates, Council, and People of Sidon."14467 A similar regard was shown for Phoenician vested rights by Anthony, who in B.C. 36, when his infatuation for Cleopatra was at its height, and he agreed to make over to her the government of Palestine and of Coelesyria, as far as the river Eleutherus, especially exempted from her control, despite her earnest entreaties, the cities of Tyre and Sidon.14468 Anthony also wrote more than one letter to the "Magistates, Council, and People of Tyre," in which he recognised them as "allies" of the Roman people rather than subjects.14469

So far the Phoenicians would seem to have gained rather than lost by exchanging the dominion of Syria for that of Rome. They gained also greatly by the strictness with which Rome kept the police of the Eastern Mediterranean. For many years previously to B.C. 67 their commerce had been preyed upon to an enormous extent by the piratical fleets, which, issuing from the creeks and harbours of Western Cilicia and Pamphylia, spread terror on every side,14470 and made the navigation of the Levant and Ægean as dangerous as it had been in the days anterior to Minos.14471 Pompey, in that year, completely destroyed the piratical fleets, attacked the pirates in their lairs, and cleared them out from every spot where they had established themselves. Voyages by sea became once more as safe as travels by land; and a vigilant watch being kept on all the coasts and islands, piracy was never again permitted to gather strength, or become a serious evil. The Phoenician merchants could once more launch their trading vessels on the Mediterranean waters without fear of their suffering capture, and were able to insure their cargoes at a moderate premium.

But their connection with Rome exposed the Phoenicians to some fresh, and terrible, perils.

The great attack of Crassus on Parthia in the year B.C. 53 had bitterly exasperated that savage and powerful kingdom, which was quite strong enough to retaliate, under favourable circumstances, upon the mighty mistress of the West, and to inflict severe sufferings upon Rome's allies, subjects, and dependencies. After a preliminary trial of strength14472 in the years B.C. 522 and 51, Pacorus, the son of Orodes, in B.C. 40, crossed the Euphrates in force, defeated the Romans under Decidius Saxa, and carried fire and sword over the whole of the Syrian presidency.14473 Having taken Apamea and Antioch, he marched into Phoenicia, ravaged the open country, and compelled all the towns, except Tyre, to surrender. Tyre, notwithstanding the mole constructed by Alexander, which joined it to the continent, was still regarded as impregnable, unless invested both by sea and land; on which account Pacorus, as he had no naval force, relinquished the idea of capturing it.14474 But all the other cities either gave themselves up or were taken, and the conquest of Phoenicia being completed, the Parthian prince proceeded to occupy Palestine. Jerusalem fell into his hands, and for three years the entire tract between the Taurus range and Egypt was lost to Rome, and formed a portion of the Parthian Empire. What hardships, what insults, what outrages the Phoenicians had to endure during this interval we do not know, and can only conjecture; but the conduct of the Parthians at Jerusalem14475 makes it probable that the inhabitants of the conquered districts generally had much cause for complaint. However, the time of endurance did not last very long; in the third year from the commencement of the invasion the fortune of war turned against the assailants. Rome, under Ventidius, recovered her lost laurels. Syria was reoccupied, and the Parthians driven across the Euphrates, never again to pass it.14476

In the struggle (which soon followed these events) between Antony and Augustus, Phoenicia had the misfortune to give offence to the latter. The terms on which they stood with Antony, and the protection which he had afforded to their cities against the greed of Cleopatra, naturally led them to embrace his cause; and it should scarcely have been regarded as a crime in them that they did so with ardour. But Augustus, who was certainly not clement by nature, chose to profess himself deeply aggrieved by the preference which they had shown for his rival, and, when he personally visited the East in B.C. 20, inflicted a severe punishment on two at least of the cities. Dio Cassius can scarcely be mistaken when he says that Tyre and Sidon were "enslaved"—i.e. deprived of freedom—by Augustus,14477 who must certainly have revoked the privilege originally granted by Pompey. Whether the privilege was afterwards restored is somewhat uncertain; but there is distinct evidence that more than one of the later emperors was favourably disposed to Rome's Phoenician subjects. Claudius granted to Accho the title and status of a Roman colony;14478 while Hadrian allowed Tyre to call herself a "metropolis."14479

Two important events have caused Tyre and Sidon to be mentioned in the New Testament. Jesus Christ, in the second year of his ministry, "arose and went" from Galilee "into the borders of Tyre and Sidon," and there wrought a miracle at the earnest request of a "Syro-Phoenician woman."14480 And Herod Agrippa, the grandson of Herod the Great, when at Cæsarea in A.D. 44, received an embassy from "them of Tyre and Sidon," with whom he was highly offended, and "made an oration" to the ambassadors.14481 In this latter place the continued semi-independence of Tyre and Sidon seems to be implied. Agrippa is threatening them with war, while they "desire peace." "Their country" is spoken of as if it were distinct from all other countries. We cannot suppose that the Judæan prince would have ventured to take up this attitude if the Phoenician cities had been fully incorporated into the Roman State, since in that case quarrelling with them would have been quarrelling with Rome, a step on which even Agrippa, with all his pride and all his rashness, would scarcely have ventured. It is probable, therefore, that either Tiberius or Claudius had revoked the decree of Augustus, and re-invested the Phoenician cities with the privilege whereof the first of the emperors had deprived them.

Not long after this, about A.D. 57, we have evidence that the great religious and social movement of the age had swept the Phoenician cities within its vortex, and that, in some of them at any rate, Christian communities had been formed, which were not ashamed openly to profess the new religion. The Gospel was preached in Phoenicia14482 as early as A.D. 41. Sixteen years later, when St. Paul, on his return from his third missionary journey, landed at Tyre, and proceeded thence to Ptolemaïs, he found at both places "churches," or congregations of Christians, who received him kindly, ministered to his wants, prayed with him, and showed a warm interest in his welfare.14483 These communities afterwards expanded. By the end of the second century after Christ Tyre was the seat of a bishopric, which held an important place among the Syrian Sees. Several Tyrian bishops of the second, third, and fourth centuries are known to us, as Cassius (ab. A.D. 198), Marinus (A.D. 253), Methodius (A.D. 267-305), Tyrannion (A.D. 310), and Paulinus (A.D. 328). Early in the fourth century (B.C. 335) Tyre was the seat of a synod or council, called to consider charges made against the great Athanasius,14484 who was taxed with cruelty, impiety, and the use of magical arts. As the bishops who assembled belonged chiefly to the party of Arius, the judgment of the council condemned Athanasius, and deprived him of his see. On appeal the decision was reversed; Athanasius was reinstated,14485 and advanced; the cause with which he had identified himself triumphed; and the Synod of Tyre being pronounced unorthodox, the Tyrian church, like that of Antioch, sank in the estimation of the Church at large.

Tyre also made herself obnoxious to the Christian world in another way. In the middle of the third century she produced the celebrated philosopher, Porphyry,14486 who, of all the literary opponents of Christianity, was the most vigorous and the most successful. Porphyry appears to have been a Phoenician by descent. His original name was Malchus—i.e. Melek or Malik, "king." To disguise his Asiatic origin, and ingratiate himself with the literary class of the day, who were chiefly Greeks or Grecised Romans, he took the Hellenic and far more sonorous appellation of Porphyrius, which he regarded as a sort of synonym, since purple was the royal colour. He early gave himself to the study of philosophy, and was indefatigable in his efforts to acquire knowledge and learning of every kind. In Asia, probably at Tyre itself, he attended the lectures of Origen; at Athens he studied under Apollonius and Longinus; in Rome, whereto he ultimately gravitated, he attached himself to the Neo-Platonic school of Plotinus. His literary labours, which were enormous, had for their general object the establishment of that eclectic system which Ammonius Saccas, Plotinus, Jamblichus, and others had elaborated, and were endeavouring to impose upon the world as constituting at once true religion and true philosophy. He was of a constructive rather than a destructive turn of mind. Still, he thought it of great importance, and a necessity of the times, that he should write a book against the Christians, whose opinions were, he knew, making such progress as raised the suspicion that they would prevail over all others, and in a short time become universal. This polemical treatise ran to fifteen books, and "exhibited considerable acquaintance with both the Jewish and the Christian scriptures."14487 It is now lost, but its general character is well known from the works of Eusebius, Jerome, and others. The style was caustic and trenchant. An endeavour was made to show that both the historical scriptures of the Old Testament and the Gospels and Acts in the New were full of discrepancies and contradictions. The history and antiquities of the Jews, as put forth in the Bible, were examined, and declared to be unworthy of credit. A special attack was made on the genuineness and authenticity of the book of Daniel, which was pronounced to be the work of a contemporary of Antiochus Epiphanes, who succeeded in palming off upon his countrymen his own crude production as the work of the venerated sage and prophet. Prevalent modes of interpreting scripture were passed under review, and the allegorical exegesis of Origen was handled with especial severity. The work is said to have produced a vast effect, especially among the upper classes, whose conversion to Christianity it tended greatly to check and hinder. Answers to the book, or to particular portions of it, were published by Eusebius of Cæsarea, by Apollinaris, and by Methodius, Bishop of Tyre; but these writers had neither the learning nor the genius of their opponent, and did little to counteract the influence of his work on the upper grades of society.14488

The literary importance of the Phoenician cities under the Romans is altogether remarkable.

Under Augustus and Tiberius—especially from about B.C. 40 to A.D. 20—Sidon was the seat of a philosophical school, in which the works of Aristotle were studied and explained,14489 perhaps to some extent criticised.14490 Strabo attended this school for a time in conjunction with two other students, named Boëthus and Diodotus. Tyre had even previously produced the philosophers, Antipater, who was intimate with the younger Cato, and Apollonius, who wrote a work about Zeno, and formed a descriptive catalogue of the authors who had composed books on the subject of the philosophy of the Stoics.14491 Strabo goes so far as to say that philosophy in all its various aspects might in his day be better studied at Tyre and Sidon than anywhere else.14492 A little later we find Byblus producing the semi-religious historian, Philo, who professed to reveal to the Greeks the secrets of the ancient Phoenician mythology, and who, whatever we may think of his judgment, was certainly a man of considerable learning. He was followed by his pupil, Hermippus, who was contemporary with Trajan and Hadrian, and obtained some reputation as a critic and grammarian.14493 About the same time flourished Marinus, the writer on geography, who was a Tyrian by birth, and "the first author who substituted maps, mathematically constructed according to latitude and longitude, for the itinerary charts" of his predecessors.14494 Ptolemy of Pelusium based his great work entirely upon that of Marinus, who is believed to have utilised the geographical and hydrographical accumulations of the old Phoenician navigators, besides availing himself of the observations of Hipparchus, and of the accounts given of their travels by various Greek and Roman authors. Contemporary with Marinus was Paulus, a native of Tyre, who was noted as a rhetorician, and deputed by his city to go as their representative to Rome and plead the cause of the Tyrians before Hadrian.14495 A little later we hear of Maximus, who flourished under Marcus Aurelius and Commodus (ab. A.D. 160-190), a Tyrian, like Paulus, and a rhetorician and Platonic philosopher.14496 The literary glories of Tyre culminated and terminated with Porphyry, of whose works we have already given an account.

Towards the middle of the third century after Christ a school of law and jurisprudence arose at Berytus, which attained high distinction, and is said by Gibbon14497 to have furnished the eastern provinces of the empire with pleaders and magistrates for the space of three centuries (A.D. 250-550). The course of education at Berytus lasted five years, and included Roman Law in all its various forms, the works of Papinian being especially studied in the earlier times, and the same together with the edicts of Justinian in the later.14498 Pleaders were forced to study either at Berytus, or at Rome, or at Constantinople,14499 and, the honours and emoluments of the profession being large, the supply of students was abundant and perpetual. External misfortune, and not internal decay, at last destroyed the school, the town of Berytus being completely demolished by an earthquake in the year A.D. 551. The school was then transferred to Sidon, but appears to have languished on its transplantation to a new soil and never to have recovered its pristine vigour or vitality.

It is difficult to decide how far these literary glories of the Phoenician cities reflect any credit on the Phoenician race. Such a number of Greeks settled in Syria and Phoenicia under the Seleucidæ that to be a Tyrian or a Sidonian in the Græco-Roman period furnished no evidence at all of a man having any Phoenician blood in his veins. It will have been observed that the names of the Tyrian, Sidonian, and Berytian learned men and authors of the time—Antipater, Apollonius, Boëthus, Diodotus, Philo, Hermippus, Marinus, Paulus, Maximus, Porphyrius— are without exception either Latin or Greek. The language in which the books were written was universally Greek, and in only one or two cases is there reason to suppose that the authors had any knowledge of the Phoenician tongue. The students at Berytus between A.D. 250 and 550 were probably, in ninety-nine cases out of a hundred, Greeks or Romans. Phoenician nationality had, in fact, almost wholly disappeared in the Seleucid period. The old language ceased to be spoken, and though for some time retained upon the coins together with a Greek legend,14500 became less frequent as time went on, and soon after the Christian era disappeared altogether. It is probable that, as a spoken language, Phoenician had gone out of use even earlier.14501

In two respects only did the old national spirit survive, and give indication that, even in the nation's "ashes," there still lived some remnant of its "wonted fires." Tyre and Sidon were great commercial centres down to the time of the Crusades, and quite as rich, quite as important, quite as flourishing, commercially, as in the old days of Hiram and Ithobal. Mela14502 speaks of Sidon in the second century after Christ as "still opulent." Ulpian,14503 himself a Tyrian by descent, calls Tyre in the reign of Septimus Severus "a most splendid colony." A writer of the age of Constantine says of it: "The prosperity of Tyre is extraordinary. There is no state in the whole of the East which excels it in the amount of its business. Its merchants are persons of great wealth, and there is no port where they do not exercise considerable influence."14504 St. Jerome, towards the end of the fourth century, speaks of Tyre as "the noblest and most beautiful of all the cities of Phoenicia,"14505 and as "an emporium for the commerce of almost the whole world."14506 During the period of the Crusades, "Tyre retained its ancient pre-eminence among the cities of the Syrian coast, and excited the admiration of the warriors of Europe by its capacious harbours, its wall, triple towards the land and double towards the sea, its still active commerce, and the beauty and fertility of the opposite shore." The manufactures of purple and of glass were still carried on. Tyre was not reduced to insignificance until the Saracenic conquest towards the close of the thirteenth century of our era, when its trade collapsed, and it became "a rock for fishermen to spread their nets upon."14507

The other respect in which the vitality of the old national spirit displayed itself was in the continuance of the ancient religion. While Christianity was adopted very generally by the more civilised of the inhabitants, and especially by those who occupied the towns, there were shrines and fanes in the remote districts, and particularly in the less accessible parts of Lebanon, where the old rites were still in force, and the old orgies continued to be carried on, just as in ancient times, down to the reign of Constantine. The account of the licentious worship of Ashtoreth at Aphaca, which has been already quoted from Eusebius, belongs to the fourth century after our era, and shows the tenacity with which a section of the Phoenicians, not withstanding their Hellenisation in language, in literature, and in art, clung to the old barbarous and awful cult, which had come down to them by tradition from their fathers. A similar worship at the same time maintained itself on the other side of the Lebanon chain in Heliopolis, or Baalbek, where the votaries of impurity allowed their female relatives, even their wives and their daughters, to play the harlot as much as they pleased.14508 Constantine exerted himself to put down and crush out these iniquities, but it is more than probable that, in the secret recesses of the mountain region, whither government officials would find it hard to penetrate, the shameful and degrading rites still found a refuge, rooted as they were in the depraved affections of the common people, to a much later period.

The mission of the Phoenicians, as a people, was accomplished before the subjection to Rome began. Under the Romans they were still ingenious, industrious, intelligent. But in the earlier times they were far more than this. They were the great pioneers of civilisation. Intrepid, inventive, enterprising, they at once made vast progress in the arts themselves, and carried their knowledge, their active habits, and their commercial instincts into the remotest regions of the old continent. They exercised a stimulating, refining, and civilising influence wherever they went. North and south and east and west they adventured themselves amid perils of all kinds, actuated by the love of adventure more than by the thirst for gain, conferring benefits, spreading knowledge, suggesting, encouraging, and developing trade, turning men from the barbarous and unprofitable pursuits of war and bloodshed to the peaceful occupations of productive industry. They did not aim at conquest. They united the various races of men by the friendly links of mutual advantage and mutual dependence, conciliated them, softened them, humanised them. While, among the nations of the earth generally, brute force was worshipped as the true source of power and the only basis of national repute, the Phoenicians succeeded in proving that as much could be done by arts as by arms, as great glory and reputation gained, as real a power built up, by the quiet agencies of exploration, trade, and commerce, as by the violent and brutal methods of war, massacre, and ravage. They were the first to set this example. If the history of the world since their time has not been wholly one of the potency in human affairs of "blood and iron," it is very much owing to them. They, and their kinsmen of Carthage, showed mankind what a power might be wielded by commercial states. The lesson has not been altogether neglected in the past. May the writer be pardoned if, in the last words of what is probably his last historical work, he expresses a hope that, in the future, the nations of the earth will more and more take the lesson to heart, and vie with each other in the arts which made Phoenicia great, rather than in those which exalted Rome, her oppressor and destroyer?

FOOTNOTES

PREFACE

01
[Die Phönizier, und das phönizische Alterthum, by F. C. Movers, in five volumes, Berlin, 1841-1856.]
02
[History and Antiquities of Phoenicia, by John Kenrick, London, 1855.]
03
[Histoire de l'Art dans l'Antiquité, par MM. Perrot et Chipiez, Paris, 1881-7, 4 vols.]
04
[Will of William Camden, Clarencieux King-of-Arms, founder of the "Camden Professorship," 1662.]
I—THE LAND
11
[See Eckhel, Doctr. Num. Vet. p. 441.]
12
[{'H ton 'Aradion paralia}, xvi. 2, § 12.]
13
[Pomp. Mel. De Situ Orbis, i. 12.]
14
[The tract of white sand (Er-Ramleh) which forms the coast-line of the entire shore from Rhinocolura to Carmel is said to be gradually encroaching, fresh sand being continually brought by the south-west wind from Egypt. "It has buried Ascalon, and in the north, between Joppa and Cæsaræa, the dunes are said to be as much as three miles wide and 300 feet high" (Grove, in Smith's Dict. of the Bible, ii. 673).]
15
[See Cant. ii. 1; Is. xxxiii. 9; xxxv. 2; lxv. 10.]
16
[Stanley, Sinai and Palestine, p. 254.]
17
[The Kaneh derives its name from this circumstance, and may be called "the River of Canes."]
18
[Robinson, Biblical Researches, iii. 28, 29.]

19

[Grove, l.s.c.]

110

[Stanley, Sinai and Palestine, p. 260.]

111

[Lynch found it eighteen yards in width in April 1848 (The Jordan and the Dead Sea, p. 64). He found the Belus twice as wide and twice as deep as the Kishon.]

112

[A more particular description of these fountains will be given in the description of the city of Tyre, with which they were very closely connected.]

113

[Robinson, Biblical Researches, iii. 410.]

114

[Robinson, iii. 415.]

115

[Ibid. p. 414. Compare Renan, Mission de Phénicie, pp. 524, 665.]

116

[Robinson, iii. 420.]

117

[Renan, Mission de Phénicie, p. 353.]

118

[See Edrisi (traduction de Joubert), i. 355; D'Arvieux, Mémoires, ii. 33; Renan, pp. 352, 353.]

119

[Gesenius, Thesaurus, p. 247.]

120

[Renan, pp. 59, 60.]

121

[Kenrick (Phoenicia, p. 8), who quotes Burckhardt (Syria, p. 161), and Chesney (Euphrates Expedition, i. 450).]

122

[Renan, p. 59:—"C'est un immense tapis de fleurs."]

123

[Mariti, Travels, ii. 131 (quoted by Kenrick, p. 22).]

124

[Strabo, xvi. 2, § 27.]

125

[Stanley, Sinai and Palestine, p. 344.]

126

[Martineau, Eastern Life, p. 539.]

127

[Van de Velde, Travels, i. 317, 318. Compare Porter, Giant Cities of Bashan, p. 236.]

128

[Ritter, Erdkunde, xvi. 31.]

129

[Grove, in Smith's Dictionary of the Bible, i. 278.]

130

[Walpole's Ansayrii, iii. 156.]

131

[The derivation of Lebanon from "white," is generally admitted. (see Gesenius, Thesaurus, p. 369; Buxtorf, Lexicon, p. 1119; Fürst, Concordantia, p. 588.)]

132

[Stanley, Sinai and Palestine, p. 395.]

133

[Tristram, The Land of Israel, p. 634.]

134

[Ibid. p. 7.]

135

[Porter, in Smith's Dictionary of the Bible, ii. 86.]

136

[Ibid. Compare Nat. Hist. Review, No. v. p. 11.]

137

[See Tristram, Land of Israel, pp. 625-629.]

138

[See Tristram, Land of Israel, p. 626.]

139

[Porter, in Dictionary of the Bible, ii. 86.]

140

[Tristram, Land of Israel, p. 621.]

141

[Ibid. p. 600. Compare Porter, in Smith's Dictionary of the Bible, ii. 87.]

142

[Such outlets are common in Greece, where they are called Katavothra. They probably also occur in Asia Minor.]

143

[Burckhardt, Travels in Syria, p. 10; Chesney, Euphrates Expedition, i. 398.]

144

[Tristram, p. 600.]

145

[Porter, Handbook for Syria, p. 571; Robinson, Later Researches, p. 423.]

146

[Tristram, p. 594.]

147

[Robinson, Biblical Researches, iii. 409.]

148

[Burckhardt, Travels in Syria, p. 161; Chesney, Euphrates Expedition, i. 450; Walpole's Ansayrii, iii. 49.]

149

[Renan, Mission de Phénicie, p. 116.]

150

[Porter, Giant Cities of Bashan, p. 289.]

151

[Ibid. p. 288.]

152

[Walpole's Ansayrii, iii. 44.]

153

[Porter, Giant Cities, p. 292; Robinson, Later Researches, p. 605; Renan, Mission de Phénicie, p. 297.]

154

[Maundrell, Travels, pp. 57, 58; Porter, Giant Cities, p. 284; Renan, Mission de Phénicie, p. 283.]

155

[Porter, p. 283.]

156

[Porter, p. 284.]

157

[Robinson, Later Researches, p. 45.]

158

[Ibid. p. 43.]

159

[Tristram, Land of Israel, p. 44.]

160

[Kenrick, Phoenicia, p. 20.]

161

[See the Transactions of the Society of Bibl. Archæology, vol. vii.; and compare Kenrick, Phoenicia, p. 14; Robinson, Later Researches, pp. 617-624.]

162

[Walpole's Ansayrii, iii. 6.]

163

[Ibid. p. 34. Compare Renan, Mission de Phénicie, who calls the pass over the spur "un véritable casse-cou sur des roches inclinées" (p. 150).]

164

[Kenrick, Phoenicia, p. 16.]

165

[Robinson, Biblical Researches, iii. 432.]

II—CLIMATE AND PRODUCTIONS

21

[Kenrick, Phoenicia, p. 32.]

22

[Grove, in Smith's Dict. of the Bible, ii. 693.]

23

[Kenrick, l.s.c.]

24

[See Canon Tristram's experiences, Land of Israel, pp. 96-115.]

25

[Ibid. pp. 94, 95.]

26

[Kenrick, p. 34.]

27

[Walpole's Ansayrii, p. 76.]

28

[Kenrick, p. 33.]

29

[Tristram, Land of Israel, p. 95.]

210

[Ibid. p. 409.]

211

[Ibid. p. 31.]

212

[Ibid. p. 34.]

213

[Ibid. p. 596.]

214

[Hooker, in Dictionary of the Bible, ii. 684.]

215

[Hooker, in Dictionary of the Bible, p. 683.]

216

[Dr. Hooker says:—"Q. pseudococcifera is perhaps the commonest plant in all Syria and Palestine, covering as a low dense bush many square miles of hilly country everywhere, but rarely or never growing on the plains. It seldom becomes a large tree, except in the valleys of the Lebanon." Walpole found it on Bargylus (Ansayrii, iii. 137 et sqq.); Tristram on Lebanon, Land of Israel, pp. 113, 117.]
217
[Hooker, in Dict. of the Bible, ii. 684. Compare Tristram, Land of Israel, p. 113.]
218
[Ibid.]
219
[See Walpole, Ansayrii, iii. 222, 236; Tristram, Land of Israel, pp. 622, 623; Robinson, Later Researches, p. 607.]
220
[Walpole, iii. 433; Robinson, Later Researches, p.. 614.]
221
[Tristram, Land of Israel, p. 6.]
222
[Ibid. p. 111; Walpole, Ansayrii, iii. 166; Hooker, in Dict. of the Bible, ii. 683.]
223
[Walpole says that Ibrahim Pasha cut down as many as 500,000 Aleppo pines in Casius (Ansayrii, iii. 281), and that it would be quite feasible to cut down 500,000 more.]
224
[Hooker, in Dict. of the Bible, ii. 684; and compare Tristram, Land of Israel, pp. 16, 88.]
225
[Robinson, Biblical Researches, iii. 383, 415.]
226
[Ezek. xxxi. 3.]
227
[Ibid. xxvii. 5. The Hebrew erez probably covered other trees besides the actual cedar, as the Aleppo pine, and perhaps the juniper. The pine would have been more suited for masts than the cedar.]
228
[1 Kings vi. 9, 10, 15, 18, &c.; vii. 1-7.]
229
[Records of the Past, i. 104. ll. 78, 79; iii. 74, ll. 88-90; p. 90, l. 9; &c. Compare Layard, Nineveh and Babylon, pp. 356, 357.]
230
[Joseph, Bell. Jud., v. 5, § 2.]
231
[Plin. H. N., xiii. 5; xvi. 40.]
232
[Compare the arguments of Canon Tristram, Land of Israel, pp. 631, 632.]
233
[Walpole, Ansayrii, pp. 123, 227.]
234
[Tristram, Land of Israel, p. 621.]
235
[Ibid. pp. 13, 38, &c.]
236
[Hooker, in Dictionary of the Bible, ii. 684.]
237
[Tristram, Land of Israel, p. 82; compare Hooker, l.s.c.]

238

[This is Dr. Hooker's description. Canon Tristram says of the styrax at the eastern foot of Carmel, that "of all the flowering shrubs it is the most abundant," and that it presents to the eye "one sheet of pure white blossom, rivalling the orange in its beauty and its perfume" (Land of Israel, p. 492).]

239

[Ibid. p. 596.]

240

[Walpole, Ansayrii, iii. 298.]

241

[Tristram, pp. 16, 28, &c.; Robinson, Biblical Researches, iii. 438.]

242

[The "terraced vineyards of Esfia" on Carmel are noted by Canon Tristram (Land of Israel, p. 492). Walpole speaks of vineyards on Bargylus (Ansayrii, iii. 165). The vine-clad slopes of the Lebanon attract notice from all Eastern travellers.]

243

[Quoted by Dr. Hooker, in Smith's Dictionary of the Bible, ii. 684, 685.]

244

[Deut. xxxiii. 24.]

245

[Tristram, Land of Israel, pp. 7, 16, 17; Walpole, Ansayrii, iii. 147, 177.]

246

[Tristram, p. 492; Stanley, Sinai and Palestine, p. 347.]

247

[Hooker, in Smith's Dictionary of the Bible, ii. 685.]

248

[Tristram, pp. 622, 633; Walpole, Ansayrii, iii. 446; Robinson, Later Researches, p. 607.]

249

[Tristram, pp. 17, 38; Walpole, Ansayrii, iii. 32, 294, 373.]

250

[Robinson, Bibl. Researches, iii. 419, 431, 438, &c.]

251

[Tristram, Land of Israel, p. 28.]

252

[Hasselquist, Reise, p. 188.]

253

[Ansayrii, i. 66.]

254

[Tristram, l.s.c.]

255

[Hooker, in Dictionary of the Bible, ii. 685.]

256

[Reise, l.s.c.]

257

[Mémoires, i. 332.]

258

[Tristram, Land of Israel, p. 493.]

259

[Tristram, Land of Israel, p. 82.]

260

[Renan, Mission de Phénicie, p. 59; Hooker, in Dictionary of the Bible, ii. 687; Tristram, Land of Israel, p. 493.]

261
[Tristram, Land of Israel, l.s.c.]
262
[Ibid. p. 82.]
263
[Ibid. p. 596. Compare Walpole's Ansayrii, iii. 443.]
264
[Tristram, Land of Israel, p. 102.]
265
[Tristram, Land of Israel, pp. 61, 599.]
266
[Ibid. pp. 38, 626, &c. Dr. Robinson notices the cultivation of the potato high up in Lebanon; but he observed it only in two places (Later Researches, pp. 586, 596).]
267
[It can scarcely be doubted that Phoenicia contained anciently two other land animals of considerable importance, viz. the lion and the deer. Lions, which were common in the hills of Palestine (1 Sam. xvii. 34; 1 Kings xiii. 24; xx. 36; 2 Kings xvii. 25, 26) and frequented also the Philistine plain (Judg. xiv. 5), would certainly not have neglected the lowland of Sharon, which was in all respects suited for their habits. Deer, which still inhabit Galilee (Tristram, Land of the Israel, pp. 418, 447), are likely, before the forests of Lebanon were so greatly curtailed, to have occupied most portions of it (See Cant. ii. 9, 17; viii. 14). To these two Canon Tristram would add the crocodile (Land of Israel, p. 103), which he thinks must have been found in the Zerka for that river to have been called "the Crocodile River" by the Greeks, and which he is inclined to regard as still a denizen of the Zerka marshes. But most critics have supposed that the animal from which the Zerka got its ancient name was rather some large species of monitor.]
268
[Kenrick, Phoenicia, p. 36.]
269
[See his article on Lebanon in Smith's Dictionary of the Bible, ii. 87.]
270
[Land of Israel, p. 447.]
271
[Houghton, in Smith's Dict. of the Bible, ad voc. BEAR, iii. xxv.]
272
[Dict. of the Bible, ii. 87.]
273
[Land of Israel, p. 116. Compare Porter's Giant Cities of Bashan, p. 236.]
274
[Cant. iv. 8; Is. xi. 6; Jer. v. 6; xiii. 23; Hos. xiii. 7; Hab. i. 8.]
275
[Land of Israel, l.s.c.]
276
[Ibid. p. 83.]
277
[Ibid. p. 115.]
278
[Walpole's Ansayrii, iii. 23.]
279
[Houghton, in Smith's Dict. of the Bible, ad voc. CONEY (iii. xliii.); Tristram, Land of Israel, pp. 62, 84, 89.]
280

[Tristram, Land of Israel, p. 106.]
281
[Ibid. pp. 88, 89.]
282
[Tristram, Land of Israel, p. 83.]
283
[Ibid. p. 55.]
284
[Ibid. p. 103. Compare Walpole, Ansayrii, iii. 34, 188, and Lortet, La Syrie d'aujourd'hui, pp. 58, 61.]
285
[Hist. Nat. ix. 36.]
286
[Kenrick, Phoenicia, p. 239. There are representations of the Buccunum in Forbes and Hanley's British Mollusks, vol. iv. pl. cii. Nos. 1, 2, 3.]
287
[Kenrick, p. 239.]
288
[Tristram, Land of Israel, p. 51.]
289
[Wilksinson, in Rawlinson's Herodotus, ii. 347, note 2.]
290
[Canon Tristram writs: "Among the rubbish thrown out in the excavations made at Tyre were numerous fragments of glass, and whole 'kitchen middens' of shells, crushed and broken, the owners of which had once supplied the famous Tyrian purple dye. All these shells were of one species, the Murex brandaris" (Land of Israel, p. 51).]
291
[Porter, in Dict. of the Bible, ii. 87.]
292
[Kenrick, Phoenicia, p. 37.]
293
[Tristram, p. 634.]
294
[Grove, in Dict. of the Bible, i. 279.]

III—THE PEOPLE—ORIGIN AND CHARACTERISTICS

31
[Histoire des Languages Sémitiques, p. 22.]
32
[Rhet. iii. 8.]
33
[Deutsch, Literary Remains, p. 160.]
34
[Renan, Hist. des Langues Sémitiques, pp. 5, 14.]
35
[Ibid. p. 16.]
36
[Deutsch, Literary Remains, p. 305.]
37
[Ibid.]
38
[Ancient Monarchies, i. 275; Deutsch, p. 306.]
39

[Herod. i. 2; vii. 89.]
310
[Strab. xvi. 3, § 4.]
311
[Hist. Philipp. xviii. 3, § 2.]
312
[Ancient Monarchies, i. 14.]
313
[Renan, Histoire des Langues Sémitiques, p. 183.]
314
[Deutsch, Literary Remains, pp. 162, 163.]
315
[Herod. vi. 47:—{'Oros mega anestrammenon en te zetesei}.]
316
[On this imaginary "monsters," see Herod. vi. 44.]
317
[Ibid. iv. 42.]
318
[Herod. vii. 85.]
319
[Ibid. ii. 112.]
320
[1 Kings xi. 1.]
321
[Ibid. xvi. 31.]
322
[Ezra iii. 7.]
323
[Is. xxiii. 15-18.]
324
[Mark vii. 26-30.]
325
[Acts xii. 20.]
326
[Herod. iv. 196.]
327
[Herod, i. 1:—{Perseon oi Lagioi}.]
328
[Ibid. ii. 190.]
329
[Ibid. ii. 4, 99, 142.]
330
[Ibid. i. 1; iv. 42; vi. 47; vii. 23, 44, 96.]
331
[As they do of being indebted to the Babylonians and the Egyptians for astronomical and philosophic knowledge.]
332
[Deutsch, Literary Remains, p. 163.]
333
[Ibid.]
334
[Compare the representation of Egyptian ships in Dümichen's Voyage d'une Reine Egyptienne

(date about B.C. 1400) with the far later Phoenician triremes depicted by Sennacherib (Layard, Monuments of Nineveh, second series, pl. 71).]

335

[Renan, Mission de Phénicie, pp. 100, 101.]

336

[The Cypriot physiognomy is peculiar. (See Di Cesnola's Cyprus, pp. 123, 129, 131, 132, 133, 141, &c.)]

337

[Herod. vii. 90.]

338

[Kenrick, Phoenicia, p. 68, note 3.]

IV—THE CITIES

41

[The nearest approach to such a period is the time a little preceding Nebuchadnezzar's siege, when Sidon, Byblus, and Aradus all appear as subject to Tyre (Ezek. xxvii. 8-11).]

42

[1 Kings xvii. 9-24.]

43

[1 Macc. xv. 37.]

44

[Gen. x. 15.]

45

[Josh. xix. 29.]

46

[Ibid. verse 28.]

47

[See Hom. Il. vii. 290; xxiii. 743; Od. iv. 618; xiv. 272, 285; xvi. 117, 402, 424.]

48

[Hist. Philipp. xviii. 3, § 2.]

49

[Kenrick, Phoenicia, p. 460.]

410

[Steph, Byz. ad voc.]

411

[Renan, Mission de Phénicie, pl. lxvii.]

412

[Scylax, Periplus, § 104. This work belongs to the time of Philip, Alexander's father.]

413

[See Renan, Mission de Phénicie, pl. lxii.]

414

[The inscription on the sarcophagus of Esmunazar. (See Records of the Past, ix. 111-114, and the Corp. Inscr. Semit., i. 13-20.)]

415

[The name "Palæ-Tyrus" is first found in Strabo (xvi. 2, § 24).]

416

[Kenrick, Phoenicia, p. 347.]

417

[Plin. H. N. v. 17.]

418

[Renan (Mission de Phénicie, p. 552) gives the area as 576,508 square metres.]

419

[Arrian, Exp. Alex. ii. 21.]

420

[Renan, Mission de Phénicie, p. 560.]

421

[So Bertou (Topographie de Tyr, p. 14), and Kenrick (Phoenicia, p. 352).]

422

[Renan, Mission de Phénicie, p. 560.]

423

[Kenrick, Phoenicia, p. 351.]

424

[See the fragments of Dius and Menander, preserved by Josephus (Contr. Ap. i. § 17, 18), and compare Arrian, Exp. Alex. ii. 24. It is quite uncertain what Phoenician deity is represented by "Agenor."]

425

[Renan, Mission de Phénicie, p. 559.]

426

[Ibid.]

427

[Ibid.]

428

[Strab. xvi. 2, § 23.]

429

[Menand, ap. Joseph. l.s.c.]

430

[Strab. l.s.c.]

431

[Eight thousand are said to have been killed in the siege, and 30,000 sold when the place was taken. (Arrian, Exp. Alex. l.s.c.) A certain number were spared.]

432

[Renan, Mission de Phénicie, p. 552.]

433

[Plin. H. N. v. 17.]

434

[Kenrick, Phoenicia, p. 348.]

435

[Renan, Mission de Phénicie, p. 22.]

436

[See Capt. Allen's Dead Sea, ii. 179.]

437

[See Capt. Allen's Dead Sea, ii. 179.]

438

[Strabo, xvi. 2, § 13.]

439

[Allen, Dead Sea, l.s.c.]

440

[Ibid. p. 180.]

441

[See the woodcut, and compare Renan, Mission de Phénicie, planches, pl. ii.; and Perrot et Chipiez, Histoire de l'Art dans l'Antiquité, iii. 25.]

442

[Allen, Dead Sea, ii. 180.]

443

[Ibid.]

444

[Strab. xvi. 2, § 13.]

445

[Strab. xvi. 2, § 13. See also Lucret. De Rer. Nat. vi. 890.]

446

[Renan, Mission de Phénicie, p. 42.]

447

[Strab. xvi. 2, § 12.]

448

[Fr. ii. 7. Philo, however, makes "Brathu" a mountain.]

449

[See Records of the Past, iii. 19, 20.]

450

[Mission de Phénicie, pp. 58-61.]

451

[Strab. l.s.c.]

452

[Ibid.]

453

[Gen. x. 18.]

454

[Eponym Canon, p. 123, 1. 2.]

455

[Renan, Mission de Phénicie, p. 115. And compare the map.]

456

[Carnus is identified by M. Renan with the modern Carnoun, on the coast, three miles north of Tortosa (Mission, p. 97).]

457

[Eponym Canon, p. 114, l. 104.]

458

[Josh. xiii. 5; 1 Kings v. 18.]

459

[Arr. Exp. Alex. ii. 15.]

460

[Strab. xvi. 2, § 18.]

461

[Fragm. ii. 8, § 17.]

462

[Corp. Inscr. Sem., i. 3 (pl 1); Philo-Bybl. Fr. ii. 8, § 25.]

463

[Strab. l.s.c.]

464

[Allen, Dead Sea, ii. 164.]

465

[Ibid.]

466

[Strab. xvi. 2, § 15.]

467

[See G. Smith's Eponym Canon, pp. 123, 132, 148.]

468

[Kenrick, Phoenicia, p. 9.]

469

[Burckhardt, Travels in Syria, p. 162.]
470
[Scylax, Peripl., § 104; Diod. Sic. xvi. 41; Pomp. Mel. i. 12.]
471
[Tristram, Land of Israel, p. 633; Perrot et Chipiez, Histoire de l'Art dans l'Antiquité, iii. 56.]
472
[Perrot et Chipiez, iii. 57, 59.]
473
[Allen, Dead Sea, ii. 152.]
474
[Renan, Mission de Phénicie, p. 295.]
475
[Lucian, De Dea Syra, § 9.]
476
[Philo. Bybl. Fr. ii. 8, § 25.]
477
[Stephen of Byzantium calls it {polin thoinikes ek mikrae megalen}. Strabo says that it was rebuilt by the Romans (xvi. 2, § 19).]
478
[Phocas, Descr. Urbium, § 5.]
479
[Cellarius, Geograph. ii. 378.]
480
[Gen. x. 17.]
481
[Eponym Canon, pp. 120, l. 25; 123, l. 2.]
482
[Josh. xix. 29.]
483
[Eponym Canon, p. 132, l. 10.]
484
[Eponym Canon, p. 132, l. 10; 148, l. 103.]
485
[Kenrick, Phoenicia, pp. 20, 21.]
486
[This seems to be the true meaning of Strab. xvi. 2, § 25; sub init.]
487
[Josh. vii. 23.]
488
[Ibid. xvii. 11.]
489
[1 Kings iv. 11.]
490
[Ancient Monarchies, ii. 132.]
491
[Steph. Byz. ad voc. DORA.]
492
[Hieronym. Epit. Paulæ (Opp. i. 223).]
493
[Josh. xix. 47.]
494
[1 Macc. x. 76.]

495
[Jonah i. 3.]
496
[2 Chron. ii. 16.]
497
[Ezra iii. 7.]
498
[See Capt. Allen's Dead Sea, ii. 188.]
499
[Eustah. ad Dionys. Perieg. l. 915.]
4100
[Compare the Heb. "Ramah" and "Ramoth" from {...}, "to be high."]
4101
[Kenrick, Phoenicia, p. 3.]
4102
[Gesenius, Monumenta Scripture Linguæque, Phoeniciæ, p. 271.]
4103
[Allen, Dead Sea, ii. 189.]
4104
[Perrot et Chipiez, Histoire de l'Art, iii. 23.]
4105
[Perrot and Chipiez, iii. 23-25.]
4106
[Perrot et Chipiez, Histoire de l'Art dans l'Antiquité, iii. 25, 26.]
4107
[The Phoenicians held Dor and Joppa during the greater part of their existence as a nation, but the tract between them, and that between Dor and Carmel—the plain of Sharon—shows no trace of their occupation.]

V—THE COLONIES

51
[Kenrick, Phoenicia, p. 71.]
52
[Gen. x. 4. Compare Joseph. Ant. Jud. i. 6.]
53
[Kenrick, p. 72.]
54
[The two plains are sometimes regarded as one, which is called that of Mesaoria; but they are really distinct, being separated by high ground in Long. 33° nearly.]
55
[Ælian, Hist. Ann. v. 56.]
56
[Strab. xiv. 6, § 5.]
57
[Theophrastus, Hist. Plant. v. 8.]
58
[Di Cesnola, Cyprus, Introduction, p. 7.]
59
[The copper of Cyprus became known as {khalkos Kuprios} or {Æs Cyprium}, then as cyprium or cyprum, finally as "copper," "kupfer," "cuivre," &c.]
510
[Ezek. xxvii. 6.]
511

[Compare Ammianus—"Tanta tamque multiplici fertilitate abundat rerum omnium Cyprus, ut, nullius externi indigens adminiculi, indigenis viribus a fundamento ipso carinæ ad supremos ipsos carbasos ædificet onerariam navem, omnibusque armamentis instructam mari committat" (xiv. 8, § 14).]
512
[Di Cesnola, Cyprus, p. 49.]
513
[Kenrick, Phoenicia, p. 75.]
514
[Di Cesnola, pp. 65-117.]
515
[Ibid. pp. 68, 83.]
516
[Perrot et Chipiez, Histoire de l'Art, iii. 215.]
517
[Ibid.]
518
[{Polis Kuprou arkhaiotate}.]
519
[Di Cesnola, Cyprus, p. 294.]
520
[Ibid. pp. 254-281.]
521
[Di Cesnola, Cyprus, p. 294.]
522
[Ibid. p. 378.]
523
[Strabo, xiv. 6, § 3; Steph. Byz. ad voc. CURIUM.]
524
[Herod. v. 113.]
525
[Apollodor. Biblioth. iii. 14, § 13.]
526
[Virg. Æn. i. 415-417; Tacit. Ann. iii. 62; Hist. ii. 2; Strab. xiv. 6, § 3.]
527
[Ps. lxxvi. 2.]
528
[Di Cesnola, Cyprus, p. 201.]
529
[Di Cesnola, Cyprus, p. 198, and Map.]
530
[Eponym Canon, p. 139, l. 23.]
531
[Ibid. p. 144, l. 22.]
532
[On the copper-mines of Tamasus, see Strab. xiv. 6, § 5; and Steph. Byz. ad voc.]
533
[Eponym Canon, ll.s.c.]
534
[Di Cesnola, Cyprus, p. 228.]
535
[Plut. Vit. Solon. § 26.]

536
[Diod. Sic. xiv. 98, § 2.]
537
[Di Cesnola, Cyprus, p. 231.]
538
[Kenrick, Phoenicia, p. 74.]
539
[Gen. x. 4.]
540
[Gesenius, Mon. Script. Linquæque Phoeniciæ, p. 278.]
541
[Strab. xiv. 5, § 3.]
542
[Ibid. xiv. 3, § 9. Mt. Solyma, now Takhtalu, is the most striking mountain of these parts. Its
bald summit rises to the height of 4,800 feet above the Mediterranean (Beaufort, Karamania,
p. 57).]
543
[Strab. xiv. 3, § 8, sub fin.]
544
[Beaufort, Karamania, p. 31.]
545
[Herod. iii. 90; vii. 77; Strab. xiii. 4, § 15; Steph. Byz. ad. voc.]
546
[Beaufort, Karamania, p. 56.]
547
[Strab. xiv. 3, § 9.]
548
[Beaufort, pp. 59, 60.]
549
[Ibid. p. 70.]
550
[As Corinna and Basilides (see Athen. Deipnos, iv. 174).]
551
[Ap. Phot. Bibliothec. p. 454.]
552
[Ap. Athen. Deipn. viii. 361.]
553
[Dict. Cret. i. 18; iv. 4.]
554
[Kenrick, Phoenicia, pp. 80, 81.]
555
[Aristid. Orat. § 43.]
556
[Acts xxvii. 12.]
557
[Steph. Byz. ad voc.]
558
[Herod. iv. 151.]
559
[Heb. {...}, Copt. labo, &c.]
560
[Steph. Byz. ad voc. {KUTHERA}; Festus, ad voc. MELOS.]

561

[Kenrick, p. 96.]

562

[Steph. Byz. ad voc. {MEMBLIAROS}.]

563

[Heraclid. Pont. ap. Steph. Byz. ad voc.]

564

[Herod. iv. 147.]

565

[Thucyd. i. 8.]

566

[Herod. iii. 57; Pausan. x. 11.]

567

[Tournefort, Voyages, i. 136.]

568

[Plin, H. N. iv. 12. Compare Steph. Byz. ad voc. {KUTHERA}.]

569

[Theophrast. Hist. Plant. iv. 2; Plin. H. N. xxxv. 15.]

570

[Strab. x. 5, § 16.]

571

[Ibid. § 19, ad fin.]

572

[Herod. ii. 44.]

573

[Ibid. vi. 47.]

574

[Hesych. ad voc. {KABEIROI}; Steph. Byz. ad voc. {IMBROS}; Strab. vii. Fr. 51.]

575

[Strab. xiv. 5, § 28; Plin. H. N. vii. 56.]

576

[Strab. x. 1, § 8.]

577

[Herod. v. 57; Strab. ix. 2, § 3; Pausan. ix. 25, § 6, &c.]

578

[Steph. Byz. ad voc. {PRONEKTOS}; Scymn. Ch. l. 660.]

579

[Apollon. Rhod. ii. l. 178; Euseb. Præp. Ev. p. 115; Schol. ad Apollon. Rhod. l.s.c.; Steph. Byz. ad voc. {SESAMOS}.]

580

[So Kenrick, Phoenicia, pp. 91, 92.]

581

[Utica was said to have been founded 287 years before Carthage (Aristot. De Ausc. Mir. § 146). Carthage was probably founded about B.C. 850.]

582

[Thucyd. vi. 2.]

583

[Strab. xvii. 3, § 13.]

584

[See the chart opposite, and the description in the Géographie Universelle, xi. 271, 272.]

585

[Ibid. p. 270.]

586

[Plin. H. N. v. 4, § 23; Géographie Universelle, xi. 157.]

587

[Géograph. Univ. xi. 275.]

588

[Ibid. p. 274.]

589

[Géograph. Univ. xi. 413, 414.]

590

[Ibid. pp. 410, 411.]

591

[See Davis's Carthage, pp. 128-130; and compare the woodcut in the Géograph. Univ. xi. 259.]

592

[Beulé, Fouilles à Carthage, quoted in the Géograph. Univ. xi. 258.]

593

["Adrymes" is the Greek name (Strab. xvii. 3, § 16), Adrumetum or Hadrumetum, the Roman one (Sall. Bell. Jugurth. § 19; Liv. xxx. 29; Plin. H. N. v. 4, § 25).]

594

[Géograph. Univ. xi. 227, 228.]

595

[Ibid. p. 227, note.]

596

[Géographie Universelle, xi. 224.]

597

[Géograph. Univ. xi. 84.]

598

[Strabo, xvii. 3, § 18.]

599

[See Della Cella, Narrative, p. 37, E. T.; Beechey, Narrative, p. 51.]

5100

[Herod. iv. 198. Compare Ovid. Pont. ii. 7, 25.]

5101

[See the chart in the Géographie Universelle, xi. 223.]

5102

[Strab. xvii. 3, § 12.]

5103

[See Daux, Recherches sur les Emporia Phéniciens, pp. 256-258; and compare Pl. viii.]

5104

[At Utica, Carthage, and elsewhere.]

5105

[Daux, Recherches, pp. 169-171; Perrot et Chipiez, Histoire de l'Art dans l'Antiquité, iii. 400-402.]

5106

[Thucyd. vi. 2.]

5107

[Perrot et Chipiez, Histoire de l'Art, iii. 336.]

5108

[Diod. Sic. xiv. 68.]

5109

[Gesenius, Monumenta Phoenicia, pp. 297, 298, and Tab. 39, xii. A, B.]

5110

[Perrot et Chipiez, Histoire de l'Art, iii. 330.]
5111
[Polyb. i. 55.]
5112
[Perrot et Chipiez, Histoire de l'Art, iii. 331. Compare the accompanying woodcut.]
5113
[Perrot et Chipiez, Hist. de l'Art, iii. 334; Woodcuts, No. 242 and 243.]
5114
[Marsala, whose wine is so well known, occupies a site on the coast at a short distance.]
5115
[Géographie Universelle, i. 552.]
5116
[Géographie Universelle, i. p. 551.]
5117
[See Gesenius, Monumenta Phoenicia, pp. 288-290, and Tab. 38, ix. Mahanath corresponds to the Greek {skenai} and the Roman castra. Compare the Israelite "Mahanaim."]
5118
[Serra di Falco, Antichità di Sicilia, v. 60, 67.]
5119
[Perrot et Chipiez, Hist. de l'Art, iii. 187-189.]
5120
[Ibid. p. 426.]
5121
[Géographie Universelle, i. 571.]
5122
[Gesenius, Monumenta Phoenicia, p. 298.]
5123
[Diod. Sic. v. 12.]
5124
[See the Corpus Inscriptionum Semiticarum, vol. i. No. 132.]
5125
[Gesenius, Mon. Phoen. Tab. 40, xiv.]
5126
[For an account of these buildings, called by the natives "Giganteja," see Perrot et Chipiez, Histoire de l'Art, iii. 297, 298.]
5127
[Ibid.]
5128
[Ibid. p. 299.]
5129
"Malte, l'île de miel" (Géogr. Univ. i. 576).]
5130
[{Kunidia, a kalousi Melitaia} (Strab. vi. 2, § 11, sub fin.).]
5131
[Perrot et Chipiez, Histoire de l'Art, iv. 2.]
5132
[Diod. Sic. xiv. 63, § 4; 77, § 6; xxi. 16, &c.]
5133
[Perrot et Chipiez, l.s.c. Compare the Géographie Universelle, i. 599, 600.]
5134
[Perrot et Chipiez, iii. 233; La Marmora, Voyage en Sardaigne, ii. 171-341.]
5135

[Strabo calls the town Sulchi ({Soulkhoi}, v. 2, § 7).]
5136
[Perrot et Chipiez, iii. 231, 232, 253, &c.]
5137
[None of the classical geographers mentions the place excepting Ptolemy, who calls it "Tarrus" (Geograph. iii. 3).]
5138
[See Perrot et Chipiez, Histoire de l'Art, iii. 231-236, and 418-421.]
5139
[Herod. i. 166.]
5140
[Kenrick, Phoenicia, p. 116; Perrot et Chipiez, iii. 46, 186.]
5141
[Géographie Universelle, i. 800.]
5142
[Strab. iii. 5, § 1.]
5143
[Kenrick, p. 118; Géogr. Univ. i. 795.]
5144
["Un admirable port natured divisé par des ilôts et des péninsules en cales et en bassins secondairs; tous les avantages se trouvent réunis dans ce bras de mer" (Géographie Universelle, i. 808).]
5145
[Ibid. p. 801.]
5146
[Ibid. p. 799.]
5147
[{Phoinikike to skhemati} (Strab. iii. 4, § 2).]
5148
[{Phoinikon ktisma} (ib. iii. 4, § 3).]
5149
[Gesenius, Mon. Phoen. pp. 308-310; Tab. 40, xvi.]
5150
[Strab. iii. 4, § 2.]
5151
[Ibid.]
5152
[Ibid. iii. 4, § 6.]
5153
[Three hundred, according to some writers (Ibid. xvii. 3, § 3).]
5154
[Plin. H. N. xix. 4.]
5155
[Gesenius, Mon. Phoen. pp. 309, 310.]
5156
[Géograph. Univ. xi. 710-713.]
5157
[Strab. ii. 3, § 4; Hanno, Peripl. § 6; Scylax, Peripl. § 112.]
5158
[See Géograph. Univer. xi. 714.]
5159
[Perrot et Chipiez, Histoire de l'Art, iii. 337.]

5160

[Ibid. p. 339.]

5161

[Ibid. p. 341.]

5162

[See Kenrick, Phoenicia, p. 118; Dyer, in Smith's Dict. of Greek and Roman Geography, ii. 1106.]

5163

[Scymn. Ch. ll. 100-106; Strabo, iii. 2, § 11; Mela, De Situ Orbis, ii. 6; Plin. H. N. iv. 21; Fest. Avien. Descriptio Orbis, l. 610; Pausan. vi. 19.]

5164

[Stesichorus, Fragmenta (ed. Bergk), p. 636; Strab. l.s.c.]

5165

[Scymn. Ch. l.s.c.]

5166

[See Herod. i. 163.]

5167

[1 Kings x. 22.]

5168

[Strab. iii. 2, § 8; Géograph. Univ. i. 741-745.]

5169

[Strab. iii. 2, § 11.]

5170

[Kenrick, Phoenicia, p. 119.]

5171

[Strab. iii. 2, § 7.]

5172

[Aristoph. Ran. l. 476; Jul. Pollux, vi. 63.]

5173

[Vell. Paterc. i. 2.]

5174

[Géograph. Univ. i. 756-758.]

5175

[Ibid. p. 758.]

5176

[Strab. iii. 5, § 5; Diod. Sic. v. 20; Scymn. Ch. 160; Mela, iii. 6, § 1; Plin. H. N. v. 19; &c.]

5177

[Gesen. Mon. Phoen. pp. 304, 370.]

5178

[Strabo, iii. 5, § 3.]

5179

[See the Géographie Universelle, i. 759.]

5180

[The name is to be connected with the words Baal, Belus, Baalath, &c. There was a river "Belus," in Phoenicia Proper.]

5181

[Gesenius, Monumenta Phoenicia, pp. 311, 312.]

5182

[Ibid. p. 311.]

5183

[I.e. towards the north-east, in the Propontis and the Euxine.]

VI—ARCHITECTURE

61
[Perrot et Chipiez, Histoire de l'Art dans l'Antiquité, iii. 101.]
62
[See Renan, Mission de Phoenicie, p. 92, and Planches, pl. 12.]
63
[Ibid.]
64
[Renan, Mission de Phénicie, pp. 62-68]
65
[Ibid. Planches, pl. 10.]
66
[1 Kings v. 17, 18.]
67
[Our Work in Palestine, p. 115. Warren, Recovery of Jerusalem, i. 121.]
68
[See the Corpus. Inscr. Semit. Pars I. Planches, pl. 29, No. 136.]
69
[As at Sidon in the pier wall, and at Aradus in the remains of the great wall of the town.]
610
[M. Renan has found reason to question the truth of this view. Bevelling, he thinks, may have begun with the Phoenicians; but it became a general feature of Palestinian and Syrian architecture, being employed in Syria as late as the middle ages. The enclosure of the mosque at Hebron and the great wall of Baalbek are bevelled, but are scarcely Phoenician.]
611
[See Renan, Mission de Phénicie, Planches, pl. vi.]
612
[Compare the enclosure of the Haram at Jerusalem, the mosque at Hebron, and the temples at Baalbek (Perrot et Chipiez, Histoire de l'Art, iii. 105, No. 42; iv. 274, No. 139, and p. 186, No. 116).]
613
[See Perrot et Chipiez, iii. 108, 299, &c.]
614
[Renan, Mission, p. 822.]
615
[See Renan, Mission, pp. 62-68; and compare Perrot et Chipiez, Histoire de l'Art, iii. 242, 243.]
616
[See Renan, Mission de Phénicie, p. 64.]
617
[See Renan, Mission de Phénicie, pp. 63, 64.]
618
[Ibid. p. 65.]
619
[See the volume of Plates published with the Mission, pl. ix. fig 1.]
620
[Di Cesnola, Cyprus, p. 110; pl. xxxv. fig. 20; xxxvi. fig. 7; xxxvii. figs. 10, 11; Perrot et Chipiez, Histoire de l'Art, iii. pp. 124, 428, 533, &c.]
621
[Renan, Mission, Planches, pl. ix. fig. 3.]
622
[See Perrot et Chipie, Histoire de l'Art, iii. 253, No. 193; p. 310, No. 233.]
623

[See the author's History of Ancient Egypt, i. 237.]
624
[Mission de Phénicie, pp. 64, 65.]
625
[See Di Cesnola's Cyprus, pp. 210-212.]
626
[The temple of Solomon was mainly of wood; that of Golgi (Athiénau) was, it is thought, of crude brick (Di Cesnola, Cyprus, p. 139).]
627
[See the plan in Perrot et Chipiez, Histoire de l'Art, iii. 267, No. 200. Explorations are now in progress, which, it is hoped, may reveal more completely the plan of the building.]
628
[As being the most important temple in the island.]
629
[Di Cesnola, Cyprus, p. 211.]
630
[Ibid. p. 210.]
631
[Ibid.]
632
[Perrot et Chipiez, iii. 269.]
633
[In M. Gerhard's plan two circular ponds or reservoirs are marked, of which General Di Cesnola found no trace.]
634
[Di Cesnola, Cyprus, p. 211.]
635
[Perrot et Chipiez, iii. 322.]
636
[As Di Cesnola, and Ceccaldi.]
637
[Ceccaldi, as quoted by Perrot et Chipiez, iii. 275.]
638
[Ceccaldi, Monuments Antiques de Cypre, pp. 47, 48.]
639
[Di Cesnola, Cyprus, p. 139.]
640
[Di Cesnola, Cyprus, p. 149; Perrot et Chipiez, Histoire de l'Art, iii. 274; Ceccaldi, l.s.c.]
641
[Di Cesnola, p. 139.]
642
[Ibid. p. 140.]
643
[Ibid. Compare Perrot et Chipiez, l.s.c.]
644
[The only original account of this crypt is that of General Di Cesnola, Cyprus, pp. 303-305.]
645
[Mephitic vapours prevented the workmen from continuing their excavations.]
646
[The length of this room was twenty feet, the breadth nineteen feet, and the height fourteen feet (Di Cesnola, Cyprus, p. 304).]
647

[Perrot et Chipiez, Histoire de l'Art, iii. 285.]
648
[See the woodcut representing a portion of the old wall of Aradus, which is taken from M. Renan's Mission, Planches, pl. 2.]
649
[In some of the ruder walls, as in those of Banias and Eryx, even this precaution is not observed. See Perrot et Chipiez, Histoire de l'Art, iii. 328, 334.]
650
[Diod. Sic. xxxii. 14.]
651
[Arrian, Exp. Alex. ii. 21, § 3.]
652
[Perrot et Chipiez, Hist. de l'Art, iii. 331, 332, 339.]
653
[Perrot et Chipiez, Hist. de l'Art, iii. pp. 333, 334.]
654
[See his Recherches sur l'origine et l'emplacement des Emporia Phéniciens, pl. 8.]
655
[Compare Renan, Mission de Phénicie, pls. 7, 16, 18, &c.; and Di Cesnola, Cyprus, p. 224.]
656
[Di Cesnola, Cyprus, p. 256, 260; Perrot et Chipiez, Hist. de l'Art, iii. 219-221.]
657
[Di Cesnola, Cyprus, p. 255.]
658
[Di Cesnola, Cyprus, pp. 255, 256.]
659
[See Di Cesnola, Cyprus, p. 260; and compare Perrot et Chipiez, Hist. de l'Art, iii. 219, No. 155.]
660
[Di Cesnola, p. 259.]
661
[Perrot et Chipiez, iii. 224.]
662
[See Ross, Reisen nach Cypern, pp. 187-189; and Archäologische Zeitung for 1851, pl. xxviii. figs. 3 and 4.]
663
[They are not shown in Ross's representation, but appear in Di Cesnola's.]
664
[See Sir C. Newton's Halicarnassus, pls. xviii. xix.]
665
[1 Macc. xiii. 27-29.]
666
[Renan, Mission de Phénicie, p. 80.]
667
[Renan, Mission de Phénicie, p. 81.]
668
[Ibid. pp. 82, 85.]
669
[See Robinson, Researches in Palestine, iii. 385.]
670
[Renan, Mission de Phénicie, p. 599.]
671

[Perrot and Chipiez remark that "the general aspect of the edifice recalls that of the great tombs at Amrith;" and conclude that, "if the tomb does not actually belong to the time of Solomon's contemporary and ally, at any rate it is anterior to the Greco-Roman period" (Hist. de l'Art, iii. 167).]

672

[See the section of the building in Renan's Mission, Planches, pl. xlviii.]

673

[Renan, Mission de Phénicie, p. 71.]

674

[Ibid. Planches, pl. 13.]

675

[Ibid. p. 72.]

676

[Perrot et Chipiez, Histoire de l'Art, iii. 153.]

677

[Renan, Mission de Phénicie, pp. 71-73.]

678

["Ce que ce tombeau offre de tout à fait particulier c'est que l'entrée du caveau, ou, pour mieux dire, l'escalier qui y conduit, est couvert, dans sa partie antérieure, par un énorme bloc régulièrement taillé en dos d'âne et supporté par une assise de grosses pierres" (Perrot et Chipiez, Hist. de l'Art, iii. 154).]

679

[Mark xvi. 3, 4.]

680

[Perrot et Chipiez, Hist. de l'Art, iii. 334.]

681

[Perrot et Chipiez, Hist. de l'Art, iii. 126, No. 68.]

682

[Di Cesnola, Cyprus, pp. 211, 301.]

683

[See Perrot et Chipiez, Histoire de l'Art, iii. 129-134.]

684

[Mission de Phénicie, p. 822.]

685

[Renan, Mission de Phénicie, p. 822.]

686

[Renan, Mission de Phénicie, p. 829.]

VII—ÆSTHETIC ART

71

[See Perrot et Chipiez, Hist. de l'Art, iii. 404, and compare pp. 428 and 437.]

72

[Di Cesnola, Cyprus, pp. 129-157, &c.]

73

[Perrot et Chipiez, iii. 510.]

74

[Ibid. p. 513: "Les figures semblent avoir été taillées non dans des blocs prismatiques, mais dans de la pierre débitée en carrière, sous forme de dalles épaisses."]

75

[Di Cesnola, p. 150.]

76

[Ibid. pp. 149, 150.]

77

[Di Cesnola, p. 157.]

78

[So both Di Cesnola (l.s.c) and Perrot et Chipiez, iii, 565.]

79

[Perrot et Chipiez, Hist. de l'Art, iii. Nos. 349, 385, 405, &c.; Di Cesnola, Cyprus, pp. 133, 149, 157.]

710

[Perrot et Chipiez, iii. 519, No. 353.]

711

[Ibid. Nos. 323, 342, 368. Occasionally an arm is placed across the breast without anything being clasped (Di Cesnola, Cyprus, pp. 131, 240).]

712

[Perrot et Chipiez, Nos. 299, 322, 373.]

713

[Ibid. Nos. 291, 321, 379, 380.]

714

[Ibid. Nos. 381, 382.]

715

[Perrot et Chipiez, Nos. 306, 345, 349, &c.]

716

[See Di Cesnola, Cyprus, pp. 141, 230, 243, &c.]

717

[Compare Perrot et Chipiez, iii. 530, No. 358; p. 533, No. 359; and Di Cesnola, pp. 131, 154, &c.]

718

[Di Cesnola, pp. 129, 145; Perrot et Chipiez, pp. 527, 545.]

719

[Di Cesnola, pp. 149, 151, 161, &c.]

720

[Perrot et Chipiez, Hist. de l'Art, iii. 201, No. 142; p. 451, No. 323; p. 598, No. 409. The best dove is that in the hand of a priest represented by Di Cesnola (Cyprus, p. 132).]

721

[Di Cesnola, Cyprus, p. 114.]

722

[Ibid. p. 331; Perrot et Chipiez, iii. 203, and Pl. ii. opp. p. 582.]

723

[Di Cesnola, Cyprus, p. 136; Ceccaldi, Rev. Arch. vol. xxiv. pl. 21.]

724

[Di Cesnola, p. 137.]

725

[Ibid. p. 133.]

726

[Ibid. pp. 110-114.]

727

[See the Story of Assyria, p. 403; and compare Ancient Monarchies, i. 395, 493.]

728

[See Story of Assyria, l.s.c.; and for the classical practice, which was identical, compare Lipsius, Antiq. Lect. iii.]

729

[So it is in a garden that Asshurbani-pal and his queen regale themselves (Ancient Monarchies, i. 493). Compare Esther i. 7.]

730

[Perrot et Chipiez, Hist. de l'Art, iii. 620.]
731
[Di Cesnola, Cyprus, pp. 259-267.]
732
[Di Cesnola is in favour of Melkarth (p. 264); MM. Perrot and Chipiez of Bes (Hist. de l'Art, iii. 610). Individually, I incline to Esmun.]
733
[See Di Cesnola, Pl. vi.; Perrot et Chipiez, iii. 450, 555, 557; Nos. 321, 379, 380, 381, and 382.]
734
[Herod. iii. 37.]
735
[Perrot et Chipiez see in it the travels of the deceased in another world (Hist. de l'Art, iii. 612); but they admit that at first sight one would be tempted to regard it as the representation of an historical event, as the setting forth of a prince for war, or his triumphant return.]
736
[A similar crest was used by the Persians (Ancient Monarchies, iii. 180, 234), and the Lycians (Fellows's Lycia, pl. xxi. oop. p. 173).]
737
[Perrot et Chipiez, Histoire de l'Art, iii. 609-611.]
738
[See the Journal le Bachir for June 8, 1887, published at Beyrout.]
739
[1 Kings vii. 14; 2 Chron. ii. 14.]
740
[1 Kings vii. 21.]
741
["In the porch" (1 Kings vii. 21); "before the house," "before the temple" (2 Chron. iii. 15, 17).]
742
[1 Kings vii. 15, 16.]
743
[Jer. lii. 21.]
744
[1 Kings vii. 17, 20.]
745
[Ibid. verse 20; 2 Chron. iv. 13; Jer. lii. 23.]
746
[1 Kings vii. 22.]
747
[See Perrot et Chipiez, Hist. de l'Art, vol. iv. Pls. vi. and vii. opp. pp. 318 and 320.]
748
[1 Kings vii. 23.]
749
[Ibid. vv. 23-25.]
750
[See the representation in Perrot et Chipiez, iv. 327, No. 172.]
751
[Perrot et Chipiez, iv. 328.]
752
[1 Kings vii. 27-39.]
753

[Ibid. verse 38.]
754
[Ibid. verse 29.]
755
[See the woodcut in Perrot et Chipiez, iv. 331, No. 173; and compare 1 Kings vii. 31.]
756
[1 Kings vii. 36.]
757
[1 Kings vii. 33.]
758
[Ibid. v. 40. Compare 2 Chron. iv. 16.]
759
[See Di Cesnola's Cyprus, Pls. xxi. and xxx.]
760
[A single statue in bronze, of full size, or larger than life, is said to have been exhumed in Cyprus in 1836 (Perrot et Chipiez, iii. 514); but it has not reached our day.]
761
[See the works of La Marmora (Voyage en Sardaigne), Cara (Relazione sugli idoli sardo-fenici), and Perrot et Chipiez (Hist. de l'Art, iv. 65-89).]
762
[Perrot et Chipiez, iv. 65, 66.]
763
[Ibid. pp. 67, 69, 88.]
764
[Ibid. pp. 67, 70, 89.]
765
[Ibid. 52, 74, 75, 87, &c.]
766
[See Di Cesnola, Cyprus, Pl. iv. opp. p. 84.]
767
[Ibid. opp. p. 345.]
768
[Ibid. p. 337.]
769
[Monumenti di cere antica, Pl. x. fig. 1.]
770
[Di Cesnola, Cyprus, p. 77.]
771
[Di Cesnola, Cyprus, Pl. xi. opp. p. 114.]
772
[In the museum of the Varvakeion. (See Perrot et Chipiez, Hist. de l'Art, iii. 782-785.)]
773
[Ibid. p. 783, No. 550.]
774
[Compare the author's History of Ancient Egypt, i. 362.]
775
[Perrot et Chipiez, iii. 779, No. 548.]
776
[See Ancient Monarchies, i. 392.]
777
[See Clermont-Ganneau, Imagerie Phénicienne, p. xiii.]
778

[See Clermont-Ganneau, Ima. Phénicienne, Pls. ii. iv. and vi. Compare Longpérier, Musée Napoléon III., Pl. x.; Di Cesnola, Cyprus, p. 329; Pl. xix. opp. p. 276; Perrot et Chipiez, Hist. de l'Art, iii. 777, 789; Nos. 547 and 552.]
779
[Clermont-Ganneau, Pl. i. at end of volume; Perrot et Chipiez, iii. 759, No. 543.]
780
[L'Imagerie Phénicienne, p. 8.]
781
[Helbig, Bullettino dell' Instituto di Corrispondenza archeologica, 1876, p. 127.]
782
[L'Imagerie Phénicienne, p. 8.]
783
[L'Imagerie Phénicienne, pp. xi, xiii, and 18-39.]
784
[Ibid. p. 151.]
785
[L'Imagerie Phénicienne, pp. 150-156. It is fatal to M. Clermont-Ganneau's idea—1. That the hunter in the outer scene has no dog; 2. That the dress of the charioteer is wholly unlike that of the fugitive attacked by the dog; and 3. That M. Clermont-Ganneau's explanation accounts in no way for the medallion's central and main figure.]
786
["Les formes et les mouvements des chevaux sont indiqués avec beaucoup du sûreté et de justesse" (ibid. p. 6).]
787
[So Mr. C. W. King in his appendix to Di Cesnola's Cyprus, p. 387. He supports his view by Herod. vii. 69.]
788
[Perrot et Chipiez, iii. 632.]
789
[Compare the cylinder of Darius Hystaspis (Ancient Monarchies, iii. 227) and another engraved on the same page.]
790
[Perrot et Chipiez, iii. 635, note.]
791
[Proceedings of the Society of Bibl. Archæology for 1883—4, p. 16.]
792
[See M. A. Di Cesnola's Salaminia, Pls. xii. and xiii.]
793
[See Perrot et Chipiez, iii. 639, No. 431.]
794
[These fluttering ends of ribbon are very common in the Persian representations. See Ancient Monarchies, iii. 351.]
795
[Ancient Monarchies, iii. pp. 203, 204, 208.]
796
[Perrot et Chipiez, Hist. de l'Art, iii. 630.]
797
[Ibid. pp. 635-639. Green serpentine is the most usual material (C. W. King, in Di Cesnola's Cyprus, p. 387).]
798
[King, in Di Cesnola's Cyprus, p. 388.]
799

[Pl. xxxvi. a.]

7100

[Di Cesnola, Cyprus, p. 277.]

7101

[See De Vogüé's Mélanges d'Archéologie Orientale, pl. v.]

7102

[Perrot et Chipiez, iii. 631.]

7103

[See Di Cesnola's Cyprus, pl. xxvi. (top line).]

7104

[See Perrot et Chipiez, iii. 645.]

7105

[Ibid. p. 646.]

7106

[De Vogüé, Mélanges, p. 111.]

7107

[Perrot et Chipiez, Hist. de l'Art, iii. 651.]

7108

[Ibid. p. 652.]

7109

[See Di Cesnola, Cyprus, pl. xxxvi. fig. 8.]

7110

[Perrot et Chipiez, iii. 646.]

7111

[Herod. vii. 61.]

7112

[Di Cesnola, Cyprus, pl. xxxv. fig. a.]

7113

[Herod. v. 113.]

7114

[That of Canon Spano. (See Perrot et Chipiez, iii. 655, note 1.)]

7115

[Perrot et Chipiez, iii. 656, 657, Nos. 466, 467, 468.]

7116

[Perrot et Chipiez, iii. p. 655.]

7117

[Ibid. p. 656, Nos. 464, 465.]

7118

[See the author's History of Ancient Egypt, ii. 47, 54, 70.]

7119

[Perrot et Chipiez, iii. 657, 658, Nos. 471-476.]

7120

[Perrot et Chipiez, iii. 655:—"La couleur parait y avoir été employée d'une manière discrète; elle servait à faire ressortir certains détails."]

7121

[Ross, Reisen auf den griechischen Inseln, iv. 100.]

7122

[Perrot et Chipiez, iii. 666:—"On obtenait ainsi un ensemble qui, malgré la rapidité du travail, ne manquait pas de gaieté, d'harmonie et d'agrément."]

7123

[See Di Cesnola, Cyprus, pp. 65, 71, 91, 181, &c.; and Perrot et Chipiez, iii. 686, 691, 699, &c.]

7124

[Cyprus, pl. xxix. (p. 333).]

7125

[Perrot et Chipiez, iii. 704.]

VIII—INDUSTRIAL ART AND MANUFACTURES

81

[Ezek. xxvii. 18.]

82

[Ibid. xxvii. 21.]

83

[See Herod. ii. 182, and compare the note of Sir G. Wilkinson on that passage in Rawlinson's Herodotus, ii. 272.]

84

[Kenrick, Phoenicia, p. 246.]

85

[Ibid.]

86

[Hom. Il. vi. 289; Od. xv. 417; Æsch. Suppl. ll. 279-284; Lucan, Phars. x. 142, &c.]

87

[Ex. xxvi. 36, xxviii. 39.]

88

[Perrot et Chipiez, Histoire de l'Art, iii. 877.]

89

[Smyth, Mediterranean Sea, pp. 205-207.]

810

[Tristram, Land of Israel, p. 51.]

811

[Lortet, La Syrie d'aujourd'hui, p. 103.]

812

[See Phil. Transactions, xv. 1,280.]

813

[Wilksinson, in Rawlinson's Herodotus, ii. 347.]

814

[Kenrick, Phoenicia, p. 258.]

815

[See Jul. Pollux, Onomasticon, i. 4, § 45.]

816

[This is the case with almost all the refuse shells found in the "kitchen middens" (as they have been called) on the Syrian coast. See Lortet, La Syrie d'aujourd'hui, p. 103).]

817

[See Réaumur, quoted by Kenrick, Phoenicia, p. 256.]

818

[Plin. H. N. ix. 38.]

819

[See Grimaud de Caux's paper in the Revue de Zoologie for 1856, p. 34; and compare Lortet, La Syrie d'aujourd'hui, p. 102.]

820

[Ibid.]

821

[Lortet, La Syrie d'aujourd'hui, p. 127.]

822

[Plin. H. N. xxxii. 22.]

823

[Ibid. ix. 37-39.]

824

[For the tints producible, see a paper by M. Lacaze-Duthiers, in the Annales des Sciences Naturelles for 1859, Zoologie, 4me. série, xii. 1-84.]

825

[Plin. H. N. ix. 41.]

826

[Ibid. ix. 39:—"Cornelius Nepos, qui divi Augusti principatu obiit. Me, inquit, juvene violacea purpura vigebat, cujus libra denariis centum venibat."]

827

[Kenrick, Phoenicia, p. 242. Compare Pliny, H. N. ix. 38:—"Laus summa in colore sanguinis concreti."]

828

[Hist. Nat. xxxvi. 65.]

829

[Wilkinson, in Rawlinson's Herodotus, ii. 82. Similar representations occur in tombs near the Pyramids.]

830

[Wilksinson, Manners and Customs, iii. 88.]

831

[Herod. ii. 86-88.]

832

[Plin. H. N. v 19; xxxvi. 26, &c.]

833

[Lortet, La Syrie d'aujourd'hui, p. 113.]

834

[Ibid. p. 127.]

835

[Perrot et Chipiez, Hist. de l'Art, iii. 735, note 2.]

836

[Plin. H. N. xxxvi. 26.]

837

[Perrot et Chipiez, iii. 739.]

838

[See Perrot et Chipiez, Histoire de l'Art, iii. 734-744.]

839

[Perrot et Chipiez, Histore de l'Art, iii. pl. viii. No. 2 (opp. p. 740).]

840

[Ibid. pl. vii. No. 1 (opp. p. 734).]

841

[Herod. ii. 44.]

842

[Perrot et Chipiez, Hist. de l'Art, iii. 745, and pl. x.]

843

[Ibid.]

844

[Perrot et Chipiez, iii. 746, No. 534.]

845

[Ibid. pp. 739, 740.]

846

[See Perrot et Chipiez, Histoire de l'Art, iii. 740, 741.]

847

[The British Museum has a mould which was found at Camirus, intended to give shape to glass earrings. It is of a hard greenish stone, apparently a sort of breccia.]

848

[Perrot et Chipiez, iii. 745.]

849

[Strabo, iii. 5, § 11.]

850

[Scylax, Periplus, § 112.]

851

[Perrot et Chipiez, Histoire de l'Art, iii. 669. (Compare Renan Mission de Phénicie, pl. xxi.)]

852

[Perrot et Chipiez, iii. 670. The vase is figured on p. 670, No. 478.]

853

[Di Cesnola, Cyprus, p. 68. Compare Perrot et Chipiez, Hist. de l'Art, iii. 671, No. 479.]

854

[Perrot et Chipiez, l.s.c.]

855

[Di Cesnola, Cyprus, appendix, p. 408.]

856

[Perrot et Chipiez, iii. 685, No. 485.]

857

[Di Cesnola, Cyprus, p. 102. Compare Perrot et Chipiez, Hist. de l'Art, iii. 675, No. 483.]

858

[So Di Cesnola, Cyprus, p. 332, and Mr. Murray, of the British Museum, ibid., appendix, pp. 401, 402.]

859

[Perrot et Chipiez, Hist. de l'Art, iii. 693-695.]

860

[Di Cesnola, Cyprus, pp. 394, 402, and pl. xlii. fig. 4.]

861

[Perrot et Chipiez, Hist. de l'Art, iii. 698.]

862

[Ibid. p. 676, No. 484; p. 691, No. 496; and p. 697, No. 505.]

863

[Ibid. p. 730.]

864

[Di Cesnola, Cyprus, p. 282, and pl. xxx.]

865

[Ibid.]

866

[Perrot et Chipiez, Hist. de l'Art, iii. 866-868. Compare Di Cesnola, Cyprus, pl. x.]

867

[Di Cesnola, Cyprus, pp. 335, 336, and pls. iv. and xxx.; Perrot et Chipiez, Hist. de l'Art, iii. 831, 862, 863, &c.]

868

[Di Cesnola, l.s.c.; Perrot et Chipiez, iii. 864.]

869

[Di Cesnola, Cyprus, pl. xx.]

870

[Perrot et Chipiez, iv. 15, 66-68, 70; Cesnola, Cyprus, p. 203.]

871

[Perrot et Chipiez, iii. 870, 871.]
872
[Ibid. p. 867, No. 633.]
8/3
[Ibid. iv. 94.]
874
[Perrot et Chipiez, iv. 94, No. 91.]
875
[Ibid. p. 67, No. 53.]
876
[Ibid. iii. 862, No. 629.]
877
[Perrot et Chipiez, iii. p. 863.]
878
[De Cesnola, Cyprus, p. 336.]
879
[See Perrot et Chipiez, iii. 133, Nos. 80, 81.]
880
[Di Cesnola, p. 335.]
881
[See Ezek. xxvii. 12; Strab. iii. 2, § 8.]
882
[Plutarch, Vit. Alex. Magni, § 32.]
883
[Ceccaldi, Monumens Antiques de Cyprus, p. 138; Di Cesnola, Cyprus, p. 282; Perrot et Chipiez, Hist. de l'Art, iii. 874.]
884
[Plutarch, Vit. Demetrii, § 21.]
885
[Hom. Il. xi. 19-28.]
886
[2 Chron. ii. 14. Iron, in the shape of nails and rings, has been found in several graves in Phoenicia Proper, where the coffin seems to have been of wood (Renan, Mission de Phénicie, p. 866).]
887
[Strab. iii. 5, § 11.]
888
[Ezek. xxvii. 12.]
889
[See Perrot et Chipiez, Hist. de l'Art, iv. 80.]
890
[Ibid. iii. 815, No. 568.]
891
[Renan, Mission de Phénicie, p. 427, and pl. lx. fig. 1; Perrot et Chipiez, Hist. de l'Art, iii. 177, No. 123.]
IX—SHIPS, NAVIGATION, AND COMMERCE
91
[Plin. H. N. vii. 56.]
92
[Perrot et Chipiez, Hist. de l'Art, iii. 517, No. 352.]
93
[Layard, Nineveh and its Remains, ii. 383.]

94
[Compare the practice of the Egyptians (Rosellini, Monumenti Storici, pl. cxxxi.)]
95
[See Mionnet, Déscript. de Médailles, vol. vii. pl. lxi. fig. 1; Gesenius, Ling. Scripturæque Phoen. Monumenta, pl. 36, fig. G; Layard, Nineveh and its Remains, ii. 378.]
96
[Layard, Monuments of Nineveh, first series, pl. 71; Nineveh and its Remains, l.s.c.]
97
[So Perrot et Chipiez, Hist. de l'Art, iii. 34.]
98
[See Di Cesnola, Cyprus, pl. xlv.]
99
[Herod. iii. 136.]
910
[In later times there must have been more sails than one, since Xenophon describes a Phoenician merchant ship as sailing by means of a quantity of rigging, which implies several sails (Xen. OEconom. § 8).]
911
[Scylax. Periplus, § 112.]
912
[Thucyd. i. 13.]
913
[Herod. l.s.c.]
914
[See Herod. vii. 89-94.]
915
[Ibid. vii. 44.]
916
[Ibid. vii. 100.]
917
[Xen. OEconom. § 8, pp. 11-16 (Ed. Schneider).]
918
[Herodotus (iii. 37) says they were at the prow of the ship; but Suidas (ad voc.) and Hesychius (ad voc.) place them at the stern. Perhaps there was no fixed rule.]
919
[The {pataikoi} of the Greeks probably representes the Hebrew {...}, which is from {...}, "insculpere," and is applied in Scripture to "carved work" of any kind. (See 1 Kings vi. 29; Ps. lxxiv. 6; &c.) Some, however, derive the word from the Egyptian name Phthah, or Ptah. (See Kenrick, Phoenicia, p. 235.)]
920
[Manilius, i. 304-308.]
921
[Strab. Geograph. xv.]
922
[Tarshish (Tartessus) was on the Atlantic coast, outside the Straits.]
923
[Ezek. xxvii.]
924
[Signified by one of its chief cities, Haran (now Harran).]
925
[Signified by "the house of Togarmarh" (verse 14).]
926

[Ionia, Cyprus, and Hellas are the Greek correspondents of Javan, Chittim, and Elishah, Chittim representing Citium, the capital of Cyprus.]
927
[Spain is intended by "Tarshish" (verse 12) == Tartessus, which was a name given by the Phoenicians to the tract upon the lower Bætis (Guadalquivir).]
928
[See the Speaker's Commentary, ad loc.]
929
[Strab. xv. 3, § 22.]
930
[Minnith appears as an Ammonite city in the history of Jephthah (Judg. xi. 33).]
931
[Herod. ii. 37, 182; iii. 47.]
932
[See Rawlinson's Herodotus, ii. 157; History of Ancient Egypt, i. 509; Rosellini, Mon. Civili, pls. 107-109.]
933
[See Herod. iii. 107; History of Ancient Egypt, ii. 222-224.]
934
[That these were Arabian products appears from Herod. iii. 111, 112. They may be included in the "chief of all spices," which Tyre obtained from the merchants of Sheba and Raamah (Ezek. xxvii. 22).]
935
[Arabia has no ebony trees, and can never have produced elephants.]
936
[See Ezek. xxvii. 23, 24. Canneh and Chilmad were probably Babylonian towns.]
937
[Upper Mesopotamia is indicated by one of its chief cities, Haran (Ezek. xxvii. 23).]
938
[Ezek. xxvii. 6. Many objects in ivory have been found in Cyprus.]
939
[Ibid. verse 7. The Murex brandaris is still abundant on the coast of Attica, and off the island of Salamis (Perrot et Chipiez, Hist. de l'Art, iii. 881).]
940
[Strab. iii. 2, § 8-12; Diod. Sic. v. 36; Plin. H. N. iii. 3.]
941
[See Gen. xxxvii. 28.]
942
[Isaiah xxi. 13.]
943
[Ibid. lx. 6.]
944
[Ibid. verses 6, 7.]
945
[Heeren, Asiatic Nations, ii. 93, 100, 101.]
946
[1 Kings v. 11; 2 Chr. ii. 10.]
947
[Ezek. xxvii. 17.]
948
[Ezra iii. 7.]
949

[Acts xii. 20.]
950
[2 Chron. l.s.c.; Ezra l.s.c.; Ezek. xxvii. 6, 17.]
951
[Ezek. l.s.c.]
952
[Gen. xxxvii. 28.]
953
[Strab. xvi. 2, § 41.]
954
[Ezek. xxvii. 18.]
955
[Strab. xv. 3, § 22.]
956
[So Heeren (As. Nat. ii. 118). But there is a Helbon a little to the north of Damascus, which is more probably intended.]
957
[Ibid.]
958
[See Amos, iii. 12, where some translate "the children of Israel that dwell in Samaria in the corner of a bed, and upon a damask couch."]
959
[Ezek. xxvii. 16.]
960
[The Hebrew terms for Syria {...} and Edom {...} are constantly confounded by the copyists, and we must generally look to the context to determine which is the true reading.]
961
[Herod. i. 1.]
962
[Ibid. ii. 112.]
963
[Ch. xxvii. 7.]
964
[Egyptian pottery, scarabs, seals, figures of gods, and amulets, are common on most Phoenician sites. The Sidonian sarcophagi, including that of Esmunazar, are of an Egyptian stone.]
965
[Herod. iii. 5, 6.]
966
[Ibid. iii. 107; Strab. xvi. 4, § 19; Diod. Sic. ii. 49.]
967
[Theophrast. Hist. Plant. ix. 4.]
968
[Wilkinson, in the author's Herodotus, iii. 497, note 6; Heeren, As. Nat. ii. 95.]
969
[Is. lx. 7; Her. xlix. 29.]
970
[Ezek. xxvii. 21.]
971
[Ezek. xxvii. 20.]
972
[Ex. xxvi. 7; xxxvi. 14.]

973

[Ezek. xxvii. 15, 19-22.]

974

[See Heeren, Asiatic Nations, ii. 96.]

975

[Ibid. pp. 99, 100.]

976

[Gerrha, Sanaa, and Mariaba were flourishing towns in Strabo's time, and probably during several centuries earlier.]

977

[Ezek. xxvii. 23, 24.]

978

[Herod. i. 1.]

979

[See Di Cesnola, Cyprus, pls. xxxi.-xxxiii.; A. Di Cesnola, Salaminia, ch. xii.; Perrot et Chipiez, Hist. de l'Art, iii. 636-639.]

980

[Layard, Monuments of Nineveh, 2nd series, pls. 57-67; Nineveh and Babylon, pp. 183-187.]

981

[Ezek. xxvii. 23.]

982

[So Heeren translates (As. Nat. ii. 123).]

983

[Ezek. xxvii. 14.]

984

[Strab. xi. 14, § 9:—{'Estin ippobotos sphodra e khora}.]

985

[Ibid.]

986

[1 Kings i. 33; Esth. viii. 10, 14.]

987

[Ezek. xxvii. 13.]

988

[Xen. Anab. iv. 1, § 6.]

989

[Hom. Od. xv. 415-484; Herod. i. 1.]

990

[Joel iii. 6.]

991

[Ezek. xxvii. 13.]

992

[Herod. v. 5.]

993

[Herod. ii. 32.]

994

[Ibid. iv. 183.]

995

[Ibid.]

996

[Ibid. iv. 181-184. Compare Heeren, African Nations, ii. pp. 202-235.]

997

[No doubt some of these may have been imparted by the Cyprians themselves, and others

introduced by the Egyptians when they held Cyprus; but they are too numerous to be accounted for sufficiently unless by a continuous Phoenician importation.]
998
[Especially Etruria, which was advanced in civilisation and the arts, while Rome was barely emerging from barbarism.]
999
[2 Chron. ii. 14.]
9100
[Dennis, Cities and Cemeteries of Etruria, ii. 204, 514; Gerhard, Etruskische Spiegel, passim.]
9101
[Schliemann, Mycenæ, Pls. 357-519.]
9102
[Ezek. xxvii. 12; Plin. H. N. xxxiv. 16; &c.]
9103
[Strabo, iii. 5, § 11.]
9104
[Ibid. In Roman times the pigs of tin were brought to the Isle of Wight by the natives, thence transported across the Channel, and conveyed through Gaul to the mouth of the Rhône (Diod. Sic. v. 22).]
9105
[Heeren, Asiatic Nations, ii. 80.]
9106
[Hom. Od. xv. 460. Some doubt, however, if amber is here intended.]
9107
[Scylax, Periplus, § 112.]
9108
[Herod. iv. 196.]
9109
[These forests (spoken of by Diodorus, v. 19) have now to a great extent been cleared away, though some patches still remain, especially in the more western islands of the group. The most remarkable of the trees is the Pinus canariensis.]
9110
[Pliny, H. N. vi. 32, sub fin.]
9111
[Pliny, l.s.c. The breed is now extinct.]
9112
[The savagery of the ancient inhabitants of the mainland is strongly marked in the narrative of Hanno (Periplus, passim).]
9113
[As Heeren (As. Nat. ii. 71, 75, 239).]
9114
[Ezek. xxvii. 15, 20, 23.]
9115
[See 1 Kings x. 22; 2 Chr. ix. 21.]
9116
[1 Kings ix. 26, 27.]
9117
[Ibid. x. 11; 2 Chr. ix. 10.]
9118
[Gen. x. 29. Compare Twistleton, in Dr. Smith's Dictionary of the Bible, vol. ii. ad voc. OPHIR.]
9119

[Ps. lxxii. 15; Ezek. xxvii. 22; Strab. xvi. 4, § 18; Diod. Sic. ii. 50.]
9¹²⁰
[Ezel. l.s.c.; Strab. xvi. 4, § 20,]
9¹²¹
[There are no sufficient data for determining what tree is intended by the almug or algum tree. The theory which identifies it with the "sandal-wood" of India has respectable authority in its favour, but cannot rise beyond the rank of a conjecture.]
9¹²²
[If Scylax of Cadyanda could sail, in the reign of Darius Hystaspis, from the mouth of the Indus to the Gulf of Suez (Herod. iv. 44), there could have been no great difficulty in the Phoenicians accomplishing the same voyage in the opposite direction some centuries earlier.]
X—MINING
10¹
[Diod. Sic. v. 35, § 2.]
10²
[Brugsch, History of Egypt, i. 65; Birch, Ancient Egypt, p. 65.]
10³
[Deut. viii. 7-9.]
10⁴
[Plin. H. N. xxxiv. 2:—"In Cypro proma æris inventio." The story went, that Cinryas, the Paphian king, who gave Agamemnon his breastplate of steel, gold, and tin (Hom. Il. xii. 25), invented the manufacture of copper, and also invented the tongs, the hammer, the lever, and the anvil (Plin. H. N. vii. 56, § 195).]
10⁵
[Strab. xiv. 6, § 5; Steph. Byz. ad voc. {Tamasos}.]
10⁶
[See the Dictionary of Gk. and Rom. Geography, i. 729.]
10⁷
[Ross, Inselnreise, iv. 157, 161.]
10⁸
[Plin. H. N. l.s.c.]
10⁹
[Herod. vi. 47.]
10¹⁰
[Plin. H. N. vi. 56; Strab. xiv. 5, § 28.]
10¹¹
[See the description of Thasos in the Géographie Universelle, i. 142.]
10¹²
[Herod. vii. 112; Aristot. De Ausc. Mir. § 42; Thuc. iv. 105; Diod. Sic. xvi. 8; App. Bell. Civ. iv. 105; Justin, viii. 3; Plin. H. N. vii. 56, &c.]
10¹³
[Col. Leake speaks of one silver mine as still being worked (Northern Greece, iii. 161).]
10¹⁴
[Perrot et Chipiez, Hist. de l'Art, iv. 99.]
10¹⁵
[Ibid. p. 100, note.]
10¹⁶
[Plin. H. N. xxxiii. 4, § 21.]
10¹⁷
[Ibid. xxxiii. 4, § 23.]
10¹⁸
[Diod. Sic. v. 35, § 1.]

1019
[Plin. H. N. xxxiii. 6, § 31.]
1020
[Ibid. § 96.]
1021
[Strab. iii. 2, § 8; Diod. Sic. v. 36, § 2.]
1022
[Ap. Strab. iii. 2, § 9. Compare Diod. Sic. v. 38, § 4.]
1023
[Strab. l.s.c.]
1024
[Plin. H. N. xxxiv. 16, § 156.]
1025
[Plin. H. N. xxxiv. 16, § 158 and § 165.]
1026
[Polyb. xxxiv. 5, § 11; Plin. H. N. xxxiv. 16, § 158.]
1027
[Plin. xxxiv. 18, § 173.]
1028
[Ibid. § 159.]
1029
[Ibid. xxxiv. 17, § 164.]
1030
[Quicksilver is still among the products of the Spanish mines, where its presence is noted by Pliny (H. N. xxxiii. 6, § 99).]
1031
[Diod. Sic. v. 36, § 2.]
1032
[Ibid. {Kai plagias kai skolias diaduseis poikilos metallourgountes}.]
1033
[Pliny says "flint," but this can scarcely have been the material. (See Plin. H. N. xxxiii. 4, § 71.)]
1034
[Ibid. § 70.]
1035
[Ibid. § 73.]
1036
[Diod. Sic. v. 37, § 3.]
1037
[Diod. Sic. v. 37, § 3. Compare Strab. iii. 2, § 9.]
1038
[Plin. H. N. xxxiii. 4, § 69.]
1039
[Ibid.]
1040
[Kenrick, Phoenicia, p. 263.]
1041
[Diod. Soc. v. 38, § 1.]
1042
[Kenrick thinks that the Carthaginians "introduced the practice of working the mines by slave labour" (Phoenicia, l.s.c.); but to me the probability appears to be the other way.]
1043

[See Wilkinson, in the author's Herodotus, ii. 504.]
1044
[Herod. iii. 96.]
XI—RELIGION
0111
[Renan, Histoire des Langues Sémitiques, p. 5.]
0112
[Ithobal, father of Jezebel, was High Priest of Ashtoreth (Menand. Ephes. Fr. 1). Amastarte, the mother of Esmunazar II. (Records of the Past, ix. 113) was priestess of the same deity.]
0113
[As figures of Melkarth, or Esmun, or dedications to Baal, as lord of the particular city issuing it.]
0114
[Herod. iii. 37.]
0115
[For the fragments of the work which remain, see the Fragmenta Historicum Græcorum of C. Müller, iii. 561-571. Its value has been much disputed, but seems to the present writer only slight.]
0116
[Compare Max Müller, Science of Religion, p. 177 et seqq.]
0117
[Gen. xiv. 18-22.]
0118
[Philo Bybl. Fr. 1, § 5.]
0119
[Records of the Past, iv. 109, 113.]
1110
[Gen. vi. 5.]
1111
[Ps. cxxxix. 2.]
1112
[Max Müller, Chips from a German Workshop, i. 28.]
1113
[Philo Bybl. Fr. 1, § 5. Compare the Corpus Ins. Semit. vol. i. p. 29.]
1114
[See Renan, Mission de Phénicie, pl. xxxii.; Gesenius, Linguæ Scripturæque Phoeniciæ Monumenta, Tab. xxi.]
1115
[2 Kings xxiii. 5. Compare verse 11.]
1116
[Gesenius, Monumenta Phoenicia, p. 96.]
1117
[Ibid. pp. 276-278.]
1118
[See Döllinger's Judenthum und Heidenthum, i. 425; E. T.]
1119
[Döllinger, Judenthum und Heidenthum, i. 425, E. T. Compare Gesenius, Mon. Phoen. Tab. xxiii.]
1120
[Herod. ii. 44; Perrot et Chipiez, Hist. de l'Art, iii. 77.]
1121
[Judg. ii. 11; iii. 7; x. 6, &c.]

1122

[2 Kings i. 2.]

1123

[Strab. iii. 5, § 5.]

1124

[Perrot et Chipiez, Hist. de l'Art, iv. 113.]

1125

[2 Kings iii. 2.]

1126

[See the representation in Perrot et Chipiez, Hist. de l'Art, iii. 73.]

1127

[Döllinger, Judenthum und Heidenthum, i. 427.]

1128

[Perrot et Chipiez, iii. 77.]

1129

[Gen. xiv. 5.]

1130

[Perrot et Chipiez, iii. 419, 450, 555, &c.]

1131

[Ibid. p. 554.]

1132

[Curtius, in the Archäologische Zeitung for 1869, p. 63.]

1133

[Kenrick, Phoenicia, p. 303.]

1134

[Menand. Ephes. Fr. 1.]

1135

[See Philo Bybl. Fe. ii. 8, § 14; {'Ilon ton kai Kronon}. Damascius ap. Phot. Bibl. p. 1050.]

1136

[Philo. Bybl. Fr. ii. 8, § 17.]

1137

[Diod. Sic. xx. 14.]

1138

[Philo Bybl. Fr. ii. 8, § 25.]

1139

[Ibid. Fr. iv.]

1140

[Ibid. Fr. ii. 8, § 14-19.]

1141

[Karth or Kartha, is probably the root of Carthage, Carthagena, Carteia, &c., as Kiriath is of Kiriathaim, Kiriath-arba, Kiriath-arim, &c.]

1142

[Melicertes is the son of Demaroüs and the grandson of Uranus; Baal-samin is a god who stands alone, "without father, without mother, without descent."]

1143

[See Perrot et Chipiez, Hist. de l'Art, iii. 567, 577, 578; Gesenius, Mon. Phoen. Tab. xxxvii. I.]

1144

[Herod. ii. 44.]

1145

[Ibid.]

1146

[Strab. iii. 5, § 4-6.]
1147
[Perrot et Chipiez, Hist. de l'Art, iii. 575.]
1148
[Ibid. p. 574.]
1149
[Strab. iii. 5, § 5.]
1150
[Sil. Ital. iii. 18-20.]
1151
[Ibid. iii. 21-27.]
1152
[1 Sam. v. 2-5; 1 Mac. x. 18.]
1153
[Philo Bybl. Fr. ii. 8, § 14.]
1154
[Ibid. § 20.]
1155
[Layard, Ninev. and Bab. p. 343; Kenrick, Phoenicia, p. 323.]
1156
[See 2 Sam. viii. 3, and 1 Kings xv. 18, where the names Hadad-ezer and Ben-hadad suggest at any rate the worship of Hadad.]
1157
[Macrob. Saturnalia, i. 23.]
1158
[So Macrobius, l.s.c. Compare the representations of the Egyptian Sun-God, Aten, in the sculpures of Amenhotep IV. (See the Story of Egypt, in G. Putnam's Series, p. 225.)]
1159
[The h in "Hadad" is he ({...}), but in chad it is heth ({...}). The derivation also leaves the reduplication of the
1160
[Philo Bybl. Fr. ii. 24, § 1.]
1161
[Zech. xii. 11.]
1162
[1 Kings i. 18; 2 Kings v. 18.]
1163
[Kenrick, Phoenicia, p. 311.]
1164
[Ezek. viii. 14.]
1165
[The Adonis myth is most completely set forth by the Pseudo-Lucian, De Dea Syra, § 6-8.]
1166
[Philo Bybl. Fr. ii. 8, § 11.]
1167
[Ibid.]
1168
["King of Righteousness" and "Lord of Righteousness" are the interpretations usually given; but "Zedek is my King" and "Zedek is my Lord" would be at least equally admissible.]
1169
[Berytus was under the protection of the Cabeiri generally (Philo Bybl. ii. 8, § 25) and of Esmun in particular. Kenrick says that he had a temple there (Phoenicia, p. 327).]

1170

[Cyprian inscriptions contain the names of Bar-Esmun, Abd-Esmun, and Esmun-nathan; Sidonian ones those of two Esmun-azars. Esmun's temple at Carthage was celebrated (Strab. xvii. 14; Appian, viii. 130). His worship in Sardinia is shown by votive offerings (Perrot et Chipiez, Hist. de l'Art, iii. 308).]

1171

[Ap. Phot. Bibliothec. Cod. ccxlii. p. 1074.]

1172

[Pausan. viii. 23.]

1173

[The name Astresmunim, "herb of Esmun," given by Dioscorides (iv. 71) to the solanum, which was regarded as having medicinal qualities, is the nearest approach to a proof that the Phoenicians themselves connected Esmun with the healing art.]

1174

[Philo Bybl. Fr. ii. 8, § 11.]

1175

[Herod. ii. 51; Kenrick, Egypt, Appendix, pp. 264-287.]

1176

[Philo Bybl. l.s.c.]

1177

[Herod. iii. 37; Suidas ad voc. {pataikos}; Hesych. ad voc. {Kabeiroi}.]

1178

[Strab. x. 3, § 7.]

1179

[Gen. ix. 22; x. 6. Compare the author's Herodotus, iv. 239-241.]

1180

[Herod. iii. 37.]

1181

[Perrot et Chipiez, Hist. de l'Art, iii. 65, 78, &c.]

1182

[Gesenius, Mon. Phoen. Tab. xxxix.]

1183

[Berger, La Phénicie, p. 24; Perrot et Chipiez, iii. 70.]

1184

[Pausan. ix. 12; Nonnus, Dionysiac. v. 70; Steph. Byz. ad voc. {'Ogkaiai}; Hesych. ad voc. {'Ogka}; Scholiast. ad Pind. Ol. ii. &c.]

1185

[As Stephen and Hesychius.]

1186

[Philo Bybl. Fr. ii. § 24.]

1187

[The "Oncæan" gate at Thebes is said to have taken its name from her.]

1188

[Gesen. Mon. Phoen. p. 113.]

1189

[Ibid. pp. 168-177.]

1190

[Prosper, Op. iii. 38; Augustine, De Civ. Dei, ii. 3.]

1191

[Gesen. Mon. Ph. Tab. ix.]

1192

[Ibid. p. 168.]

1193

[Apul. Metamorph. xi. 257.]

1194

[Gesen. Mon. Ph. Tab. xvi.]

1195

[Ibid. pp. 115-118.]

1196

[See the author's History of Ancient Egypt, i. 400]

1197

[See the Fragments of Philo Bybl. Fr. ii. 8, § 19.]

1198

[Ibid. § 25.]

1199

[See Sir H. Rawlinson's Essay on the Religion of the Babylonians and Assyrians, in the author's Herodotus, i. 658.]

11100

[So Gesenius, Mon. Phoen. p. 402; Kenrick, Phoenicia, p. 301, and others.]

11101

[There seems also to have been a tendency to increase the number of the gods by additions, of which the foreign origin is, at any rate, "not proven." Among the deities brought into notice by the later Phoenicians are—1. Zephon, an equivalent of the Egyptian Typhon, but probably a god of Phoenician origin (Ex. xiv. 2); 2. Sad or Tsad, sometimes apparently called Tsadam; 3. Sakon or Askun, a name which forms perhaps the first element in Sanchon-iathon (= Sakon-yithan); 4. Elat, a goddess, a female form of El, perhaps equivalent to the Arabian Alitta (Herod. i. 131) or Alilat (ibid. iii. 8); 5. 'Aziz, a god who was perhaps common to the Phoenicians with the Syrians, since Azizus is said to have been "the Syrian Mars;" and 6. Pa'am {...}, a god otherwise unknown. (See the Corpus Inscr. Semit. i. 122, 129, 132, 133, 144, 161, 197, 333, 404, &c.)]

11102

[Gesenius, Mon. Phoen. pp. 96, 110, &c.; Corpus Ins. Semit. Fasc. ii. pp. 154, 155.]

11103

[Ibid. p. 99 and Tab. xl. A.]

11104

[Steph. Byz. ad voc. {'Amathous}.]

11105

[Lucian, De Dea Syra, § 7.]

11106

[Plut. De Is. et Osir. § 15, 16; Steph. Byz. l.s.c.; Gesen. Mon. Phoen. pp. 96, 110.]

11107

[Gesen. Mon. Phoen. Tab. xxi.]

11108

[Ibid. pp. 168, 174, 175, 177.]

11109

[Ibid. Tab. xxi.]

11110

[Ibid. pp. 197, 202, 205.]

11111

[Ibid. Tab. xxi. and Tab. xxiii.]

11112

[Lucian, De Dea Syria, § 54.]

11113

[Clermont-Ganneau, in the Journal Asiatique, Série vii. vol. xi. 232, 444.]

11114
[Lucian, § 42.]
11115
[Ibid. Compare the 450 prophets of Baal at Samaria (1 Kings xviii. 19).]
11116
[Lucian, l.s.c.]
11117
[Ibid. Lucian's direct testimony is conined to Hierapolis, but his whole account seems to imply the closest possible connection between the Syrian and Phoenician religious usages.]
11118
[Lucian, § 49.]
11119
[Lucian, § 50: {'Aeidousi enthea kai ira asmata}.]
11120
[Gesenius, Scripturæ Linguæque Phoeniciæ Monumenta, Tab. 6, 9, 10, &c.; Corp. Ins. Semit. Tab. ix. 52; xxii. 116, 117; xxiii. 115 A, &c.]
11121
[Gesen. Tab. 15, 16, 17, 21, &c.; Corp. Ins. Semit. Tab. xliii. 187, 240; liv. 352, 365, 367, 369, &c.]
11122
[Revue Archéologique, 2me Série, xxxvii. 323.]
11123
[Jarchi on Jerem. vii. 31.]
11124
[Diod. Sic. xx. 14.]
11125
[2 Kings iii. 27; xvi. 3; xxi. 6; Micah vi. 7.]
11126
[Plutarch, De Superstitione, § 13.]
11127
[Döllinger, Judenthum und Heidenthum, i. 427, E. T.]
11128
[Judenthum und Heidenthum, book vi. § 4 (i. 428, 429 of N. Darnell's translation).]
11129
[Herod. i. 199; Strab. xvi. 1058; Baruch vi. 43.]
11130
[De Dea Syra, § 6.]
11131
[Judenthum und Heidenthum, l.s.c. p. 429; Engl. Trans.]
11132
[Euseb. Vit. Constantin. Magni, iii. 55, § 3.]
11133
[See 1 Kings xiv. 24; xv. 12; xxii. 46; 2 Kings xxiii. 7.]
11134
[Lucian, De Dea Syra, § 50-52; Corp. Ins. Semit. vol. i. Fasc. 1, p. 92; Liv. xxix. 10, 14; xxxvi. 36; Juv. vi. 512; Ov. Fast. iv. 237; Mart. Ep. iii. 31; xi. 74; Plin. H. N. v. 32; xi. 49; xxxv. 13; Propert. ii. 18, l. 15; Herodian, § 11.]
11135
[Lucian, § 51.]
11136
[Ibid. § 50.]
11137

[Döllinger, Judenthum und Heidenthum (i. 431; Engl. Tr.). Compare Senec. De Vita Beata, § 27; Lact. § 121.]

11138

[Liban. Opera, xi. 456, 555; cxi. 333.]

11139

[Compare Perrot et Chipiez, Histoire de l'Art, iii. 210, 232, 233, 236; Di Cesnola, Cyprus, pp. 66, 67, &c. In the anthropoeid sarcophagi, a hole is generally bored from the cavity of the ear right through the entire thickness of the stone, in order, apparently, that the corpse might hear the prayers addressed to it (Perrot et Chipiez, iii. 139).]

11140

[One of Esmunazar's curses on those who should disturb his remains is a prayer that they may not be "held in honour among the Manes" (Corps. Ins. Semit. vol. i. Fasc. 1, p. 9). A funereal inscription translated by Gesenius (Mon. Phoen. p. 147) ends with the words, "After rain the sun shines forth."]

11141

[Perrot et Chipiez, iii. 139.]

11142

[Job iii. 11-19.]

11143

[The compilers of the Corpus Ins. Smit. edit 256 of these, and then stop, fearing to weary the reader (i. 449).]

11144

[Di Cesnola, Cyprus, p. 325.]

11145

[Ibid. p. 146.]

11146

[Di Cesnola, Cyprus, pp. 306-334.]

XII—DRESS, ORNAMENTS, AND SOCIAL HABITS

0121

[See also Di Cesnola, Cyprus, p. 233; Perrot et Chipiez, Hist. de l'Art, iii. 405, 447, 515, &c.]

0122

[Perrot et Chipiez, iii. 428, 527, 531, 533, 534, &c.]

0123

[Ibid. pp. 527, 545; Di Cesnola, Cyprus, p. 145.]

0124

[Perrot et Chipiez, p. 538.]

0125

[Ibid. pp. 539, 547; Di Cesnola, pp. 143, 145, 149, 151, &c.]

0126

[Di Cesnola, pp. 141, 145, 149, 151, 153, 240, 344.]

0127

[Ibid. pp. 141, 143, 149; Perrot et Chipiez, pp. 511, 513, 531, &c.]

0128

[Perrot et Chipiez, pp. 519, 523, &c.]

0129

[Ibid. pp. 531, 533; Di Cesnola, pp. 129, 131, &c.]

1210

[Perrot et Chipiez, pp. 527, 533, 539; Di Cesnola, pp. 129, 145, 154.]

1211

[Di Cesnola, p. 306.]

1212

[Ibid. Pls. xlvi. and xlvii.; Perrot et Chipiez, pp. 205, 643, 837.]

1213

[Di Cesnola, p. 132.]

1214

[Perrot et Chipiez, pp. 64, 450, 555, 557; Di Cesnola, Pls vi. and xv.; also p. 275.]

1215

[Perrot et Chipiez, Hist. de l'Art, iii. 431.]

1216

[Perrot et Chipiez, pp. 202, 451, 554.]

1217

[Ibid. pp. 473, 549; Di Cesnola, Cyprus, p. 230.]

1218

[Perrot et Chipiez, iii. 549.]

1219

[Ibid. pp. 189, 549, 565.]

1220

[Di Cesnola, Cyprus, 141, 190, 230.]

1221

[Ibid. pp. 141, 191.]

1222

[Ibid. p. 141.]

1223

[Is. iii. 18-23.]

1224

[Perrot et Chipiez, pp. 257, 450, 542, 563, 824.]

1225

[Di Cesnola, Cyprus, pl. xxiii.; Perrot et Chipiez, Histoire de l'Art, iii. 819, A.]

1226

[Di Cesnola, pl. xxii.; Perrot et Chipiez, iii. 819, B.]

1227

[Di Cesnola, p. 315.]

1228

[See plate x. in Perrot et Chipiez, iii. opp. p. 824.]

1229

[Ibid. pp. 826, 827.]

1230

[Compare Di Cesnola, pl. xxv.; Perrot et Chipiez, iii. 826.]

1231

[Perrot et Chipiez, iii. 826.]

1232

[Di Cesnola, Cyprus, p. 311.]

1233

[Ibid. Compare Perrot et Chipiez, p. 832.]

1234

[These bracelets are in Paris, in the collection of M. de Clercq (Perrot et Chipiez, iii. 832).]

1235

[Ibid.]

1236

[This bracelet is in silver, but the head of the lion has been gilded. It is now in the British Museum.]

1237

[Perrot et Chipiez, p. 836; No. 604.]

1238

[Di Cesnola, Cyprus, pp. 311, 312.]
1239
[Ibid. p. 312. Compare Perrot et Chipiez, p. 835.]
1240
[Perrot et Chipiez, l.s.c. (No. 603.)]
1241
[Perrot et Chipiez, p. 818: "Il y a dans les formes de ces boucles d'orielles une étonnante variété."]
1242
[See his Cyprus, pl. xxv., and compare Perrot et Chipiez, iii. 819, fig. D.]
1243
[Perrot et Chipiez, p. 821; No. 577.]
1244
[Ibid. Nos. 578, 579.]
1245
[Di Cesnola, pl. xxvi.]
1246
[Perrot et Chipiez, p. 823.]
1247
[See Perrot et Chipiez, iii. 822; No. 582.]
1248
[Ibid. pp. 821, 822. Compare Di Cesnola, Cyprus, p. 297, and pl. xxvii.]
1249
[Perrot et Chipiez, p. 823.]
1250
[Di Cesnola, p. 310; Perrot et Chipiez, p. 818; No. 574.]
1251
[Perrot et Chipiez, p. 818; No. 575.]
1252
[Di Cesnola, pl. xxviii.]
1253
[Ibid. pl. xxi.]
1254
[Perrot et Chipiez, pp. 830, 831.]
1255
[Perrot et Chipiez, p. 831; No. 595.]
1256
[Di Csnola, p. 316.]
1257
[Ibid. pl. xxi (opp. p. 312).]
1258
[Ibid. pl. xxx.]
1259
[Ibid. pl. ix.]
1260
[Compare Di Cesnola, p. 149.]
1261
[Ibid. pl. x.]
1262
[Ibid. p. 77; Perrot et Chipiez, iii. 783.]
1263
[Di Cesnola, p. 149.]

1264
[Ibid. pl. xiv.]
1265
[Ibid. pl. x.]
1266
[See Perrot et Chipiez, iii. 769, 771, 789.]
1267
[Perrot et Chipiez, iii. 798.]
1268
[C. W. King, in Di Cesnola's Cyprus, pp. 363, 364.]
1269
[Mr. King says of it: "No piece of antique worked agate hitherto known equals in magnitude and curiosity the ornament discovered among the bronze and iron articles of the treasure. It is a sphere about six inches in diameter, black irregularly veined with white, having the exterior vertically scored with incised lines, imitating, as it were, the gadroons of a melon" (ibid. p. 363).]
1270
[Renan, Mission de Phénicie, Pls. xii. xiii.; Di Cesnola, Cyprus, pls. iv. and xxx.; and pp. 335, 336.]
1271
[Perrot et Chipiez, iii. 846-853.]
1272
[1 Kings xxii. 39.]
XIII—PHOENICIAN WRITING, LANGUAGE, AND LITERATURE
0131
[This follows from the fact that the Greeks, who tell us that they got their letters from the Phoenicians, gave them names only slightly modified from the Hebrew.]
0132
[See Dr. Ginsburg's Moabite Stone, published in 1870.]
0133
[See Quarterly Statement of the Palestine Exploration Fund for October 1881, pp. 285-287.]
0134
[Corp. Ins. Semit. i. 224-226.]
0135
[Herod. v. 58; Diod. Sic. v. 24; Plin. H. N. v. 12; vii. 56; Tacit. Ann. xi. 14; Euseb. Chron. Can. i. 13; &c.]
0136
[Capt. Conder, in the Quarterly Statement of the Palestine Exploration Fund, Jan. 1889, p. 17.]
0137
[Encycl. Britann. i. 600 and 606.]
0138
[Conder, in Quarterly Statement, &c. l.s.c.]
0139
[See Gesenius, Mon. Phoen. Tab. 19 and 20.]
1310
[See the Corpus Ins. Semit. i. 3, 30, 73, &c.; Gesenius, Mon. Phoen. Tab. 29-33.]
1311
[See on this entire subject Gesenius, Scripturæ Linguæque Phoeniciæ Monumenta, pp. 437-445; Movers, article on Phoenizien in the Cyclopädie of Ersch and Gruber; Renan, Histoire des Langues Sémitiques, pp. 189-192.]
1312

[Renan, Histoire, &c., p. 186.]
1313
[Philo Byblius, Fr. i.]
1314
[Philo Byblius, Fr. ii. § 5-8.]
1315
[Ibid. Fr. v.]
1316
[The Voyage of Hanno translated, and accompanied with the Greek Text, by Thomas Falconer, M.A., London, 1797.]
1317
[Quoted by Falconer in his second "Dissertation," p. 67.]
1318
[See the Histoire des Langues Sémitiques (p. 186):—"Les monuments épigraphiques viennent heureusement combler en partie cette lacune."]
1319
[See the Corpus Inscr. Semit. i. 13.]
1320
[Corpus Inscr. Semit. i. 20.]
1321
[Story of Phoenicia, p. 269.]
1322
[On the age of Jehavmelek, see M. Renan's remarks in the Corpus Inscriptionum Semit. i. 8.]
1323
[Ibid. p. 3.]
1324
[I have followed the translation of M. Renan (Corp. Ins. Semit. i. 8).]
1325
[See the Corpus Inscr. Semit. i. 226-236.]
1326
[See the Corp. Inscr. Sem. i. 30-32.]
1327
[Gesenius, Script. Linguæque Phoen. Monumenta, p. 177.]
1328
[Ibid. p. 96.]
1329
[See the Corpus Inscr. Semit. i. 36-39.]
1330
[Ibid. pp. 110-112.]
1331
[Ibid. p. 69.]
1332
[Ibid. p. 76.]
1333
[See the Corpus Inscr. Semit. pp. 67, 68.]
1334
[Gesenius, Scripturæ Linguæque Phoen. Mon. p. 144.]
1335
[Ibid. p. 147.]
1336
[Ibid. p. 187.]
1337

[See the fragments of Dius and Menander, who followed the Tyrian historians (Joseph. Contr. Ap. i. 18).]
1338
[Ap. Strab. xvii. 2, § 22.]
1339
[Ibid.]
1340
[See Sallust, Bell. Jugurth. § 17; Cic. De Orat. i. 58; Amm. Marc. xxii. 15; Solin. Polyhist. § 34.]
1341
[Columella, xii. 4.]
1342
[Ibid. i. 1, § 6.]
1343
[Plin. H. N. xviii. 3.]
1344
[As Antipater and Apollonius, Stoic philosophers of Tyre (Strab. l.s.c.), Boëthus and Diodotus, Peripatetics, of Sidon (ibid.), Philo of Byblus, Hermippus of Berytus, and others.]
XIV—POLITICAL HISTORY
0141
[Gen. x. 15-18.]
0142
["Canaanite" is used in a much wider sence, including all the Syrian nations between the coast line and the desert.]
0143
[Mark vii. 26.]
0144
[Ezra iii. 7.]
0145
[1 Kings v. 18 (marginal rendering).]
0146
[Ezek. xxvii. 11.]
0147
[Gen. x. 17, 18.]
0148
[Judg. i. 31.]
0149
[Brugsch, Hist. of Egypt, i. 222, et seq.]
1410
[See Records of the Past, ii. 110, 111.]
1411
[Josh. xi. 8; xix. 28.]
1412
[Judg. xviii. 7, 8.]
1413
[Ibid. i. 31.]
1414
[Ramantha (Laodicea) in later times claimed the rank of "Metropolis," which implied a supremacy over other cities; but the real chief power of the north was Aradus.]
1415
[Hom. Il. xxiii. 743.]
1416

[Ibid. 743-748.]
1417
[Hom. Od. iv. 613-619.]
1418
[Ibid. xv. 460 (Worsley's translation).]
1419
[Hom. Il. vi. 290-295 (Sotheby's translation).]
1420
[Scylax, Periplus, § 104.]
1421
[Cl. Julius, quoted by Stephen of Byzantium, ad voc. {DOROS}.]
1422
[Justin, Hist. Philipp. xviii. 3.]
1423
[Strab. xvi. ii. § 13.]
1424
[Appian, De Rebus Punicus, § 1, &c.]
1425
[Gesenius, Mon. Phoen. p. 267.]
1426
[The Sidonian vessel which carries off Eumæus quits the Sicilian haven after sunset, and continues its voyage night and day without stopping—{'Exemar men onos pleomen nuktas te kai e mar} (Hom. Od. xv. 471-476).]
1427
[Strabo, xvi. 2, § 24.]
1428
[Ibid.]
1429
[Manilius, i. 304-309.]
1430
[Herod. i. 1.]
1431
[See Hom. Odyss. xv. 455.]
1432
[Herod. l.s.c.]
1433
[Hom. Odyss. xv. 403-484.]
1434
[Strabo, xvi. 2, § 14.]
1435
[We find hereditary monarchy among the Hittites (Records of the Past, iv. 28), at Tyre (Menand. ap. Joseph. Contr. Ap. i. 18), in Moab (Records, xi. 167), in Judah and Israel, in Syria (2 Kings, xiii. 24), in Ammon (2 Sam. x. 1), &c.]
1436
[1 Sam. viii. 20.]
1437
[When kings are priests, it is noted as exceptional. (See Menand. l.s.c.; Inscription of Tabnit, line 1.)]
1438
[Judg. x. 12.]
1439
[Kenrick, Phoenicia, p. 343.]

1440

[Josh. xix. 29.]

1441

[Records of the Past, ii. 111.]

1442

[Justin, Hist. Phil. xviii. 3.]

1443

[Claudian, Bell. Gild. l. 120.]

1444

[Solinus, Polyhist. § 29; Plin. H. N. v. 76.]

1445

[Herod. i. 1 ({nautiliai makrai}).]

1446

[Maspero, Histoire Ancienne des Peuples de l'Orient, p. 321.]

1447

[See the fragments of Philo Byblius, passim.]

1448

[Euseb. Præp. Ev. x. 9, § 12.]

1449

[Tatian, Adv. Græc. § 58.]

1450

[Cinyras and Belus are both connected with Cyprus as kings. The Assyrians found kings there in all the cities (G. Smith, Eponym Canon. p. 139). So the Persians (Herod. v. 104-110).]

1451

[Dius, Fr. 2; Menand. Fr. 1.]

1452

[Justin (xviii. 3) is scarcely an exception.]

1453

[See the fragments of Dius and Menander above cited.]

1454

[1 Chr. xiv. 1.]

1455

[2 Sam. vii. 2.]

1456

[1 Chr. xxii. 4.]

1457

[1 Kings v. 1.]

1458

[Joseph, Ant. Jud. viii. 2, § 6; 1 Kings, l.s.c.]

1459

[Ibid. viii. 2, § 8.]

1460

[See Joseph. Ant. Jud. viii. 2, § 7, and compare the letters with their Hebrew counterparts in 1 Kings v. 3-6 and 7-9.]

1461

[1 Kings v. 10-12.]

1462

[Ezek. xxvii. 17; Acts xii. 20.]

1463

[Menander, Fr. 1.]

1464

[1 Kings v. 15, 18; 2 Chr. ii. 18.]

1465
[1 Kings v. 17, 18.]
1466
[Ibid. vi. 18, 29.]
1467
[Ibid. verses 23-28.]
1468
[Ibid. verse 35.]
1469
[2 Chron. iii. 14.]
1470
[Ibid. ii. 14.]
1471
[1 Kings vii. 13.]
1472
[1 Kings vii. 14; 2 Chron. ii. 14.]
1473
[1 Kings vii. 46.]
1474
[Menander, Fr. 1; Dius, Fr. 2; Philostrat. Vit. Apoll. v. 5; Sil. Ital. Bell. Pun. iii. 14, 22, 30.]
1475
[1 Kings vii. 15-22.]
1476
[Ibid. verses 27-37.]
1477
[Ibid. vi. 38.]
1478
[Ibid. vii. 1. Compare ix. 10.]
1479
[Stanley, Lectures on the Jewish Church, ii. 165-167.]
1480
[See the Fragment of Menander above quoted, where Hiram is said to have been fifty-three years old at his decease, and to have reigned thirty-four years.]
1481
[Strabo, xvi. 2, § 23.]
1482
[Menander, l.s.c.]
1483
[So M. Renan, Mission de Phénicie, p. 369.]
1484
[Herod. ii. 44.]
1485
[Arrian, Exped. Alex. ii. 16, 24.]
1486
[So M. Renan, after careful examination (Mission, l.s.c.). The earlier opinion placed the smaller island, with its Temple of Baal, towards the north (Kenrick, Phoenicia, p. 347).]
1487
[Menander, l.s.c.]
1488
[Arrian, Exp. Alex. ii. 23, sub fin.]
1489
[Josh. xix. 27.]

1490
[See Robinson, Later Researches, pp. 87, 88.]
1491
[1 Kings ix. 10-13.]
1492
[Justin, Dial. c. Tryph. § 34.]
1493
[Menand. ap. Clem. Alex. Strom. i. 386.]
1494
[1 Kings xi. 1.]
1495
[Ibid. ix. 27.]
1496
[See 1 Kings x. 22. The distinctness of this navy from the one which brought gold from Ophir
has been maintained by Dean Stanley (Lectures on the Jewish Church, ii. 156) and the Rev. J.
Hammond (Pulpit Commentary, Comment on 1 Kings, p. 213), as well as by the present writer
(Speaker's Commentary, ii. pp. 545, 546).]
1497
[Mela. iii. 1; Plin. H. N. iv. 22, § 115; Catull. xx. 30, &c.]
1498
[See Plin. H. N. iii. 3; xxxiii. 6; Polyb. x. 10; Strab. iii. 2, § 3 and 10.]
1499
[Herod. iv. 191; Plin. H. N. viii. 11.]
14100
[Hanno, Periplus, p. 6.]
14101
[Ibid. pp. 13, 14.]
14102
[1 Kings ix. 26.]
14103
[1 Kings x. 11.]
14104
[The case is excellently stated in Mr. Twistleton's article on OPHIR in Dr. Smith's Dictionry
of the Bible, vol. ii.]
14105
[As almug or algum which is "the Hebraised form of a Deccan word for sandalwood"
(Stanley, Lectures, ii. 157).]
14106
[1 Kings ix. 28.]
14107
[Contr. Ap. i. 18.]
14108
[Kenrick argues in favour of {Kitioi} (Phoenicia, p. 357).]
14109
[See Encycl. Britann. ad voc. PHOENICIA, xviii. 807.]
14110
[Menander, Fr. 2.]
14111
[Ibid.]
14112
[1 Kings xvi. 31.]
14113

[The Assyrians probably found their way into Phoenicia through the gap in the mountain line between Bargylus and Lebanon. Botrys occupied a strong position between this gap and the southern Phoenician cities, Gebal, Sidon, and Tyre.]
14114
[Menander, l.s.c. Aüza, which at a later date became Auzen, is mentioned by Tacitus (Ann. iv. 25) and Ptolemy (Geograph. iv. 2).]
14115
[The Greek lamda, {L}, readily passes into delta {D}. Baal-azar is found as a Phoenician name in an inscription (Corp. Ins. Semit. i. 335, no. 256).]
14116
[See Gesen. Mon. Phoen. p. 410. Mattan, "a gift," was the name borne by Athaliah's high priest of Baal (2 Kings xi. 18). It is found as an element in several Phoenician names, as Mattan-elim (Corp. Ins. Semit. i. 298, no. 194); Mattan-Baal (ibid. p. 309, no. 212), &c.]
14117
[See Justin, Hist. Phil. xviii. 5.]
14118
[Menander, Fr. 1.]
14119
[Kenrick, Phoenicia, pp. 363-367.]
14120
[Contr. Ap. i. 18.]
14121
[Ancient Monarchies, ii. 84-89.]
14122
[Histoire Ancienne, pp. 347, 348.]
14123
[Ancient Monarchies, ii. 90-99.]
14124
[Ancient Monarchies, ii. 102-106; Eponym Canon, pp. 108-114.]
14125
[Eponym Canon, p. 112, l. 45.]
14126
[Ibid. p. 108, l. 93.]
14127
[Ibid. p. 115, l. 14.]
14128
[Ibid. p. 120, ll. 33-35.]
14129
[When Assyria became mistress of the Upper Syria, the Orontes valley, and the kingdom of Israel, she could have strangled the Phoenician land commerce at a moment's notice.]
14130
[Is. xxiii. 2-8.]
14131
[Eponym Canon, p. 64.]
14132
[Eponym Canon, pp. 117-120.]
14133
[Ibid. p. 123, ll. 1-5.]
14134
[Ibid. p. 120, l. 28.]
14135
[In B.C. 720. (See Eponym Canon, p. 126, ll. 33-35.)]

14136
[Ezek. xxviii. 14.]
14137
[Menander ap. Joseph. Ant. Jud. ix. 14, § 2; Eponym Canon, p. 131.]
14138
[Eponym Canon, p. 132.]
14139
[Menander, l.s.c.]
14140
[Joseph, Ant. Jud. l.s.c. {'Epelthe polemon ten te Surian pasan kai Phoiniken}.]
14141
[Ibid.]
14142
[A slab of Sennacherib's represents the Assyrian army entering a city, probably Phoenician, at one end, while the inhabitants embark on board their ships at the other (Layard, Monuments of Nineveh, 1st series, pl. 71; Nin. and its Remains, ii. 384).]
14143
[Menander, l.s.c.]
14144
[Compare Perrot et Chipiez, Hist. de l'Art, iii. 357, and Lortet, La Syrie d'aujourd'hui, p. 128.]
14145
[Menander, ut supra.]
14146
[This folows from his taking refuge there when attacked by Sennacherib (Eponym Canon, p. 136).]
14147
[Since Sennacherib calls him persistently "king of Sidon" (ibid. p. 131, l. 2; p. 135, ll. 13, 17), not king of Tyre.]
14148
[It was the same army which lost 185,000 men by miracle in one night (2 Kings xix. 35).]
14149
[2 Kings xix. 23.]
14150
[Eponym Canon, p. 134, l. 11.]
14151
[Records of the Past, i. 35.]
14152
[Eponym Canon, p. 132.]
14153
[Ibid.]
14154
[Eponym Canon, p. 132, l. 14; p. 136, ll. 14, 19. "Tubaal" is probably for Tob-baal, "Baal is good," like "Tabrimon" for Tob-Rimmon, "Rimmon is good" (1 Kings xv. 18), and "Tabeal" for Tob- El, "God is good" (Is. vii. 6).]
14155
[Eponym Canon, p. 132, ll. 15, 16.]
14156
[Ibid. ll. 19, 20.]
14157
[From the fact that Abd-Milkut is king of Sidon at the accession of Esarhaddon (Records of the Past, iii. 111).]
14158

[Abd-Melkarth is one of the commonest of Phoenician names. It occurs, either fully, or in the contracted form of Bod-Melkarth, scores of times in the inscriptions of Carthage. The meaning is "servant of Melkarth."]

14159

[Records of the Past, iii. 112.]

14160

[Ancient Monarchies, ii. 186.]

14161

[Rec. of the Past, iii. 111, 112.]

14162

[Eponym Canon pp. 139, 140.]

14163

[Ibid. p. 140, Extract xxxviii. ll. 1-3.]

14164

[Eponym Canon, p. 140, Ext. xxxviii. ll. 4-9.]

14165

[Ibid. p. 141, Ext. xl.]

14166

[Ibid. p. 142, ll. 12, 13.]

14167

[Eponym Canon, p. 142, l. 14.]

14168

[See Ancient Monarchies ii. 193.]

14169

[Ibid. p. 195.]

14170

[Eponym Canon, p. 143, Extr. xli. l. 3.]

14171

[Eponym Canon, pp. 143, 144. Six names are lost between the eleventh line and the eighteenth. They may be supplied from the broken cylinder of Esarhaddon (Records of the Past, iii. 107, 108.)]

14172

[Eponym Canon, pp. 144, 145, ll. 84-98.]

14173

[Ibid. p. 139, l. 17.]

14174

[Records of the Past, vol. i. p. 100.]

14175

[Records of the Past, i. 66; ix. 41.]

14176

[Ibid. iii. 67, ll. 116, 117.]

14177

[Ibid. i. 67, 68.]

14178

[See Judg. xix. 29; Eponym Canon, p. 132, l. 9.]

14179

[Eponym Canon, pp. 149, 149.]

14180

[Eponym Canon, p. 70.]

14181

[Herod. i. 103. B.C. 633 was, according to Herodotus, the year of the accession of Cyaxares. His attack on Nineveh seems to have followed shortly after.]

14182
[Herod. l.s.c. and iv. 1; Ezek. xxxviii. 2-16; Strabo, xi. 8, § 4; Diod. Sic. ii. 34, § 2-5.]
14183
[Ancient Monarchies, ii. 221.]
14184
[Stanley, Lectures on the Jewish Church, ii. 432, 433.]
14185
[Herod. i. 105; Strabo, i. 3, 16; Justin, ii. 3.]
14186
[Herod. l.s.c.; Hippocrat. De Aëre, Aqua, et Locis, vi. § 108.]
14187
[Herod. i. 73.]
14188
[Strabo, xi. 767; Arrian, Exp. Alex. iii. 8, § 4.]
14189
[Polyb. v. 70, § 4.]
14190
[Ancient Monarchies, ii. 228, note.]
14191
[Ancient Monarchies, ii. 232.]
14192
[Herod. ii. 157; and compare the author's History of Ancient Egypt, ii. 467, note 6.]
14193
[Ezek. xxvii. 8.]
14194
[Ibid. verse 11.]
14195
[Ibid. verse 9.]
14196
[Ibid. xxviii. 2-5.]
14197
[Ezek. xxvii. 3-6, and 25.]
14198
[See the author's History of Ancient Egypt, ii. 472, note 1.]
14199
[Herod. ii. 159; 2 Kings xxiii. 29; 2 Chron. xxxv. 20-24.]
14200
[Herod. ii. 157.]
14201
[See Jer. xlvii. 1. Gaza, however, may not have been taken till the campaign of B.C. 608.]
14202
[Herod. i. 105 raises the suspicion that Askelon, which was nearer Egypt than Ashdod, may have belonged to Psamatik I.]
14203
[Ibid. ii. 159.]
14204
[2 Kings xxiii. 19; 2 Chron. xxxiv. 6.]
14205
[History of Ancient Egypt, ii. 228.]
14206
[Judg. iv. 15; v. 19.]
14207

[2 Chron. xxxv. 21.]
14208
[See Jer. xlvi. 2.]
14209
[Berosus, Fr. 1; 2 Kings xxiv. 7.]
14210
[Herod. iv. 42.]
14211
[Ibid. ii. 112.]
14212
[Berosus, l.s.c.]
14213
[Habakkuk, i. 6-10.]
14214
[Jer. xlvi. 3, 4.]
14215
[Ibid. verse 5.]
14216
[Ibid. verse 6.]
14217
[Jer. xlvi. 10.]
14218
[Ibid. verse 16.]
14219
[Ibid. verse 21.]
14220
[Stanley, Lectures on the Jewish Church, ii. 455.]
14221
[Ibid.]
14222
[Berosus, l.s.c. The extreme haste of the return is indicated by the fact, which is noted, that Nebuchadnezzer himself, with a few light troops, took the short cut across the desert, while his army, with its prisoners, pursued the more usual route through the valley of the Orontes, by Aleppo to Carchemish, and then along the course of the Euphrates.]
14223
[See History of Ancient Egypt, ii. 480.]
14224
[Habak. i. 6.]
14225
[Menander ap. Joseph. Contr. Ap. i. 21.]
14226
[Ezek. xxvii. 8, 9, 11.]
14227
[So Joseph. l.s.c. Mr. Kenrick disputes the date on account of Ezek. xxvi. 2, which he thinks must refer to the final siege and capture of Jerusalem; but the reference may be to the breaking of the power of Judæa, either by Neco in B.C. 608 or by Nebuchadnezzar in B.C. 605.]
14228
[2 Kings xxiv. 2; 2 Chr. xxxvi. 6.]
14229
[Ezek. xxviii. 21-23.]
14230
[Menander, l.s.c.]

14231
[Ezek. xxvi. 8-12.]
14232
[Isaiah xliii. 14; Æschyl. Pers. l. 54.]
14233
[As Kenrick (Phoenicia, p. 390).]
14234
[See especially, ch. xxviii. 2, 12.]
14235
[Ibid. verses 2-10, 17, 18.]
14236
[Ezek. xxvii. 26.]
14237
[Herod. vii. 44, 96, 100, 128.]
14238
[Ibid. ii. 161; vii. 98; Ezra iii. 7.]
14239
[Menander, Fr. 2.]
14240
[Herod. ii. 182.]
14241
[Ibid. i. 201-214; Ctesias, Ex. Pers. § 6-8.]
14242
[Herod. i. 177; Arrian, Exp. Alex. iii. 27.]
14243
[Herod. i. 201-214; Ctes. Ex. Pers. l.s.c.]
14244
[Ezra i. 1-11.]
14245
[Kenrick, Phoenicia, p. 393.]
14246
[Herod. iii. 19, 34.]
14247
[Ezra iii. 7.]
14248
[Ezra iii. 7.]
14249
[Herod. i. 153.]
14250
[Ibid. ii. 177.]
14251
[See Berosus, ap. Joseph. Ant. Jud. x. 11, § 1.]
14252
[Hence the sacred writers speak of the Assyrians and Babylonians as "God's northern army," "a people from the north country." (Jer. i. 15; vi. 22; Ezek. xxvi. 7; Joel ii. 20, &c.)]
14253
[See Herod. iii. 5.]
14254
[Ibid. ii. 159.]
14255
[Ibid. ii. 161.]
14256

[Ibid. ii. 182.]
14257
[Herod. ii. 150, 154; iii. 11.]
14258
[Ibid. iii. 19.]
14259
[Ibid. vii. 98; viii. 67, § 2; Diod. Sic. xvi. 42, § 2; xvii. 47, § 1; Arrian, Exp. Alex. ii. 13, 15, &c.]
14260
[Herod. iii. 19.]
14261
[Ezek. xxix. 10.]
14262
[Herod. iii. 17.]
14263
[Herod. iii. 19.]
14264
[Ibid.]
14265
[Kenrick, Phoenicia, p. 394.]
14266
[Diod. Sic. xvi. 41.]
14267
[Kenrick, p. 391, note 3.]
14268
[Herod. iii. 91.]
14269
[Diod. Sic. xvi. 41, § 2.]
14270
[Herod. v. 52.]
14271
[See the author's Herodotus, iv. 30, note 1.]
14272
[Herod. vii. 28.]
14273
[Ibid. iv. 166.]
14274
[Herod. v. 37-104.]
14275
[Phoenicia could furnish 300 triremes, Cyprus 150, Ionia at this time 283 (Herod. vi. 8), Æolis at least 70 (ibid.), Caria the same number (ib. vii. 93)—total, 873. Against these Darious could only have mustered 200 from Egypt (ib. vii. 89), 100 from Cilicia (ib. 91), 50 from Lycia (ib. 92), and 30 from Pamphylia (ib. 91)—total, 380.]
14276
[Herod. i. 28, 176; Appian, Bell. Civ. iv. 80.]
14277
[Herod. iii. 14-16, 27-29, 37, &c.]
14278
[Ibid. v. 108.]
14279
[Ibid.]
14280

[Ibid. v. 112.]

14281

[See the author's Herodotus, i. 268, 269, 3rd ed.]

14282

[Herod. vi. 9.]

14283

[Ibid. ch. 6.]

14284

[Herod. ch. 8.]

14285

[Ibid. chs. 9-13.]

14286

[The Lesbians and most of the Samians (Herod. v. 14).]

14287

[Ibid. ch. 15.]

14288

[Ibid. chs. 31-33.]

14289

[Herod. v. 41.]

14290

[Ibid. iii. 135-138.]

14291

[Herod. vi. 43-45.]

14292

[See the author's Herodotus, iii. 494, note 3.]

14293

[The fleet which accomponied Mardonius lost nearly three hundred vessels off Mount Athos (Herod. vi. 44), and therefore can scarcely have fallen much short of 500; that of Datis and Artaphernes is reckoned at 600 by Herodotus (vi. 95), at a thousand by Cicero (Orat. in Verr. ii. 1, § 18), and Valerius Maximus (i. 1).]

14294

[So Herodotus (vi. 95).]

14295

[Herod. vi. 118.]

14296

[Herod. vii. 23.]

14297

[Ibid. vii. 34-36.]

14298

[Ibid. viii. 117.]

14299

[Æschyl. Pers. l. 343; Herod. vii. 89.]

14300

[Herod. vii. 89-95; Diod. Sic. xi. 3, § 7.]

14301

[Herod. vii. 44.]

14302

[Ibid. vii. 100, 128.]

14303

[Ibid. viii. 85.]

14304

[Ibid. viii. 17.]

14305

[Diod. Sic. xi. 13, § 2: {'Aristeusai Phasi para men tois 'El-lesin 'Athnaious, para de, tois barbarois Sidonious}.]

14306

[Herod. viii. 84; Æschyl. Pers. ll. 415-7.]

14307

[Herod. viii. 86-90.]

14308

[Ibid. ch. 90.]

14309

[Ibid. ch. 90.]

14310

[Diod. Sic. xi. 19, § 4.]

14311

[Herod. ix. 96.]

14312

[Diod. Sic. xi. 60, § 5, 6.]

14313

[So Diodorus (xi. 62, § 3); but the mention of Cyprus in line 6 renders this somewhat doubtful.]

14314

[Thucyd. i. 110.]

14315

[See Ancient Monarchies, iii. 501.]

14316

[See the Corpus Inscriptionum Semiticarum, i. 139-148.]

14317

[Nos. 115, 116, 117, 119, 120.]

14318

[Ibid. No. 118.]

14319

[Corp. Ins. Sem. i. 132, 145.]

14320

[Dionys. Halicarn. De Orat. Antiq. "Dinarch." § 10.]

14321

[Corp. Ins. Sem. i. 145, No. 119.]

14322

[See the Corpus Inscriptionum Græcarum, i. 126, No. 87.]

14323

[Nefaheritis or Nefaa-ert. (See the author's Story of Egypt, pp. 385, 386, and compare Ancient Monarchies, iii. 481, 482.)]

14324

[Isocrates, Paneg. and Evag.; Theopompas, Fr. 111; Diod. Sic. xiv. 98; Ctesias, Exc. Pers. Fr. 29, § 63.]

14325

[Diod. Sic. xv. 9, § 2. (See Grote's Hist. of Greece, x. 30, note 3.)]

14326

[Diod. Sic. xv. 9, § 2.]

14327

[Isocrates, Paneg. § 161; Evag. §§ 23, 62.]

14328

[See Diod. Sic. xiv. 98; xv. 2; Ephorus Fr.; 134 Isocrates, Evag. §§ 75, 76.]

14329
[Kenrick, Phoenicia, p. 405.]
14330
[See Ancient Monarchies, iii. 504.]
14331
[Ancient Monarchies, iii. 505, 506.]
14332
[Diod. Sic. xv. 90, § 3.]
14333
[Ibid. xv. 92, § 5.]
14334
[Ibid. xvi. 41, § 1.]
14335
[Diod. Sic. xvi. 42, § 2.]
14336
[Ibid. xvi. 41, § 5.]
14337
[Ibid. xvi. 32, § 2.]
14338
[Ibid. § 5.]
14339
[Ibid. xvi. 40, § 5, ad fin.]
14340
[Ibid. xvi. 44, § 6, ad fin.]
14341
[Diod. Sic. xvi. § 5.]
14342
[Diodorus is our authority for all these facts (xvi. 45, § 1-6).]
14343
[See the author's Story of Egypt, pp. 396-401.]
14344
[Diod. Sic. xvi. 42, § 6; 46, § 3.]
14345
[Scylax, Periplus, § 104.]
14346
[Ibid.]
14347
[See Arrian, Exp. Alex. ii. 13, sub fin.; 15, sub fin.; 30, sub init.]
14348
[See Encycl. Brit. xviii. 809.]
14349
[Quint. Curt. iv. 4; Justin, xi. 10. Diodorus by mistake makes Strato II. king of Tyre (xvii. 47, § 1).]
14350
[Arrian, Exp. Alex. i. 1, § 2.]
14351
[See Grote, History of Greece, xii. 102.]
14352
[Ibid. pp. 29-51.]
14353
[Diod. Sic. xvii. 7.]
14354

[Four hundred were actually brought to the relief of Miletus a few weeks later (Arrian, Exp. Alex. i. 18, § 5).]
14355
[Ibid. § 4.]
14356
[Diod. Sic. xvii. 22; Arrian, Exp. Alex. i. 18-20.]
14357
[Diod. Sic. xvii. 23-26; Arrian, Exp. Alex. i. 20-23.]
14358
[Diod. Sic. xvii. 29, § 2; Arrian., Exp. Alex. ii. 1, § 1.]
14359
[See the remarks of Mr. Grote (History of Greece, xii. 142, 143.)]
14360
[Diod. Sic. xvii. 29, § 4.]
14361
[Arrian, Exp. Alex. i. 20, § 1; Diod. Sic. i. 22, § 5.]
14362
[Arrian, ii. 8-13.]
14363
[Arrian, ii. 13, 87; Diod. Sic. xvii. 40, § 2.]
14364
[As Ger-astartus, king of Aradus (Arrian, l.s.c.); Enylus, king of Byblus (ibid. ii. 20, § 1); and Azemileus, king of Tyre (ibid. ii. 15, ad fin.)]
14365
[Arrian, Exp. Alex. ii. 13, ad fin.]
14366
[Ibid. ii. 15, § 6.]
14367
[Arrian, l.s.c.]
14368
[Ibid. ii. 15, § 7; Q. Curt. iv. 2, § 3.]
14369
[Arrian, Exp. Alex. ii. 16, ad fin.; Q. Curt. iv. 2, § 5; Justin, xi. 10.]
14370
[Diod. Sic. xvii. 40, § 2.]
14371
[See Diod. Sic. xv. 73, § 4; 77, § 4.]
14372
[In point of fact, he only obtained, towards the fleet which he collected against Tyre, twenty-three vessels that were not either Cyprian or Phoenician (Arrian, Exp. Alex. ii. 20, § 2).]
14373
[Herod. viii. 97.]
14374
[Compare Arrian, Exp. Alex. ii. 15, § 7, with ii. 24, § 5.]
14375
[Diod. Sic. xvii. 41, § 3.]
14376
[Ibid. § 4.]
14377
[Q. Curt. iv. § 20; Diod. Sic. xvii. 41, § 1, 2.]
14378
[Diod. Sic. xvii. 40, § 5.]

14379
[Arrian, Exp. Alex. ii. 18, § 3.]
14380
[Arrian, Exp. Alex. ii. 18, § 3.]
14381
[Diod. Sic. xvii. 42, § 1; Arrian, Exp. Alex. ii. 18, § 5.]
14382
[Arrian, ii. 18, sub fin.]
14383
[Ibid. ii. 19, § 1.]
14384
[This seems to be Arrian's meaning, when he says, {ai keraiai periklastheisaiexekhean es to pur osa es exapsin tes phlogus pareskeuasmena en} (ii. 19, § 4).]
14385
[Grote, History of Greece, xii. 185, 186.]
14386
[Kenrick, Phoenicia, p. 418.]
14387
[Q. Curt. iv. 3, § 8.]
14388
[Arrian, l.s.c.]
14389
[Arrian, ii. 20, § 1.]
14390
[Ibid. § 2.]
14391
[Arrian, ii. 20; § 3; Q. Curt. iv. 3, § 11.]
14392
[{'Epibibasas tois katastromasi ton upaspiston osoi ikanoi edokoun es to ergon} (Arrian, ii. 20, § 6).]
14393
[The Tyrians had but eighty vessels against Alexander's 224.]
14394
[Arrian, Exp. Alex. ii. 20, ad fin.]
14395
[Ibid. ii. 21, § 8.]
14396
[Q. Curt. iv. 3, § 7-9.]
14397
[Diod. Sic. xvii. 42, § 6; Q. Curt. l.s.c.]
14398
[See Kenrick, Phoenicia, pp. 421, 422.]
14399
[Arrian, Exp. Alex. ii. 21, § 1.]
14400
[Arrian, Exp. Alex. ii. 21, § 4-7.]
14401
[Arrian, Exp. Alex. ii. 21, § 8.]
14402
[Some editions of Arrian gave {Pasikratous tou Thourieos}, "Pasicrates the Thurian," but the right reading is undoubtedly {tou Kourieos}, "the Curian, or king of Curium." (See the note of Sintenis ad loc.)]

14403
[Arrian, Exp. Alex. ii. 22, § 2.]
14404
[Six triremes and all the quinqueremes (Arrian, ii. 22, § 3).]
14405
[Arrian, Exp. Alex. ii. 22, § 5.]
14406
[Diod. Sic. xvii. 42, § 7.]
14407
[Ibid. xvii. 45, § 4.]
14408
[Diod. Sic. xvii. 45, § 3.]
14409
[Ibid. xvii. 43, § 7, 8.]
14410
[Ibid. xvii. 44, § 4.]
14411
[Ibid. xvii. 44, § 1-3.]
14412
[Ibid. § 4.]
14413
[Ibid. xvii. 45, § 6.]
14414
[Ibid. xvii. 43, § 3.]
14415
[Arrian, Exp. Alex. ii. 22, sub fin.]
14416
[{Kateseise tou teikhous epi mega} (Ibid. ii. 23, § 1).]
14417
[Diod. Sic. xvii. 46, § 1.]
14418
[Arrian, ii. 23, § 2.]
14419
[Ibid. ii. 23, § 5.]
14420
[Not "the foremost," as Diodorus says (xvii. 46, § 2).]
14421
[Arrian, Exp. Alex. ii. 23, ad fin.]
14422
[Ibid. ii. 24, § 1.]
14423
[Ibid.]
14424
[Arrian, Exp. Alex. ii. 24, § 4.]
14425
[Diod. Sic. xvii. 46, § 4.]
14426
[So Arrian (l.s.c.) Diodorus reduces the number to thirteen thousand (xvii. 46, § 4).]
14427
[Diod. Sic. xvii. 46, § 5; Arrian, ii. 24, § 6.]
14428
[See Kenrick, Phoenicia, p. 428, note 3.]

14429
[See Diod. Sic. xvii. 46, § 6. The name Abd-elonim, "servant of the gods," is common. The Greeks and Romans generally render it by Abdalonymus.]
14430
[Arrian, Exp. Alex. iii. 6, § 3.]
14431
[Ibid. vi. 1, § 6.]
14432
[Arrian, Exp. Alex. vi. 22, § 4.]
14433
[Ibid. vii. 19, § 3.]
14434
[Ibid. § 5.]
14435
[Diod. Sic. xviii. 3, § 1.]
14436
[Ibid. 43, § 2.]
14437
[Diod. Sic. xix. 58, § 1.]
14438
[So Kenrick, Phoenicia, p. 433. Compare Diod. Sic. xviii. 37, § 4.]
14439
[Diod. Sic. xix. 58, § 2-4.]
14440
[Ibid. 61, § 6.]
14441
[Plutarch, Vit. Demetr. § 32.]
14442
[Diod. Sic. xxx. 17; Polyb. v. 40.]
14443
[Polyb. v. 60.]
14444
[Ibid. v. 62.]
14445
[Polyb. xvi. 18; Joseph. Ant. Jud. xii. 3, § 3.]
14446
[See Kenrick, Phoenicia, p. 436.]
14447
[Herod. i. 1. Egypt never sent trading ships into the Mediterranean. All her commerce with Syria, Asia Minor, and Europe was carried on either in Greek or Phoenician bottoms.]
14448
[Kenrick, Phoenicia, l.s.c.]
14449
[As that of the Red Sea, Arabia, and the East African coast.]
14450
[2 Macc. iv. 18.]
14451
[Ibid. verses 44-50.]
14452
[Gesenius, Mon. Phoen. pls. 32-34.]
14453
[Kenrick, Phoenicia, pp. 437, 438.]

14454

[Livy, xxvii. 30.]

14455

[2 Macc. iv. 49.]

14456

[1 Macc. iii. 34-36; 2 Macc. viii. 9; Joseph. Ant. Jud. xii. 7, § 2,]

14457

[2 Macc. viii. 11.]

14458

[1 Macc. iii. 41.]

14459

[2 Macc. viii. 25; Joseph. Ant. Jud. xii. 7, § 4.]

14460

[Strab. xvii. 2, § 22.]

14461

[Joseph. Ant. Jud. xii. 4, § 3.]

14462

[Ibid. § 4.]

14463

[By Theodotus in B.C. 219 (Polyb. v. 61, § 5), by Cleopatra, queen of Syria, about B.C. 85 (Joseph. Ant. Jud. xiii. 13, § 2), by Tigranes in B.C. 83 (ibid. xiii. 16, § 4), &c.]

14464

[Justin, Hist. Philipp. xl. 1; Appian, Syriaca, § 48.]

14465

[Kenrick, Phoenicia, p. 438.]

14466

[Or, sometimes, under a proprætor.]

14467

[Joseph. Ant. Jud. xiv. 10, § 2.]

14468

[Ibid. xv. 4, § 1, ad fin.]

14469

[Ibid. xiv. 12, §§ 4, 5.]

14470

[Mommsen, History of Rome, iv. 113-115, Engl. Tr.; Merivale, Roman Empire, i. 36.]

14471

[Thucyd. i. 4.]

14472

[See the author's Sixth Oriental Monarchy, pp. 178-180.]

14473

[Dio Cass. Hist. Rom. xlviii. 25.]

14474

[Ibid. § 26.]

14475

[Joseph. Ant. Jud. xiv. 13.]

14476

[Dio. Cass. xlviii. 39-41.]

14477

[Ibid. liv. 7.]

14478

[Ramsay, in Smith's Dict. of Greek and Rom. Geography, i. 11.]

14479

[Suidas ad voc. {Paulos Turios}.]
14480
[Mark vii. 24-30. Compare Matt. xv. 21-28.]
14481
[Acts xii. 20, 21.]
14482
[Acts xi. 19.]
14483
[Ibid. xxi. 3-7.]
14484
[See Robertson, History of the Christian Church, i. 195, 196.]
14485
[Ibid. p. 201.]
14486
[Some doubts have been entertained as to whether Porphyry was really a Tyrian, but his own statement (Vit. Plotini, ii. 107), backed as it is by the testimony of Eunapius and Suidas, should be regarded as settling the question.]
14487
[Mason, in Smith's Dict. of Greek and Rom. Biography, iii. 502.]
14488
[See the article on PORPHYRIUS in Smith's Dict. of Greek and Rom. Biography, iii. 498-502.]
14489
[Strab. xvi. 2, § 24.]
14490
[See the lines quoted by Kenrick (Phoenicia, p. 440, note) from Cramer's Anecdota Græca (iv. 19, § 6):—]
{Oi tes Stoas bullousin 'Akademian, Purronas outoi, pantas o Stegeirites. 'Alloi de touton Phoinikes te kai Suroi.}]
14491
[Strabo, l.s.c.]
14492
[Ibid. Strabo's words are: {Nuni de pases kai tes alles philosophias euporian polu pleisten labein estin ek touton ton poleon.}]
14493
[Smith's Dict. of Greek and Rom. Biography, ii. 417.]
14494
[Kenrick, Phoenicia, p. 440.]
14495
[Suidas, s.v. {Paulos Turios}.]
14496
[Smith's Dict. of Greek and Rom. Biography, ii. 1000.]
14497
[Smith's Gibbon, ii. 317.]
14498
[Heineccius, Ant. Rom. Synt. Proëm, § 45.]
14499
[Ibid.]
14500
[See Eckhel, Doctr. Num. Vet. iii. 366; Mionnet, Description des Médailles, Supplement.]
14501
[Note that the "Syro-Phoenician woman" who conversed with our Lord is spoken of as also

{'Ellenis}, one whose language was Greek (Mark vii. 26).]
14502
[De situ orbis, i. 12; "Sidon adhuc opulenta."]
14503
[Ulpian, Digest. Leg. de Cens. tit. 15.]
14504
[Exp. totius Mundi in Hudson's Geographi Minores, iii. 6.]
14505
[Hieronymus, Comment. ad Ezek. xxxvi. 7.]
14506
[Hieronymus, Comment. ad Ezek. xxvii. 2.]
14507
[Ezek. xxvi. 14.]
14508
[Euseb. Vita Constantin. Magni, iii. 58.]

Printed in Great Britain
by Amazon